Just Wars

Just Wars

From Cicero to Iraq

ALEX J. BELLAMY

polity

First published in 2006 by Polity Press

Reprinted 2008, 2011, 2012

Polity Press
65 Bridge Street
Cambridge CB2 1UR, UK.

Polity Press
350 Main Street
Malden, MA 02148, USA

ISBN-10: 0-7456-3282-3
ISBN-13: 978-07456-3282-7
ISBN-10: 0-7456-3283-1 (pb)
ISBN-13: 978-07456-3283-4 (pb)

A catalogue record for this book is available from the British Library.

Typeset in 10 on 12 pt Stempel Garamond
by SNP Best-set Typesetter Ltd, Hong Kong
Printed and bound in Great Britain by the MPG Books Group

For further information on Polity, visit our website: www.politybooks.com

To my darling wife Sara.
My Lúthien
'Lúthien Tinúviel
more fair than mortal tongue can tell'.

Contents

Preface and Acknowledgements   *viii*

Introduction   1

Part I: Mapping the Just War Tradition   **13**

1   Antiquity   15

2   The Middle Ages   30

3   Renaissance and Reformation   49

4   From Holy War to Enlightenment   67

5   Modernity and Beyond   88

Part II: Contemporary Issues   **115**

6   The Just War Tradition Today   117

7   Terrorism   135

8   Pre-emption   158

9   Aerial Bombing   180

10 Humanitarian Intervention   199

Conclusion   229

Bibliography   *232*

Index   *262*

Preface and Acknowledgements

It seems a long time since I started this project, though it was only three years ago. So much has changed since then, yet the urgency of the issues dealt with in this book has not diminished. Four authors in particular inspired me and shaped the way that I think about the normative dilemmas presented by war. The work of J. R. R. Tolkien, particularly his account of the War of the Ring, provided me with a salutary reminder that whilst there are some things that are worth fighting for, worth killing for, war is always a tragedy. Although it is all too often tragically necessary, war always comes at a cost. Above all, it is vital in war to avoid becoming the very thing we are fighting. In a letter to his son Christopher in 1944, Tolkien wrote:

[T]here was a solemn article in the local paper seriously advocating systematic exterminating of the entire German nation as the only proper course after military victory: because, if you please, they are rattlesnakes, and don't know the difference between good and evil! (What of the writer?) The Germans have just as much right to declare the Poles and Jews exterminable vermin, subhuman, as we have to select the Germans. Of course, there is a difference here. The article was answered, and the answer printed.... You can't fight the Enemy with his own Ring without turning into an Enemy. (H. Carpenter (ed.), *The Letters of J. R. R. Tolkien* (London: HarperCollins, 1995, p. 94))

Until such a time as it is eradicated, the imperative will be to limit war as far as possible, bearing in mind the responsibilities that political and military leaders have to protect their own citizens and uphold the common good wherever possible.

At the very beginning of my work on this book, my wife Sara, who as I write this is reorganizing my bibliography, bought me a pristine copy of James Turner Johnson's *Ideology, Reason and the Limitation of War* (1975). This opened my eyes to a new universe. Since its inception in 1919, the discipline of International Relations has purportedly attempted to assist the effort of ridding humankind of the scourge of war, yet we have seldom engaged with those in earlier times who confronted many of the dilemmas we face today. Johnson's brilliant work introduced me to a wealth of insight that I hope I have done justice to here. Michael Walzer's *Just and Unjust Wars* (1977) remains, thirty years on, the definitive work on the ethics of war. Although I have tried to contribute to Walzer's work by endeavouring to make sense of what the Just War tradition actually is, how it evolved over time, and where the main points of controversy are, I was unable to resist returning to Walzer for insights on innumerable issues. Not least, my understanding of double-effect and due care owe everything to Walzer's inspiring work. I will be contented if this book is seen as a footnote to Walzer's. I spent the final six months or so wrestling with the big questions about the meaning, nature and role of the Just War tradition. Thankfully, Ian Clark's *Legitimacy in International Society* was published in 2005 and helped me to clarify the idea of the Just War tradition as a legitimacy framework, an idea I had long been toying with but had been unable to put into words in a coherent fashion. I was fortunate enough to tutor international history for Ian whilst I studied for my Ph.D. at Aberystwyth in the 1990s; he is a model of integrity, professionalism and scholarship and I am happy to have learnt from him and hope I have done justice to his arguments in the defaced way I have presented them here.

I was able to write this book thanks to the financial and academic support provided to me by the University of Queensland, in Brisbane, Australia. The Faculty of Social and Behavioural Sciences funded an enlightening trip to Geneva and enabled me to employ research assistants throughout the project. The School of Political Science and International Studies not only provided a very amiable environment for the writing of this book but also supported my taking six months' study leave to complete writing this volume. The staff at the Social Science library provided wonderful assistance in obtaining all manner of volumes necessary to write this one, many of them not available in Australia. Finally I am grateful to my students, particularly the honours students who, in 2003, sat through twelve weeks of seminars on the ethics of war almost entirely related to elements of this volume. They proved expert and patient critics as week after week I used them as guinea pigs as I developed the arguments that follow. I consider myself very fortunate to teach and research at such a wonderful university in such an amazing city.

Polity Press have supported this project from the outset and I am deeply grateful to Rachel Kerr, who first commissioned this work, Louise Knight, Ellen McKinlay and Emma Hutchinson, whose professionalism and astute assistance have helped marshal it to its conclusion, and Justin Dyer, who was meticulous and kind in providing advice about the final stages of putting the book together. I am also grateful to the two anonymous reviewers, whose comments were very useful indeed.

Although many colleagues and friends have read, commented on, criticized and helped amend every aspect of this book, five deserve particular mention. Paul Williams has been a colleague, collaborator and friend since we began our Ph.D.s together at Aberystwyth in 1997. I am deeply privileged to have Paul as a friend and colleague. Paul read and commented on the entire manuscript, going over some chapters several times. He was generous, as ever, in sharing his immense expertise, and his influence can be seen on every page of this book. Roland Bleiker, my colleague and friend at the University of Queensland, also read the entire manuscript and provided sage advice at a number of critical junctures. It is a delight to work alongside Roland and he has forced me to push my horizons beyond my comfort zone: a little, at least. Shannon French at the US Naval Academy also read significant parts of the manuscript and offered superbly detailed comments. Toni Erskine read and offered detailed and apposite comments on the introduction and main argument. Finally, I owe Nicholas Wheeler a debt of gratitude for his support, encouragement and wise words about all matters relating to war and peace. Nick also offered detailed and thought-provoking comments on several chapters.

Besides these, I was also helped by many people who commented on individual parts of the book or spin-off projects directly related to it. The introduction was helped by comments and suggestions by Christian Reus-Smit, Ian Clark and Matt McDonald.

I was rather overwhelmed when conducting research for the first few chapters by the sheer volume and complexity of early thinking about the ethics and laws of war. Fortunately, I found a mentor in the shape of James Muldoon. Jim graciously shared his extensive expertise on medieval politics, ethics and law, read and commented on all the early chapters, engaged with and suggested revisions to the argument and sent me personal papers and references of important works that I was missing. The first part of the book was also helped by comments and suggestions from another Queensland colleague, Richard Shapcott.

Likewise, many friends and colleagues took the time to read and comment on different chapters in Part II or on related projects. I would like to thank Abraham Sofaer, David Rodin, Cian O'Driscoll, Nils Petter Gleditsch, Justin Morris, Luke Glanville, Tony Coady and Brian Orend for their help and advice.

The book greatly benefited from the group of research assistants who performed so brilliantly. Thanks go to Mariano Griva, Brian Adams and Regan Neal.

Some of the key arguments in this volume have been aired before, and I am grateful to a number of people for inviting me to present my ideas. Parts of this project were presented at Griffith University, May 2004 (thanks to Brendon O'Connor), Australian National University, May 2005 (thanks to John Ravenhill and Kathy Morton), and Monash University, June 2005 (thanks to Richard Devetak and Christian Enemark).

Alan and Marie are the best parents a son-in-law could ask for and provided unfaltering support and help throughout this project. Likewise Jane,

Tony, Clair and James are the best siblings a brother-in-law could ask for. Little puppy Polly has been a consistent supplier of joy, love and presents.

There are no words that can describe the gratitude I have for my darling wife, Sara, to whom this volume is dedicated. Sara's influence on this book is too great to measure. She is a wonderful scholar, and as well as reading and providing excellent and detailed comments on many drafts of the manuscript, she was my longest-serving research assistant – I only wish I could have paid her more, employed her longer and read as quickly as she found things. Sadly, this volume does no justice to the quality of Sara's research and commentary. Sara has lived and breathed this project for the entirety of our married life. At the beginning she spurred it on by buying me Johnson's book, which I have grown to treasure and admire more with every reading. She has patiently discussed every element of the argument and provided wise counsel at every roadblock. Sara is my wife, my best friend and most treasured source of inspiration. She sat alongside me as every word of this book was written: *'Lúthien was the most beautiful of all the Children of Ilúvatar. . . . As the light upon the leaves of trees, as the voice of clear waters, as the stars above the mists of the world, such was her glory and her loveliness; and in her face was a shining light'* (J. R. R. Tolkien).

AJB
Brisbane, December 2005

Introduction

This book has two principal aims. The first is to map the evolution of the Just War tradition and the many controversies that shaped it. The second is to investigate the normative dilemmas posed by contemporary wars with reference to the Just War tradition.

Writing around 45 BC, Cicero (1961: x–xiv) argued that there were two ways of resolving a dispute: through discussion or physical force. He concluded that

since the former is characteristic of man, the latter of the brute, we must resort to force only in case we may not avail ourselves of discussion. The only excuse, therefore, for going to war is that we may live in peace unharmed; and when the victory is won, we should spare those who have not been blood-thirsty and barbarous in their warfare.

Without ethical and legal constraints on both the decision to wage it (*jus ad bellum*) and its conduct (*jus in bello*), war is nothing more than the application of brute force, logically indistinguishable from mass murder. War often appears this way. From the sacking of Jerusalem by the Christian Crusaders in 1099 and the Thirty Years War that wracked seventeenth-century Europe, to the murder of millions in the Second World War and more recently in sub-Saharan Africa and the Balkans, war has descended into genocidal violence, prompting some to argue that it is always thus (Booth 2001; Shaw, M. 2003: 103). But it need not always be this way (Keegan 1993). During the Middle Ages, the chivalric code governed relations between knights, creating a complex system of rules concerning their capture, treatment and ransoming. The carnage of the First World War was almost entirely aimed at combatants; though brutal and horrific, it was not unrestrained. Even during the dark days of the Second World War, there were glimpses of restraint. For the first eighteen months of the war, Britain and Germany observed a prohibition on bombing each other's cities and throughout the war treated each other's prisoners of war with a basic level of humanity (Paskins and Dockrill 1979: 203–4; Thomas, W. 2001: 122–5).

According to the famous Prussian strategist, Carl von Clausewitz (1993: 77), 'war' is best understood 'as nothing but the continuation of policy by other means'. War reflects the politics that drive it. When wars are driven by religious or ideological absolutism, doctrines of racial superiority, nationalist claims to territory, the accumulation of economic and political power through terror, or disputes about the nature of international order itself, they are likely to descend into barbarism. Indeed, most of the twentieth century's mass killing was carried out by states attempting to impose a particular ideology or racial orthodoxy on others, often their own citizens. It is important to recognize that the nature of war is shaped by the politics that underpin it and that, as such, war can be more or less limited and rule-governed (see Bonanate 1995: 17). It is this possibility of distinguishing between 'better' and 'worse', legitimate and illegitimate, war that sets it apart from 'brute force' and opens the door to normative engagement.

The Just War Tradition

The Just War tradition is a two-thousand-year-old conversation about the legitimacy of war (see Nardin 1992: 6–21; Rengger 2002: 362) that has over time crystallized around several core principles and sub-traditions. Michael Walzer based his landmark account of just and unjust wars on what he described as the 'war convention', the customary embodiment of the Just War tradition. According to Walzer (1977: 44), the war convention arose out of the 'articulated norms, customs, professional codes, legal precepts, religious and philosophical principles and reciprocal arrangements that shape our judgments of military conduct'. It shapes our judgements about war. It provides a justificatory framework; a meaningful language that soldiers and politicians use to legitimize their actions and that friends, foes and bystanders alike use to evaluate those claims. Through the war convention, actors from a range of diverse cultural backgrounds can communicate their normative judgements about war (see Kratochwil 1989: 6).

The war convention does more than provide a framework for judgement, however. It can also constrain and enable certain types of activity. As Walzer put it (1977: 45), 'though chivalry is dead . . . professional soldiers remain sensitive (or some of them do) to those limits and restraints that distinguish their life's work from mere butchery'. Thus, armed forces and political leaders are inhibited from acting in ways that cannot be justified by reference to the war convention (Skinner 1988: 117). This claim comes with three caveats. First, it assumes that actors wish to be considered legitimate within the prevailing international order. Actors that wish to change the order through force, that have little interest in establishing or maintaining themselves as legitimate international actors, or that believe that their rule-breaking will not provoke a negative response are less likely to be constrained by the war convention. Second, it makes no judgement about the plausibility of justificatory arguments. Arthur Watts (2000: 8) famously declared that a legal argument need only be 'not demonstrably rubbish' and thereafter political considerations would determine whether a particular act was deemed acceptable or not. This is pertinent for the war convention. The continuing prevalence of the idea of military necessity and what Walzer (2004a: 33–50) described as 'emergency ethics' within the war convention grants soldiers and politicians considerable leeway to justify actions that may otherwise be proscribed. Third, there is the problem of indeterminacy: whilst there might be broad agreement about the nature of the war convention, common reference points are not enough to generate agreement in specific cases (Wheeler, N. J. 2004a: 47). In the absence of an authoritative global judge to adjudicate competing claims, such claims cannot be resolved by appeal to the rules alone (Higgins 1994: 7–8; Wheeler, N. J. 2004b: 194–5). In short, the Just War tradition creates the possibility for meaningful discussion about the legitimacy of war and can inhibit actions that cannot be justified by reference to it, but it cannot determine political outcomes or judgements in every case.

According to Hedley Bull (1979), Walzer's account of the war convention was both unsupported and ahistorical. Bull argued (1979: 598–9) that Walzer repeatedly invoked the war convention to make judgements about the normative merits of different types of activity, but he assumed that his readers both knew what the war convention proscribed and agreed that those proscriptions required no further justification. To understand and utilize the war convention, Bull argued, we need to comprehend its historical evolution. This is the primary purpose of the first part of this book.

It is important at this juncture to recognize that in some important respects what is commonly referred to as 'Just War theory' (e.g. Elshtain 1992; Evans 2005) is not about 'Just' wars and is only 'theory' in the very loosest sense. The tradition's use of the word 'just' should not be read as implying that its function is to justify war or that it holds war to be a good in itself. Most thinkers associated with the tradition abhorred war but acknowledged it as a social fact. They investigated the circumstances that made some wars 'justifiable' and others not. The criteria they developed were tools for evaluating and critiquing the actions of political leaders and soldiers (Johnson 2001: 110). They did not praise warriors, but sought to ascertain the conditions that made the warrior's work more or less blameworthy. The Just War tradition is, therefore, concerned with the lesser evil (see Ignatieff 2004). It acknowledges that war always has evil consequences, principally the deaths of non-combatants, but that there are some wrongs that are worse than the wrong of war itself.

The Just War is also only a 'theory' in the very loosest sense. The tradition is fragmented, comprising many different sub-traditions, and indeed sub-sub-traditions (see Figure 1 on p. 8), none of which permanently prevail over the others. In this sense, it is the conversation that is important (Rengger 2002: 362). According to Hidemi Suganami (2005: 30), a normative theory is one that 'elucidates the steps through which some fundamental normative presuppositions lead to conclusions about what should be done in world politics'. The Just War tradition as a whole contains many such theories: secular and divine; legal and moral; consequentialist and deontological. It offers several ways of generating normative presuppositions about war. Its different sub-traditions are united by three common factors: first, they share a concern that recourse to war ought to be limited and conduct of war made as humane as possible; second, they originated in Western traditions of theological, legal and philosophical reasoning; and, third, they subscribe to a common set of rules governing the decision to wage war (*jus ad bellum*) and its conduct (*jus in bello*), though they differ in both their interpretation of the rules and the relative weight they attach to them. Within the Just War tradition as a whole, there are myriad sub-traditions, including scholasticism, neo-scholasticism, canon law, chivalry, holy war, secular natural law, positive law, various types of 'reformism', and realism (see Figure 1). Today, these sub-traditions can be broadly categorized into three types (positive law, natural law and realism), which are discussed in greater detail below.

It is necessary to comment briefly on the second commonality mentioned above. Some critics complain that the tradition is distinctly European and Christian and therefore incapable of providing a common, global, framework. Robert Myers (1996: 122), for instance, insists that the tradition was constructed to suit the interests of Church and state, whereby the Church sanctioned the use of force in the service of Machiavellian statecraft and in return enjoyed the state's patronage and protection. Whilst it is true that the tradition has European origins, there are at least four reasons to doubt the claim that this undermines its role. First, as Jack Donnelly argues (1989: 60), it is unreasonable to claim that an idea that has its origins in one place cannot be adopted elsewhere. If it were true, many ideas and traditions that are adhered to and practised cross-culturally would never have travelled. Second, the Just War tradition encompasses positive law, and almost all the world's states are parties to the UN Charter and the Geneva Conventions and Protocols that govern *jus ad bellum* and *jus in bello*. Thus, at least in a formal sense, almost all the world's communities have consented to the most basic positive laws governing war. Third, most of the world's religious and philosophical traditions contain rules not dissimilar to the Just War tradition (see, e.g., Hashimi and Lee 2004; Lepard 2002). There is therefore an 'overlapping consensus' around the Just War tradition's basic ideas: many peoples arrive at similar sets of rules from very different perspectives (Rawls 1993: 133–72, Caney 2005: 87). Finally, my argument is that the Just War tradition provides a set of common referent points, not that it determines political or moral outcomes. In practice, the tradition affords many different ways of interpreting its rules, opening a space for political dialogue.

The Just War tradition fulfils two roles. It provides a common language that actors can use to legitimize recourse to force and the conduct of war and that others use to evaluate those claims. It can also inhibit actions that cannot be legitimated. The Just War tradition itself is a protracted normative conversation about war that has crystallized around a number of principles, labelled the 'war convention' by Walzer. This book develops a novel account whereby what is considered legitimate in any given case is dependent on the balance between the three sets of values embedded in the Just War tradition's main sub-traditions: positive law, natural law and realism.

Does the tradition only apply to *wars* in the Clausewitzian sense? My view is that the tradition applies to all forms of political violence whether or not they earn the label of war. There are three reasons for this. First, formally separating war from other forms of political violence seems arbitrary. Second, some aspects of positive law relating to war, such as the 1977 Geneva Protocols, apply to all 'armed conflicts'. Finally, disputes about whether a given armed conflict amounts to war or not usually take place within the realm of positive law and are important because they determine which types of laws should apply, peacetime law or the very different war laws. Such arguments are very important, but according to the approach developed in this book they take place at a secondary level. They make a contribution to, but do not determine, wider debates about the legitimacy of violent acts.

The Just War Tradition and Legitimacy

Because the Just War tradition is primarily concerned with restraining war by legitimating certain types of actions and de-legitimating others, it is important to question how we understand legitimacy. There are at least two ways of approaching this question, which Ian Clark (2005: 18–19) describes as 'substantive' and 'procedural' approaches (see also Bellamy and Williams 2005). The substantive approach, widely favoured by the earliest Just War writers, holds that an act is legitimate if it conforms to certain rules. Such rules may be divinely prescribed, grounded in natural law or approved by authoritative legislators (Clark, I. 2005: 18; Donagan 1977: 149–57; Nardin 2005: 252). Rules are important, this approach insists, because they reflect embedded moral truths or because they are created by authoritative bodies. However, political realists would argue that because world politics is anarchic (in that there is no world government), international rules cannot be enforced and therefore lose their binding character (e.g. Art and Waltz 1983: 6; Morgenthau 1951). As noted earlier, rules alone cannot resolve disputes.

In practice, their applicability and meaning in specific cases are interpreted and contested.

Procedural approaches attempt to overcome this apparent disconnection between rules and practice by focusing on the manner in which decisions are reached. There are a number of different procedural approaches. The most basic holds that legitimacy can be elided with consensus (Osiander 2001: 9–10). This approach creates the logical possibility that decisions that produce intuitively immoral consequences may nevertheless be legitimate. A different take on this theme suggests that an act is legitimate if the decision-making procedure that produced it conformed to particular moral principles (Linklater 1998; Shapcott 2001). Decisions may be considered legitimate if they are made on the basis of a genuine consensus among all the parties likely to be affected by the proposed course of action. Sadly, present conditions in world politics are so alien to the ideal environment that underpins this approach that virtually every decision would be rendered illegitimate. Furthermore, as Gerry Simpson (2004) has convincingly argued, small and medium-sized states have often recognized the legitimacy of 'legalized hierarchies' that grant powerful states special rights and responsibilities for the maintenance of international order. What this second approach captures, though, is the idea that legitimacy and consensus cannot be elided; that consensus must be founded to some extent on agreed moral rules to reflect legitimacy (Clark, I. 2005: 206).

My approach to the Just War tradition holds that in war, acts are legitimate if they are justified in terms of the common referents and perspectives provided by the Just War tradition and if those justifications are validated by other actors (Clark, I. 2003: 80). I reject both the substantive claim that rules can be applied in a neutral fashion and the dialogic insistence on entirely inclusive consultation. When actors proffer justifications for their actions, others serve as 'judges and juries' weighing the balance of the different claims (see Franck 2002: 185). 'Judges' are those entities capable of backing up their judgements with serious material rewards or punishments; in particular, the world's most powerful states. 'Juries' comprise the rest of world opinion. Jurors debate and form their own opinions, can impose some relatively minor penalties and rewards and can attempt to influence judges' decisions. In the second part of the book, I will act as a juror – evaluating the claims levelled to justify particular types of action, claims for rules changes and the arguments put forward by other jurors.

My approach is therefore based on two ideas: (1) actors tend to use a common normative language to justify their behaviour to others; and (2) actors use these common reference points (among other things) to assess the legitimacy of others' actions, which in turn frame their responses to them. Actors that accept the legitimacy of a particular act are more likely to provide material and diplomatic support; those that believe an act to be illegitimate may condemn it, impose sanctions or try to punish the perpetrators. It is important to reiterate here that the common language provided by the Just War tradition does not guarantee that judges and jurors will agree in particular cases.

According to Clark, legitimacy claims are articulated and assessed by reference to three subordinate sets of norms, none of which is permanently prioritized over the others. Clark describes these as legality, morality and constitutionality. The first two are self-evident. Constitutionality refers to the interplay of power and interests in political relations. At the core of constitutionality 'are political sensibilities about what can properly be done, and how affairs should be conducted' (Clark, I. 2005: 220). Constitutionality therefore points towards the political aspects of legitimacy judgements. In relation to war, these sensibilities are best captured by political realism. The Just War tradition provides a *legitimacy* framework for war that encompasses these three norms through its three main sub-traditions. This is illustrated by Figure 1.

As set out in Figure 1, my starting point is the claim that judgements about the legitimacy of particular wars are framed by the Just War tradition. In turn, what is considered 'just' depends on the interplay between the tradition's legal sub-tradition (positive law), moral sub-tradition (natural law) and political sub-tradition (realism). According to Clark (2005: 207–8),

legitimacy is a composite of, and an accommodation between, a number of other norms, both procedural and substantive, and does not possess its own independent standard against which actions can be measured. For that reason, it is never in direct tension with other norms: it is amongst those norms that any tension exists. . . . From this point of view, legitimacy denotes a combination of values, and represents some balance amongst them, when these individual normative standards might tend to pull in opposite directions.

As illustrated, the nature and content of these sub-traditions change over time, as does the relationship between them. What the Just War tradition has to say about a particular matter depends upon the appropriate balance between the three sub-traditions at any given time or place.

Structure of the Book

The first part of this book maps the evolution of different streams of thought that comprise the Just War tradition in order to provide a foundation for an evaluation of contemporary normative dilemmas about war.

Chapter 1 focuses on the earliest Just War thinkers in ancient Greece, the Roman Empire and the early Christian Church. Like earlier, non-European civilizations, the Greeks and Romans developed customs and

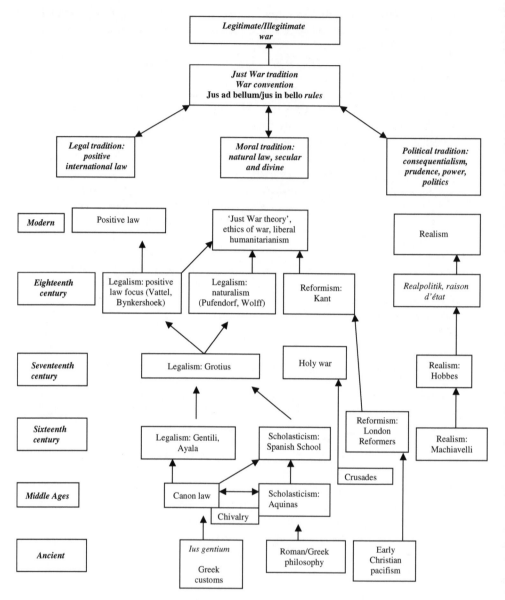

Figure 1: The Just War tradition as a legitimacy framework

laws governing war. Many of these ideas directly influenced the earliest non-pacifist Christian writers, including Ambrose and Augustine. Indeed, other than providing Christian foundations, the earliest Christian Just War writers added little that was substantively new to the prescriptions set out by Roman law and Cicero. Augustine and other early Christian Just War writers were primarily concerned with countering the pacifism that dominated early Christian teaching and focused on the moral justification of individual participation in war. Augustine argued that war was only licit for the purpose of preserving peace or righting a wrong and that it must be conducted by a proper authority, which in Augustine's time meant the Roman Empire. Augustine was all but silent on the *jus in bello*, insisting only that soldiers obey commands from their superiors and fight with right intention.

It was during the Middle Ages, discussed in Chapter 2, that Just War teaching was codified and different sub-traditions began to emerge: canon law, scholasticism, the chivalric code and the doctrine of holy war. Canon law governed the conduct of the Church and individuals who fell under its jurisdiction. Among other things, it claimed jurisdiction over war. The two main problems that troubled canon lawyers were the questions of who had authority to wage war and what the permissible role of the Church was. By the thirteenth century, a consensus emerged around the proposition that wars could only be waged by princes with the authority to do so. The role of the Church was more carefully limited. The law insisted that clerics must not themselves participate in war, though they could exhort others to do so and the papacy had a right to declare divinely sanctioned wars. With the exception of the 'Peace of God' and 'Truce of God' movements, *jus in bello* played a secondary role for canon lawyers. The main sources of its development in this period were the scholastic writings of Thomas Aquinas and the chivalric tradition. Aquinas contributed two pivotal ideas: the doctrine of double-effect and the proportionality rule. The chivalric code developed as a customary practice within the knightly class and was gradually transformed into a statutory code (Meron 1998: 5). The fourth sub-tradition was holy war. During the Middle Ages, holy war was an integral part of the Just War tradition enabled by the insight that wars directly commanded by God were justifiable. This idea persisted until the sixteenth century, though scepticism grew as to how humans could definitively know that God had commanded war.

The sixteenth century was an important period of contestation and change among the different sub-traditions, and this is detailed in Chapter 3. The decline of medieval governance structures, rise of new technologies, discovery of the Americas, emergence of sovereign states and development of new methodologies that challenged scholasticism and introduced secularism contributed to a more open intellectual climate. Three medieval traditions went into decline, two of them permanently: the use of artillery eroded the distinctiveness of the knightly class and in turn the impact of chivalry on the conduct of war; the Christian reformation and bifurcation of the western Church into Catholic and Protestant reduced canon law's jurisdiction; and the loss of the holy lands to the Turks in the fourteenth century temporarily reduced the fervour for holy wars. In their place, the so-called 'Spanish school' refined scholasticism, as Francisco de Vitoria developed an almost complete neo-scholastic account of the Just War. Scholasticism competed with three relatively new traditions, two of which (realism and legalism) were inspired by the growing centrality of states and the third (reformism) by the renaissance spirit of critique. Significantly, all three of these new traditions made use of a secular account of natural law, but between the sixteenth and nineteenth centuries theological and secular approaches cohabited.

The relatively open and broad-ranging debates that epitomized the Just War tradition in the sixteenth century were gradually brought to an end by the re-emergence of holy war thinking in the late sixteenth and early seventeenth centuries. Chapter 4 charts the impact of this on the Just War tradition from the seventeenth century to the end of the eighteenth century. In part, the wars that wracked Europe during this period were a contest between Protestants and Catholics over the meaning of the 'one true faith', but in greater part they were about fashioning a new European political order to replace the irretrievably decayed feudal order (Bonney 1991). The resurgence of holy war throughout Europe inspired an important intellectual reaction. Both holy war thinking itself and Catholic scholasticism were widely discredited. In their place, realism and legalism took centre stage, epitomized by the deeply influential work of Hobbes and Grotius. The idea of common Christendom was gradually replaced by the idea that Europe was divided into territorially discrete states ruled by sovereigns. Although Grotius continued the legalist tradition of coupling natural and positive law, post-Grotian legalists tended to bifurcate into those prioritizing natural law (Pufendorf) and those who tended towards positive law (Vattel and Bynkershoek), though both coupled natural and positive law to some extent.

The final chapter in the first part of the book charts the solidification of legalism and realism as central tenets of the Just War tradition and the decisive shift within legalism towards positive law. This shift was manifested in the increasing body of international positive law designed to constrain both recourse to force and its conduct. In relation to *jus ad bellum*, the apex of this trend came with the UN Charter's prohibition on the use of force except in self-defence or for collective enforcement measures. Positive law in relation to *jus in bello* continues to develop. The 1949 Geneva Conventions and subsequent Protocols created a comprehensive system of basic law that has since been added to in an *ad hoc* fashion. In 2002, states established the International Criminal Court to prosecute individuals guilty of grave breaches of *jus in bello*. For much of the twentieth century, however, the persistence of realist ideas among political leaders and strategists alike limited the impact of positive law on the actual conduct of war. More recently, natural law-type arguments have re-emerged under different guises, insisting that positive law does not cover the full spectrum of normative decision-making about war and that there may occasionally be moral imperatives for acting in ways prohibited by positive law. Today, the Just War tradition comprises three broad sub-traditions (positive law, natural law, realism), each of which offers different ways of interpreting and valuing the tradition's core rules.

The second part of the book explores some of the most important normative dilemmas posed by contemporary war by reference to the Just War tradition. It begins in Chapter 6 by detailing the content of the sub-traditions and the relationship between them. Chapter 6 also explores ways of addressing four major problems raised by this way of viewing the Just War tradition: the potential for conflict between the sub-traditions, the relationship between *jus ad bellum* and *jus in bello*, the place of emergency ethics, and the question of how rules change. The remainder of Part II focuses on contemporary normative dilemmas associated with terrorism, pre-emptive self-defence, aerial bombardment and humanitarian intervention.

Chapter 7 explores whether terrorism, understood as the intentional targeting of non-combatants, is ever justified. After defending this definition, the chapter moves on to reject different justifications for terrorism (based on consequentialism, collective responsibility, supreme emergency and holy wars, respectively) on the grounds that none of these arguments provide a sound case for overriding the fundamental principle of non-combatant immunity. With this in mind, the question becomes not so much one of whether the act of terrorism itself is ever justifiable but whether terrorist tactics undermine the causes for which they are used. This chapter identifies three types of terrorism based on the extent to which *jus in bello* violations undermine the terrorist's *jus ad bellum* case for using violence in the first place.

Chapter 8 asks whether states have a right of pre-emptive self-defence in the face of a terrorist threat. Traditionally, both positive law and natural law have conceded only a narrow right of pre-emption when the impending threat is imminent and overwhelming, leaving no room for manoeuvre. Since September 11, many writers have complained that this formula prevents states from effectively defending their citizens from terrorism because it is much harder to identify specific emerging threats. While such approaches point to important limitations in the traditional account of pre-emption, they offer overly permissive alternatives that could undermine international order. In their place, I offer an account of pre-emption whereby states may act against terrorists (be they states or non-state actors) so long as modified imminence and necessity tests are satisfied. The amended imminence test insists that pre-emptive force may only be used against terrorists who have the means and clearly demonstrated intention to strike, even if a particular attack is not temporally imminent and it is not known what the precise target will be. The second test requires that those using pre-emptive force demonstrate its necessity.

Chapter 9 explores the ethical questions associated with the use of air power in the war on terror, focusing on the US-led intervention in Afghanistan. This chapter takes us from the relatively abstract discussions of earlier chapters and demonstrates how the Just War tradition also shapes judgements about the minutiae of war. Combating terrorism presents some unique challenges to military leaders. Terrorists are difficult to distinguish from non-combatants, hide amongst non-combatants and launch attacks from bases in civilian settings, do not abide by the rules of war, and employ violence sporadically. Combined, this makes it very difficult for rule-abiding militaries to prevail in battle against terrorists. This chapter focuses on the problems of discrimination and proportionality during Operation *Enduring Freedom* in Afghanistan. I argue that whilst the US Air Force discriminated between combatants and non-combatants, doubts remain about whether it demonstrated due care by taking every reasonable measure to reduce the risks faced by Afghan non-combatants. This case demonstrates how difficult it is in practice to make judgements about how much extra risk combatants should be prepared to accept in order to reduce the risks faced by enemy non-combatants.

The final chapter turns to the question of humanitarian intervention. This is one of the most complex and hotly contested issues in contemporary world politics. I ask whether states have a right and/or duty to intervene in humanitarian crises characterized by mass killing and ethnic cleansing. After a brief survey of many different positions on this question, I attempt to articulate a Just War framework for evaluating the legitimacy of humanitarian intervention based on the idea that in these cases there is a close relationship between right authority and just cause. The chapter then applies the proposed framework to three cases: Kosovo, Iraq and Darfur. I argue that states that invoke a right of humanitarian intervention in one case incur a duty to protect endangered civilians in similar future cases, but that this duty is constrained by considerations of prudence and proportionality.

The purpose of this book is to inform debates about the legitimacy of today's wars. The challenge is to understand the relationship between rules and practice; to identify the rough edges, the points where different sub-traditions pull in different directions and where those different traditions have plausible cases to make, and to navigate a way through seemingly intractable dilemmas.

PART I

MAPPING THE JUST WAR TRADITION

1

Antiquity

This chapter traces the development of normative thinking about war from the early European civilizations of Greece and Rome to the work of Augustine at the end of the Roman era in the fifth century. Although the Just War tradition has its origins in ancient Greece and Rome, earlier civilizations also attempted to limit war. For a brief period, the Aztecs fought battles with fixed numbers of soldiers, on predetermined days, and pre-arranged battlefields (Christopher 1994: 9). Sun Tzu (1963: 76–8), the renowned fifth-century Chinese strategist, insisted that armies treat prisoners and non-combatants with respect. Ancient Hindu, Egyptian and Hebrew civilizations created rules governing the humane treatment of prisoners and non-combatants in wartime (Christopher 1994: 9–10). However, these customs of war often only applied to wars fought within a particular civilization and even then could be overridden by necessity. These conventions were primarily concerned with ensuring that the individual polities within a particular civilization could resolve their differences violently with minimal damage to the civilization as a whole. Moreover, these rules and traditions were constitutive of a warrior's calling and helped to distinguish between warriors (generally respected by society) and murderers (generally reviled). Thus, what Shannon French (2005) labelled the 'warrior's code' was meant to both protect society from the warriors and protect the warriors themselves.

This chapter charts the earliest Just War thinking in four parts. The first focuses on the development of customary practices and philosophical ideas in ancient Greece. The second evaluates the contribution of Roman law and ethics to the Just War tradition. The third section discusses the professed pacifism of the early Christian Church. The fourth and final section assesses Augustine's contribution to the early Just War tradition.

Ancient Greece

Between 700 and 450 BC, Greek city-states observed loose traditions aimed at limiting war. Restraints on war were derived from Hellenic customs and written treaties, though as Greek society fragmented during the Peloponnesian War, there was a growing focus on written treaties at the expense of custom (Fleiss 1960: 3). Breaches of the customs elicited 'indignant comments' from writers and political leaders (Ober 1994: 13). These customs, which only pertained to war between the city-states and not to the Hellenic wars against Persia, covered both recourse to war and its conduct. The Greek code insisted that war should be formally declared, truces should be respected, especially during the Olympic Games, and battles should only be fought during the campaigning season (summer). The code also covered the conduct of war. It held that erecting a battlefield trophy was a mark of victory and should be respected as such, a battle should be prefaced by a ritual challenge, non-combatants should not be the primary target of attacks, and prisoners should be offered for ransom rather than executed (Ober 1994: 13).

The Peloponnesian War caused these customary practices to break down (see Bury et al. 1927: 165ff.). There were many reasons for this, but three stand out. First, the development of Athenian democracy and its leaders' belief in the superiority of democracy over oligarchy created ideological strife, particularly between Athens and the two principal oligarchic states, Thebes and Sparta. Second, social and strategic changes within Athens reduced the centrality of the warrior class on whom the traditional customs rested (Ober 1994: 19–20). Athens, for instance, built a citizen army and also used mercenaries (Russell, A. G. 1941: 103–12). Finally, the transformation of the 'Delian League' into the Athenian Empire and its open desire for imperial expansion made war a matter of survival for many city-states, not a mechanism for resolving petty disputes (Gregor 1953: 27–32). In this context, armies used terror, deception and insurgency tactics to improve their chances of success (Ashworth 1996).

The Greek historian Thucydides recounted the Peloponnesian War in detail and is sometimes labelled the first important realist (e.g. Gilpin 1981: 227–8). Thucydides portrayed the war as a story of Athens' moral decay and the dramatic erosion of the customs of war. This point can be demonstrated by briefly considering one of the most oft-cited passages of his history: the 'Melian dialogue'. The Melian dialogue took place in 416 BC on the island of Melos. Melos had remained neutral during the war, offering assistance to neither Athens nor Sparta. The Athenians sent envoys to secure the island state's allegiance. The Melians refused to ally with Athens, insisting that their independence be respected. They argued that if Athens acted unjustly towards them, others would unite against the Athenians and overrun them. The Athenians rejected this argument, giving the famous retort that 'you know as well as we do that right, as the word goes, is only in question between equals in power, while the strong do what they can and the weak suffer what they must' (Thucydides 1954: 98). Still the Melians refused to forgo their independence and the Athenians attacked, slaying all the island's inhabitants. Although the Athenians succeeded in this instance, they paid a heavy price for their hubris. As the Melians predicted, the injustices of the Athenian actions in Melos encouraged other states to ally against them. Alcibiades, who had led the Melian expedition, later invaded Sicily with the intent of colonizing it. The Sicilians and a growing number of allies defeated Athens, and in 404 BC, the Peloponnesian War came to an end.

For Thucydides, the war was a tragedy of epic proportions, an internal war that destroyed the Hellenic society of city-states (see Price 2001). As demonstrated by the Melian dialogue, the war caused the breakdown of the customs of war that had characterized earlier Greek warfare. Although the 'might is right' doctrine can be found in Thucydides, the underlying story is one of moral decay. The war was devastating for both the Athenian empire and wider Hellenic society. In the long run, it irretrievably weakened Greece's ability to unite against external enemies. The Greek customs of war had been developed to satisfy the city-states' shared interest in preserving Hellenic society and their erosion damaged Greek civilization as a whole (Bainton 1960: 28).

The war's aftermath brought new forms of philosophy to the fore in Athens, prompting new ways of thinking about war. Plato (2003: § 351) argued that the path to happiness lay in justice, and that justice was not simply a matter of opinion, as the Sophists claimed, but a matter of knowledge. He concurred with the Melians that injustice did not serve the interests of the powerful because it caused fragmentation and wasteful conflict (Plato 2003: §§ 351–2). Plato insisted that democracy could not be trusted to provide knowledge and the requisite good life because, as Athens' recent history demonstrated, the democratic will (*demos*) tended towards the most unjust forms of governance. The same reasoning resonated in *The Laws*, in which Plato directly addressed the question of war. Here, Plato (2005: § 631) argued that war was an eternal feature of human society and reflected the two sides of man – one better, one worse. The aim of the state was to establish peace by subjugating the worse side of people's nature and promoting the positive. According to Plato, war should only be waged for the sake of peace.

Plato also addressed the question of how wars should be fought. In *The Republic*, Plato's Socrates outlined a series of restraints on the conduct of war. They included refraining from burning habitations and only killing foes and not all the men, women and children of the enemy state (Plato 2003: § 471). Plato insisted that these restraints were only valid amongst Greeks, who spoke the same language. However, in a later text Plato lamented the 'arbitrary' division of humanity into Greeks and barbarians and noted that many Greek words had non-Greek origins, suggesting that there may be a thin duty to act humanely even in wars with non-Greeks (see Pappas 1995: 109–10).

Aristotle distilled these ideas further. He replaced Plato's deontological conception of justice with a relational conception whereby justice was found 'in relation to a friend. For justice belongs to persons who have [something] in common' (Miller, F. D. 1995: 84). According to Aristotle, justice depended on human relations and all humans had their own position within nature. From this perspective, Aristotle formulated the first ideas about the legitimate causes of war and even used the term 'just war'. He argued (Aristotle 1998: § 199) that there were five pretexts for waging war legitimately: in self-defence, to take vengeance on those who have injured us, to help allies, to gain advantage for the *polis* in the form of glory or resources, and to maintain authority over those not fit to rule themselves. The fourth and fifth causes derived directly from Aristotle's belief that humanity had a natural order, with some fit to be rulers and others not, and that war aimed at restoring or maintaining that order was legitimate (see Hamburger 1951: 172–5).

The ancient Greek period therefore saw restraints placed on both recourse to war and conduct of war and witnessed their breakdown, with devastating consequences for both Athens and the Hellenic world more generally. After the Athenian disaster in 404 BC, philosophers refuted the idea that there was a profound connection between justice and power, which had become prevalent during the war and had been at least partly responsible for Athens' demise. This resuscitated the idea that city-states should exercise restraint in warfare with one another, though the philosophers continued to insist that such restraints were only valid in internal Greek wars.

The Roman Empire

Roman rules about war moved beyond the Greek in at least two important respects. First, the Roman philosopher Cicero developed a more comprehensive account of the laws of war. Second, the promulgation of *ius gentium* (law of peoples) suggested the possibility of *universal* legal restraints on the conduct of war (Bederman 2001).

At the time that Athens fell, Rome was itself undergoing distressing times. In 390 BC, the Gauls sacked Rome. In the years that followed, Rome embarked on a series of almost continuous wars and conquests, until it dominated virtually all of Europe, much of the Middle East, and North Africa (Scullard 1951). During this period of expansion, Roman leaders launched new offensives almost every year. New wars and conquests fulfilled three purposes: they kept the legions busy, reducing the likelihood of civil war; they secured important resources; and they brought glory to successful conquerors. Rome valued military glory. Roman writers and politicians celebrated emperors who pursued expansionist policies and vilified those who did not or were unsuccessful. Security, it was believed, rested on the empire's appearance of greatness, which in turn depended on demonstrations of military might (Mattern 1999: 162–210). This did not mean, however, that there were no rules about the decision to wage war. The early Romans believed that victory depended on satisfying the gods and therefore followed fetial law (*ius fetiale*) to please the gods when deciding to wage war (Halliday 1922: 114).

Under fetial law, the Senate was obliged to send emissaries with Rome's demands to enemy states and wait thirty-three days for a response. If the demands were rejected or if no reply was forthcoming, the republic could issue a declaration of war, and even then only once religious leaders (the *fetiale*) endorsed the proposed action (Harris 1979: 167). Roman apologists argued that this procedure ensured that Rome only fought wars for defensive purposes or to rectify a prior injury received (e.g. Davie 1929: 292–3). Others have argued that fetial law was more or less uniformly practised and provided an 'objective' measure of the justice of war (e.g. Christopher 1994: 14; Nussbaum 1954: 21–3). However, even in the heyday of the republic, the fetial procedure was only applied in special cases, notably in the Punic Wars against Carthage, the war against Phillip V and the attack on Perseus. In the same period, the procedure was not used in the war against Antiochus III in 191 BC or in the war against the Aetolians. The procedure disappeared entirely from the historical record around 171 BC (Harris 1979: 167). What is more, the conditions that Rome offered were non-negotiable and often set at unacceptable levels, so there is only one case of a state accepting the demands. The fetial procedure, therefore, 'had nothing to do with any philosophically conceived system of impartial equity' (Harris 1979: 170). It was a precautionary measure taken to persuade the gods to support wars that Rome was not certain of winning.

Rome was always keen to assert the justice of its wars. However, formal justice was not primarily found in the fetial procedure, as has often been suggested, but in the belief that Rome's wars were defensive. Polybius argued that it was important always to have a pretext for war, because pretexts satisfied humanity as well as the gods (Harris 1979: 172). This encouraged a subtle shift away from fetial law to a concern with creating pretexts for war that seemed to demonstrate their justice. What is clear, as Harris points out (1979: 172), is that neither approach restrained Roman expansionism or limited Rome to fighting defensive wars only.

Like the Greek philosophers before him, Cicero believed that the proper role of the state was to maintain a balance between nature and law in order to facilitate the pursuit of justice and hence happiness (see Wheeler, M. 1952: 49–56). He argued that war may only be fought to protect the safety or honour of the state (Cicero 1928: 211–3). Echoing Plato, Cicero (1961: 38) insisted that 'the only excuse ... for going to war is that we may live in peace unharmed'. Even wars fought for glory must be motivated by the desire to live in peace, and Cicero insisted that such wars be prosecuted with less brutality than wars for survival. Expansionist wars were justified 'to enlarge the boundaries of peace, order and justice' (Wilkin 1947: 65). By bringing more lands into the empire, he reasoned, greater peace and happiness could be brought to humanity. Thus, for Cicero, there was no contradiction between fighting for the glory of Rome and fighting to preserve the peace.

Cicero had two other principal concerns. First, in order to minimize the potential for civil war, he insisted that wars be formally declared by the proper authorities and that only soldiers on active duty for the state were entitled to fight (Cicero 1961: 39). Second, he argued that there should be limits on what the state may do even to its enemies in the form of retribution and punishment. Specifically he urged soldiers to 'take consideration' of the inhabitants of conquered lands and offer protection to enemies who laid down their arms (Cicero 1961: 37).

Although there were many cases where Cicero's prescriptions were not followed, Roman practice bequeathed the idea that there were certain laws binding on all. These were the *ius gentium*, which were grounded in natural law derived from the conscience of mankind (see Aristotle 2004: §§ 5–13). Cicero argued that *ius gentium* was also grounded in Roman jurisprudence and developed over time as a response to the necessities of governing a large and multinational empire. *Ius gentium* attempted to maintain equity between the peoples of Rome by allowing magistrates to moderate the civil law (*ius civile*) to take local customs, languages and procedures into account. According to Gaius (in Johnston 2000: 619), *ius gentium* also applied beyond Rome's borders. *Ius gentium* is important because it framed thinking about the legality of war until the sixteenth century: the rights-bearer under *ius gentium* was the individual and it was not until the sixteenth century that the sovereign entities became the principal bearer of rights (Chroust 1941–2: 22–8). However, its enforcement presupposed the existence of a universal empire, which is indeed how Rome perceived itself.

Whilst the empire persisted, Roman law and ethics provided a useful guide to *jus ad bellum*, containing many of the core elements of the later Just War tradition (especially just cause and right authority). One of the main problems that animated canonists and theologians after the empire's fall was the issue of who had the authority to wage war and enforce *ius gentium*. Moreover, adherents to the new Christian religion were confronted with the challenge of ascertaining whether killing itself was ever justified. Restraints on the conduct of war in the post-Roman period were predominantly pioneered by the ecclesiastical peace movements and chivalric tradition (see Chapter 2).

The Early Christians

When considering the morality of war, the earliest Christians confronted the dilemmas of deciding how to interpret scripture and relate to the government of the time. There was something of a contradiction between Christian teaching and practice. Christian leaders such as Origen and Tertullian preached pacifism, whilst some Christians served in increasing numbers in the Roman army from as early as 173. At the heart of the problem for Christians was the fact that the New Testament contained no definitive answer to the question of whether a Christian may participate in war. The God of the Old Testament was partially a God of war. Yahweh sometimes exhorted the Jews to war and urged them to show no restraint, on one occasion telling them: 'If thou wilt indeed deliver this people into my hand, then I will utterly destroy their cities' (Numbers 21:2). On other occasions, however, God instructed the Jews to offer peace before attacking a city and refrain from destroying fruit-bearing trees (Deuteronomy 20:10, 19). The Gospels are equally ambiguous. On the one hand, Jesus' teachings at the Sermon of the Mount can be interpreted as demanding non-violence (e.g. Matthew 5:5, 9, 39). Jesus also rebuked Peter for drawing his sword in Gethsemane with the phrase, 'all they that take the sword shall perish with the sword' (Matthew 26:52). Elsewhere, however, the Gospels and epistles were uncritical of military service. Neither the centurion who came to John the Baptist (Luke 3:14), the centurion at Capernaum (Matthew 8:5–13) nor the centurion Cornelius (Acts 10) were admonished for their profession. Jesus also said, 'Think not that I am come to send peace on earth: I came not to send peace, but a sword' (Matthew 10:34). However, whatever one thinks of the balance of New Testament teaching, there is no evidence of Christian participation in military service before 173. Four principal explanations have been offered for this absence.

The first is eschatological. Many Christians believed that the Second Coming of Christ was close at hand and that until that time Christians should remove themselves from public life, reject the ways of man and retain an 'other-worldliness' (Bainton 1960: 62–3). Christian eschatology demanded sectarianism and withdrawal from human affairs (Johnson 1987: 12–13). Thus, prior to 173 Christians tended to refrain from all forms of public service, not just the military.

The second explanation focuses on idolatrous practices in the military. Before Constantine, military officers were expected to follow the cult of the deified emperor, and officers of centurion rank and above were obliged to perform sacrifices (Bainton 1960: 74). Pagan idolatry was clearly inadmissible for the early Christians, making it impossible for them to serve in the military. In *On the Soldier's Crown*, Tertullian responded to a question about whether a Christian in the military may wear the military's laurel crown. He answered in the negative, arguing that the crown was implicitly idolatrous. In doing so, however, he revealed both the Christian's aversion to idolatry in the military and the fact that there were Christians in the army at this time (Tertullian 1885a: 61–78; 1885b: 93–104).

The third explanation for Christian reluctance to serve in the military was the relationship between the Christian community and Rome. In the first two centuries AD, the empire often persecuted Christians. Why, Roland Bainton (1960: 74) asked, would Christians volunteer to serve in the army of an empire that persecuted them? Moreover, the book of Revelation identified Rome as the anti-Christ. This perspective was probably most powerful during the persecutions of the first century, but by the second and third centuries there is evidence that although Church leaders believed military service to be unsuitable for a Christian life, they also welcomed Roman law as a barrier against anarchy (Bainton 1960: 74).

The final, and most popular, explanation is the argument that the early Church leaders were pacifists because they interpreted the New Testament teaching as calling upon Christians to renounce violence. Twentieth-century historians such as Hershberger (1969) and Cadoux (1919) argued that the early Christians were doctrinally committed to non-resistance and pacifism. The move away from pacifism after the conversion and succession of Constantine was seen as a 'fall' from the purity of pacifism inspired by imperial pressure (Cadoux 1919: 256). Although talk of the Church's fall from grace is exaggerating the point because it assumes that scripture's teachings on the matter were clear, until the mid-third century most prominent Church leaders argued that Christians should not serve in the military. However, the leaders (Clement of Alexandria, Origen, Tertullian, Lactantius, Hippolytus and Cyprian) based their aversion to war on different grounds. For instance, Tertullian was principally concerned with the danger of idolatry, whereas Origen argued that Christians should be exempt from military service because of their special affinity with God but nevertheless implied that pagans could (indeed, should) engage in military service to protect the empire. Moreover, we cannot derive a universal Christian idea about pacifism from the surviving work of six writers spread over more than a century. For all the professed pacifism of their leaders, there were definitely Christians in the army after 173, as we have noted.

Christian writers began to write about their attitudes to war in response to criticism by the pagan writer Celsus, around 180. Celsus accused Christians of not pulling their weight in defence of the empire, insisting that 'if everyone followed your example, nothing would prevent his [the emperor's] being left all alone and deserted while all earthly affairs fell under the same sway of the most lawless and uncivilized barbarians' (in Swift 1983: 38–9). Both Tertullian and Origen replied directly to this criticism. Tertullian's *Apology*, written around 197, argued that Christians played an important part in the life of the empire, and that although they could not participate in war, they prayed 'without ceasing' for the prolonged life of all emperors and defence of the law. He went on to argue that there were two principal reasons why Christians could not serve in the military. The first was the danger of idolatry. The second was that military service contravened biblical teachings. Tertullian argued that Jesus' injunction to 'turn the other cheek' forbade Christians from serving in the military (in Swift 1983: 44).

Origen levelled three main arguments against Celsus. First, he accepted the argument that scripture forbade Christians from military service. Second, he argued that if everyone behaved as Christians, Rome would not be imperilled because the 'barbarians' would be Christianized and would cease their violent attacks. Finally, he echoed Tertullian in arguing that although Christians could not directly participate in war, they played a crucial role in determining its outcome through prayer. Like Tertullian, therefore, Origen insisted that it was wrong for Christians to take part in war but did not condemn pagans who did so in defence of Rome (see Johnson 1987: 25–9).

By contrast, Cyprian of Carthage advanced a more standard pacifist argument. He rejected the separation between public and private morality on which the justification of individual participation in war depends and insisted that Jesus' commands extended to both private dealings and public service. Killing was no less immoral, Cyprian argued, if committed in the name of the state (Swift 1983: 48). Likewise, in one of the earliest pieces of canon law, written in the early part of the third century, Hippolytus of Rome wrote that Christian soldiers should not kill even when ordered to and should be dismissed from the Church if they did (Swift 1983: 47).

These points go a long way to explaining the absence of Christians from the military before 173. After that date, however, a Roman legion (the 'Thundering Legion') recruited Christians in southern Armenia (Bainton 1960: 70). The historical record is then somewhat sparse until 312, at which date, during a civil war, Constantine marked his legions with the sign of the cross and won an important victory at Milvian Bridge that helped him secure the leadership in Rome twelve years later. Constantine converted to Christianity, which became the empire's religion. Although this was an important turning point in Christian attitudes towards war, it was not quite the cataclysmic event that Christian pacifists tend to suggest. By this date, Christians had been in the Roman army for almost 140 years, and were well represented among Constantine's troops. This gradual trend towards Christian participation in the military was prompted by three main impulses. First, military service was professionalized, making a military career an attractive prospect for lower-class citizens of the empire (Johnson 1987: 33–47). Second, pagan barbarians on the empire's borders were threatening the rule of law. Especially after Constantine, Christianity flourished under the protection of Roman law but was endangered by the pagan invaders. Christians entered public service (including the military) in greater numbers to help protect the empire (Windass 1964: 20–1). Third, the early Church's eschatological expectations had receded by the fourth century. As the perceived likelihood of an imminent Second Coming retreated, so Christians became less sectarian (Brown, P. R. L. 1995). In short, therefore, the change in Christian attitudes towards military service occurred over a number of decades (if not centuries) and for a variety of reasons.

This changed situation was reflected in the writings of Church leaders from the fourth century onwards – particularly those of Ambrose of Milan and Augustine of Hippo. Ambrose became Bishop of Milan in 374, having previously been governor, demonstrating that within sixty years of Constantine's rise to power, Christians had begun to take up senior offices in the empire. Ambrose was the first thinker systematically to blend Christian teachings with Roman law and philosophy (Johnson 1987: 54). He followed Cicero in acknowledging the possibility of justifiable wars and recognizing the difference between abhorrent civil wars and wars fought against barbarians (Swift 1970: 533–4). Wars against barbarians, Ambrose argued, were legitimate because they protected both the empire and Christian orthodoxy.

Ambrose argued that there were two grounds for justifying war. First, he found evidence in the Old Testament to support the view that not only was violence sometimes justified in order to protect others from harm, it was sometimes *required* on moral grounds or even directly commanded by God (Swift 1970: 535). Second, Ambrose agreed that Jesus' teaching forbade an individual from killing another in self-defence and counselled against the wholesale adoption of Cicero's laws of war, which had presumed that killing in self-defence was always legitimate. Nevertheless he argued that whilst an individual may not kill to save himself, he must act in the defence of others even if that meant killing his assailant. As Swift (1970: 537) points out, 'this is a remarkable statement in that it denies to an individual in his own case a right which he *must* exercise on behalf of another'. The source of this apparent contradiction was the dualism between inward disposition and outward action later developed by Augustine. To kill an attacker in self-defence implied that the individual in question preferred earthly life to a spiritual relationship with God. Acting in defence of others, however, was an act of love, and 'he who does not keep harm off a friend, if he can, is as much in fault as he who causes it' (Ambrose 1896: 36). The justified anger of the intervener must be directed against the wrong being committed, not the wrongdoer. For Ambrose, 'the principle of turning the other cheek pertains more properly to the inward disposition of the heart than to outward actions' (Swift 1970: 541). This dualism formed a crucial tenet of Augustine's thinking and plays an important role in the Just War tradition today, reflected in principles such as double-effect, right intention and proportionality (see Chapters 2–6).

Ambrose followed Cicero on the question of whether and under what conditions war might be justified, arguing that wars could only be fought in self-defence (broadly understood, as in the Roman tradition) when directly commanded by God, or in defence of religious orthodoxy. He argued that combatants must respect treaties, show mercy to their enemies, and treat the innocent amongst the enemy population with care, even when doing so risked the soldier's own life. Moreover, Ambrose insisted that those who held office within the Church were never to take up arms because it was not their vocation to do so (Ambrose 1896: 35–49).

To reiterate: the early Christians began as a sectarian community, divorcing themselves from the world of men and refusing to serve Rome primarily because they expected the imminent return of Christ and rejected the idolatry that accompanied military service. Within the Church leadership, there was a strong tendency towards pacifism. However, from at least 173 Christians began joining Roman armies. For more than a century, there was a contradiction between Christian teaching and practice in this area, but as Christians began to play a part in the functioning of the empire and persecution decreased, the perceived gap between the world of God and the world of men lessened. By the time of Constantine, there were already many Christians in the military and it was not long before Christians began taking up senior public positions. These political changes removed many of the key reasons for Christian non-participation in the military. A new generation of theologians was therefore confronted with the question of whether it was right for a Christian to use force to protect the empire, the faith and the law, questions that had lacked relevance when the state was pagan and persecuted Christians. Ambrose was the first to deal with these questions in depth and his methodology shaped Christian thinking about war until the rise of legal positivism in the eighteenth and nineteenth centuries. However, it was his contemporary, Augustine, who is credited with fleshing out the first Christian doctrine of the Just War.

Augustine

There can be little doubting the significance of St Augustine of Hippo (354–430) to the development of the Just War tradition. Given this, it is surprising to discover that within his work there is no coherent ethics of war. Instead, references to war and military service are dotted throughout his writings, and it was his commentators from Gratian onwards who were most responsible for articulating a systematic Augustinian account of war. Many of Augustine's comments on war were responses to specific questions, such as his letters to Boniface, a Christian officer in the Roman army who wrote to Augustine asking whether he should fight against the barbarians. Moreover, Augustine's teachings about whether it was ever right to kill and when a war may be considered justifiable drew heavily on Cicero and Ambrose. Thus, Augustine's work represents a refinement of earlier work rather than a break with the past. Augustine lived in a time of imperial decline and rapid growth of Christianity (Griffith 1993: 273). In 410,

Alaric's Visigoths sacked Rome for three days, and at the time Augustine died, the Vandals were besieging his home city of Hippo in North Africa.

The best starting point for understanding Augustine's justification of war is his position on whether an individual could permissibly kill in self-defence. In a treatise on free will, Augustine (1955a: 44) argued that 'the law is not just which authorises a traveller to kill a robber in self-protection, or any man or woman to kill an assailant'. Such an act is legitimate in the eyes of temporal law, which aims to maintain a degree of earthly peace (which could never be as pure as divine peace), but not in the eyes of the higher unwritten law. Augustine's justification for rejecting the right of an individual to kill in self-defence, something that is a moral given today, was that

as for the life of the soul, it is at least doubtful whether it can be taken away by killing the body ... whatever the man who is killed was going to take away is not wholly in our power, so I cannot understand how it can be called ours. [Also] how can they [those who kill to defend themselves] be free from sin against Divine Providence, if they are stained with human blood in defence of things which ought to be despised? (Augustine 1955a: 46).

When an individual killed in self-defence, he killed to protect earthly things (life, honour, property) that those close to God ought not to want to protect. An assailant could not take away the most important thing, one's virtue. However, it was not the *act* of killing in self-defence that was itself sinful but the *inward disposition* that drove the act – the love of earthly above spiritual things.

This dualism between inward disposition and outward action shaped Augustine's views about the ethics of war. In a letter to Faustus, who was a heretical Manichaean, he asked:

What is the evil in war? Is it the death of some who will soon die in any case, that others may live in peaceful subjection? This is merely cowardly dislike, not any religious feeling. The real evils in war are love of violence, revengeful cruelty, fierce and implacable enmity, wild resistance, and the lust of power, and such like; and it is generally to punish these things, when force is required to inflict the punishment, that, in obedience to God or some lawful authority, good men undertake wars. (Augustine 1876: 74)

Following his argument on self-defence, it was not the killing that made war sinful, for it only shortened the life of those doomed to die anyway. For Augustine, the sin of war lay in the hatred, avarice, greed and lust for power that it generated.

When individuals acted violently to defend others, public order or the common good, Augustine believed that it was possible that they might do so without committing any of these sins (see Deane 1963: 154). As he put it in a letter to Publicola, 'in regard to killing men so as not to be killed by them, this view does not please me, unless perhaps it should be a soldier or a public official. In this case he does not do it for his own sake, but for others or for the state as a whole' (in Rist 1994: 233). This position draws immediate criticism from pacifists, expressed most eloquently by Robert Holmes. Holmes (1989: 121–2) asks why it is morally impermissible to use force to save oneself or other earthly things that one should not ordinarily desire, but permissible to use force to save others or to protect the state, both of which are as bound to the temporal world as the desire for self-preservation. Augustine's response to questions like this began with the assertion that social life was an essential part of humanity. Society, law and order were necessary, for without them there could be no advancement towards human purity and a closer relationship with God (Markus 1970: 99). Earthly law, Augustine argued, guaranteed public order, security and property rights and thereby assisted the individual on his or her path towards God (Markus 1970: 89–90). Augustine's views on this matter were clearly shaped by his time. Watching the destruction wreaked by the pagan barbarians, he believed that without law and society there could be no organized Christianity and thus no chance of divine redemption. Using violence to defend another or the state was not only justified, therefore, it was a moral necessity.

From this brief assessment we can derive Augustine's two principal insights on the ethics of war. The first was that war must be waged with right intentions. An individual engaged in war must not act out of feelings of hatred, envy, greed or a will to dominate but from a feeling of love and wish to maintain peace and justice. *All* wars, Augustine argued (1972: 866), even unjust wars, were fought from a desire for a just peace and it was this desire that marked out the legitimacy of war from the illegitimacy of killing for individual self-preservation or gain. The central difference between a just and unjust war was that a just war attempted both to restore peace and to repair an injury received. Such wars not only helped to preserve the temporal law but were also acts of love towards the wrongdoers, as it prevented them from committing further sins:

But, say they, the wise man will wage just wars. As if he would not all the rather lament the necessity of just wars, if he remembers that he is a man; for if they were not just he would not wage them, and would therefore be delivered from all wars. For it is the wrong-doing of the opposing party which compels the wise man to wage just wars; and this wrong-doing, even though it gave rise to no war, would still be a matter of grief to man because it is man's wrong-doing. (Augustine 1972: 850)

The key for Augustine, therefore, was the inward disposition that drove one to war. Most of the wars in his time were internecine struggles for power or riches and came nowhere near to satisfying his demands. A truly just king, Augustine believed, would not wage war to expand his kingdom, enslave peoples or steal plunder; he would fight only just wars to uphold justice and maintain the peace (Deane 1963: 158). A just king only fought wars of necessity, not of choice (Augustine 1955b: 269).

How are we to tell a war fought with right intentions? Augustine argued that a war could be just if it aimed to accomplish either one of four objectives. First, it could be just if waged in self-defence, because such wars aimed to punish the unjust actions of the aggressor. Second, apparently aggressive wars could be just if waged against a state that refused to make reparations for previous wrongs or if a state refused to return property that had been wrongfully taken. Third, wars that were directly ordered by God, such as the Israelites' wars recounted in the Old Testament, were just. Finally, wars to maintain religious orthodoxy might be just (Deane 1963: 160). In all four cases, just wars were fought with the intention of maintaining peace and ending injustice. Because a war had to be either a response to a prior wrong or commanded by God in order to be just, it followed that for Augustine a war might ever only be just on one side (Ramsey 1961: 28).

If killing was only justified on behalf of the state and in the service of the common good, it follows that war could only be just if authorized by the appropriate public authority. Augustine argued that soldiers and public officials did not sin when they acted on an order to use violence because they acted with the intent of promoting the common good. Indeed, killing could only be justified when it was either directly ordered by God or commanded by a just law issued by the appropriate authorities (Augustine 1876). According to Augustine, only monarchs had the right to decide whether an injustice warranting war had been committed. When war was properly declared, soldiers were obliged to fight. In doing so they committed no wrong, even if they suspected that the war was unjust (Deane 1963: 163). Indeed, Augustine allowed very little (if any) room for conscientious objection, implying that if a monarch launched an unjust war he would receive divine retribution but that his soldiers would not (see Burnell 1993: 177–88). However, Augustine was ambivalent on the question of whether a soldier should obey an order that he *knew* to be unjust, assuming that soldiers would either always agree with the order or only have doubts. In either of these cases, a soldier should obey orders. Augustine did not consider the possibility of a soldier knowing an order to be unjust with certainty, despite elsewhere writing that one was not obliged to respect unjust laws (see Swift 1983: 140).

Augustine's ethics of war therefore revolved around two basic principles. First, killing was justified when conducted with right intentions, to correct an injustice and restore peace. Augustine did not discuss in detail what might count as a just cause, presumably because any war fought by an appropriate authority for the common good must logically be a war fought for a just cause. Second, wars must be declared by appropriate authorities. In Augustine's time, it was relatively simple to identify the legitimate authority (whoever held power in Rome). However, the fall of the empire and rise of feudalism with its complex and overlapping authority structures made this question much more difficult to answer.

Augustine's thinking on just conduct in war was far less developed. He argued that agreements should always be respected (even those concluded with enemies), that soldiers should show mercy to defeated enemies once war was over and the wrong righted, but that ambushes were legitimate because God had instructed them in the Old Testament (Swift 1983: 139). Nowhere did Augustine discuss the principle of non-combatant immunity, leading one commentator to conclude that Augustine was 'unconcerned with the fate of the innocent so far as the necessities of the just war is concerned' (Hartigan 1966: 203). This does not mean that Augustine approved of killing the innocent, only that he was primarily concerned with the question of whether it was ever right for individual Christians to kill and when they might wage war.

Conclusion

Although there were many attempts to limit recourse to war and its conduct in antiquity, there was no framework of legitimacy comparable to that provided by the modern Just War tradition. Augustine undoubtedly made an important contribution to the tradition, but it is important to recognize that he did not put forward a single and coherent theory. Nor did he spend much time on the question of just conduct. Similarly, those expecting a theory of *jus ad bellum* in Augustine's writings are surprised to find a doctrine reducible to two core elements: that a war is justified only if it is inspired by right intentions and declared by a proper authority. Nevertheless, Augustine combined Christian theology with Roman law and philosophy and provided the basic ideas that would inform judgements about the legitimacy of war for many centuries to come. In particular, he demonstrated that although wars could be justified, they were not necessarily just simply because they were waged by the emperor. For the next thousand years or so, thought about the legitimacy of war fragmented into several camps, charted in the following chapter.

2

The Middle Ages

This chapter charts the development of the Just War tradition in the Middle Ages (from around the tenth to the fifteenth centuries). This was an era characterized by the feudal system that developed from the remnants of the Roman Empire. Formally, feudalism was a system of individual relations between people of unequal status based on trust and loyalty (Pennington 1993: 24). Feudalism demanded that every piece of land have an owner who would profit economically and exercise primary jurisdiction over it. This lordship was neither absolute nor independent, since the landowner acquired the right to own land from a higher authority and provided military service and paid homage and money in return for that right. The superior lord was often himself the vassal of another, with the most senior position held by a king or emperor (Nederman and Forhan 1993: 10–11).

During the twelfth and thirteenth centuries, there was a struggle between centralizing and particularist forces – the former pulling towards the establishment of a unified Christian society or empire, the latter towards a society of equal sovereigns. Both the Church and the Holy Roman Empire proposed a common Christian republic under the leadership of the papacy or Holy Roman Emperor, respectively. The papacy asserted an overarching jurisdiction in moral and spiritual matters throughout Christendom, whilst the empire attempted to unite feudal lords under its banner (Morrall 1960: 81). The two clashed in the 'investiture contest' of the late eleventh century during the papacy of Gregory VII. This was ostensibly a conflict over who had the authority to appoint local bishops but actually concerned the much deeper question of whether the Church was subject to the emperor, or vice versa. Meanwhile, technological advances in agriculture led to the growth of cities and a shift in the machinery of political administration. The old system of feudal allegiance, whereby the prince or king would enter into agreements with each of his feudal lords, was replaced by new systems of representation that allowed kings to extract revenue from these groups. What emerged was a centralized bureaucratic and legislative authority that had jurisdiction over a political community (Morrall 1960: 59–61).

In theology, canon law and Christian practice, three strains of thought – pacifism, holy war and Just War – developed into coherent bodies of thought. Pacifist tendencies were evident in the French-led Christian anti-war movement of the twelfth and thirteenth centuries that produced the 'Peace of God' and 'Truce of God', which aimed to limit the brutality and duration of war. The holy war tradition spawned the crusades, which began in earnest in 1095 (Housley 2002). Most important for the development of the Just War tradition was the evolution of canon law, addressing primarily the circumstances that made war legitimate. Beyond the Church, the chivalric tradition attempted to govern the way that knights conducted themselves. This chapter explores each of these sub-traditions (canon law, scholastic philosophy, the chivalric code; and the doctrine of holy war and crusades) in turn.

Canon Law

Canon law was a system of law governing the Church and individuals who fell under its jurisdiction. Among other things, canon law claimed jurisdiction over wills, offences against God, oaths and war. The impetus to formalize canon law came in the late eleventh century when Pope Gregory VII renounced secular control of some of the Church's institutions and established the Church as an independent legal authority (Reid and Witte 1999: 647). Throughout much of this period, therefore, there was not one but two structures of government – the secular authorities and the Church (Tierney 1982: 10). Schools of law were created in Provence, Lombardy, Ravenna and Bologna where scholars combined elements of Roman law with biblical and theological teachings and customary practice to produce important legal tracts (Post 1964: 3–24). Bologna in particular became an important centre for canon law, especially after the production of Gratian's *Concordantia Discordantium Canonum* (A Harmony of Discordant Canons), commonly referred to as the *Decretum* (decree), around 1140 (Coriden 1990: 17).

The first sustained attempt by bishops to regulate the conduct of war in an immensely violent, almost anarchic, Europe began more than one hundred years before the *Decretum*. In the final decades of the tenth century, churchmen associated with the Abbey of Cluny established a peace movement known as the 'Peace of God'. The movement was a response to the increasingly violent nature of feudalism towards the defenceless and the Church especially (Lea 2001: 335). The Peace of God was initially promulgated at a series of synods held in southern and central France, where it was given official sanction by many Church and secular leaders. The synods forbade all acts of warfare or vengeance against clerics, pilgrims, merchants, Jews, women and peasants (farmers), and the despoliation of ecclesiastical and agricultural property (Berman 1983: 90). Nobles were required to swear a solemn 'pact of peace and justice', in which they promised to protect society from feudal violence and to punish their own barons for any infractions (Mackinney 1930: 186).

The Peace of God movement spread throughout much of Western Europe and even touched the lives of peasants. In 1038, the Council of Bourges decreed that every adult Christian male should place himself in the service of a militia that would enforce the Peace (Berman 1983: 90). This project was short-lived, as the militia itself became a menace to public order when it began burning castles (popularly believed to be the source of lawlessness). The feudal lord Odo de Déols massacred the militia after it burned an entire village (Barber 1995: 251). Moreover, the Church's highest bodies did not support the movement (Magnou-Nortier 1992). For instance, Pope Gregory VII chastised the Abbot of Cluny for bringing the Duke of Burgundy into the peace movement, because it prohibited the Duke from providing military service to the Church (Kaeuper 1999: 65).

As it spread, the movement aimed at more that just the protection of certain groups of non-combatants. Under the banner of the 'Truce of God' – created by Abbot Odilo of Cluny – the Church forbade the conduct of war from Saturday noon until Monday morning, during Lent and Advent, and on other holy and saints' days. In the twelfth century, the Church also attempted to limit the use of particular weapons. The Second Lateran Council in 1139 banned the use of crossbows and siege machines in wars between Christians (Bachrach 1994: 119–33).

Although both the Peace of God and the Truce of God spread across Western Europe and many nobles swore oaths, they did not have much of an impact on the actual conduct of war. The spoiling of agricultural lands and terrorization of the peasantry remained key elements of war fighting. Moreover, acts of violence against the clergy and ecclesiastical property continued, and where they abated this was due more to the start of the crusades than to the Peace of God. As for the Truce of God, there is no evidence of a leader choosing not to fight on a particular day because the Church forbade it. Although the peace movement ceased to carry much weight in its own right in the twelfth century, it did, however, make two lasting contributions to the Just War tradition, forming the cornerstones of canon law's *jus in bello*: it forbade the targeting of clerics and insisted that certain groups of people be immune from the ravages of war.

Canon law began to take shape as a more coherent body of rules in the twelfth century. The most significant contribution to this process was Gratian of Bologna's *Decretum*, produced, as noted, around 1140. The *Decretum* remains one of the most influential sources of guidance in the Just War tradition (Gallagher 2002: 122–3; Keen 1965). Gratian adopted a scholastic method, posing questions and answering them by demonstrating the contradictory viewpoints of past canons and theologies before attempting to reconcile them (Brooke 1969: 75–89). He focused on four central questions related to war: whether war and killing were ever justified; the nature of the just war; the question of right authority; and conduct in war (Russell, F. H. 1975: 57).

Gratian's concept of the just war began with the same question as Augustine's: is military service a sin? Gratian noted that, on the one hand, the canons of Origen forbade participation in war, whilst, on the other, Augustine had insisted that it was justified. Scripture, Gratian concluded, did not forbid all military service because the scriptural passages denouncing killing referred to the inward disposition of the soldier not to his outward actions. Because of the early canons pointing in the opposite direction, however, Gratian placed important limits on military service. He insisted that people who killed excommunicates should undergo penance and that a knight who had undergone penance should not return to military service without special permission from the Church (Russell, F. H. 1975: 59).

Gratian's discussion of the just causes of war drew on the Roman idea that war was justified only when it furthered peace. Given this, Gratian permitted only three legitimate causes of war, all of which demanded that fault be found on the part of those whom war was being waged against. First, war was justifiable if it aimed to recover stolen goods. Second, wars fought to avenge injuries were justifiable. Finally, it was legitimate for political communities to resort to force in self-defence. The Augustinian influence is evident in all three of these just causes, as is the view, drawn from the Roman legal tradition, that justifiable war was a 'quasi-legal' procedure for defending the rights of individuals in contexts where no higher authority was able to arbitrate effectively (Johnson 1975: 37).

Whilst Gratian followed Augustine in arguing that only soldiers ordered to war by a legitimate authority could justly kill, it was much more difficult by Gratian's time to identify precisely where that authority lay. There were two principal questions in this regard: was it legitimate for the Church to wage war? And which secular authorities had the right to wage war? The *Decretum* did not offer much specific insight on which secular authorities might wage war, though its insistence that a war be declared beforehand suggested that only those with the material power to make such a declaration could wage a just war. However, Gratian was imprecise about who precisely held this authority, and the *Decretum* could be read as suggesting that the emperor, the kings, princes, barons, and even vassals could all legitimately launch wars in certain circumstances (Russell, F. H. 1975: 71).

The *Decretum* provided more insight into the proper role of the Church. Gratian argued that war could be directly commanded by God through the pope, his representative on earth. Such wars might be fought to defend the Church against material attack or heresy. On the question of whether bishops could legitimately authorize war (a common occurrence in Gratian's time), Gratian argued that whilst clerics could not legitimately wield anything other than the spiritual sword (an idea that Gratian took from Origen), bishops who held secular as well as ecclesiastical office were obliged to fulfil their secular duties, using war if necessary. Moreover, all clerics could exhort the secular authorities to wage war on behalf of the Church (Russell, F. H. 1975: 76–80). Nevertheless, clerics continued to participate in war. For example, in 1145 Pope Lucius II died at the head of an army attempting to seize Rome (Tyerman 1995: 558).

Gratian was even sketchier on the question of how war should be conducted. He argued that if a war was declared by a legitimate authority and aimed to avenge an injury, it could be waged at any time, even during Lent. The closest Gratian came to a concept of non-combatant immunity was the demand that pilgrims, clerics, monks, women and unarmed peasants be immune from violence, on pain of excommunication. However, he implied that these exemptions could be overridden by military necessity and rejected the Second Lateran Council's ban on the use of crossbows on similar grounds (Russell, F. H. 1975: 71).

The *Decretum* made at least three important contributions to the Just War tradition. First, it reinforced the idea that war was only justified in response to a prior injury received. Gratian omitted 'right intent', which was so crucial to Augustine's schema, presumably assuming that a war to reverse or avenge an objective wrong was necessarily fought with right intentions. Second, by separating secular and ecclesiastical sources of authority, Gratian formalized the idea that there were two types of justifiable war, though both were understood as 'just wars': 'just wars' were declared by secular authorities to right a prior wrong, and 'holy wars' were declared by ecclesiastical authorities to defend the faith and its orthodoxy. Finally, the *Decretum* developed the principle of non-combatant immunity by insisting that certain groups be immune from the violence of war because of their social function unless necessity dictated otherwise. It was what Gratian left out, however, that most exercised the canonists that followed him: precisely which secular authorities had the right to wage war?

This question was of practical as well as theoretical significance. War was one of the primary ways in which lesser nobles enriched themselves and most nobles could muster an army of peasants or mercenaries, making war between them the norm rather than the exception (Strickland 1996: 183–96). Restricting the authority to wage war was therefore key to limiting warfare in Europe. One path, adopted by the papacy, was to summon Christians to crusades against the infidel – thereby asserting the Church's authority and redirecting the energies of the fractious nobles. Another, pursued by the canon lawyers who succeeded Gratian (known as Decretists and, after around 1190, Decretalists) was to resolve the gaps in the *Decretum*.

The Decretists were commentators on the *Decretum* who presented summaries and glosses of the great work of canon law between approximately 1140 and 1190 (Tierney 1964: 117). The bulk of their work elaborated on two elements of the *Decretum:* the nature of the just cause and the rightful authority for war. By and large, the Decretists followed Gratian, though some members of the Bolognese School challenged the idea that one side must always be in the wrong (Russell, F. H. 1975: 89). For instance, some argued that a war might be unjustly launched against one who nevertheless deserved punishment. Moreover, given the complexity of the feudal system, some scholars recognized that it was possible for more than one noble legitimately to claim a particular territory or good. Although this view presaged later ideas about invincible ignorance, it was rejected by most Decretists. Huguccio, for instance, denounced the idea that a war might be just on both sides, arguing that if one side attacks justly, the other cannot justly defend itself; if one side attacks unjustly, the other might defend itself justly. Likewise, although Stephen of Tournai admitted that an unjust war might be inadvertently launched in good faith, he too insisted that one side must have a monopoly on justice (Russell, F. H. 1975: 91).

In relation to just cause, the Decretists limited themselves to explaining and justifying Gratian's findings. Huguccio insisted that any war fought with direct clerical participation or where the enemy had not committed an objective wrong was unjust. What counted as a just cause was expanded to include defence of the right to free passage (denial of which breached *ius gentium*), the imprisonment of heretics, preservation of the peace, suppression of rebellion, and recovery of lost property. Defence of the *patria* (political community) was expressly identified as a just cause, though the Decretists made little headway in identifying what the *patria* was in practical terms (Russell, F. H. 1975: 98–100).

The Decretists had a difficult time making sense of Gratian's views on the nature of proper authority. They followed him in prohibiting clerical participation in war and most agreed that whilst bishops who also held secular office must exercise that office to the full, they should not themselves participate in war. One of the major developments was the view that the Church itself could legitimately wage war and did not need to receive a prior injury to do so. Some canonists believed that heretics, pagans, infidels, schismatics and excommunicates posed a constant threat and that the Church was invested with divine authority to initiate war against them. Clerics, they argued, might initiate wars but not participate in them, whilst Christian princes were obliged to heed the Church's call to arms.

What, though, of secular authority? The primary secular authority was the Holy Roman Emperor, who, along with the pope, held the ultimate authority to wage war. According to the Decretists, this authority was delegated through custom to the many Christian princes. This did not go a long way towards solving the problem, as the thorny question of who qualified as a 'prince' remained. The Decretists tended to take a tautological approach to this question, holding that a prince was someone who controlled land and had the ability to wage war. What they did provide, though, was a clearer picture of the ideal just warrior: he was a layman, acted under proper authority (in accordance with the instructions of his superiors), with right intent, and followed orders (except in exceptional circumstances) (Russell, F. H. 1975: 103). Beyond this, the Decretists remained as ambiguous as Gratian as to the nature of legitimate authority.

The Decretalists took up these problems at the end of the twelfth century. Scholars began compiling lists of criteria that constituted a just war, none of which were particularly novel. Laurentius Hispanus provided five such criteria: war should be initiated by a layman; the object of war should be recovery of lost goods or defence of the *patria;* wars should be products of necessity; the desire to punish was not a rightful intent; and war should be fought by a princely authority (Russell, F. H. 1975: 128). Though there was little new in Decretalist thought about just cause, defence of the *patria* and the vindication of legal rights took on greater prominence.

The Decretalists expanded the role of the Church in relation to the question of legitimate authority. Hostiensis argued that the proper role of civil power was to do the work necessary for the well-being of the Church that was too sordid for the clergy to do themselves (Tierney 1964: 152). He believed there to be a basic solidarity between the Christian Roman peoples and that the pope headed a form of 'world-empire' (see Muldoon 1972: 485). Several Decretalists used this sentiment to argue that only the pope, emperor and kings had the authority to wage war. They developed the Decretist argument that a just warrior obeys orders by insisting that only those with no secular superior had a right to wage war. Even these figures, however, might only wage war when the conditions outlined above were met. Thus, Hostiensis provided the first clear resolution to the question of legitimate authority in the post-Roman era: only those with no judicial superior might wage war (Russell, F. H. 1975: 142).

Being almost entirely absorbed with the question of legitimate authority and the proper role of the Church, the Decretalists did not spend much time on the conduct of war. They reiterated the earlier view that when a war was just, any *necessary* means might be used to ensure victory. Decretalists rejected the ban on the use of crossbows, though some later argued that the prohibition held in unjust wars (Russell, F. H. 1975: 157). This view is striking because most writers at the time argued that if a war was unjust, every act of violence unleashed by the unjust party was illicit. Following Roman custom, the Decretalists acknowledged that agreements with the enemy were to be upheld, but beyond that their concept of *jus in bello* extended only to the prohibition of 'unnecessary' harm.

Canon lawyers therefore went some way to formalizing the rules of war by synthesizing material drawn from canon law, scripture, theology and philosophy. By replacing the primacy of right intent with just cause, the canonists provided what they thought of as objective benchmarks by which to judge actions. The core questions that pervaded this period related to the relationship between the Church and war and the question of what, precisely, counted as a legitimate authority. On the former, canonists agreed with Origen's insistence that clerics not participate in war but acknowledged that clerics with secular responsibilities must fulfil those responsibilities by enjoining others to wage war if necessary. By the mid-thirteenth century, canon lawyers began to argue that the Church was the primary authority for waging war. The question of secular authority was more problematic because of the sheer complexity of the feudal system. For much of the period, canon lawyers remained ambiguous on this question, assuming perhaps that feudal society would recognize an unjust authority when it saw one. Towards the end of the period, however, Decretalists began further to delimit the authority to wage war, suggesting that only those with no earthly superior enjoyed this right. As for the question of conduct in war, the most significant progress was made in the Peace of God movement. When it declined in importance, so too did interest in *jus in bello*. Gratian and his followers made only passing reference to the idea that some groups should be immune from the ravages of war and that its conduct be limited to actions deemed necessary.

Scholasticism: Thomas Aquinas

Scholasticism refers more to a methodology than a set of substantive ideas. Scholastic teaching tried to make human experience intelligible through reason and to incorporate this into a Christian philosophy. Its central presupposition was that whilst nothing that challenged theological dogma could be held true, precepts of theology ought to be defensible in terms of human reason (D'Arcy 1930: 30). As a scholastic scholar, Thomas Aquinas (1225–c. 1274) blended theology with philosophy and used each to support and justify the other. This, in part, helps to explain the lasting significance of his account of the just war. Unlike Augustine, it is not essential to agree with Aquinas' belief in God in order to accept his arguments. Moreover, Aquinas' account of the just war was much more 'earthly' than Augustine's and addressed many of the practical dilemmas with which the canonists wrestled. Aquinas was not particularly influential in his own time. Even after canonization, he was not venerated. Indeed, so upset did he become about the negative reception that his ideas received that he refused to complete his monumental work *Summa Theologica* (Kenny 1980: 27). In his own time, Aquinas' work on war was much less significant than canon law, the chivalric code and the doctrine of holy war.

Aquinas agreed with Augustine that private persons and public officials were bound by different rules. He accepted that public officials acting as representatives of the state might kill people because he understood the scriptural command of non-resistance as placing an obligation on individuals not governments (Tooke 1965: 183). Like Augustine, Aquinas derived this position from a belief in the inherent sociability of man and the need for government, arguing that 'man is by nature a political and social animal' who uses reason and speech to build political communities that satisfy important human needs (in Sigmund 1993: 218). Men need to cooperate in order to achieve their basic needs and ultimate ends. To do so effectively 'a directing mind is needed to show the right way to the goal' (in Grabmann 1928: 163). Thus, Aquinas argued that government had a value of its own, independent of religion. If mankind was to achieve virtuous life through the proper application of divinely guided reason, government was required to provide order and direct it towards the common good (see D'Entrèves 1959: 24).

Although Aquinas built his approach to war on similar foundations to Augustine, his starting point was a 'presumption against war'. According to Rowan Williams (2003), the current Archbishop of Canterbury, Aquinas assumed violence to be an evil 'which is only resolved by appeal to the duty of the ruler to preserve peace internally and externally by the literal use of the sword'. Understood in this sense, the use of coercive violence always requires special justification. From the point of view of the victim, Aquinas argued, violence is never justifiable. It is only justifiable from the point of view of the assailant if it aims to produce a greater benefit to the community. As Joan Tooke summarized (1965: 156): 'any killing, even in war and even if unintentional, is only half just'. Aquinas suggested that war could never be *just*, because the very act of killing always contained some element of injustice, but that in certain circumstances it might be *justifiable* in that the total injustice inflicted by war might be less than the total justice delivered by it. In order to sustain this argument, Aquinas offered two further ideas: the doctrine of double-effect and the associated principle of proportionality.

Like Augustine, Aquinas addressed the question of whether it is ever right for a Christian to serve in the military by asking whether a Christian might kill an assailant in self-defence. His answer was quite different to Augustine's, primarily because Aquinas insisted that self-preservation was 'natural':

Nothing hinders one act from having two effects, only one of which is intended, while the other is beside the intention. Now moral acts take their species according to what is intended, not from what is beside the intention, since this is accidental. . . . Accordingly the act of self-defence may have two effects, one is the saving of one's life, the other is the slaying of the aggressor. Therefore this act, since one's intention is to save one's own life, is not unlawful, seeing that it is natural to everything to keep itself in being. . . . And yet, though proceeding from good intention, an act may be rendered unlawful, if it be out of proportion to the end. Wherefore if a man, in self-defence, uses more than necessary violence, it will be unlawful: whereas if he repel force with moderation his defence will be lawful. (Aquinas 2002: 264)

As formulated by Aquinas, the doctrine of double-effect has two fundamental elements. The first is that any act may have two consequences: one
that is intended and one that is not. The only legitimate intent that an individual may have is self-preservation. Even then it is incumbent upon the
killer to demonstrate through his actions that he intended to defend himself
and not kill his assailant. For their part, governments must demonstrate
that they intend to promote the common good and must act only when they
have a just cause. The second element of double-effect concentrates on the
objective consequences of an act and asks whether they were proportionate.
Even if we intend good, we must be sure that the likely good outweighs the
possible negative consequences. War may only be waged if the injustice it
is being waged to halt outweighs the likely injustices of the war itself
(Aquinas 2002: 264).

The doctrine of double-effect did not do away with the need for the other
elements of *jus ad bellum*, and much of Aquinas' explicit discussion of the
just war reflected the canonists' concern with the nature of just cause and
legitimate authority. Aquinas outlined three conditions for a just war: legitimate authority, just cause and right intent. He argued that for a war to be
just it must be declared by a ruler within 'whose competence it lies to declare
war' (Aquinas 1998: 41). Private individuals may not legitimately declare
war because they have superiors with greater rights and do not have the
right to mobilize the people into an army. Aquinas also argued that war
was only justifiable in circumstances where no arbitration was possible. As
private individuals could always enjoy the arbitration of their king, only
kings with no superiors had the authority to wage war. Aquinas incorporated the requirement that wars be properly declared under the rubric of
legitimate authority. It served two purposes. First, it reinforced the principle of legitimate authority because a noble who lacked the authority to
declare war would be unable to do so legitimately. Second, it contributed
to ensuring the just cause by forcing leaders to articulate their case
for war.

Aquinas' second condition was that wars be fought for a just cause. A
just war was one aimed at either avenging a wrong, punishing someone who
had failed to make amends for a wrong, or recovering something unjustly
taken. Significantly, self-defence was not singled out as a just cause in its
own right chiefly because Aquinas (2002: 15) insisted that wrongdoers,
including tyrannical rulers, had no inherent right to defend themselves
against potentially legitimate assailants. Although Aquinas held onto the
idea that actions could be described as more or less objectively right or
wrong, he acknowledged the idea that human justice may be approximate
(see O'Connor 1967: 57). He shared Augustine's view that a war must be
unjust on one side, but suggested that it was more a question of degrees than
absolutes. As we noted earlier, Aquinas admitted that killing could never
be wholly just. Thus, a war could never be wholly just. The converse was

also true. Aquinas argued that rationality directed individuals to do good and thus people did not deliberately wage unjust wars. Therefore he permitted the possibility that injustice could be done unintentionally owing to the perpetrator's ignorance and that a war might *appear* just to both sides (Tooke 1965: 127).

The third condition for a just war was 'right intention'. That is, 'there is required a right intention on the part of the belligerents: either of achieving some good or of avoiding some evil' (Aquinas 1998: 41). Following Augustine, Aquinas argued that virtue and evil resided in the will and the intellect. Moreover, he argued that intent and motive were bound together, so that what compels one to do something very much shapes what it is that one is trying to do (see Tooke 1965: 151).

As with the canonists, Aquinas said much less about *jus in bello*. In one passage, he forbade the killing of the innocent and righteous (Aquinas 2002: 262). Whilst this marked an important expansion of non-combatant immunity, implying that there was a complete prohibition on killing the innocent, not one that depended on their social function (canon law) or relative weakness (chivalry), it begged the question of who could be legitimately labelled 'innocent' or 'righteous'. Most interesting was the inference that slaying the innocent and otherwise violating the laws of war rendered unjust otherwise just wars. For Aquinas, a government's willingness to violate the laws of war entailed an unjust decision to wage war, presumably because such wars were fought without right intention (see Finnis 1998: 285, n. 63).

Aquinas' major contribution to the Just War tradition was to offer a philosophical justification for restraining war. The concepts of double-effect and proportionality became cornerstones of the Just War in the sixteenth century and remain so today. At the time, however, Aquinas was challenged by his peers and his ideas contained none of the weight of canon law or chivalric custom. It was another three centuries before his importance to the Just War tradition became fully evident.

The Chivalric Code

During the Middle Ages, the principles governing the conduct of war were based more on chivalric customs than Church law or scholastic philosophy. Just as ancient Greek customs of war were embedded in a distinct warrior class, the chivalric code was partly produced by the emergence of a distinct social class of knights around the mid-thirteenth century (Bumke 1977: 39). The emergence of the knight and his rise to aristocracy was intimately linked with the growing military importance of cavalry and the financial burdens it entailed. Between the fall of the Roman Empire and the mid-thirteenth century, the principal method of war fighting entailed the mobilization of feudal militias supplemented by mercenaries. In the eleventh century, the improvement of castle design made siege warfare more expensive and increased the significance of winning open battles and hence of mounted soldiers. The elevation of cavalry had a profound social effect that far outweighed its military significance. To be effective, mounted soldiers required much higher levels of skill than had previously been necessary for soldiers. The new mounted soldiers required expensive mail shirts, a number of good horses and squires to look after both the knights and their steeds. As most knights needed to acquire their equipment before engaging in battle, this required either that they already had substantial wealth or that they enjoyed the patronage of a wealthy noble (Keen 1984: 25–6). By the end of the thirteenth century, the knightly class had been incorporated into the nobility (Turner 1990). John of Salisbury (1909) argued that chivalry was a professional order, instituted by God, to protect human well-being, and that the knighthood was a brotherhood of warriors bound to defend the Church, the clergy and the poor. Thus, chivalry was determined by function not status and, whilst secular, was closely linked to the Church (Keen 1984: 5). A useful place to start our exploration is with three authorities in the thirteenth and fourteenth centuries that introduced chivalry as a particular way of life. All three suggest a close link between chivalry and the Church.

The first, *Ordene de chevalerie*, probably written before 1250, detailed the ritual that men underwent to become knights. It insisted that the knight be re-baptized, dressed first in a white robe (to signify the cleanliness of the body) and then a scarlet robe (to signify the shedding of blood in defence of the Church), and carry a double-edged sword to remind him that justice and loyalty must go together. Finally, the knight was given four instructions: he must not consent to false judgement; he must never be treasonous; he must honour all women and aid them whenever possible; and he must hear mass every day (Keen 1984: 7).

The second authority, Ramon Lull, who wrote in the second half of the thirteenth century, was a teacher in a Franciscan college. Lull went into more detail about the duties of chivalry. He offered a theological account of the origins of chivalry: after the fall of man, one in every thousand was designated by God to restrain and protect the people. They were the knights. The primary duty of the knight, Lull argued, was to defend the Church against unbelievers. The knight must also protect his secular ruler, the weak, women and children. The knight must be prepared to uphold the king's laws, protect roads and pursue thieves. In his conduct, the knight should prize honour above all else, eschewing falsehood, treachery, greed and idleness. The knighting ritual was to take place in church, the knight should be adorned with the symbols outlined in the Ordene and should be versed in Christian virtue (Keen 1984: 9–11).

The third authority, Geoffrey de Charny, was a professional soldier. De Charny wrote three works on chivalry between 1340 and the late 1350s.

Contra Augustine, he argued that earthly goods were significant and that soldiers would be rewarded for chivalrous action. Thus, the wealthier a knight, the more chivalrous he should be considered. Chivalry provided salvation, and the soldier who bore arms for a just cause, to defend his honour, that of his superior and the Church, or against the infidel would find redemption. As for the requirements of chivalry, de Charny's account was similar to earlier texts, with the notable difference that it extended to all soldiers, not just knights (Keen 1984: 12–14).

These accounts suggest a close affinity between ecclesiastical and secular authorities. The primary justification for chivalry was theological, and the knighting rituals were deeply religious and usually conducted by clerics. By the fourteenth century, the requirement that knights be trained in the art of mounted warfare prompted a need for military education and manuals (Hernshaw 1928: 21). These texts marked a significant departure from the earlier justifications of chivalry because they set forth a military law, replacing theological tenets with the idea that knights should be guided by a professional ethic. For instance, knights were forbidden from breaking formation in order to loot, unless it was safe to do so. *Knyghthode and Bataile*, published in England in the mid-fifteenth century, insisted that knights obey their king and that their main duty was to sacrifice themselves to protect the monarch and suppress rebellion (Bornstein 1975: 32–6). What is particularly interesting about these manuals is that they said very little about the actual conduct of war, especially on the treatment of non-combatants. Moreover, whilst remaining firmly within the Christian tradition, these later texts demanded fealty to the king not the Church.

The two most important and comprehensive works of this type were Honoré Bonet's *L'Arbre des battailes*, written between 1382 and 1387, and Christine de Pisan's *Les Faits d'armes et de chivalrie*, probably written in the early fifteenth century. Writing during the Hundred Years' War between England and France, Bonet rejected the Augustinian idea that war required special justification, arguing instead that God ordained all war (not just holy war) (Johnson 1975: 67). Bonet followed Lull in arguing that God gave victory to those he liked best. On the question of the rituals and virtues that made a knight, Bonet's thought was consistent with earlier works, but he furnished a concept of non-combatant immunity more complete than any previous work connected with either chivalry or canon law. He expanded the canonical idea that certain groups should be immune from war because of their social function in peacetime (clerics, farmers, merchants) to include the chivalrous idea that groups that were too weak to bear arms should also be exempt (Bonet 1949: 115). He called upon kings to enforce the immunity of both classes of non-combatant, arguing that failure to do so robbed war of its legitimacy in the eyes of God.

Christine de Pisan was the first woman to make an important contribution to normative debates about war, and her ideas were widely circulated in France, Burgundy and England (Bornstein 1975: 39). Pisan's justification of war was less vitriolic than Bonet's, concurring with Augustine and Aquinas that God *permitted* war in certain circumstances rather than ordained it (Johnson 1975: 73). The knight, Pisan argued, was a member of a Christian profession bound by his oaths to uphold chivalry. War could only be waged by a sovereign prince in defence of the Church, his subordinates or his allies. Interestingly, Pisan expanded the traditional understanding of 'ally' to include 'women, widows, orphans and all them that may have necessity' (in Johnson 1975: 73). She retained Bonet's expansive list of non-combatants, but removed the distinction between the two classes – the first based on social function and derived from canon law, the second based on weakness and derived from chivalric custom – producing a more complete concept of non-combatant immunity.

By the fifteenth century, therefore, the chivalric code had developed from a largely religious legitimization of the knightly class into a more secular convention based on a mixture of canon law and customary practice. The key question is whether chivalry had a positive impact on the actual conduct of war. Strickland (1996: 183–96) claimed that chivalry played an important part in restraining violence *between knights.* In particular, the tradition of ransoming noble prisoners rather than killing them made war much less dangerous for knights. Unfortunately there is no evidence to suggest that knights showed much restraint when it came to non-knights. Common soldiers were often massacred, towns burnt and churches attacked. Apologists for chivalry such as Philippe de Mézières (c. 1395) insisted that 'countless ills and cruelties ... occur in war, against and outside the laws of chivalry' (in Kaeuper 1999: 176, n. 92). Similarly, Richard Barber (1995: 238) insisted that massacres were carried out by common soldiers against the wishes of their knights. However, such privations were too regular an occurrence to be explained away in this way. Even Bonet (1949: 189) recognized that soldiers showed very little restraint in war. The customary practice of chivalry extended to fulfilling many of the rituals outlined in the early works and extending courtesy to one's fellow nobles. It evidently did not extend to the treatment of non-combatants aspired to by Bonet and Pisan (see Kaeuper 1999: 185).

Not only did the chivalric code not do much to restrain the conduct of war, it may have had some entirely negative consequences. First, by venerating knighthood, chivalry glorified war for its own sake. Furthermore, the ransom system made war financially appealing, encouraging knights to wage war for private financial gain. Second, chivalry only applied to an exclusive class, creating contempt for social inferiors and helping to justify atrocities against them. Third, Christian rituals were used to legitimize knighthood, but few of the restrictions on war laid out by Augustine, canon law and Aquinas were observed (Hernshaw 1928: 31). On the other hand, the military manuals represented the first sustained attempt to apply legal and moral thinking to the actual conduct of war. Bonet and Pisan in particular made an important contribution to the development of thinking about non-combatant immunity that expanded the categories of protected people and offered further justification for their immunity. Finally, the idea of a distinct warrior class opened up the possibility of thinking about a professional soldiery, creating the potential for military law.

Crusades and Holy War

A holy war, according to Carl Erdmann (1977: 3), 'is any war that is regarded as a religious act or is in some way set in a direct relation to religion'. The term 'crusade' should not be applied to every holy war waged by Christians but rather to those specific wars proclaimed by the pope in the name of God or Christ (Riley-Smith, L. and J. 1981: 1). The crusade and holy war were not considered wholly separate types of warfare in the Middle Ages (Riley-Smith, J. 1995: 16). Indeed, the word 'crusade' was a product of a much later era and was not used by contemporaries of the eleventh and twelfth centuries to describe their activities (Riley-Smith, J. 1997: 67). Holy war doctrine drew upon the Just War idea that a war was justifiable if directly commanded by God (Erdmann 1977: 7). It also made considerable use of the chivalric code and Peace of God movement. Thus, holy war doctrine was part of the Just War tradition, not antithetical to it (see Walters 1973).

The crusades' origins lay in the shift in the Church's attitude towards war during Gregory VII's papacy, which was dominated by the 'investiture contest' between the Church and the Holy Roman Emperor. Gregory VII proclaimed the pope to be the primary source of authority, and to support his claim he proclaimed a soldiery of Christ answerable to Rome, the *militia sancti Petri* (Mayer 1988: 19). Between 1090 and 1095, Bishop Bonizo of Sutri wrote a manual outlining the special roles and responsibilities of the *militia*, replete with Christian knighting ceremonies, a professional code and a code of honour. The consensus in the Middle Ages held that God could directly command war (and that such wars were obviously justifiable), and under Gregory and Urban the papacy claimed the right to act as God's spokesman on earth and command the *militia* (see Riley-Smith, J. 1998: 3).

Before Pope Urban II summoned a great army of Western Christendom to save the Church in the east, crusades of a sort had already been waged against Muslims in Spain. Gregory VII had urged knights to help free Spain from Muslim control, promising remission of sins for those who answered the call (Tyerman 1998). This proved successful, and these first crusaders retook much of Spain from the Muslims. Gregory VII failed, however, to summon an army to assist the eastern Church in its struggles against the

Muslims. Although he often floated the idea, there was little support amongst the kings and princes of the west for such an endeavour.

That changed at the Council of Clermont in 1095, when Pope Urban II preached the crusade to the massed gathering and received a rapturous response. Urban was motivated by two primary considerations. First, he was committed to the idea of reunifying the western (Roman) and eastern (Greek/Byzantine) halves of the Church and believed that sending an army to help the eastern Christians would bring the two Churches together under Rome. Second, the Byzantine Empire was being put under enormous military pressure by the Muslim Seldjuks and Turks, who had seized almost all Asia Minor. The Byzantines repeatedly requested aid, their propaganda insisting that the Muslims were oppressing and massacring Christians in the east, threatening the very existence of Christianity in the holy lands (Saunders 1962: 61–8). Whether or not this was true is an entirely different matter. There are reports of Christians reaching the Middle East to find, with some surprise, thriving Christian communities (Mayer 1988: 5).

At Clermont, Urban proclaimed a holy war aimed at 'the liberation of the Church of God [in Jerusalem]' (in Riley-Smith, J. 1997: 60–1). One of the key puzzles is why so many knights, peasants, clerics, women and children took up Urban's call – so many, indeed, that the crusaders put together a force of approximately 50,000 to 60,000 combatants, an army of a scale not seen since the Roman Empire (France 1994: 3). Some claim that the principal motivation was economic. The crusades, they argue, offered the opportunity for lower nobles and knights to acquire land and untold riches. Western Europe was undergoing an economic and demographic expansion, and nobles, particularly those who were not first in line to inherit the land and wealth of their fathers, welcomed the papal sanction to enrich themselves in the east (Finucane 1983: 15–16). According to this view, crusaders' motives were not that dissimilar to the motivations that underlay war in Western Europe. This view is problematic, though. Most crusaders knew nothing of the east, there was little likelihood of success in the first crusade, and the vast majority of crusaders returned west once their oaths were fulfilled. Going on crusade was very expensive; many nobles had to sell land to accumulate enough wealth to sustain them on their journey. Moreover, the nature of the feudal system meant that from a noble's perspective, prolonged absence, an inevitable consequence of going on crusade, jeopardized the security of the land, the castles and the peasants that were left behind (France 1994: 7; Riley-Smith, J. 1997: 47). Viewed from an eleventh-century perspective, there was very little material wealth to be gained by crusading and a lot to be risked.

The most likely explanation is that religious fervour was the principal motivation for crusaders. Particularly important in this regard was the link between holy war and penance. Penitential warfare was premised on the idea that fighting a holy war was meritorious in God's eyes (Riley-Smith,

J. 1997: 49). This idea, one of the cornerstones of holy war doctrine, was established before the Gregorian reforms by Pope Leo IX, who promised absolution of sins for soldiers who assisted him in battle. The general idea was that anyone who died whilst serving as a *militia Christi* would be absolved of his sins. Gregory developed these ideas when he was planning to form an army to march to the defence of Byzantium and portrayed the proposed war as one fought to defend Christ. Taking part in such a war was an act of merit that would be recompensed by God (Riley-Smith, J. 1997: 50). This created a new category of war fought for the remission of sins.

The idea that going on crusade would absolve the crusader of his sins was put forward by Urban and publicized by other preachers (France 1994: 10). As Jonathan Riley-Smith put it (1997: 69), 'there can be no doubt that the crusaders understood that they were performing a penance and that the exercise they were embarking on could contribute to their future salvation'. Imploring knights to wage war against Muslims in Spain, Urban proclaimed that 'no one must doubt that if he dies on this expedition for the love of God and his brothers his sins will surely be forgiven and he will gain a share of eternal life through the most compassionate mercy of our God' (in Riley-Smith, J. 1997: 71). At the turn of the twelfth century, the idea that taking up the crusade and marching to an uncertain fate in the east would lead to the remission of sins was very powerful. As one noble – Guibert of Nogent – put it in 1108, the crusade offered 'a new means of attaining salvation' (in Bull, M. 2002: 174).

The crusaders proceeded by different routes to Constantinople and then set out across Asia Minor, defeating two Muslim armies. By 1099 they had taken Antioch but found themselves besieged. Facing starvation, many crusaders climbed the walls and fled, many others succumbed to disease. Just as all seemed lost, there was 'divine' intervention when Peter Bartholomew claimed to find the 'holy lance' that had pierced Christ's side, beneath Antioch's church. The ruse worked and the newly inspired crusaders stormed their Turkish besiegers, defeating them and breaking out of Antioch (Fulcher of Chartres 1941). This incident reinforces the view that the crusaders were heavily influenced by the ebb and flow of religious pronouncements. Within months of the breakout, they reached Jerusalem and took it after a short siege.

The fall of Jerusalem was instructive in the conduct of holy war. It was quite normal in European war for peasant soldiers to be massacred after the fall of a city. Such acts were not prohibited by the chivalric code or canon law. If massacring Christians was an acceptable element of war, how much more acceptable was the massacre of infidels in a penitential war? After the fall of Jerusalem, the crusaders killed every Muslim they could find and showed delight in doing so. As Raymond of Aguilers exclaimed, 'it was a just and splendid judgment of God that this place should be filled with the blood of unbelievers. . . . The city was filled with corpses and blood' (in

Finucane 1983: 100). It is estimated that 70,000 people were massacred by the crusaders at Jerusalem (Seward 1972: 13).

The Christian success was relatively short-lived. Most crusaders returned home, leaving small Frankish colonies in the Middle East. Military religious orders such as the Hospitallers, Templars and Knights of St John were created to defend the holy lands. They were supported by the papacy on the grounds that a permanent holy war was needed to protect the new colonies from the infidels. By the mid-twelfth century, however, the colonies were again under threat and in 1145 the Syrian city of Edessa fell to the Muslims. St Bernard began preaching a new crusade and in doing so offered a classic definition of what holy wars were all about:

They can fight the battles of the lord and can be of surety the soldiers of Christ. Let them kill the enemy or die; they need have no fear! To embrace death for Christ or to cause His enemies to submit to it is naught but glory – it is no crime! Moreover it is not without reason that the soldier of Christ carries a sword; it is for the chastisement of the wicked and for the glory of the good. If it bring death to the malefactor, the soldier is not a homicide but (excuse the word) a 'malicide'! And we must recognise in him the avenger who is in the service of Christ, and the liberator of the Christian people. (In Gautier 1959: 3)

Bernard travelled Europe preaching the second crusade as a penitential war, as Urban had done prior to the first. Louis of France answered the call first but his campaign went badly and he withdrew in 1149 (Odo of Deuil 1948). He was followed by Germans, Englishmen and Flems, who had somewhat more success. By 1187, however, the Muslims had been united under Saladin and further crusades were needed (Mayer 1988: 137–50). Crusades were repeatedly launched between 1187 and 1229, with Pope Innocent IV reiterating the idea of penitential war and the pope's right to summon soldiers to fight in Christ's name. After five formally pronounced crusades and dozens of crusading sorties into the Middle East, the Latin Christians were finally driven from the Holy Land in 1291 (Riley-Smith, L. and J. 1981: 17–34). As Christian kingdoms began to evolve from the fractured feudal properties of Europe, European leaders became less concerned with affairs in the east. Neither the first crusade nor the ones that followed it precipitated the unification of the western and eastern branches of the Church, and the divide took on an air of permanence. By the fourteenth century, crusading energies were directed against the pope's enemies closer to home, in Italy and the Baltic region, for instance. When the 'great Schism' divided western Christendom in 1378, rival popes began declaring 'crusades' against each other, and in the seventeenth century the doctrine of holy war furnished justification for the carnage of the Thirty Years' War between Catholic and Protestant Christians (Housely 1995: 270).

Successive popes made crusades possible by claiming that the papacy had the right to speak for God and command wars and that participation was penitential. The holy war doctrine effectively gave the pope the highest authority to wage war and rejected the idea of constraints on conduct. As Christianity continued to fracture, however, the crusading impulse came to be directed against other Christians. By the seventeenth century, the holy war idea was almost exclusively used by Catholics and Protestants against each other.

Conclusion

At the beginning of the Middle Ages, the European political order was chaotic and complicated. Feudal lords competed with one another for land, power and privilege and both the Church and empire laid claim to political authority. War was frequent but small-scale. The Middle Ages contributed at least three significant ideas of the Just War tradition. First, a consensus emerged on the question of who had the legitimate authority to wage war. Canon lawyers and Aquinas agreed that only sovereign leaders, kings with no temporal superior, might wage war. Although private wars continued well into the eighteenth century, they diminished significantly from the fourteenth century onwards. In many respects, Augustine, the canonists and Aquinas agreed on the question of *jus ad bellum*, and their ideas concerning legitimate authority, right intent and just cause remain central to the tradition today. The second key contribution was Thomas Aquinas' doctrine of double-effect and his philosophical defence of the just war. Double-effect remains central to the Just War tradition today. Furthermore, it created the space for subsequent jurists to formulate practicable laws of war because of the distinction between intentions and outcomes. By basing his ethics of war on a philosophical rather than theological doctrine, Aquinas formulated a justification of war that withstood attack from both pacifists and later rationalists. The third key contribution was the chivalric code's development of customary *jus in bello* rules. Although we should not over-state the impact of chivalry's rules on the conduct of war, particularly in relation to non-knights, they established the idea that soldiers constituted a discrete professional class governed by its own code of ethics.

In the fourteenth and fifteenth centuries, there were significant changes in the way Europe was governed and its wars fought. The wider use of gunpowder and the consolidation of political power in the hands of a few powerful kings changed both the destructiveness and purpose of warfare (France 1999: 1–15). Amidst all this, new ways of thinking about the regulation of warfare began to emerge. The following chapter focuses on one of the most creative periods of debate within the Just War tradition. During the sixteenth century, four distinct sub-traditions emerged and competed with one another: the neo-scholasticism of the Spanish School, legalism, realism and reformism.

3

Reformation and Renaissance

This chapter maps Just War thinking in the sixteenth century. This period witnessed the decline of medieval structures of governance, the discovery of the Americas, the emergence of nascent modern states and important transformations in the conduct of war (see Hirst 2001: 14–15). Whilst there was a keen sense that laws and customs were decaying, there was little agreement about what would replace them. The period is sometimes characterized as one in which the Just War tradition was secularized, as the tradition's foundations shifted from canon law and scholasticism towards natural law grounded in human reason and positive law based on the voluntary agreements of sovereigns (e.g. Christopher 1994: 49–110; Coates 1997: 76–122). This characterization masks the complexity of the tradition's transformation. Moreover, it downplays the extent to which theological precepts continued to shape Just War thinking. It was not until the nineteenth century that the Just War tradition was fully 'secularized'. Before then, secular ideas co-existed with theological doctrines within the Just War tradition. The common denominator was a reliance on natural law, and one of the principal controversies of this period was the question of where natural law came from: human reason or divine inspiration? Most of the writers considered in this chapter and Chapter 4 suggested that it was a combination of both.

Three of the sub-traditions discussed in the previous chapter became less central during this period. The increasing use of artillery eroded the distinctiveness of the knightly class and thus the impact of the chivalric code (Parker 1988). The Christian reformation, which bifurcated the western Church into Catholic and Protestant, reduced canon law's authority. For its part, holy war doctrine faded into the background in the fourteenth century with the loss of the holy lands to the Turks. Scholasticism, though, remained central to the Just War tradition. However, at precisely the time that scholastic approaches to war reached their apex in terms of refinement and comprehensiveness, the methodology itself was challenged by proponents of new, humanist, methodologies.

The Church's main competitor for universal jurisdiction in Europe – the Holy Roman Empire – was also in what proved to be terminal decline. Although the emperor continued to claim sovereignty over his empire, many of the larger principalities, such as Venice, Pisa and Florence, asserted their independence (see Post 1954). On the empire's borders, the kingdoms of England, France and Spain all grew in strength and rejected imperial supremacy (Keen 1967: 212). Whilst a vague idea of imperial unity remained for much of the sixteenth century, the empire no longer extended beyond Germany (Van Der Molen 1968: 2).

This chapter traces the development of scholasticism and the emergence in turn of three new sub-traditions that had a profound effect on the Just War tradition: realism, legalism and reformism.

Neo-Scholasticism and the Spanish School

Scholastic thinking enjoyed a renaissance in sixteenth-century Spain led by Francisco de Vitoria, a Dominican friar who spent much of his life as *prima* Professor of Theology at the University of Salamanca. Twentieth-century debates about Vitoria's contribution centred on the fruitless question of whether he should be considered the 'father' of modern international law. The leading advocate of this position was James Brown Scott, head of the Carnegie Council's programme on the ethics of war (see Boyle 1999; Rossi 1998). According to Scott, Vitoria was the first to think of the European world as comprising a rule-governed international society of sovereign equals (Scott, J. B. 1922: 98; 1928: 136–9). Arthur Nussbaum, who reserved the title of 'father' of international law for Hugo Grotius, vigorously rejected this thesis. Nussbaum (1954: 296–306) argued that Scott simply misunder-stood Vitoria and overlooked the medieval and conservative tone of his work. This debate obscured more than it illuminated. Indeed, it clouded Vitoria's contribution to the Just War tradition. Vitoria provided an almost complete scholastic account of the Just War. Importantly, in popular modern renderings of the natural law approach to the Just War tradition, virtually all of Vitoria's ideas remain intact in one form or another.

Vitoria's interest in war was a by-product of his concern about the legitimacy of the Spanish conquest of the Americas. In his lecture on the American Indians, delivered in 1539, he investigated the Spanish claims to the Americas, first addressing the unfounded claims and then the plausible ones. He rejected the papal and imperial claims to universal jurisdiction on the grounds that they did not have dominion throughout Europe, let alone beyond. He also rejected claims based on the argument that the 'barbarians' could not be true masters of their land, arguing that the existence of laws, rulers and rites in the New World meant that the American Indians had dominion. Vitoria went on to reject the 'right of discovery' as a legitimate title and the supposed right forcibly to convert non-believers. The barbarians, he argued, committed no sin through their non-belief prior to being preached the Christian faith. Under no circumstances, then, could the Spanish use force to convert the American Indians. As Vitoria (1991a: 272) put it, 'war is no argument for the truth of the Christian faith. Hence the barbarians cannot be moved by war to believe, but only to pretend that they believe.' Vitoria conceded that if Spanish missionaries presented reasonable proofs of the faith 'accompanied by manners both decent and observant of the law of nature', the American Indians sinned if they still refused to convert. However, he found no evidence that the Spanish were presenting the faith in a decent fashion, and even if they were, the 'sins' of the American Indians did not necessarily provide justifiable grounds for war (Vitoria 1991a: 270–1). Vitoria (1991a: 272–7) went on briefly to reject three other claims – the sins of the barbarians (because not all sins provide cause for war), the free choice of the barbarians to be ruled by the Spanish (because in reality it would be a coerced choice), and the divine gift of God (because there is no precedent for it and it cannot be proven). He therefore expressly ruled out the idea that the Church or empire had a universal right to wage war (a pivotal idea in the crusades), the claim that wars of conversion were just, and the argument that non-believers had fewer rights than believers.

In the second half of his lecture, Vitoria turned to the potentially legitimate Spanish titles. First, he argued that the Spanish had a right to travel and dwell in the new lands, predicated on a right to trade, which, Vitoria argued, was grounded in natural law (Muldoon 1991: 74). In certain specific circumstances, this right might lend itself to a just cause for war. As Vitoria (1991a: 283) explained:

Once the Spaniards had demonstrated diligently both in word and deed that for their own part they have every intention of letting the barbarians carry on in peaceful and undisturbed enjoyment of their property, if the barbarians nevertheless persist in their wickedness and strive to destroy the Spaniards, then they may treat them no longer as innocent enemies, but as treacherous foes against whom all rights of war can be exercised.

On the basis of the evidence of Spanish behaviour in the Americas, Vitoria argued that this theoretical right could not be exercised because the Spaniards had not fulfilled their side of the bargain. Indeed, given *actual* Spanish practices in the Americas, the American Indians were entitled to use force in self-defence (see Reichberg 2003: 197–8). Many of the other potentially legitimate titles were predicated on this one. The settlers were permitted to preach the Christian faith and to wage war if they were violently prohibited from preaching, to protect converts from attack or to protect the innocent from tyranny. A Christian prince might come to power only if freely elected by the majority of American Indians (Vitoria 1991a: 278–91).

Vitoria's discussion of the Spanish conquest of the Americas stands as a practical application of Just War thinking and – until that point – a rare case in which a public intellectual criticized official policy (see Norena 1997: 257–71). Importantly, as an example of applied morality it demonstrates Vitoria's belief that states did not have a *carte blanche* to wage war, even against infidels. In particular, Vitoria expressly ruled out three potential just causes: religious differences, claims of universal jurisdiction and the personal ambitions of sovereigns (see Ballis 1937: 80, 84). In his lecture on the American Indians, Vitoria only permitted war in self-defence or to protect the innocent.

Vitoria viewed his lecture on the law of war as a continuation of his investigation of the Spanish claims to dominion over the American Indians. The lecture, delivered on 19 June 1539, explored four questions: whether Christians might wage war; where authority to wage war lay; what counted as a just cause and what should happen in times of doubt; and how wars should be conducted. We need not be detained by the first question, because Vitoria offered only a brief explanation based on well-established precepts. He also followed canon law on the question of who had the authority to wage war, arguing that only sovereigns were entitled to do so (Vitoria 1991b: 302–3).

It was on the questions of just cause and proper conduct that Vitoria made significant improvements to scholastic teachings. He viewed war as a quasi-judicial activity properly resorted to only in cases where there was no judiciary to adjudicate disputes. Following Augustine, he argued that the only just cause for war was to right a prior wrong (Vitoria 1991b: 303). However, he insisted that not every injury received created sufficient grounds for war. As he explained, 'since all the effects of war are cruel and horrible – slaughter, fire, devastation – it is not lawful to persecute those responsible for trivial offences by waging war upon them. The wicked man "shall be beaten according to his fault, by a certain number" (Deut. 25:2)' (Vitoria 1991b: 304). In other words, war was only justifiable if the injury it sought to redress was greater than the probable evil the war would unleash.

However, Vitoria was not satisfied with leaving his discussion of just cause with a simple assertion of what that cause might consist of. At the time he was writing, princes waged wars over lands that were plausibly claimed by many. Unravelling feudal agreements and inheritance lineages was a complex business. For instance, when Henry VIII attacked France in 1512 claiming inheritance to the French throne, he presented a sophisticated legal justification demonstrating his family's claim. The King of France, of course, rejected this claim, but both claims had a degree of plausibility (see Adams 1962: 62–6). Difficult disputes such as this raised the thorny question of whether a war might be just on both sides.

Vitoria prefaced his answer to this question with the idea that just causes have objective and subjective qualities. Objectively speaking, a war might only be just on one side, but in difficult cases, only God could know who acted justly. What people *thought* about the war did not affect this 'objective justice'. 'Subjective justice' referred to what people believed. Vitoria argued that humans lived behind a veil of ignorance because they could never *know* as perfectly as God. Humans might therefore believe their actions to be just when in fact they were not. In relation to the just causes of war, 'where there is provable ignorance either of fact or of law, the war may be just in itself for the side which has true justice on its side, and also just for the other side, because they wage war in good faith and are hence excused from sin. Invincible error is a valid excuse in every case' (Vitoria 1991b: 313). James Turner Johnson (1975: 20–1) described this position as 'simultaneous ostensible justice', the notion that due to invincible ignorance a war might *appear* just on both sides. As Johnson notes, in the hands of Vitoria this doctrine carried two consequences. First, because sovereigns needed to make difficult decisions in cases where the truth was veiled by ignorance, it became important to pay more attention to the process by which decisions to wage war were taken. Second, if it is conceded that the enemy might have justice on its side, it becomes imperative to conduct the war with maximum restraint.

If a sovereign could never be certain of the justice of his cause, could a war be justified if he merely *believed* his cause just? If the answer to this were affirmative, Vitoria's theory could have been used by clever sovereigns to justify virtually any war. However, Vitoria argued that the sovereign's belief alone did not constitute grounds for war. Rather, a sovereign should consult as widely as possible with good and wise men, and must listen to the counsel of those who oppose war. Furthermore, senators, public officials and advisers should consult with the wise so that they might better advise their sovereign (Vitoria 1991a: 235–7). This idea was later revised and developed by one of Vitoria's successors, Molina. Molina espoused 'probabilism', the idea that in doubtful cases subjects and sovereigns should ask whether it is 'probable' that they have a just reason for war (see Hale 1962: 22).

In doubtful cases, do subjects have a right to selective conscientious objection? This was an important and difficult question for Vitoria, particularly given his views on invincible ignorance. He concluded that political and religious leaders were bound to examine the legitimacy of the cause and offer frank advice to the sovereign. If they failed to do so they would be culpable for the war's injustice because they had the power to avert unjust wars and would be consenting parties to an unjust act (see Norena 1975: 130). What he described as 'lesser folk', however, were not required to examine the causes of war. Such people might rely on their 'betters' to make these judgements and committed no sin when they participated in unjust wars. Vitoria offered three reasons to support this view: first, it would be impractical to expect sovereigns to explain the matters of statecraft to all their subjects; second, 'lesser people' were in no position to stop the war; third, the fact that war was waged by a legitimate authority should be proof enough of its legitimacy for such people (Vitoria 1991b: 308).

Ordinary subjects were therefore not expected to assess the causes of war and were not held responsible when their sovereign waged an unjust war. How, though, should subjects behave when they were unsure of the legitimacy of a war they were ordered to fight? Pope Adrian VI argued that in doubtful cases, subjects should not serve in the army. Vitoria disagreed, arguing that if doubt alone were enough to prevent military service, no state would be able to muster an army to defend itself. When there was *doubt*, Vitoria argued that subjects should trust their sovereign. However, in cases where subjects believed a war to be *manifestly unjust*, they should refuse to participate, though sovereigns retained a right to punish conscientious objectors (Vitoria 1991b: 307–9).

Arguably the most significant consequence of Vitoria's discussion of just cause and invincible ignorance was its impact on the position of *jus in bello* within the Just War tradition. If we can never be entirely sure of our case and there is a chance that our enemy might have a degree of justice on its side, it stands to reason that we should conduct ourselves in a restrained fashion, only targeting those we must in order to achieve our aims. It was precisely this type of argument that contributed to the shift away from the focus on *jus ad bellum* towards a conception of the just war almost entirely predicated on *jus in bello* in the nineteenth century.

Vitoria's *jus in bello* employed the doctrine of double-effect first proposed by Aquinas. Accordingly:

It is occasionally lawful to kill the innocent not by mistake, but with full knowledge of what one is doing, if this is an accidental effect. . . . This is proven since it would otherwise be impossible to wage war against the guilty, thereby preventing the just side from fighting . . . care must be taken to ensure that the evil effects of war do not outweigh the possible benefits sought by waging it. (Vitoria 1991b: 315)

Although the innocent might not be deliberately targeted, Vitoria permitted their accidental killing in certain circumstances. For example, they may be killed during a siege when they intermingle with enemy soldiers. Once the siege is over, however, the innocent may not be killed because they are not complicit in any wrong. The victors may judge and slay the guilty but they must let the innocent live unharmed. Once again, however, considerations of proportionality came into play. Vitoria (1991b: 315–16) argued that if a besieged city housed so few of the guilty that its taking would not affect the outcome of the war, it could not be considered lawful to attack it. Moreover, he argued that it was wrong to kill the innocent pre-emptively to prevent, for instance, the enemy's male children from bolstering its military ranks at some later date.

Vitoria influenced a significant revival in scholasticism, and several subsequent Spanish intellectuals developed his ideas. The most famous of these was Francisco Suárez. Suárez's most significant addition to Vitoria's work was his more rigorous discussion of the nature of international law (Suárez 1944a: 380). Writing in the early seventeenth century, Suárez argued that the law of nations was universal and predicated on customs common to all peoples that included both natural law and human positive law. He retained the Roman idea that *ius gentium* was binding on individuals rather than states (*ius inter gentes*). Paving the way for later conceptions of law, he argued that *ius gentium* was a voluntary positive law grounded in the customary practices and consent of humans rather than in natural or divine law, but that this was only one of four types of law, with the other types including divine and secular natural law.

Suárez's account of the Just War was very similar to Vitoria's. He relaxed Vitoria's insistence that a sovereign be certain of his cause by endorsing Molina's 'probabilism' (Suárez 1944b). Like Vitoria, Suárez insisted that a sovereign should consult widely about the legitimacy of his cause before deciding to wage war. Indeed, Suárez obligated sovereigns to do so whereas Vitoria only suggested that they 'ought' to do so, though Suárez placed fewer obligations on the sovereign's counsellors than Vitoria (Johnson 1975: 179). Suárez's position on *jus in bello* was similarly Vitorian, combining a rule of non-combatant immunity with a doctrine of double-effect that permitted the unintentional killing of the innocent (see Bailey 1972: 14).

Though still grounded in medieval scholasticism, therefore, the Spanish School made an important contribution to the Just War tradition. Whilst it is inappropriate to label Vitoria the 'father' of international law, he did begin to enunciate the idea of a universal international society of sovereign equals in his lecture on the American Indians. Suárez developed this view more systematically, as did legalists such as Gentili and Grotius. Vitoria's discussion of invincible ignorance and simultaneous ostensible justice unwittingly paved the way for later realists and legalists to argue that as objective knowledge of just causes was impossible, it should be assumed that war waged by sovereigns was just, placing the normative emphasis on its conduct. The insistence that sovereigns consult their advisers, churchmen and other intellectuals before deciding to wage war added an important safeguard against embarking on conflict opportunistically. Moreover, Vitoria and Suárez opened the possibility of selective conscientious objection since they accepted the idea that an individual should refuse to fight if he was convinced of a war's illegitimacy. Also, Vitoria was the first writer to accord an important role to proportionality at both the *jus ad bellum* and *jus in bello* levels and to discuss its practical implications. Finally, Vitoria and

Suárez clarified the nature of just causes by according them a quasi-judicial function. War was only justifiable when a significant injury was received that could not be rectified by arbitration.

Realism

The most important, though certainly not the only, proponent of realism in the sixteenth century was Machiavelli (see Skinner 1978: 253). Machiavelli rejected scholastic methodology and the place of theology in political theory more generally. He claimed that humans were basically selfish and driven by their own self-interest to an insatiable quest for wealth, honour and power (see Zeitlin 1997: 55). For Machiavelli, the law of nature did not point to common rules about appropriate behaviour but to a continual quest for survival and enrichment. This quest, Machiavelli argued, produced recurring patterns of action. History should be used to identify these patterns and proffer advice about how best to harness them (Zeitlin 1997: 55). Machiavelli also insisted that the state itself was a source of good. He argued that although all human history was characterized by civil strife, it could be directed towards profitable ends by the good state. What was good for the state was therefore good for humankind, and *raison d'état,* properly understood and used, provided justification enough for most of the prince's actions (see Bien 1981: 200–1). Given human nature, however, the achievement of this good must necessarily involve the commission of acts that were traditionally thought immoral (Machiavelli 1940: 138–9).

Machiavelli therefore had a very different concept of virtue to that held by the scholastics and canon lawyers. He accepted that it was important for a prince to appear to conform with the traditional Christian virtues of 'compassion, faith, integrity, humanity and *religione*' in order to maintain domestic legitimacy. However, these qualities could actually damage the prince if he insisted on observing them at all times, for it was sometimes necessary to act 'against faith, against charity, against humanity, and against *religione*' (Machiavelli 1940: 18). To be successful, a prince needed to learn a new set of public virtues, different to the private virtues taught by religious leaders. 'Virtue' in the Machiavellian sense referred to the ability to understand the nature of necessity and have the strength and cunning to turn it to one's advantage (see Ball, T. 1984: 525).

Although some critics have argued that Machiavellian virtue required a 'willingness to discount the demands of justice' (Skinner 1984: 216), Machiavelli did propose a theory of justice, though one greatly at odds with the prevalent ideas of his day. Machiavelli wrote that a state required justice and arms to survive: justice, 'to restrain and correct the subjects', and arms, 'to protect them from foreign attack' (Parel 1990: 531). What Machiavelli meant by 'justice' was outlined in part in the *Discourses*, which he wrote between 1515 and 1520. He argued that in the beginning, humans lived like beasts without society and states and endured a permanent sense of insecurity. In this condition, physical power became the primary virtue and was gradually concentrated until political communities were formed, at which point humans began to distinguish between good and evil. Thus, morality and law were products of political communities (Parel 1990: 531). Humans created laws within such communities to punish wrongdoers and protect the community. Whilst justice was not part of the innate human condition, it was a first-order component of political community. Physical force was essential for the creation of those communities, but justice was its primary product, and both force and justice were essential for the state's survival and growth (Parel 1990: 532). This was positive justice based on volitional law. It was relative rather than universal and did not extend beyond the state.

The prince's primary role in this schema was to protect the political community through force of arms and justice. To do this, however, he must remain 'above' the law and be free to act however necessity dictated. The requirement to sometimes get 'dirty hands' was nowhere stronger than in matters of war and peace. Machiavelli maintained that as justice was confined to the state, the world beyond was an ungoverned anarchy. In order to protect the political community in this environment, princes must be directed by the virtue of necessity and guided only by considerations of prudence, not of law and morality (Linker 1992: 18). Thus, in Machiavelli's approach to war everything was subordinated to military power and its prudential use (Scott, J. 1992: 567).

Machiavelli placed no universal moral or legal constraints on the prince's decision to wage war or its conduct. The only guide was necessity. For Machiavelli, this meant that morally evil means were permissible if they accomplished good consequences (Hancock 1994: 14). That is not to say that he argued that it was always wise to fight in an unrestrained manner. In cases 'when it is absolutely a question of the safety of one's country, there must be no consideration of just or unjust, or merciful or cruel, of praiseworthy or disgraceful; instead, setting aside every scruple, one must follow to the utmost any plan that will save her life and keep her liberty' (Machiavelli 1965: 519). Of course, most wars were not wars of national survival, and in such wars *prudence* dictated that princes fight in a limited fashion. In *The Prince*, written in 1513, Machiavelli (1940: 62) criticized Agathocles of Syracuse for his brutality, arguing that 'it cannot be called prowess to kill fellow citizens, to betray friends, to be treacherous, pitiless, irreligious'. He went on to condemn Agathocles for his 'brutal cruelty, inhumanity, his countless crimes, which altogether forbid his being counted among eminent men'. Machiavelli argued that a prince's cruelty must only be of a level dictated by necessity. In other words, *raison d'état* did not provide permission for *any* act of cruelty on behalf of the state, only what was necessary and proportionate (see Jackson, M. 2000: 433). Nevertheless, Machiavelli eschewed classic Just War teachings by arguing that cruelty was not intrinsically wrong but wrong only in relation to its consequences (Hancock 1994: 15). Excessive cruelty might inspire opposition and disunity but cruel, necessary acts that accomplished their goals were not wrong.

Machiavelli explicitly turned to the question of war in a short piece entitled *The Art of War* (1521). Recalling that a successful state rested on justice and arms, he insisted that the prince be proficient in military strategy and tactics. Machiavelli suggested that the state was best defended by an army comprising skilled citizens and led by officers well versed in the strategies and tactics of the ancients. He argued against the use of mercenaries on the grounds that they created a potential source of weakness because their primary motivation was financial gain not loyalty to the state (Machiavelli 1969: 130). Machiavelli went on to discuss how the army should be formed, what sort of units should comprise it, and how it should march, camp and conduct battles, building a schema predicated entirely on ancient methods of warfare. He was scathing about the use of cavalry and argued that artillery was 'useless' (Machiavelli 1969: 215). Unsurprisingly, Machiavelli did not address the ethics of war, assuming that anything that prudently contributed to its successful prosecution was legitimate. Nevertheless, in places he expressed a chivalric attitude to subjects such as military hierarchy and tactics, not least in his discussion of artillery. As Sidney Anglo (1969: 131) pointed out, Machiavelli's view on war was more an account of a dying mode of medieval warfare than a doctrine for future conflict.

Whilst Machiavellianism did not become popular for at least another two centuries and differed from Machiavelli's writings in important respects, Machiavelli's realism provided an important counterpoint to scholasticism. Not least, it proffered a historicist methodology that rejected the relevance of scripture and canon law; it rejected universal deontology; it insisted that all acts conducted in the interests of the state were licit; and it prioritized consequences over intentions. That is not to say that Machiavelli endorsed unrestrained war. Instead, he argued that only those acts that were prudently deemed necessary were justifiable. In Just War terms, therefore, Machiavelli discarded just cause and right intentions from *jus ad bellum*, and replaced them with the twin assertions that any war fought by a sovereign in the service of the state constituted just cause and proper intent and that war itself must be proportionate to the desired ends. Likewise, he reduced the *jus in bello* to proportionality considerations derived from a *prudential* and not a moral basis.

Legalism

Legalists broadly accepted the Machiavellian view that states were inherently valuable but departed from realism by insisting that they comprised an international society constituted by laws and norms governing their mutual relations. Legalists differed from scholastic writers in their rejection of theology as a foundation for earthly law. The best-known advocates of legalism during the sixteenth century were Balthazar Ayala and Alberico Gentili. Not unlike Machiavelli, Ayala argued that the question of whether recourse to war was justified was a matter for the ruler alone. If a sovereign sincerely believed a cause to be just, then it should be considered so (Duchhardt 2000: 286). The logical corollary of this was that if a war was waged by two sovereigns who believed their cause to be just, then the war must be considered just on both sides (see Delos 1950: 548). Ayala therefore accepted Vitoria's doctrine but removed the distinction between objective and ostensible justice. Divine law, he maintained, governed the metaphysical world, and since there were no earthly authorities higher than sovereigns, it made no sense to think of the sovereign's choices as only 'ostensibly' just.

Ayala argued that if a war could be just on both sides, the most pertinent legal questions related to its conduct. A just army might only unleash the full horror of war on unjust enemies. Given that armies confronted a 'just enemy' in most wars, war had to be waged in a limited fashion. Moreover, once war was over, Ayala argued, the victor was obliged to follow precise rules. No longer could the victor destroy and pillage from the vanquished, for it must be assumed that the vanquished also had justice on their side. For Ayala, post-war settlements should be viewed as political compromises, not as a form of quasi-judicial punishment (Duchhardt 2000: 286).

This line of thinking was echoed in emerging Protestant approaches to war. Calvinist theories of the state proposed by writers such as Althusius and Daneau suggested that war was 'legally sanctioned self-help' conducted by sovereigns, and proposed the concept of 'necessary war' in opposition to the Just War tradition (Duchhardt 2000: 287). For Ayala and the Calvinists, the key tests of a war's justice were whether it had been authorized by a sovereign and whether the belligerents conducted themselves justly. Ayala went as far as to argue that it was simply inappropriate to judge a sovereign's causes for waging war (see Draper 1992: 189).

The best-known legalist writer of the sixteenth century was Alberico Gentili, whose most celebrated work, *De Jure Belli*, was published in 1589. Gentili rejected the realist idea that sovereigns could justifiably wage war whenever they saw fit and argued that such decisions were subject to scrutiny under international law, because whilst princes were 'above' positive law, they remained 'below' natural law and international law (D'Entrèves 1951: 68). For Gentili, international law governed relations between states and comprised rules that they consented to. It was volitional law, grounded in both written law and custom (Van Der Molen 1968: 116).

Gentili argued that no war was just unless it was absolutely necessary, but rejected the view that any war deemed necessary by a sovereign was just. For Gentili, a war became necessary when every other avenue for resolving a conflict had been explored and there was no means of arbitration. Before waging war, a sovereign must be prepared to present his case to impartial arbitration and must show willingness to compromise. According to Gentili, a reluctance to submit to impartial arbitration exposed a sovereign's doubts about the justice of his own case (Van Der Molen 1968: 116–17).

Gentili wrote at length on the specific causes that might justify war, and there is a striking similarity between his permissions for war and Vitoria's. Gentili permitted three types of defensive war and three types of offensive war. The most obvious and unproblematic just cause was 'necessary defence': defence against an enemy who has attacked or who is preparing to do so (Gentili 1933: 59). In these latter situations ('expedient defence'), sovereigns must have a well-grounded fear of imminent attack. Neither general fear nor the increased power of a neighbour constituted grounds for war. The threat must be either 'meditated and prepared', or, if not meditated, 'probable and possible' (Gentili 1933: 66). For Gentili, all sovereigns enjoyed these basic rights to self-defence regardless of other issues. He also permitted a third type of defence: defence of 'honour', which was closely linked to defending foreign subjects against their sovereign. For Gentili, this type of defensive war was permissible under natural law, which bound states to protect individuals in other states. It is 'lawful for any one', Gentili (1933: 73) argued, 'to aid a neighbour against injury', and those that refuse aid might even share in the guilt. The just causes for offensive war also followed the tripartite doctrine of necessity, expediency and honour, but each involved war to uphold legal rights. War might be waged to maintain the existence of the political community by reclaiming property unjustly taken (necessity), to take vengeance on those who have committed a wrong (expediency), to enforce customary and natural rights in cases where they are denied, and to punish crimes (Gentili 1933: 79–92). Finally, like Vitoria, Gentili (1933: 36–7) accepted the possibility of divine war, but was concerned about the potential for abuse, and insisted that whilst God clearly had a right to command war, earthly progenitors were obliged to provide compelling evidence of divine command. Failing that, Gentili (1933: 41) ruled out the legality of war for religion on the grounds that no injury is done to others by a community's choice of religious practice.

Where scholasticism and legalism parted company in the most pronounced way was on the question of whether a war could be just on both sides. Vitoria insisted that this was a logical impossibility but that the veil of invincible ignorance might make wars *appear* just on both sides. This option was not open to Gentili because of his radical separation of divine and human laws into the metaphysical and physical worlds, respectively. Thus, Gentili agreed with Ayala that a war could be *objectively* just on both sides. Indeed, he insisted that it was most unlikely that one side would enjoy a monopoly of justice. Most wars were not fought to right clear wrongs but to enforce contested legal rights. Moreover, even in wars of the first type (to right wrongs) the state that had war waged upon it had a right to defend itself (Gentili 1933: 31–3). This view reduced the relative importance of *jus ad bellum* vis-à-vis *jus in bello*. If war could be objectively just on both sides, the interrogation of just causes was less important than just conduct in determining its overall legitimacy.

This translated into a slightly more rigorous doctrine of *jus in bello* than that offered by scholasticism. Gentili (1933: 142–4) contended that all strategies that directly contributed to achieving a war's objectives were legitimate. However, he insisted that prisoners should not be killed, even if their numbers were so large that they could not be guarded, because soldiers were not guilty of anything other than defending the rights of their sovereign (Gentili 1933: 231). This stood in contrast to Vitoria's view that enemies guilty of injustices could be justly killed. Gentili was slightly less restrictive on the question of non-combatant immunity and his logic mirrored the canon law view that people should enjoy immunity from the ravages of war according to their peacetime function. Whilst arguing that women and children in general should not be killed, he permitted the killing of women if they undertook male duties or led the people into fornication (Gentili 1933: 251–60). Likewise, clerics, farmers, traders and travellers should be immune because they performed important peacetime functions and played no part in the hostilities (Gentili 1933: 261–9). This did not amount to a complete ban on killing non-combatants, and Gentili offered more than ten instances where such killing was legitimate. Principal among them was reciprocity: one was not obliged to respect the enemy's non-combatants if they did not do likewise (see Renick 1994: 453–4).

Gentili and the other legalists discarded both the Just War tradition's theological foundations and the Machiavellian idea that all that was left was unrestrained sovereigns guided only by prudence and necessity. Although Gentili considered the doctrine of necessity to be valid, he insisted that sovereigns were constrained by natural law and volitional international law. The result was a normative approach to war remarkably similar to Vitoria's in substance but very different in methodology and epistemology. Most crucially, eschewing the separation of objective and subjective justice meant that wars could be objectively just on both sides. Not only did legalist writers admit to this possibility, they also contended that most, if not all, wars had a degree of justice on both sides. This perspective contributed to the decline of the relative importance of *jus ad bellum*, which until then had been the predominant preoccupation for Just War writers. Whilst legalists suggested that sovereigns ought to consult their advisers or seek arbitration before waging war, they admitted that the sovereign had the ultimate right to determine the justice of his case. The justice of a war could not be evaluated by interrogating its causes and the authority that waged it, an assumption that had underpinned the classic Just War tradition. Instead, a just war was one waged by sovereigns and conducted in a just fashion. Despite this change of focus, by the end of the sixteenth century legalists had not elaborated on earlier ideas about *jus in bello* found in canon law, the chivalric code and scholasticism. Indeed, it was not until the nineteenth century that significant progress was made in this area.

Reformism

The fourth tradition that emerged in the sixteenth century epitomized the intellectual creativity of the time. In England especially, the king's right to wage war was challenged on the basis of its anti-humanist consequences (Lowe 1990: 174–7). Reformists such as Erasmus, More, Colet, Vives and even Shakespeare disputed the legitimacy of European wars. They employed historical, fictional, satirical and political methods to convey their arguments, eschewing the formalism of scholasticism and legalism and the anachronistic historicism of Machiavelli's realism. The humanists were not the only source of opposition to war during this period. Other traditions included Hussitism, which espoused the doctrinal pacifism of the earliest Church leaders, and the Anabaptists, who insisted that Christians must never associate themselves with the shedding of blood or with governments that might order such things (Hale 1962: 19). The humanists differed from these perspectives because they accepted that war might be legitimate in some circumstances; they simply doubted that any of the wars of their time were justifiable.

These humanists are sometimes referred to as the 'London Reformers' because they were active together in London at the beginning of the sixteenth century (Adams 1962). They received royal audiences and were widely published. Although others are better known, John Colet was the first to gain notoriety for his outspoken opposition to the wars of his day. Before becoming Dean of St Paul's (1504–19), Colet lectured in Oxford and used renaissance thought directly to challenge scholasticism. He proffered a novel methodology for interpreting scripture: rather than discussing the voluminous interpretations of past theologians as scholasticism demanded, he returned directly to the biblical text. Doing so, he found that much of what passed for canonical 'truth' about war was actually the product of generations of scholastic interpretation. Colet found that there was very little in the scripture to support the view that 'evil was a good, just and Christian means for overcoming evil' (Adams 1962: 22). As he put it: '[I]t is not by war that war is conquered, but by peace, and forbearance, and reliance in God. And in truth by this virtue we see that the apostles overcame the entire world' (in Adams 1962: 23).

Colet's most significant contribution to the Just War tradition came in a sermon given before the king in 1513 at a time when Henry VIII of England was contemplating war against France. We have only Erasmus' account of that sermon, but there is every reason to think that it is an accurate account because Colet and Erasmus were close friends and colleagues:

Exhorting all Christians to war and conquer under Him their proper King. For they had, he said, who through hatred or ambition were fighting, the bad with the bad, and slaughtering one another by turns, were warring under the banner, not of Christ, but of the Devil. At the same he pointed out to them, how hard a thing it was to die a Christian death, how few entered on a war unsullied by hatred or love of gain; how incompatible a things it was, that a man should have that brotherly love without which no one would see God, and yet bury his sword in his brother's heart. (In Adams 1962: 69)

Colet challenged both popular images of war and the Church's view that those who died whilst fighting a just war achieved salvation. He pointed out how unlikely it was in practice that a soldier killed another with a sense of Christian love (a necessary condition for Augustine). Amazingly, Henry applauded Colet's sermon and the Dean was invited for subsequent private discussions with the king. Henry invaded France nevertheless, but not before his legal advisers had provided a detailed document justifying his claim to the French throne.

It is difficult to do justice to Erasmus' thought on war because he wrote so many, sometimes contradictory, pieces. He insisted that the role of the ideal Christian prince was to promote concord on earth and that war was the cause of many social ills. The prince was in a position to cure those ills but would only be able to do so if he were educated in humanism (Fernandez 1973: 211). This education involved recognizing that war was a 'disease of man's wit' (Erasmus 1968: 189), a product of perverted individual psychologies, not the necessities of international anarchy. If society was to be rid of its ills, it must be rid of war. Echoing Colet, Erasmus (1907: 46) argued that it was all but impossible to conduct war whilst maintaining Christian values of peace, charity and love.

Erasmus stopped short, however, of endorsing pacifism. He recognized that princes had rights that must not be violated and admitted that good princes might justly wage war to vindicate those rights. According to Erasmus (1907: 51), princes must be sure that rights vindication would recompense the exceedingly great harm caused by war before embarking on that course of action. He considered war in itself to be always evil and calamitous, lifting the proportionality bar much higher than either the scholastics or legalists had placed it (Erasmus 1968: 252). Whilst some wars might be just, Erasmus (1962: 1) maintained that most wars did not pass the proportionality test and that most princes deceived themselves into thinking that their cause was just. The only type of war that Erasmus identified as potentially justifiable was defensive wars against the Turks. These wars protected the Christian way of life and therefore satisfied his exacting proportionality criteria, which, however, did not seem to be the case for any of the wars fought among Christian princes in his own time.

By the 1520s, the war between England and France and deteriorating relations between England and Spain made anti-war agitation more difficult. As Erasmus (1964: 151) himself lamented in 1521, 'matters are come to such a pass, that it is deemed foolish and wicked to open one's mouth against war, or to venture a syllable in praise of peace; the constant theme of Christ's eulogy'. Nevertheless, Erasmus and his supporters continued to publish their anti-war humanism anonymously, though such ideas were suppressed (Marx, S. 1992: 56). At the end of the century, the tension between patriotic 'warism' and humanist 'anti-warism' was evident in the plays of William Shakespeare. Steven Marx has eloquently demonstrated Shakespeare's transition from support for militarism in the early 1590s, through a balanced position that partly mirrored scholasticism and legalism in *Henry V* in 1599, towards anti-warism from 1602–3 onwards, encapsulated by some of Shakespeare's most famous plays, including *Othello* and *Macbeth* (Marx, S. 1992: 59). *Henry V* was a particularly important play because, whilst it is imbued with nationalism and militarism, Shakespeare portrayed the king as being particularly concerned to prove the justice of his cause – even employing scholars to research and present his case in detail – and conduct himself with the utmost regard for chivalric values (Meron 1992). However, in later works such as *Othello* and *Macbeth*, Shakespeare demonstrated the ultimate folly of war and the problematic nature of its values. For instance, Othello was portrayed as a good soldier but his sense of confidence was based almost entirely on war, a shaky dependency intimately linked to his ultimate downfall (Marx, S. 1992: 79).

Reformist writers questioned the foundations of classic Just War thinking, realism and legalism. They argued that predominant justifications for war deviated from scriptural teachings. Whilst war might be justifiable in certain circumstances, reformists poked fun at the martial values of the time, insisting that militarism should never be prized. In relation to the Just War tradition, Colet pointed to the problematic nature of one of the tradition's central foundations – the idea that one can kill without feeling hatred towards the enemy. In the vast majority of cases (if not all), Colet quite correctly pointed out, those involved in killing others 'hated' and wished harm upon those they were striking. At the level of the individual soldier, therefore, killing could not be considered an act of Christian charity. The full import of Colet's argument was clearly not recognized in his own time and has been overlooked since, as Christian concepts of the Just War retain the basic Augustinian justification for killing that Colet so convincingly questioned. For his part, Erasmus raised the bar of proportionality so high that only wars fought in defence of the Christian way of life itself could be justified. In normal circumstances (conflicts between Christian princes), Erasmus argued that an unjust peace was morally preferable to a just war. Importantly, these ideas were very much in the public realm. Colet preached regularly in London; Erasmus' pamphlets were published and sold very well in England; and the presence of humanist anti-war ideas in Shakespeare's plays demonstrates that they both were well known and enjoyed a degree of popularity. So dangerous were these ideas that they were actively suppressed throughout Europe after the 1520s.

Conclusion

The sixteenth century was a period of profound contestation within the Just War tradition. Although scholasticism was in terminal decline, the 'Spanish School' produced its most coherent and sophisticated account of the Just War and introduced the notion of simultaneous ostensible justice, contributing to the subtle shift in the relative weight afforded *jus ad bellum* and *jus in bello*. Vitoria continued to privilege *jus ad bellum*, and his work on both American Indians and the laws of war imposed important substantive and procedural constraints on recourse to war. Not least, Vitoria insisted that considerations of just cause should be tempered by proportionality and war should not be waged on the whim of the sovereign alone. Realists and legalists insisted that scholasticism used unsustainable theological arguments where reasoning grounded in human experience was necessary. It was evident to them that the most cherished aspects of human existence (social life, prosperity, religious worship) were protected by states. For Machiavelli, any act that was good for the state was good in itself. Thus, in their dealings with one another princes should only be constrained by prudential considerations. For legalists, however, the Machiavellian schema was problematic because it could not provide order between states. Whilst Gentili and others accepted Machiavelli's basic ontological proposition, they nevertheless argued that states were constrained by natural law and international law: products not of divine providence but human nature and volition, respectively. These developments further weakened the *jus ad bellum*, for in cases where there was no recourse to arbitration and both sovereigns believed their cause to be just, it was acknowledged that a war was objectively just on both sides. By removing the theological component central to Vitoria's assertion that one side must always have objective justice on its side, legalists and realists moved towards a position which held that any cause properly espoused by a sovereign must be just. Machiavelli and Ayala articulated this view clearly, whilst Gentili maintained that some constraints remained. The weakening of the *jus ad bellum* had a corollary in the growing importance of *jus in bello*. If a war might be justified on both sides, one must evaluate the justice of a war by focusing upon its conduct.

In the seventeenth century, these debates were overtaken by a resurgence of holy war thinking, as Europe was ravaged by a series of wars including the Thirty Years War and the English Civil War. The holy wars of the seventeenth century brought these sixteenth-century debates to an abrupt end and gave rise to two types of response that had a profound effect on the Just War tradition. The first was a resurgent realism found in the work of Thomas Hobbes, and the second was the further elaboration of legalism in the work of Hugo Grotius, Christian Wolff, Samuel Pufendorf and Emmerich de Vattel, and its bifurcation into naturalist and positivist schools, both of which utilized natural and positive law but lent different weight to them.

4

From Holy War to Enlightenment

The period between 1570 and 1660 was one of almost incessant holy war in Europe (Hale 1985: 28). England fought wars with France, Spain and the Netherlands and endured a civil war. Between 1618 and 1648 disputes about Spanish hegemony erupted into a series of wars collectively labelled the 'Thirty Years' War'. The war began as a conflict between a 'Union' of Protestant principalities and a 'League' of their Catholic counterparts and spread to engulf much of Europe (Jackson, R. 2000: 162–3). These wars both inspired and were inspired by a resurgence in holy war thinking in England and on the continent. Their destructiveness generated an important intellectual and political backlash that led to the demise of both holy war thinking in Europe and Catholic scholasticism. The wars were brought to an end by two treaties collectively known as the 'Peace of Westphalia'. These treaties reaffirmed the principle of *cujus regio ejus religio* (to each sovereign his own religion), first enunciated in the Peace of Augsburg (1555). This principle laid the foundation for the idea of sovereign inviolability and an account of the Just War predicated on agreements between states.

Between 1660 and 1789, the kingdoms of France and England continued to grow in power and territory and the number of principalities in the Holy Roman Empire shrank whilst the power of individual principalities (such as Prussia) grew considerably. Realism and legalism came to the fore within the Just War tradition. Machiavellian teachings, once thought almost satanic, became more popular, as did the doctrine of *raison d'état*. At the same time, legalist thought bifurcated into naturalist and positivist streams, with the latter predominant by the end of the period. In the late eighteenth century, an alternative to realism and legalism appeared in the reformist work of Immanuel Kant.

This chapter maps the Just War tradition's transformation in three parts. The first charts the return of holy war doctrine to Europe. The second focuses on the intellectual reaction to holy war in the influential work of Thomas Hobbes and Hugo Grotius. The final section charts post-Grotian

Just War thinking, focusing on the bifurcation of legalism and Kant's reformist writings.

Holy War Returns to Europe

Holy war returned to prominence in Europe from the end of the sixteenth century until approximately 1660 with the end of the puritanical regime in England and the restoration of the monarchy. Holy war thinking in England and Spain was given added impetus by nationalism and religious reform in England; England itself was wracked by the puritan revolt and civil war; and between 1618 and 1648 central Europe endured the Thirty Years' War precipitated by the collapse of the Treaty of Augsburg. The Treaty of Augsburg, concluded in 1555, had recognized French victories over the Habsburgs and put an end to the Holy Roman Emperor's ambition to establish a *respublica Christiana* across the continent. In essence, Augsburg (not Westphalia in 1648) put an end to the universalist aspirations of both Church and empire (Bobbitt 2002: 487).

The Thirty Years' War (1618–48) was actually a number of separate wars between the kingdoms and principalities of central Europe and Scandinavia, mostly waged for territorial aggrandizement or the vindication of succession rights. The wars comprised a conflict between Habsburg aspirations to maintain their possessions in Germany and eastern Europe and the principalities' claims for independence (supported by Sweden), a religious struggle between Protestants and Catholics, and a contest over the type of order that would replace the medieval system. The religious dimension certainly contributed to its brutality (Howard, J. 1976: 37). Around one-third of the entire population of the Holy Roman Empire died in the war. One study showed that prior to the war there were 35,000 villages in Bohemia; by war's end only 6,000 remained (Bobbitt 2002: 119). Likewise the puritanical revolution and civil war between Monarchists and Parliamentarians in England was characterized by 'atrocity, war crime and treason' (Montross 1960: 293–5).

The return of holy war to Europe brought an end to the era of intellectual creativity mapped in the previous chapter. Opposition and even indifference to war was viewed as treachery. In the early seventeenth century, Harward complained that 'England hath many seditious malcontents which, being wearie of their own welfare, doe repine against those meanes whereby our prosperity is preserved' (in Hale 1983: 496). Meanwhile, the traditional rules of war broke down almost completely. Stephen Gosson, one of the leading advocates of holy war thinking in England, insisted that when the issue of just cause was not in doubt, 'al the means are lawful that are requisite to the attaining of victory; sleights, shifts, stratagems, burning, wasting, spoiling, undermining, battery, blows and bloud' (in Hale 1983: 497).

One of the key holy war thinkers of this period was the Swiss writer Heinrich Bullinger. In 1586, Bullinger argued that war was justified in self-defence, to punish those condemned by God and to correct religious error. Of all causes, though, the highest was the protection of true religious faith (Bullinger 1849: 376–7). This view challenged the one point that many legalists, realists and reformists agreed on – the illegitimacy of religious wars. Bullinger's view predominated, though. In England, the renowned statesman Francis Bacon argued that the concept of defence should be expanded to include defence of right religion as well as defence of the state (Johnson 1975: 90). Likewise, Gosson argued that 'just wars' were not just permitted by God, they were directly commanded by him (Johnson 1975: 98).

The devastation wrought by Europe's holy wars produced a profound intellectual reaction that reshaped the Just War tradition. Thomas Hobbes' *Leviathan* (1651) was a self-conscious reaction to the anarchy that accompanied the English Civil War, whilst Grotius' *De Jure Belli et Pacis* (1625) attempted to construct a system of law that would prevent future cataclysms. In the diplomatic field, the Westphalian treaties attempted to restructure European society by reconfiguring its borders and restating the sovereignty principle enunciated at Augsburg.

Reactions to the Holy Wars

Realism – Thomas Hobbes

Hobbes was influenced by his experiences of the English Civil War and exile in France. He rejected scholasticism because of its appeal to divine authority and tendency towards 'nonsensical and empty terms', preferring reason and history instead (Cahn 1997: 79). When there was no civil authority, he argued, individuals inhabited a state of nature where life was determined by physical power. In this state of nature, individuals could never be sure of their security and were forced to wage a constant war upon all (Hobbes 1994: 76). Within this context, natural law was limited to the desire for self-preservation. Recognizing that they could not meet their most fundamental needs in the state of nature, individuals established states through a contract between the people and their rulers. The people agreed to place a monopoly of power and the right to rule in the hands of a sovereign. In return, the sovereign promised to protect the political community from the twin dangers of internal anarchy and external aggression (Cahn 1997: 79). This view of the origins of states lent itself to two important propositions about international politics. First, Hobbes had an absolutist conception of sovereignty, any derogation from which threatened a return to the state of nature. Second, whilst the creation of states removed individuals from their personal state of nature, the multiplicity of states created an international state of nature. Both these propositions flowed from the insight that although humans had reason enough to establish states and escape the condition of anarchy, their egoism and self-interestedness remained unchanged (Haslam 2002: 56).

In this context, the sovereign defended both himself and his citizens (Tuck 1979: 129–30). To make this possible, the contracting parties yielded all their rights bar one – individual self-defence – to the sovereign (Tierney 1982: 396). The sovereign was therefore granted wide authority to make and enforce the law with the only source of law being the sovereign's will. If the law was the will of the sovereign and depended on the exercise of power legitimated by the original contract between sovereign and people, and natural law extended only to the duty of self-preservation, it followed that for Hobbes there could be no law guiding relations between sovereigns. Sovereigns, he argued, inhabited an anarchic society and endured constant fear for their security, which could only be mitigated by military preparations. To increase their chances of survival, states should seek to maximize their power. This was an important departure that reflected political changes in post-Westphalian Europe. Prior to Westphalia, European international society was not widely considered to be anarchic. It was a hierarchical society with the empire and Church at the pinnacle, followed closely by powerful kingdoms such as France, Spain and England, and then an admixture of principalities, city-states, federations and republics (Pennington 1993). All were tied together in a web of hierarchical relations. Although the degree of hierarchy diminished after Westphalia, it remained a feature of European international society for a considerable time after. However, Hobbes' depiction of the international realm as anarchic became predominant among thinkers – a long time before it became a practical reality.

The Hobbesian reaction to the civil strife of the seventeenth century was to view it as an inevitable result of the breakdown of sovereign power. The primary barrier against war and tyranny was therefore held to be the preservation of sovereign states. As such, Hobbes insisted that there were no legal constraints on what sovereigns could do to maintain their rule. In the Hobbesian schema, sovereign states became goods in themselves. Although states made treaties, sovereigns could never be confident that others would abide by them. Thus, Hobbes advised states to maintain a constant readiness for war.

What did this mean for the Just War tradition? According to Hobbes, it was pointless to attempt to restrain war because that assumed moral and legal bonds between units that had no such bonds. In the absence of an authority able to enforce legal or moral rules, those rules had no force. In relation to civil wars, Hobbes rejected any right of rebellion, though he admitted that individuals retained their natural right to defend themselves (individually) against sovereign power. In relation to wars between sovereigns, the Hobbesian position was that such wars were an enduring feature of an anarchic international society. This had three important consequences for the Just War tradition. First, the assertion of anarchy challenged legalist ideas about the existence of law in relations between states. Second, Hobbes' absolutist conception of sovereignty negated any potential role for *jus ad bellum* and *jus in bello*. *Jus ad bellum* was reduced to the principle of right authority, with the presumption that any war waged by a sovereign for the good of the state was justifiable, whilst *jus in bello* was overlooked entirely. An absolute sovereign was bound only by whatever laws he consented to. Finally, because the Hobbesian world was divided into distinct political units, each guided by its own laws, sovereigns did not have international duties.

Legalism – Hugo Grotius

Grotius' major work on the ethics of war, *De Jure Belli et Pacis*, was also a reaction to Europe's holy wars, self-consciously aimed at redressing what he saw as the disturbing trend towards the realist view that sovereigns could wage war for any reason and fight in an unconstrained fashion (Edwards 1981: 116). Grotius believed that war itself was neither inherently right nor wrong. Correctly used, it could be an instrument used by rational people to preserve society. International law, Grotius believed, provided a framework for evaluating when and how war could be legitimately used. The existence of such law, he argued, 'is similar to that for unwritten municipal law; it is found in unbroken custom and the testimony of those who are skilled in it' (Grotius 1925: 44).

Grotius understood international law as a law that bound states to one another, not a universal law that bound individuals. He argued that this law was a complex system that covered a wide variety of activities in international relations (Nussbaum 1954: 109). International law comprised two elements, natural law and human law (comprising human and divine law), the first governing what was *just*, the latter determining what was *legal* (Grotius 1925: 44–5). Grotius has often been misinterpreted as offering an entirely secular theory of natural law because of his oft-repeated statement in the *Prolegomena* to *De Jure Belli et Pacis* that 'what we have been saying [about natural law] would have a degree of validity even if we should concede that which cannot be conceded without the utmost wickedness, that there is no God or that the affairs of men are of no concern to him' (Grotius 1925: 13). That this 'impious hypothesis' was not meant as a prelude to a secular doctrine of natural law is revealed later in *De Jure Belli*, where he defined natural law in traditional terms as reason applied to understanding the will of God (Grotius 1925: 39). Beyond this statement, however, Grotius was happy to locate natural law in human reason (see Haakonssen

1985: 247). Although he considered natural law binding on all people, only acts that were clearly repugnant and 'unambiguously destructive of society' were forbidden by it (Ballis 1937: 110). The second, and more comprehensive, element of international law was human law. In the domestic realm, human law referred to those rules constituted by states/civil power, which Grotius (1925: 44) understood to be voluntary associations of men 'joined together for the enjoyment of rights and for their common interest'; in the international sphere it referred to the agreement of states manifested in treaties and customs (Boukema 1983: 69–73).

Within this schema, it was quite possible for natural law and human law to contradict one another. For instance, under volitional law an oppressed people might not revolt because they consented to the sovereign's rule. However, if the sovereign breached natural law by committing heinous crimes, another sovereign might lawfully intervene (Forde 1998: 642). What, then, was the relationship between human and natural law, and which took precedence? Grotius suggested that human law was created by practical reflection on natural law. Sometimes, human law permitted things outlawed by natural law – such as slavery. Occasionally, as in the case of slavery, volitional law might even appear to sanction breaches of natural law. In other cases, though, volitional law 'tightened' natural law, for instance in its prohibition of polygamy (Forde 1998: 643).

The complex relationship between natural and volitional law was shaped by Grotius' notion of 'permissions'. Grotius argued that 'human law cannot *command* what natural law forbids or forbid what natural law commands' (in Forde 1998: 644). Volitional law may *permit* things that are forbidden by natural law (but not command them) and may *command* things that are only permitted by natural law. Permissions did not make an act morally right; they merely suspended the operation of the rule forbidding the act (Forde 1998: 644). This made international law more responsive to political realities, making it less likely, Grotius hoped, that the law would be simply jettisoned in wartime.

Grotius' account of how law operated in international society began with the assertion that law constituted a society of states (Grotius 1925: 17). He followed Vitoria and Gentili in defining the just war in quasi-judicial terms. The only just cause for war, he argued, was an injury received in a context where tribunals were either ineffective or without jurisdiction (Knight 1925: 196). Grotius thus conceived three 'images' of Just War: war as judicial act; war as litigation; and war as defence of the common good (Kingsbury and Roberts 1992: 16).

At the beginning of his treatise, Grotius asked whether it was ever legitimate to use force. He shared what was to become Hobbes' view that self-preservation was the first principle of natural law, an idea first presented by Cicero (Tooke 1965: 210). This did not mean, however, that an individual's right to self-preservation was straightforwardly transferred to the sovereign once states were established. If this proposition were accepted, Grotius argued, it would be impossible to justify war because defending the state would jeopardize the lives of people who would not otherwise be personally threatened (Tooke 1965: 211, cf. Rodin 2004a: 107). In other words, war was inimical to individual self-preservation. Grotius therefore argued that war in defence of the state was justifiable because the state itself had value beyond the amalgamation of individual rights to self-preservation, which derived from its role as protector of society, economy, culture, and the like. Thus, he maintained that war was not forbidden by either natural law or volitional law but that the contradictions inherent in the concept of collective self-preservation necessitated laws governing recourse to war and its conduct.

My discussion of *jus ad bellum* in *De Jure Belli et Pacis* is prefaced by three observations. First, Grotius recognized the problem of 'abuse'. He noted that all too often sovereigns offered just causes as pretexts for war (e.g. Grotius 1925: 551). Such wars could be considered objectively unjust and might give other sovereigns a right under natural law to wage war upon the 'abusers'. Second, Grotius accepted Vitoria's argument that not all just causes justified war, but whereas Vitoria based his proposition on the proportionality principle, Grotius (1925: 556) argued that wars fought for just causes might be waged without right intention and would therefore be unjust (though not necessarily unlawful). Moreover, he argued that a sovereign must be sure that he could satisfy his rights through force of arms (Grotius 1925: 574–5). Finally, echoing Aquinas, Grotius argued that a war fought for just causes might *become* unjust if waged in an unjust manner (e.g. Grotius 1925: 494).

The conception of war as a quasi-judicial activity led Grotius to espouse a principle of right authority that encompassed the conditions of last resort and proper declaration. Grotius (1925: 170) argued that war might only be waged by sovereigns and only when they have properly declared their intentions and causes, offering the enemy an opportunity to provide restitution. Linked to this, he insisted that war was only justifiable when there was no possibility of effective arbitration. He argued that it was much better for disputes to be settled by conference, arbitration, lots or combat between champions (see Knight 1925: 198). War was unjust if these measures were available but left unused. However, whenever these conditions were satisfied, Grotius argued that a war must be considered *legal* because the legal right of sovereigns to wage war was recognized by volitional law. That did not mean, however, that the war was necessarily *just*. To accomplish that, a sovereign needed to satisfy the other *jus ad bellum* requirements.

Grotius identified four specific just causes for war and, like some of his predecessors, rejected the legitimacy of both 'divinely commanded' war and war to enforce religious orthodoxy. Two of his just causes were grounded in natural law: the right of self-defence (grounded in the principle of self-preservation) and the right to punish wrongdoers. The right of self-defence included a limited right of pre-emption in situations where there was a clear, specific and imminent threat, but, like Gentili, Grotius argued that a generalized fear of some future threat did not provide grounds for war (see Chapter 8). The right to punish wrongdoers pertained only to circumstances where the wrong committed was 'unambiguously destructive' of society. The other two just causes were grounded in human law: the enforcement of legal rights and the reparation of injuries where no other avenue was available.

Grotius' response to the question of whether a war could be just on both sides was more restrictive than Ayala's and Gentili's and mirrored the Vitorian distinction between objective and ostensible justice. Moreover, his distinction between moral justice and legal justice added a further level of complexity. Grotius (1925: 557) argued that only one side could have 'right' on its side in an objective *moral* sense. In such cases, justice lay with one side only and the forceful resistance of the other only compounded its wrong, because in cases where objective justice lies on one side only the other side has no right of self-defence (see Remec 1960: 96). Such cases were quite rare, however, for two reasons. First, for justice to be on one side only in an objective sense required both legal and moral justice. However, each sovereign had a *legal* right to wage war. In terms of legal justice, if both belligerents were sovereigns, it stood to reason that both sides might have legal justice on their side (Bailey 1972: 29). This meant that privateers, brigands and lower aristocrats who waged private wars did so unjustly, but that in most wars between sovereigns, both sides had a degree of legal justice on their side.

Second, Grotius admitted that human ignorance could cloud perceptions of justice and that from a subjective perspective most wars appeared just on both sides. In such cases both sides acted without guilt, but also without avoiding moral blame. As Grotius (1925: 75) put it: 'In a general sense that is usually called just which is free from all blame on the part of the doer. However, many things are done without right and yet without guilt, because of unavoidable ignorance' and 'sometimes the doer himself is said to act justly so long as he does not act unjustly, even if that which he does is not just'. Guided by 'unavoidable ignorance', a sovereign might wage war when he genuinely believed his cause to be morally just. Even if the cause turned out to be objectively unjust in moral terms, the sovereign did not commit blameworthy deeds providing the conduct of war was not manifestly unjust. As Grotius (1925: 76) explained: 'Yet it may actually happen that neither of the warring parties does wrong. No one acts unjustly without knowing that he is doing an unjust thing, but in this respect many are ignorant. Thus, either party may justly, that is in good faith, plead his case.' Grotius' position on this was very close to Vitoria's. In relation to 'the thing itself', or 'objective moral justice', only one side in a war acted justly, though both might act legally. However, objective justice was clouded by unavoidable ignorance (see Ballis 1937: 115). Whenever a state acted in good faith believing that it acted justly, it had ostensible subjective justice on its side and committed no wrong. It was theoretically possible therefore that both sides wage war unjustly in an objective sense yet neither does any wrong (Hodges 1956: 39).

What should we do when confronted by indeterminacy in such cases? Grotius argued that people should not do things when they do not know whether those things are right or wrong. This prescription is fine when an actor is confronted with a choice between doing something and nothing, and where doing nothing is morally neutral. In war, however, sovereigns are confronted with situations where failing to act might facilitate a wrong or let a wrong go unpunished. In such cases, Grotius argued, the sovereign must choose the least evil option (Edwards 1981: 125).

The novelty of Grotius' position on *jus ad bellum* lay in the following:

1 *Its foundations.* Grotius built a system of morality and law predicated on both natural and volitional law. Although Grotius' discussion of *jus ad bellum* contained few new contingencies, his *system* could be applied to make ethical and legal sense of virtually any type of conflict.
2 *The relationship of the different aspects of* jus ad bellum *to one another.* Grotius attempted to deal with simultaneous ostensible justice by emphasizing the procedural aspects of *jus ad bellum*. Just cause, right intention and proportionality of ends played a secondary role to right authority and proper declaration. If these procedural elements were satisfied, a war could be said to have legal justice. If the other *jus ad bellum* criteria were satisfied, a party could stake a claim to moral justice as well.
3 *The impact of the conduct of war on its overall justice.* Whereas Aquinas grounded his defence of a relationship between *jus ad bellum* and *jus in bello* in right intentions, Grotius insisted that if both sides had potential justice on their side, the conduct of war became the more powerful normative test in itself.

Grotius' doctrine of *jus in bello* was entirely based on natural law. Perhaps surprisingly given the greater role accorded to it in his overall schema, he did not add much to traditional Just War thinking about the conduct of war. Grotius admitted that killing everyone found in the enemy's territory was not illegal because it was not expressly forbidden by volitional law (Lawrence 1908: 330). This did not mean that such actions were just. Indeed, Grotius believed that killing the innocent was manifestly unjust because it violated principles of Christian charity (Johnson 1975: 226). To make this point, Grotius adopted Aquinas' doctrine of double-effect without revision and followed the canon law and chivalric traditions by identifying specific groups who should be immune from deliberate attack. Such groups included children and women (unless they had committed crimes deserving punishment), old men, merchants, artisans and other workers, prisoners of war and the citizens of neutral states. Grotius expressly forbade the use of poison, deception, terrorism and the destruction of artistic and sacred artefacts (Bailey 1972: 32). In order to operationalize these restraints, he ordered soldiers to refuse to carry out commands that manifestly violated either natural law or God's commands (Kingsbury and Roberts 1992: 24).

The Grotian reaction to the holy wars of the seventeenth century produced an important transformation within the Just War tradition. Explicitly theological arguments were marginalized in favour of arguments based on natural and volitional law. Although Grotius only permitted a universal natural law that prohibited acts 'destructive of society', natural law played a significant part in his substantive rules of war because the emerging positive law of nations remained underdeveloped. Grotius used natural law to justify killing, as well as two types of just cause, and as the entire basis for his *jus in bello*. The problem was that in the hands of realist-minded sovereigns, secular natural law arguments were as malleable as theological claims. The tendency towards abuse that this engendered was only encouraged by the doctrine of simultaneous ostensible justice. Thus, subsequent writers attempted to close the gaps by making wider legal claims, a task made easier in the nineteenth century by the proliferation of international treaties. Grotius himself tried to constrain the sovereign's discretion by emphasizing that a war could only be just if it was launched in a procedurally correct fashion and – echoing Ayala and Gentili – justly conducted.

Towards Enlightenment

After Grotius, legalism bifurcated into two sub-traditions that prioritized natural law and positive law, respectively. The first, manifested in the works of Pufendorf and Wolff, attempted to develop a more coherent natural law theory and predominated in European intellectual circles for much of the eighteenth century, though by the beginning of the following century it was very much in decline. The second, evident in the works of Vattel and Bynkershoek, minimized the role of natural law in favour of what would later be called positive law (Grotius' 'human law') – a conception of international law based on sovereign consent. This second strand became increasingly popular in intellectual circles and in the twentieth century was also preferred by state leaders. By 1789, the practical regulation of war had become predominantly a matter for positive international law which focused almost entirely on *jus in bello* as it assumed that wars waged by sovereigns were by definition lawful. These changes were reflected in the practice of war. Sovereigns waged frequent but limited wars for often spurious reasons.

Such wars were fought by small armies of volunteers, officers and mercenaries and often had little impact on domestic life.

This part of the chapter proceeds in three sections. The first considers legalist writers who emphasized natural law (Wolff and Pufendorf). The second focuses on legalists who insisted that positive law ought to be central (Vattel and Bynkershoek). The third section focuses on the reformist work of Immanuel Kant, who married a call for the radical reorganization of world politics with the decidedly positivist idea that law received its binding power from the reciprocal relations of sovereigns.

Legalism – Natural Law Focus

Writing towards the end of the seventeenth century, Samuel Pufendorf attempted to construct a complete system of natural law. Like Grotius, Pufendorf argued that natural law could be studied without appeal to theological argument but also that religion was not irrelevant to international law (Schneewind 1990: 156–7). Again like Grotius, Pufendorf drew a distinction between two types of law: civil/positive law and natural law. In *The Law of Nature and Nations* (1672), Pufendorf argued that sovereigns inhabited a state of nature in which civil/positive law was entirely absent because there was no global sovereign to make and enforce authoritative laws (Rommen 1947: 96). The customs observed by states were based on natural law, he argued. Pufendorf insisted that natural law did not consist of biological urges for self-preservation alone but was grounded in right reason and therefore had a significant moral component. This led him to reject the relevance of treaties and customs aimed at restraining the conduct of war, which he declared to be 'repugnant to nature' (in Nussbaum 1954: 149). Moreover, he insisted that 'a person who trusts in a treaty whose preservation is not in another's interest is even a fool' (Pufendorf 1994: 260).

On the law of war, Pufendorf (1994: 257) argued that nature permitted wars waged for the end of peace. The criteria he laid down for establishing when a war was legitimate did not depart much from those of his predecessors. He argued that even when a wrong was committed, war was only justifiable when more good than evil was likely to arise (proportionality of ends) (Pufendorf 1994: 257). He also echoed his predecessors in arguing that the only just causes for war were a wrong received, the satisfaction of rights, reparation for wrongs, and to guarantee future peace. Like Grotius, Pufendorf (1994: 258) admitted that a genuine fear of imminent threat could provide a warrant for war, though he was much more circumspect in delimiting the circumstances in which such a claim could be asserted.

Rather than expanding Grotius' conception of *jus in bello*, Pufendorf actually limited the constraints on conduct. He argued that an army fighting for a just cause had the right to 'apply whatever means seem to be most appropriate'. However, right reason and what he described as the 'law of humanity' dictated that 'one must, to the extent that it can be done and our defence and future security allow, take care that the evils which will be inflicted on an enemy be adjusted to the measure customarily followed by a civil court in assessing crimes' (Pufendorf 1994: 258). Thus, Pufendorf essentially made the application of non-combatant immunity conditional on military necessity without clearly delineating the extent to which military necessity might override the discrimination principle, as Vitoria had done.

Pufendorf's successor in the naturalist school, Christian Wolff, writing in the first half of the eighteenth century, articulated a cohesive account of the laws of war but this still fell well short of what was needed to 'fill the gaps' in Grotius' work and produce a secular doctrine of restraint in battle. Like Pufendorf, Wolff owed an intellectual debt to Hobbes and prefaced his approach on a Hobbesian account of the state of nature. Thus, like Hobbes, Wolff's first precept of natural law was that individuals and states had a right of self-preservation and perfection. However, for Wolff this right entailed a duty to assist others. This was an 'imperfect duty' inasmuch as a state had a right to request assistance but others were not obliged to assist if doing so prejudiced their own preservation and perfection. Given the existence of such rights and duties, Wolff concluded that sovereigns inhabited a world society (*civitas maxima*) predicated on an original contract and body of rules. This body of rules comprised volitional law, which overrode what Wolff described as the 'necessary law' governing the state of nature. Thus, for example, whereas the 'necessary law' insisted that a war might only be just on one side, volitional law held that two sovereigns in a war might have justice on their side and that this latter law should prevail (Nussbaum 1954: 152–6).

What contribution did Pufendorf and Wolff make to the Just War tradition? Substantively, they offered very little that was new. Their discussion of specific constraints on the use of force did not noticeably depart from Grotius. Their principal contribution therefore lay in the naturalist schema that they attempted to construct in order to overcome the perceived gaps in Grotius' work. In this endeavour they failed by and large because they were unable to articulate a doctrine of natural law that went beyond scholasticism. This failure helped to seal the demise of naturalism and the rise to predominance of legal positivism, for at least two reasons. First, the idea of a rule-governed *civitas maxima* stood in sharp contrast to European statecraft, dominated as it was by *raison d'état* (e.g. Rousseau 1927: 19). Second, there was growing recognition of the need for some form of enforcement to give the law weight beyond the conscience of sovereigns (Reddy 1975: 38). For these reasons, by the nineteenth century natural law had ceased to play an overt role in the laws of war, though natural law-type injunctions remained commonplace, embedded – for example – in the so-called 'Martens clause' (Kingsbury and Roberts 1992: 33; see also Chapter 5 below).

Legalism – Positive Law Focus

The second strand of thought within post-Grotian legalism was more positivist in its understanding of the law in that it gave more weight to the customs and treaties of states, though natural law retained a place. It proved more successful than naturalism both in terms of the intellectual development of the Just War tradition and in terms of restraining the actual conduct of war. The most significant of these writers was Emmerich de Vattel. Vattel's *Le Droit des gens* (1758) provided the most comprehensive post-Grotian reworking of the laws of war. Between them, Grotius and Vattel dominated thinking about the laws of war until the twentieth century. During the eighteenth century, for example, courts in both Europe and the United States frequently cited Vattel as a legal authority (Reeves 1909: 547). Indeed, one of Vattel's most vocal critics opined that 'the most disheartening fact of all is that Vattel was enormously successful'; he was so favoured that 'the second stage of the Law of Nations (1770–1914) may be safely called after him' (Van Vollenhoven 1919: 32).

Vattel's system of international law was predicated on the view that nations were free, independent and equal in nature. From this he drew the idea that separate nations should be considered sovereign and that such entities ought to be regarded as equal (Vattel 1916: 11). Developing the thought of earlier writers (particularly Vitoria and Grotius), Vattel argued that any self-governing nation warranted the title 'sovereign' and that all sovereigns enjoyed equivalent rights regardless of their type or relative power. Sovereignty was based on a relationship between a ruler and a nation and derived its authority from the delegation of power from the ruled to the ruler. International law Vattel (1916: 3) understood as 'the science of the rights which exist between Nations or States, and of the obligations corresponding to those rights'. The laws of war were therefore grounded in relationships between sovereigns and the rights and duties that they owed one another.

From Wolff, Vattel took the idea that there were four types of law. First, there was the 'necessary' or 'natural' law of nations, which was binding on rulers in their conscience (Vattel 1916: 4–5). This aspect of law gave Vattel's approach the escape clause used by the scholastics. In indeterminate cases (where two subjective views of justice collided) or in cases where human law was insufficiently complete, natural law would be the final, metaphysical, arbiter. The second type of law was 'voluntary law', a phrase Vattel (1916: 8) borrowed from Wolff. This was the practical interpretation of natural law in international relations. The third type of law was treaty law and the fourth customary law. Voluntary, treaty and customary law all depended on the consent of states and coalesced to make what Vattel labelled the 'positive law of nations' (Covell 1998: 87). Although states were considered generally free (in that they were not answerable to a higher authority), Vattel (1916: 9) argued that the law made them accountable to one another.

Unsurprisingly, Vattel (1916: 235) insisted that sovereigns had an inherent right to wage war. Moreover, he agreed with the Grotian premise that the *jus ad bellum* was a largely procedural matter dependent on the satisfaction of the rightful authority and prior declaration criteria, though this did not entirely exonerate sovereigns from their culpability under natural law. Vattel (1916: 236) considered both defensive and offensive wars to be potentially legitimate, with the key criteria being that 'the cause of every just war is an injury either already received, or threatened'. Reiterating the classic Just War doctrine on just cause, Vattel (1916: 236) argued that there were three such causes: claiming rightfully owned property; punishing the aggressor or offender; and self-defence (1916: 236). For a war to be just it also had to be supported by proper motives, a secularized version of right intention. For Vattel (1916: 244), 'proper motives' were expediency, advisability and prudence.

On the question of whether a war could be considered just on both sides, Vattel (1916: 247) followed Wolff in arguing that whilst in 'necessary law' ('objectively') a war may only be just on one side, in voluntary law ('subjectively') a war may be just on both sides because states were not entitled to judge their sovereign equals when disputes are entered into in good faith. Whilst a war might be objectively wrong (wrong according to 'necessary law', to use Vattel's terminology), such a wrong was only punished in conscience. As noted earlier, the fact that a war was not illegal according to voluntary law did not mean that a sovereign who waged an unjust war should be excused. Indeed, the waging of unjust (but legal) wars could give another sovereign a right to wage justifiable war in order to punish the wrongdoing.

Vattel's approach to *jus in bello* held that because of the close linkage between the nation and the sovereign, all enemy citizens were potential enemies. However, he rejected the idea that all enemy citizens were therefore legitimate targets, and proposed two safeguards. The first was a rearticulation of the doctrine of non-combatant immunity not dissimilar to canon law. Individuals who offered no resistance, or clergy, whose manner of life was 'wholly apart from the profession of arms', were to be immune from violence (Vattel 1916: 282–3). The second was an early form of *jus in bello* proportionality (Johnson 1975: 246–53). Vattel (1916: 293) expressly ruled out the wanton destruction of cities and agricultural land, insisting that he who committed such acts 'declared himself an enemy to mankind'. To be legitimate, any use of force had to be directed towards the accomplishment of military aims and must not cause harm beyond that which was necessary. As with earlier writers, Vattel's insistence that both sides in a war may (and usually do) have a degree of justice on their side meant that the overall justice of war was determined more by each side's relative adherence to *jus in bello* than by the non-procedural aspects of *jus ad bellum* (Reddy 1975: 122).

'The writings of Vattel', one commentator has observed, 'practically mark the end of any dominant influence of natural law in international relations' (Kahn, R. 1944: 94). Certainly, one of Vattel's primary contributions was his rejection of the idea of a universal world community predicated upon either Christianity or rationality and advocacy of the idea of an international society of sovereign equals bound by voluntary rules. Equally significant was the idea that sovereigns owed each other legal explanations for their actions and had a right to judge the actions of others and enforce the law. This decentralized vision of international law had been implied by many of Vattel's predecessors from Gentili onwards, but most writers were reluctant to dispense with universalism completely and maintained an earthly role for natural law. As we saw earlier, this presented problems for Grotius and certainly created ambiguities in Vattel's theory. For example, Vattel's theory of simultaneous ostensible justice was much less precise than either Vitoria's or Gentili's. Overall, however, Vattel preserved the main precepts of the Just War tradition and grounded them on a secular basis whilst eschewing naturalism. More than any other writer, therefore, Vattel paved the way for the predominance of legal positivism.

This shift was perhaps more evident in the work of one of Vattel's contemporaries, the Dutch jurist Cornelius van Bynkershoek (1673–1743). Bynkershoek joined Vattel in arguing that *ius gentium* was 'nothing but law made among persons of free will by tacit agreement' (in Akashi 1988: 21). As there were no authorities or laws beyond what sovereigns had themselves consented to, there were few restraints on warfare. Sovereigns, Bynkershoek argued, enjoyed an unlimited right to wage war primarily because there was no customary law forbidding it (Akashi 1988: 66). Furthermore, he argued that once war was embarked upon, every type of force was lawful (Renick 1994: 457). He did not deny that there should be restraints on the conduct of war but insisted that such restraints were dictated by 'charity' rather than law and that soldiers were not obliged to respect them.

After Grotius, therefore, the Just War tradition was dominated by legalism, which was itself divided along broadly naturalist and positivist lines. The result was that although there were virtually no substantive developments in constraints on the use of force (except Vattel's *jus in bello* proportionality rule), the tradition's core ideas were planted on secular foundations. This accelerated many of the trends identified earlier. First, it enhanced the importance of *jus in bello* vis-à-vis *jus ad bellum*. Second, it perpetuated a shift towards the procedural elements of *jus ad bellum* at the expense of the substantive aspects. Third, in the absence of deontological rules derived from God or reason, realist ideas about the primacy of state interests and importance of military necessity had a growing influence on the construction of international law. Finally, the role of voluntarism was increased to such an extent that by the end of the eighteenth century the idea that sovereigns had an inherent right to wage war became an established part of the Just War tradition. Although each of these transformations demanded a more coherent and comprehensive *jus in bello*, none was forthcoming. At its most comprehensive, the *jus in bello* extended as far at the end of the eighteenth century as it had at the end of the fifteenth century, but in many post-Grotian works much less protection was afforded and the grounds for protection were weakened to either self-interest or charity. Given this, it is unsurprising that intellectuals looked beyond the philosophy of law for a new ethics of war. The final section of this chapter considers one attempt to do so that was widely read in its own time and continues to shape Just War thinking today: Immanuel Kant's plan for 'perpetual peace'.

Reformism – Immanuel Kant

Kant's *Perpetual Peace* (1795) made a lasting contribution to the Just War tradition, though this has been long disputed. For instance, Fernando Tesón (1992: 90) argued that Kant dismissed 'the idea that there could be a just war', whilst W. B. Gallie (1978: 19–20) insisted that, for Kant, 'nothing but confusion and harm resulted from regarding wars as just'. There is no doubt that Kant rejected the central tenets of Just War thinking in his own time. It is worth quoting *Perpetual Peace* on this point:

Hugo Grotius, Pufendorf, Vattel and the rest (sorry comforters as they are) are still dutifully quoted in *justification* of military aggression, although their philosophically or diplomatically formulated codes do not and cannot have the slightest *legal* force, since states as such are not subject to a common external constraint. Yet there is no instance of a state ever having been moved to desist from its purpose by arguments supported by the testimonies of such notable men. (Kant 1903: 131)

Thus, Kant's direct engagement with the Just War tradition consisted of a basically realist attack which insisted that international law could not constrain states because it had no binding power. For Kant it was not enough to simply argue that the law of nations *did* constrain states; the challenge was to show *how* it could do so.

In the process, Kant also made an important contribution to the philosophy of law. His discussion of war made no appeal to natural law, insisting instead that the only sources of law were customary practice, treaties and the opinions of 'recognized authorities' (Covell 1998: 94). For Kant, the law of nations rested on the voluntary agreement of states, and the task that he confronted was persuading states willingly to accept the creation of a normative order that would constrain them in matters of war and peace. His key move was to enunciate a modern conception of sovereignty whereby states, enjoying the rights and duties associated with it, ought to bind themselves to the rule of law because those rules were constitutive of their sovereign independence (Covell 1998: 97). In other words, the rights enjoyed by states were bestowed upon them by the society of states itself. Kant argued that state rights were exclusively grounded in relations of recognition between sovereigns. In the Kantian schema – as today – a state's international legitimacy was linked to it acting in accordance with the law of nations. From the nineteenth century onwards, it was this Vattelian conception of law as grounded in the consensual relations of states that came to replace naturalism and dominate thinking about the laws and ethics of war. Amplifying Vattel, Kant held that international law's normative force lay in the politics of mutual recognition. The key question that Kant and the legal positivists of the nineteenth century disagreed upon was the content of that law and the potential for reshaping it. Kant's two key contributions to the substantive restraints on war – *Perpetual Peace* and the categorical imperatives (Orend 2000a) – were in effect efforts to shape the law's *content*. The rest of this section will consider these contributions in turn.

The basic argument of *Perpetual Peace* was that *if* states were voluntarily to bind themselves to the rules Kant laid down, international society would become more peaceful, to the benefit of all. The argument consisted of six articles outlining practices that should be abolished and three 'definitive' articles demanding positive actions. Kant did not believe that he could abolish war immediately. Instead, his approach was based on the liberal belief in progress and he maintained that if enlightened states adhered to the first six articles, war between them could be lessened. This would create a normative impetus to implement the three definitive articles which would abolish war altogether. Once other states saw the benefits that could accrue from perpetual peace, they too would voluntarily bind themselves to its rules.

The six preliminary articles were:

1 No treaty of peace shall be regarded as valid if made with the secret reservation for a future war.
2 No state having an independent existence – whether it be great or small – shall be acquired by another through inheritance, exchange, purchase or donation.
3 Standing armies shall be abolished in the course of time.
4 No national debt shall be contracted in connection with the external affairs of the state.

5   No nation shall violently interfere with the constitution and administration of the other.
6   No state at war with another shall countenance modes of hostility as would make mutual confidence impossible in a subsequent state of peace. (Kant 1903: 109–42)

The three definitive articles demanded that: (1) states should have republican constitutions, because democratic states were much less likely to fight one another; (2) free states should establish a federation to discuss the possibility of collective enforcement of international law; and (3) universal human rights should only be extended to a right to hospitality. Through hospitality, Kant (1903: 134ff.) thought that distant territories would be brought closer together and come to share common values.

In *Perpetual Peace*, therefore, Kant attempted to add content and normative force to his conception of international law. Unlike his predecessors, Kant was not satisfied with simply describing the state of international law or assuming that prohibitions on particular types of action existed in natural law. *Perpetual Peace* attempted to outline a legal order that, like domestic legal orders, would abolish war (Habermas 1997: 114). It was precisely this desire to abolish war that led so many writers to insist that Kant had nothing to contribute to the Just War tradition. There are at least two responses to this assertion. The first is that *Perpetual Peace* was itself an important contribution to Just War thinking. Not only did it enunciate a convincing novel approach to international law that avoided reliance on natural law, it also provided a blueprint of what that law should look like. The second response is that *Perpetual Peace* did not exhaust the limits of Kant's engagement with the Just War tradition. Kant recognized that many obstacles stood in the way of obtaining his ideal, not least human selfishness, the imperialist tendencies of states and the folly of absolutist rulers (Armstrong 1931: 199). As Brian Orend (2000a) has demonstrated, Kant's wider philosophy based on the categorical imperatives offered a Just War theory as an interim measure for guiding action before perpetual peace could be established.

The second Kantian approach to war was informed by natural law and involved two 'categorical imperatives' which Kant argued formed the basis of universal moral law. The first imperative was to act only on maxims that could be applied universally, and the second was always to treat humans as ends in themselves, never as means (Paton 1962: 133–45). From these two basic maxims and Kant's wider philosophy, Kant proposed basic rights relating to war, such as the right for a state not to be invaded, to be self-governing, to use its natural resources however it sees fit, to enjoy its own property, and to make treaties with others voluntarily. Each of these rights has a correlative duty (do not invade others, do not interfere in others' domestic matters, etc.) (Orend 2000a: 29).

Orend argues that based on these propositions it is possible to construct a Kantian Just War theory comprising *jus ad bellum*, *jus in bello* and *jus post bellum* (the justice of the post-war settlement). On *jus ad bellum*, a Kantian Just War doctrine holds that a just cause is created when the rights of one of the states are violated. The intention of such wars must be limited to the satisfaction of those breached rights and the sovereign must properly declare war after due consultation with citizens. Expanding Vitoria's demand that the sovereign seek advice, the injunction that individuals not be seen as mere means created a requirement for sovereigns to wage war only with the consent of their citizens (Orend 2000a: 51–2). Orend's Kantian *jus ad bellum* also insisted that force be a last resort and be consistent (or at least not inconsistent) with the pursuit of perpetual peace.

Kant's *jus in bello* was much less well developed, but two general principles can be derived. First, we can plausibly infer the principles of non-combatant immunity and proportionality from the categorical imperative that humans never be treated as means. To kill non-combatants in order to spread fear or lower morale is to use them as means. Moreover, the first categorical imperative (only follow maxims that are universalizable) supports the view that a Kantian Just War doctrine endorses non-combatant immunity and proportionality. Secondly, the sixth preliminary article of *Perpetual Peace*, forbidding the use of strategies inconsistent with the long-term ideal, also places important restrictions on *jus in bello*, as did the requirement to abide by treaties (Orend 2000).

According to Orend, Kant introduced an innovative third component to his Just War doctrine: *jus post bellum*. This requirement flowed directly from the view that a justifiable war must be consistent with the long-term aim of perpetual peace. *Jus post bellum* demanded that the victor afford the vanquished a right of self-determination. That is, the vanquished must be allowed to select their own form of government and must not have the will of the victor imposed on them (Orend 2000a: 58–9).

Kant therefore implied that war could be regulated until such a time as perpetual peace was established. In articulating a vision both of how international law could govern peaceful relations between states and of how war may be constrained in the interim, Kant made at least two important contributions to the Just War tradition that have often been overlooked. First, he articulated a modern (Vattelian) conception of international law grounded in reciprocal relations between states. Kant's second contribution to the Just War tradition was the schema outlined in *Perpetual Peace*. He systematically explored the conditions that were required for a law of peace to come into effect, and, as we will see in the following chapter, many of his ideas were tacitly adopted by states in the aftermath of the two world wars in the twentieth century.

Conclusion

By the time of the French Revolution in 1789, the Just War tradition had undergone its own transformation. It had confronted two critical challenges: how to adapt to the rise of sovereign states and the global expansion of the European worldview. The second challenge was much more problematic. After the Enlightenment, Just War writers could no longer base their arguments on divine commands, opening a significant window for realists to argue that sovereigns must do whatever is necessary to satisfy their interests.

For most of the period discussed in this chapter, mainstream Just War thinking depended on a mixture of human/volitional law and natural law as a substitute for God, but naturalism became less tenable largely because it was unable to put forward a convincing explanation of *why* there should be constraints on war and, as Kant pointed out, it exerted little normative force. Therefore, writers such as Vattel, Bynkershoek and Kant eschewed natural law, grounding international law almost entirely on the voluntary will of states instead. This concept of law – which also played a significant role in the work of Gentili and Grotius – became the predominant mode of thought and practice in the Just War tradition over the next two centuries. It created the rigid distinction between legalism and moralism that persists today.

In the course of this transformation, two components of the medieval Just War tradition disappeared entirely. The return of holy wars to Europe in the seventeenth century had devastating consequences and provoked a powerful intellectual backlash. As a result, from the mid-seventeenth century onwards, holy war thinking became peripheral in Europe. The other casualty of the tradition's transformation was scholasticism. By the seventeenth century, scholasticism was not widely accepted as a legitimate methodology.

There were three particularly noteworthy changes to the Just War tradition's criteria as a result of these transformations. The first was the rise of subjectivism. Put simply, if God was dead, how could we know for sure that what we do is just or unjust, especially in uncertain cases? For much of the period, most Just War thinkers did not believe that God was dead, only that divine revelation was impossible to prove. For them, the question was that if we cannot know God's judgements during our earthly life, how can we know for sure that what we do is just or unjust? This was the veil of invincible ignorance, which was first raised by Vitoria and informed the work of virtually every subsequent Just War writer. For most (with the exception of Ayala and Gentili, who argued that a war could be objectively just on both sides and thereby dispensed with the need to distinguish between objective and ostensible justice) the answer was that although logically a war may only be just on one side, our inability to ascertain this for certain meant that we should content ourselves with simultaneous ostensible justice.

Second, there was a shift in the relative weight given to *jus ad bellum* criteria. The criteria that medieval scholars and canon lawyers had thought crucial (just cause, right intention) became secondary because, given invincible ignorance, cause and intent could never be accurately judged and, given the ascendancy of absolutist sovereignty, it was assumed that there was no temporal authority empowered to judge the causes and intention of sovereigns. In their place, the procedural elements of *jus ad bellum*, especially right authority and proper declaration, rose in prominence.

The third transformation was the shift in the relative weight given to *jus ad bellum* and *jus in bello* (see Johnson 1973: 461–2). In the periods covered in Chapters 1, 2 and 3, the Just War tradition (with the exception of chivalry) was more concerned with the justice of the decision to wage war than it was with the justice of the way the war was conducted, often rejecting the idea that the two were separate domains. The rise of subjectivism shifted the balance in favour of *jus in bello*. Curiously, however, the substantive constraints on force were neither expanded nor made more comprehensive. Non-combatant immunity remained almost identical in form to that at the end of the medieval period (based on the twin ideas of weakness and social function), and although Vattel introduced the principle of *jus in bello* proportionality, it hardly amounted to a comprehensive system of rules. However, there was a growing tendency for international treaties on war to mention the protection of non-combatants. For example, Article II of the Treaty of Ryswick (1697) between William III of England and Louis XIV of France declared that both states would abstain 'from all plundering, depredation, harm-doing, injurys [*sic*], and infestation whatsoever', and the subsequent treaties of Utrecht (1713) and Rastadt (1714) contained similar provisions (Reddy 1975: 176).

Into the nineteenth century, the Just War tradition faced two challenges. On the one hand, it needed to demonstrate that the laws of war carried normative force. This was achieved through the rise of legal positivism and the careful delineation between law and morality. On the other hand, it needed to develop a more comprehensive system of *jus in bello*. This was accomplished by different actors, including lawyers, philosophers, political leaders, liberal humanitarians and professional soldiers, as the following chapter demonstrates.

5

Modernity and Beyond

This chapter maps the Just War tradition from the French Revolution to the present. From the end of the eighteenth century, technological changes dramatically increased military firepower whilst advances in communications and logistics enabled states to field much larger armies, more rapidly and for longer periods (Black 1998: 164–70). Revolutionary France's *levée en masse* made war-waging a duty of every citizen. The Napoleonic wars that followed pitted nations rather than mercenary armies against each other. Success in modern warfare hinged as much on the industrial might of the state as on the prowess of its military commanders. The apex of modern war was the development of nuclear weapons after the Second World War. Nuclear warfare would be 'total' in ways not contemplated by earlier strategists. As a result, after 1945 many strategists, ethicists and politicians moved away from ideas of total war to embrace different types of limited conflict.

Modern war often required the mobilization of entire societies. This raised important questions about the principle of non-combatant immunity because even those sections of society not engaged in war-fighting – such as farmers – were nevertheless deeply engaged in the war effort (Janda 1995: 8). Moreover, this mobilization required a unifying ideology. Throughout Europe, nationalism was converted from an ideology of anti-monarchist resistance into the ideology of the state. National wars required grander ambitions. Wars could no longer be fought to 'correct the balance of power' or 'redeem matters of honour'. They aimed to 'defend democracy', 'eradicate tyranny' or protect the nation (Bond 1996: 106). Although most wars of the nineteenth century fell short of Clausewitz's understanding of total war as a war of annihilation, this trend reached its logical conclusion in the carnage of the twentieth century's two world wars and in the Cold War concept of mutually assured destruction. In short, modern war dramatically increased the number of potential combatants and the number of civilians who could be legitimately targeted.

The Second World War was an important watershed in this regard. The Holocaust, terror bombing of cities and the dawning of the atomic age combined brutality with a degree of mechanical mass killing on a scale not seen before. With a few notable exceptions, the laws of war proved incapable of restraining the belligerents (Kunz 1951). Even some Church leaders justified the deliberate killing of non-combatants (e.g. Temple 1940) and upwards of 40 million people died as a direct result of the war. This created a post-war impetus to further codify positive law on the use of force and create new mechanisms to enforce it. Moreover, it saw a move away from the doctrine of total war towards the idea of limited war. After the end of the Cold War, many scholars and Church leaders returned to more traditional ways of thinking about just and unjust wars, as positive law and realism appeared unable to provide answers to some of the most pressing moral dilemmas.

This chapter explores the impact of these changes on the Just War tradition by focusing on the realist and legalist sub-traditions first in the industrial era (1789–1945) and then in the post-Second World War era (1945–present).

The Industrial Age: 1789–1945

Realism dominated for most, if not all, of this period. Sovereigns believed that they enjoyed an unlimited right to wage war wherever they deemed it prudent and that normative restrictions on the conduct of war should be tempered by military necessity. From the mid-nineteenth century onwards, however, these prerogatives were challenged by legalists who argued that states had a responsibility to care for the wounded and sick in war and limit war's violence. Into the twentieth century, significant progress was made towards codifying *jus in bello* in positive law, but its development was shaky and collapsed almost completely during the Second World War especially.

Realism

During the nineteenth century, realism was transformed from a broad philosophical worldview into an ideology of the state combining nationalism and militarism. Hegel's concept of the state, set out in a series of works at the very beginning of the nineteenth century, provides a useful way of caricaturing this shift. It began with a denunciation of the natural law claim that states were worth protecting because of the good they yielded to individuals. Hegel (1946: 324) argued that to accept the Hobbesian view that states were created to protect the life and property of individuals would make it senseless for individuals to sacrifice their own life and property to protect the state. He got around this problem by putting forward a very different conception of the state. According to Hegel, the state was not just an amalgam of institutions but an ethical community that situated individuals within a timeless cosmos (see Armstrong 1933: 685). This view of the state as an organic community had an important effect on the place of war in human relations. If human happiness was directly related to the shared identities that individuals enjoyed as citizens of states, then there should be a welcome for phenomena that 'raise us above the level of mere civil association with its rootedness in material possessions' into a timeless ethical community (Smith, S. B. 1983: 628). Moreover, Hegel argued that without a common will to hold it together, a state was constantly in danger of descending into an aggregate of private interests (Smith, S. B. 1983: 628). For Hegel (1946: 324), therefore, war played a central role in maintaining this common will:

War is the state of affairs which deals in earnest with the vanity of temporal goods and concerns. . . . War has the higher significance that by its agency, as I have remarked elsewhere, the ethical health of the peoples is preserved in their indifference to the stabilization of finite institutions; just as the blowing of the winds preserves the sea from the foulness which would be the result of prolonged calm, so also corruption in nations would be a product of prolonged, let alone 'perpetual' peace.

Hegel rejected the Just War tradition's principles, insisting that there were no *a priori* moral standards governing combat (Smith, S. B. 1983: 630). However, he did not argue that war was amoral, and identified two types of justifiable war: wars of self-defence and wars waged by 'higher' civilizations against lower ones (Gilbert 1986: 127–8). Thus, Hegel went one step further than Machiavelli and Hobbes by arguing that war fulfilled a positive function by unifying the ethical community. International law, he insisted, remained in the realm of the 'ought' and not the 'is' because law could only bind members of ethical communities (Hasner 1994: 745).

This Hegelian position provides a neat caricature of realist views in the nineteenth and early twentieth centuries. Whereas earlier realists were generally sceptical about nationalism and militarism, Hegelians embraced them. These and similar views were widely held during this period. To give one, perhaps unlikely, example, Theodore Roosevelt (1916: 12) argued that although 'no intelligent man desires war', the ability to wage war was essential for the preservation of a nation's core values. Echoing Hegel, Roosevelt insisted that 'the man fit for self-government must be fit to fight for self-government'. War, in other words, was the ultimate test of a nation's ability to govern itself.

The guiding idea for political leaders in the nineteenth and early twentieth centuries was the doctrine of *raison d'état*. It followed from the Hegelian argument that defending the state and its interests was the most important human endeavour. As Friedrich Meinecke (1957: 2) put it in 1924, for realism 'the well-being of the state and of its population is held to be the ultimate value and the goal'. The well-being of the state, Meinecke (1957: 3) argued, could be secured 'at the expense of a complete disregard for moral and positive law' if necessary (1957: 3). That is not to say that the pursuit of *raison d'état* should be entirely unconstrained. Echoing Machiavelli, Meinecke insisted that both prudential and moral considerations play a part in shaping the policy and that *raison d'état* be conceived as the bridge between power-seeking and moral behaviour. Ultimately, though, states can only satisfy their legal and moral rights if they have the physical wherewithal to do so (Meinecke 1957: 14). Although prudence, morality and power did not always conflict, the doctrine of *raison d'état* suggested a clear hierarchy when they did. The actual conduct of war remained constrained by the lingering tradition of chivalry, Church law and emerging codes of military law, but realists insisted that these constraints could be overridden if *raison d'état* dictated.

The doctrine of *raison d'état* was widely defended by political leaders and scholars. The Napoleonic *levée en masse* justified mass mobilization for war in these terms, and the French government's position in the notorious 'Dreyfus affair' was similarly framed (Vagts 1969: 88). Mazzini used a Hegelian conception of the state as a manifestation of the sovereignty of nationality to justify agitating for a united Italy, warning that he would be prepared to 'decimate, purge, punish a whole population' if they rejected the idea (in Vagts 1969: 98). *Raison d'état* was also evident in Britain's support for the balance of power and its engagement in the Crimean War.

Raison d'état shifted normative discussion about war in the nineteenth and early twentieth centuries. The central constraints on war-fighting in this period were domestic political and moral concerns, prudence and utility. This helped to limit some types of war by militating against aggression aimed at restoring or preserving justice, but it encouraged states to engage in combat whenever they believed it in their interests. The key determinant of the conduct of war was strategic, which had a number of implications for the way actors viewed the Just War tradition. First, necessity provided a permanent justification for acts that were otherwise forbidden, such as waging war without just cause or using terror tactics to 'pacify' non-combatants (see Raymond, G. A. 1998–9: 675). Second, this approach privileged strategic and militarist thinking over moral and legal thinking.

Raison d'état allowed political and military leaders to invoke 'necessity' to justify overriding the Just War tradition's rules. Examples of this are numerous, so I will briefly focus on the American Civil War (1861–5) as an example of necessity arguments in relation to *jus in bello* and on German justifications for the violation of Belgian neutrality in 1914 as an example of the same type of argument in relation to *jus ad bellum*.

At the beginning of the US Civil War, the Union's political and military leaders supported the prevailing European view that it was wrong to target non-combatants directly (Weigley 1973: 82). During the course of war, however, Union commanders, particularly William T. Sherman and Ulysses S. Grant, gradually came to the view that total war eroded the distinction between combatant and non-combatant. Sherman is most famous for his statement that 'war is hell'. Indeed, he said much the same thing on many occasions (e.g. Sherman 1957: 660). Sherman insisted that war could not be made less inhumane and that responsibility for its carnage and bloodshed must rest with those who caused the war. The only possible remedy, he insisted, was victory (Bower 2000: 1020). Soldiers who used force to resist aggression or rebellion 'can never be blamed for anything they do that brings victory closer' (in Walzer 1977: 32). This doctrine implied an aggressor–defender concept of *jus ad bellum* that placed justice on the side of the defenders and provided them with a blanket justification for violating the *jus in bello*.

Sherman's siege of Atlanta provides one example of the use of military necessity arguments to override established rules of war. In order to pacify the local population, Sherman directed artillery fire over the heads of Hood's defending Confederate army into residential parts of the city. Despite evidence to the contrary, Sherman repeatedly claimed that Hood's defences were too close to the city, so shells that missed their target inevitably landed in residential areas (Bower 2000: 1022). However, he later fell back on the 'war is hell' doctrine, insisting that 'I had no hand in making this war and I know that I will make more sacrifices than any of you ... to secure peace' (in Merrill 1971: 259). In other words, military necessity obliged Sherman to bombard non-combatants in Atlanta (excusing him) but it was the Confederate decision to wage war in the first place that had forced him to take that course of action (condemning Hood). Sherman and Grant used similar arguments to justify burning the crops and property of non-combatants to lessen the enemy's ability to fight and weaken its morale, with Sherman conducting what one commentator described as a 'terror war' (Hanson 1999: 2).

Jus ad bellum was also affected by *raison d'état*. Justifying his decision to invade Belgium in 1914, thereby violating that country's neutrality, the German Chancellor, Theobald von Bethmann-Hollweg, argued that:

We are in a state of legitimate defence. *Necessity knows no law.* Our troops have occupied Luxembourg and have perhaps already penetrated into Belgium. This is against the law of nations. . . . A French attack on our flank in the region of the lower Rhine might have been fatal. It is for that reason that we have been compelled to ignore the just protests of the Governments of Luxembourg and Belgium. The injustice which we thus commit we will repair as soon as our military object has been attained. (In Garner 1915: 77)

Amongst legal scholars at the time there was considerable sympathy for the right being claimed by Germany. Oppenheim admitted that in cases of self-defence, necessity could override the law, and even some French jurists concurred. Indeed, prior to 1914 the UK, the US and Japan had all invoked necessity arising out of self-preservation as a justification for law-breaking (in Garner 1915: 78). The crucial difficulty for Germany in 1914 was not the legal principle but the empirical credibility of its claim.

Another feature of nineteenth- and early twentieth-century realism was the prioritization of strategic over moral considerations. The best-known thinkers on war from this period are strategists, not moralists or lawyers, and arguably the most influential was Carl von Clausewitz (1780–1831). Clausewitz was wholly sceptical about the relevance of moral and legal rules to war. He described international law as 'cumbersome' and famously defined war itself as an instrument of policy that required no special justification (Clausewitz 1993: 38). Clausewitz insisted that there were neither legal nor moral constraints on the conduct of war and was widely criticized by British thinkers for doing so. Liddell Hart (1934: 120–1) referred to him as 'the Mahdi of mass and mutual massacre', whilst John Keegan (1999: 42) described Clausewitz's view as 'pernicious' because it presented war as a 'value-free' activity. Like other realists, Clausewitz did not argue that war had no limits, only that it had no *universal moral* limits. For Clausewitz, the conduct of war ought to be limited by its ends (Howard 1983: 34–5). It should be waged only for limited political purposes and directed at the accomplishment of those ends. This had implications for both *jus ad bellum* and *jus in bello*. In relation to the former, Clausewitz shared the view that war may be waged whenever it is in the interests of the state. However, he insisted that political leaders stipulate clear political objectives when ordering their armies to war. He argued, for instance, that it was Napoleon's failure to set limited goals that lay behind the French dictator's demise at Waterloo (see Herberg-Rothe 2001: 177). Clausewitz also maintained that the conduct of war be determined by its ends. The achievement of those ends often depended on the destruction of the enemy's army, imposing important limits on the conduct of war. Hence, Clausewitz did not countenance the targeting of non-combatants, though he did not expressly forbid it (see Ignatieff 1998: 116). For the nineteenth-century strategists, war had limits but they were set by domestic political considerations not by universal morality or law.

In the early nineteenth century, therefore, realism was transformed into an ideology that combined militarism and nationalism. Whilst it recognized constraints on war, it insisted that established rules could – indeed should – be violated in the service of the state because the preservation of the state was a higher good than the preservation of universal moral rules. Politicians and soldiers were not only entitled to do whatever they could to preserve the state, they were *morally obliged* to. *Jus ad bellum* concerns were almost entirely subverted, with only proportionality left intact as a prudential check on reckless war. In relation to *jus in bello*, realists argued that war be limited only by its political goals.

Legalism

Although realism was dominant in the nineteenth and early twentieth centuries, legalism also continued to develop. Legal positivists believed that the best way of creating an authoritative legal regime governing war was to accept the centrality of the state as a basic social fact and insist on state consent as the basis for a limited yet authoritative international law (Boyle 1999: 11). Recognizing that states had a legal right to wage war, legalists attempted to create a compulsory arbitration system to enable them to resolve their differences peacefully. These efforts were unsuccessful prior to 1914. Indeed, the right of a state to decide when to wage war for self-preservation was widely accepted as a legal principle (Brownlie 1963: 42). Legalism had a more profound impact on the conduct of war. By the twentieth century, most militaries were governed by military law prohibiting unnecessary attacks on non-combatants and inhumane treatment of prisoners.

   In this section I will briefly chart the development of legalism by focusing on the three main sources of law in the nineteenth and early twentieth centuries: military codes, liberal humanitarianism and international treaties. Between them, they created a partial law of war, with myriad circumstances not legislated for. Because of this, for all their pretensions to positivism, the legalists of the nineteenth and early twentieth centuries filled the gaps in positive law by recourse to natural law, disguised as the principle of humanity formalized by the 'Martens clause'. First proposed by the Russian delegate F. F. de Martens at the 1899 Hague peace conference, the Martens clause stipulates that:

Until a more complete code of the laws of war is issued, the High Contracting parties [to the 1899 Hague Convention] declare that in cases not included in the Regulations adopted by them, populations and belligerents remain under the protection of the principles of international law, as they result from the usages established between civilized nations, from the laws of humanity, and the requirements of public conscience. (In Meron 2000: 79)

The clause has been invoked in many subsequent treaties, including the 1949 Geneva Conventions, its additional Protocols (1977) and the terms of reference of the post-Second World War Nuremberg tribunal. It holds that simply because a particular act or weapon is not expressly outlawed by positive law, it should not be assumed that the act or weapon is legal. To determine this, two further criteria must be met: the laws of humanity and requirements of public conscience. The clause is significant because it demonstrates the continuing role of natural law within a broadly legal positivist approach to the Just War, further challenging the view that law and ethics are entirely separate modes of thought (see Chapter 6; cf. Aldrich and Chinkin 2000: 97). I will now turn to the three main sources of law identified earlier: military codes, humanitarianism and international treaties.

Although military laws were developed by most modern militaries in the nineteenth century, the most significant example came in the context of the American Civil War. On 24 April 1863, the US government published the General Orders No. 100. Better known as the 'Lieber code' after its author, Francis Lieber, it has been described as the first 'complete' code of military law (e.g. Levie 1962: 436; Raymond, J. M. and Frischolz 1982: 817). It was adopted in 1870 by the Prussian government and formed the basis of the 1874 'Brussels declaration' (Carnahan 1998: 215). The pivotal concept in the Lieber code was military necessity. Lieber defined military necessity as 'those measures which are indispensable for securing the ends of the war, and which are lawful according to the modern law and usages of war' (Article 48, reproduced in Hartigan 1983: 48). He argued that unnecessary suffering and damage to property should be avoided because the victims were fellow Americans (Nys 1911: 383). The 'Code' went on to state that:

All wanton violence committed against persons in the invaded country, all destruction of property not commanded by the authorised officer, all robbery, all pillage or sacking, even after taking a place by main force, all rape, wounding, maiming, or killing of such inhabitants, are prohibited under the penalty of death. (Article 44)

The scope of the protection provided by Lieber's schema depended on the definition of 'wanton violence' and military necessity, which were not at all clear.

This problem was not helped by the fact that Lieber actually changed his position. In *Political Ethics*, he denounced 'all suffering inflicted upon persons who do not impede my way' (1839: 657). Whilst echoing the two pillars of the principle of non-combatant immunity (social function and inability to fight), this approach permits wide discretion in cases where the war aims are very broad (Johnson 1981: 300). However, in the 'code', Lieber articulated an altogether different, and novel, basis for distinguishing between those who may be legitimately targeted and those who may not: 'Military necessity admits of all direct destruction of life and limb of *armed* enemies, and of other persons whose destruction is incidentally *unavoidable* in the armed contests of the war' (Article 15). However, that same article went on to permit 'all destruction of property, and obstruction of the ways and channels of traffic, travel or communication, and of all withholding of sustenance or means of life from the enemy; of the appropriation of whatever an enemy's country affords necessary for the subsistence and safety of the army'. In other words, whilst the 'code' forbade the direct targeting of non-combatants (defined as such for the first time), it permitted indirect measures such as the destruction of property, crops and other supplies which could directly cause mass suffering amongst non-combatants on the grounds that such measures contributed to the military effort (see Millett 1945).

The 'code' also made provisions for the humane treatment of prisoners of war. However, the apparently broad level of protection offered by Article 56 ('a prisoner of war is subject to no punishment for being a public enemy') had two crucial caveats attached to it. First, 'a prisoner of war remains answerable for his crimes committed against the captor's army' (Article 59), including the crime of aggression. Second, the prisoner remained subject to 'retaliatory measures'. The captor may carry out reprisals on prisoners in response to acts carried out by the enemy (Article 59).

The Lieber code was therefore far from a complete set of *jus in bello* rules. It was a product of its time whose principal aim was to provide guidance for the Union's new mass army. Its overarching aim was less about advancing the laws of war than teaching the fundamental basics – particularly the importance of following orders – to military beginners (Johnson 1981: 306–7). That said, it made one crucial contribution to our understanding of *jus in bello*, though subsequent caveats did much to unravel it. In place of civilian immunity based on either social function or inability to bear arms, Lieber introduced the distinction between combatant (defined as one bearing arms) and non-combatant (all others). This latter group was to be immune from direct attack, subject to the caveats noted above.

Our assessment of Lieber needs to be tempered in at least two respects. First, those looking for a comprehensive law of war will not find it in the 'code'. The 'code' said little about belligerents' obligations to non-combatants, prisoners of war and other vulnerable groups (Johnson 1981: 312). Second, the 'code' was not immune from the influence of realism. As Confederate Secretary of War James Seddon put it: 'In this code of military necessity . . . the acts of atrocity and violence which have been committed by the officers of the United States and have shocked the moral sense of civilized nations are to find an apology and defence' (in Hartigan 1983: 120). Moreover, whilst the Prussian military's adoption of the 'code' in 1870 was widely applauded, by 1902 scholars were expressing concern about the growing tendency of the German army to use military necessity as a justification for violating the laws of war (Carnahan 1998: 218). The main challenges to this approach came from the other two sources of legalism in this period: liberal humanitarianism and international treaties.

The most significant manifestation of increasing humanitarian concern amongst Europe's middle class was the creation and growth of the Red Cross. After writing about his experiences of the battle of Solferino in June

1859, a Swiss banker, Henry Dunant, attempted to persuade states and societies to assist the victims of war (Forsythe 2005: 15–16). He proposed two ways of doing so. First, he asked whether it would 'be possible, in time of peace and quiet, to form relief societies for the purpose of having care given to the wounded in wartime by zealous, devoted and thoroughly quali- fied volunteers' (Dunant 1959: 17). Second, he called for a conference to establish principles to limit war and provide relief to its victims (Dunant 1959: 21). Both proposals were quickly taken up (Kewley 1984: 4). Dunant originally printed 1,600 copies of *Memory of Solferino* at his own expense in 1862 and distributed them among his friends. It received such a warm response that publishers in Paris, Turin, St Petersburg and Leipzig began distributing it. The French historian Ernest Renan told Dunant: 'you have created the greatest work of the century', a sentiment echoed by Victor Hugo (Moorhead 1998: 9). The head of the Geneva Society of Public Welfare, Gustave Moynier, summoned a meeting to explore how the Society could take up Dunant's challenge to establish relief societies for wounded soldiers. A committee of five was established, including Moynier and Dunant, with the latter feverishly touring Europe to summon support for the initiative. From the outset, the committee recognized the importance of winning the support of powerful states, and one of the key debates at that time, as today, was how the organization could do this without com- prising its principles (Pitteloud 1999: 17–18). In 1863, a conference of inter- national experts was held in Geneva and the Red Cross was born.

A year later, political leaders were invited to Geneva to consider how best to put Dunant's vision into practice. After intense lobbying by Dunant and his fellow committee members, the Geneva conference produced a conven- tion that formally established the International Committee of the Red Cross (ICRC) and awarded it a special role in the provision of assistance to the war wounded (Moorhead 1998: 30). The Convention called for the 'amelioration of the condition of the wounded' and offered protection to medical personnel working under the Red Cross emblem. It also insisted that wounded enemies be handed over for medical treatment and repatriated to their home country on the proviso that they would play no further part in the hostilities. The 1864 Geneva Convention therefore made two impor- tant contributions to the *jus in bello*. First, it granted recognition to the ICRC, which became a key player in the development of the laws of war (Sandoz 1987: 287). Second, it extended the idea of non-combatant immu- nity to medical personnel and wounded soldiers. Unfortunately, it said nothing about non-combatants and only enjoyed declaratory status, drawing criticism from Florence Nightingale (Moorhead 1998: 47).

Although the Convention was heavily circumscribed, the size and influ- ence of the Red Cross movement grew. National committees were created throughout Europe and North America, and the movement established itself in every continent (see Wylie 2002: 188). National committees pressured governments to adopt more humane practices in war and the ICRC started to incorporate care for the non-combatant victims of war into its mandate. (Today, the ICRC's charter gives the organization a duty to protect both military and civilian victims of war (Lavoyer and Maresca 1999: 503).) The Red Cross movement not only placed pressure on states to restrain themselves by setting norms and verifying compliance, it also provided invaluable material assistance to victims in war zones (see Finnemore 1996: 69–88).

The effect of the mobilization of humanitarian sentiment through the ICRC was evident in the third source of legalism: international treaties and declarations. From the 1860s onwards, states regularly convened to discuss ways of limiting war. Between the 1860s and 1914, the focus of this effort was directed almost solely towards *jus in bello*, because states recognized one another's legal right to wage war. After the First World War, however, efforts were made to restrict that right through a short-lived system of compulsory arbitration and collective security.

The period between the 1860s and the outbreak of the First World War was something of a 'golden era' for international treaty-law governing war conduct (see Scott, J. B. 1924). In relation to *jus ad bellum*, the 1899 and 1907 Hague Conventions tacitly accepted a state's legal right to wage war, but attempted to limit recourse to war through a system of arbitration (Wright 1924: 757–8). The *jus in bello* elements of these treaties and declarations attempted to limit the 'unnecessary suffering' caused by war. After the First World War, the focus changed and *jus ad bellum* became the priority. The League of Nations Covenant attempted to strengthen the principle of compulsory arbitration and introduced collective security. In the 1920s, the Kellogg–Briand Pact went one step further and outlawed the use of force except in self-defence.

Four years after the 1864 Geneva Convention, Tsar Alexander II invited states to attend an International Military Commission to discuss the manufacture and use of 'dum dum' bullets. These bullets, developed by Russia for use against ammunition wagons, exploded on impact with a hard surface and, after 1867, with a soft surface as well. The Russian War Ministry recognized that such weapons could do great harm to soldiers and ordered that their use be restricted (Roberts, A. and Guelff 2000: 53). At the conference itself, Prussia called for a wider inquiry into the application of scientific discoveries in war, a view rejected by Britain and France. A Swiss compromise was finally accepted which broadened the prohibition to all inflammable projectiles under 400 grams in weight. Although nothing like a comprehensive treatment on *jus in bello*, the resulting St Petersburg Declaration was important because it imposed 'obligatory' requirements upon its signatories for the first time and its preamble reiterated the Lieber code's invocation of military necessity as a restraint on war, stating that the only legitimate object of war was the enemy's military (in Roberts, A. and Guelff 2000: 54–5).

Although the sovereign prerogative to wage war was widely recognized, there were attempts to curtail it. The so-called 'Monroe Doctrine' issued by the US in 1823 declared that European powers were not free to wage war in the Americas. Also, from the mid-1800s, states made increasing use of voluntary arbitration to avoid war for the enforcement of legal rights. The most notable case was the so-called 'Geneva arbitration' in 1872, where the UK was instructed to pay $15.5 million of reparations to the US for the damage caused by the UK's collusion with Confederate shipbuilding during the US Civil War. The UK accepted the judgment and a potential war was averted (Chadwick 1999). For many legalists in the US and Europe, compulsory arbitration was an attractive solution to the problem of limiting recourse to arms whilst acknowledging the sovereign's inherent right to wage war.

Attempts to codify the laws of war accelerated at the end of the nineteenth century with the first of two conferences on peace and disarmament at The Hague. The first Hague peace conference (1899) produced three conventions, three declarations and a final act, covering both *jus ad bellum* and *jus in bello*. The conventions created a procedure for the arbitration of disputes between states and the declarations prohibited particular weapons. There was a major disagreement about what type of arbitration system should be created. The UK and US proposed a permanent tribunal. France accepted the idea but insisted that recourse to arbitration be voluntary and that the parties be free to select the arbitrators. Russia argued that arbitration should be compulsory on those matters likeliest to lead to war (Caron 2000: 15–16). Whilst these four states worked towards a compromise, Germany rejected the very idea of arbitration because it believed that it placed it at a disadvantage by cancelling out its military superiority. The four put considerable pressure on Germany and the result was the creation of a Permanent Court of Arbitration. The court satisfied demands for an arbitration process but allayed Germany's fears by making the process voluntary (Boyle 1999: 34–5). The declarations proved less controversial and simply expanded the scope of the St Petersburg Declaration. In Declaration II, the parties agreed not to use asphyxiating or deleterious gases and Declaration III forbade the use of bullets that expanded on impact.

A second Hague peace conference was convened in 1907 with the aim of including states not represented in 1899, developing the arbitration procedures and limiting the conduct of war (Rifaat 1979: 28). As in 1899, the 1907 meeting was shaped by important differences between the UK, US and Russia on one side and Germany on the other. Germany rejected the idea of disarmament and remained hostile to compulsory arbitration (Brailey 2002: 204). Nevertheless, the conference passed thirteen conventions (three of which reiterated the three 1899 conventions), one declaration (renewing

Declaration I of 1899) and a final act. Although the second Hague conference failed to establish a system of obligatory arbitration, it strengthened commitment to the procedural elements of *jus ad bellum* and slightly restricted a sovereign's right to wage war (Lauterpacht 1933: 27–8). In particular, Article I of Convention III provided that 'the contracting powers recognize that hostilities between themselves must not commence without previous or explicit warning, in the form either of a reasoned declaration of war, or of an ultimatum with conditional declaration of war'. Furthermore, parties were obliged to inform neutral states before launching hostilities. This system forced those intent on waging war to make their case publicly and afforded an opportunity for other parties to the conflict to make restitution (Corbett 1951: 213). The Hague Conventions also slightly curtailed a sovereign's right to wage war by prohibiting the use of force to recover debts (Scott, J. B. 1908: 15–16).

Most of the Hague Conventions related to the conduct of war. The most significant of these was the Convention on the Laws and Customs of War on Land, which marked an important step towards codifying long-established principles of *jus in bello*. Article 25 forbade the bombardment of undefended towns and villages, Article 26 required that military commanders give due warning before commencing a bombardment, and Article 27 insisted that commanders take measures to spare, as far as possible, damage to protected buildings. Furthermore, the Convention granted protection to the vanquished at the end of hostilities.

There is much debate about the significance of the 1907 Hague Conventions for the development of *jus in bello*. Sceptics point to the fact that the Conventions were not primarily concerned with protecting non-combatants and that the use of terms like 'undefended towns' gave attackers considerable latitude (Aldrich 2000: 50). British jurist T. E. Holland declared its *jus in bello* restrictions 'defective' because each signatory added reservations and there were no mechanisms for enforcement (in Karsten 1978: 23). James Brown Scott (1908: 25), one of the Conventions' leading votaries, admitted that peace activists would be concerned about the failure to include provisions for arms control. Others, however, point out that whilst the Conventions did not confer a level of protection commensurate with that offered by natural law or canon law, they widened the scope of protection afforded by positive law and therefore increased – however marginally – the likelihood of the restrictions having practical effect (Johnson 2000: 431). Protected groups included the ill, wounded, prisoners of war, inhabitants of undefended places (all of them non-combatants), those in defended places who were given an opportunity to leave, and all inhabitants once hostilities ceased (except spies and insurgents). In relation to *jus ad bellum*, the Conventions outlawed a largely outdated cause of war and strengthened the arbitration process, but failed to establish compulsory arbitration or to significantly limit a sovereign's right to wage war.

It is difficult to overestimate the impact that the First World War had on the legalist approach. The war saw the demise of four formerly powerful European empires (Russian, Austro-Hungarian, Turkish and German), the rise of the US as a major world power, the emergence of Bolshevik communism in Russia, and the spread of the idea of self-determination to the colonies. The industrial-scale killing in the trenches made the First World War the first indisputable 'total war'. Entire societies were pitted against one another. On the first day of the Somme alone, 20,000 British soldiers were killed. Seven hundred thousand French and German soldiers lost their lives in the battle for Verdun, yet the front line hardly moved. In total, upwards of six million people were killed. Although approximately 90 per cent of them were combatants, many were conscripts and volunteers (Keegan 2000: 5). Given these figures, the key challenge after the war was not so much to develop stronger *jus in bello* rules but to reduce the likelihood of war significantly through compulsory arbitration, collective security and legal prohibition.

Although it is misleading to portray the post-First World War era as one dominated by idealists and reformists – a portrayal that owes more to E. H. Carr's (1960) trenchant critique of idealism than the actual influence of reformist work – the period did see a resurgence of reformist thought, which fed into the legalist project. Immediately before the war, reformist-minded writers such as Norman Angell (1972: 368) had expressed dismay at the Hague conferences' inability to achieve their goals and laid the blame squarely at the feet of political leaders. Reformists argued that the war had been a product of the balance of power system. They reasoned that had Europe's publics known the likely costs, they would have forced their leaders not to fight. For post-war reformists, therefore, the challenge was to construct a legal and institutional structure that would prevent accidental wars in the future (Boucher 1994; cf. Schuman 1932: 149). After the First World War, therefore, the Just War tradition's attention shifted from *jus in bello* back towards *jus ad bellum*.

Created in the immediate aftermath of the First World War, the League of Nations system was predicated on the assumption that there were two types of war. First, there were blatantly unjust wars of aggression. To prevent these, the League established a system of collective security. US President Woodrow Wilson envisaged a system whereby aggressive war would be countered by the automatic and determined opposition of all other states (Claude 1964: 262–9). In Article 10 of the League's Covenant, member states undertook to respect the territorial integrity and political independence of others and act collectively against transgressors. At first glance, this article placed important restraints on a state's right to wage war. As Lord Curzon told the British House of Lords in 1919, 'aggressive war, aiming at territorial aggrandisement or political advantage, is expressly forbidden' (in Brownlie 1963: 62).

In practice, these provisions amounted to much less. Article 10 did not ban the use of force. Although it gave states an obligation to resist aggression, it left the sovereign's legal right to wage war intact. Moreover, the determination of whether a particular use of force constituted an act of aggression was to be made by a unanimous decision of the League Council, comprising the organization's most powerful member states. In practice, unanimity was almost impossible to achieve even in the most blatant cases, such as the Japanese invasion of Manchuria (1931) and Italy's invasion of Abyssinia (1935). In the former case, the UK and France were reluctant to coerce a friendly Asian power and doubted whether the invasion of Manchuria amounted to aggression, and in the latter case the League's most powerful states placed their economic interests before their obligations to uphold the peace (Bennett 1984: 19–20). As a result, collective security did not function as Wilson and Curzon had envisaged.

The second type of wars that the Covenant attempted to prevent were those caused by genuine disputes over rights. It attempted to prevent these wars by establishing a system of compulsory arbitration. Under Article 12, members pledged to submit any dispute likely to lead to war for arbitration, judicial settlement or to the League Council. If a dispute was submitted to the Council and a judgment unanimously agreed by Council members, or if a judicial settlement or arbitration agreement was reached, the parties were obliged not to use force for a period of three months (Arend and Beck 1993: 20). This system was clearly aimed at avoiding a repeat of the First World War's 'war by timetable' by creating a cooling-off period that forced states to attempt a negotiated settlement. Sadly, the League's structure for dealing with genuine disputes was flawed. Sovereigns retained a legal right to wage war and could use the cooling-off period to make preparatory military deployments (Kaplan and Katzenbach 1961: 210).

The League system did not therefore mark a revolutionary shift in the way that states thought about war. The most significant innovation was the requirement that states justify their decision to wage war to their peers, who would in turn choose whether or not to accept those justifications (Miller, L. H. 1964: 261). This was arguably the most important development in *jus ad bellum* since Ayala, Vitoria and Gentili agreed that questions relating to just cause and right intention were subjective. That finding had led scholars and sovereigns to accept as just any war waged by a sovereign so long as *jus ad bellum*'s procedural elements were satisfied. Whether consciously or not, the Covenant pointed towards an alternative: justice was inherently subjective but to justify war it was necessary to persuade others of the case. The main problem with the League was that the requirement for unanimity meant that a sovereign wishing to wage war only had to persuade a few others to avoid collective sanctions.

The League's arbitration system simply developed the Hague Conventions and formalized the procedural elements of *jus ad bellum*. Whilst on the one hand this placed important constraints on sovereigns willing to play by the rules, it did not dampen the assumption that sovereigns had a legal right to wage war. Many states recognized this problem, and in 1928 the US and France concluded the so-called Kellogg–Briand Pact, which was eventually signed by sixteen states (Wright, Q. 1953). The parties to the Pact agreed to renounce war 'as an instrument of national policy in their relations with one another'.

The exclusive focus on *jus ad bellum* in the Covenant and Pact turned attention away from efforts to codify *jus in bello* rules into positive law. Between the two world wars, there were only two developments of note in this arena. The draft 1923 Hague rules governing aerial warfare attempted to forbid aerial bombardment to terrorize the enemy's civilian population and the 1924 Geneva Protocol outlawed the use of chemical and biological weapons. In all other areas of combat, the principle of military necessity continued to guide military operations.

By the time of the Second World War, the Just War tradition had crystallized around two positions: realism and positive law. Although the positive laws of war had developed significantly since the mid-1800s, they remained partial in their coverage and subordinate to the realist dictates of *raison d'état* and military necessity. The problem was that positive law was derived directly from the wishes and actions of realist-minded sovereigns. Indeed, some of the period's prominent legalists argued that the society of states had lost its 'moral bearings' due to the rupture between law and ethics inspired by legal positivism (e.g. James Brown Scott, see Rossi 1998: 21, 99–103). Although the First World War had shaken people's faith in their sovereigns, it had not produced a radical transformation in the way states thought about war. The League system did not fail because it was too utopian; it failed because it was not utopian enough. The League only slightly amended a sovereign's right to wage war without proving a just cause, right intent or proportionality and did nothing to expand the scope of *jus in bello*. It insisted that states persuade their peers of their case for war but set the threshold too low. The twentieth century's second cataclysm, the Second World War, further propelled the legalist agenda. Between 1945 and 1950, states agreed to outlaw force and create a comprehensive code of law for the conduct of war; they even agreed – in principle – that the violation of those laws was universally punishable. Once again, however, that agenda was constrained by realism.

The Contemporary Era: 1945 and After

Realism

There were significant differences between nineteenth- and early twentieth-century realism and its post-Second World War successor (Gilpin 1984).

According to Elshtain (1985), the Just War tradition became a form of 'modified realism'. Another way of looking at it is that realism became imbued with Just War thinking. There were several reasons for this. First, nuclear weapons exponentially increased the inherent danger attached to war (Garnett 1975: 115). Second, Nazi Germany had demonstrated the excesses produced by the unbridled pursuit of national interests. Hannah Arendt (1964) was not alone in arguing that, far from an aberration, Nazi Germany was a logical consequence of modernist and realist dogma. Whilst post-war realists subscribed to concepts such as the national interest and necessity, many argued that the application of these ideas rested on moral judgements about the relative weight of different values (e.g. Wolfers 1949: 187–90). Others suggested that *raison d'état* and necessity were not self-evident and did not 'compel' political leaders to pursue certain courses of action (Morgenthau 1945: 5). The third main reason for the discernible shift in realism during and after the Second World War was that many new realists combined an interest in the betterment of the human condition with a deep sense of the tragic nature of human life. Writers such as Morgenthau, Niebuhr and Wolfers confronted an 'elemental realist dilemma' – how to oppose the power of tyrants such as Hitler and Stalin with power (the only means of opposing power) without becoming the very thing one is standing against (Craig 1992: 688)?

For these reasons, among others, some realists began to engage with two types of moral question: (1) How can we make moral and prudential sense of strategic dilemmas such as those posed by nuclear weapons? (2) How can we place more effective constraints on human behaviour? It is important to note, however, that some strategists, such as Hermann Kahn (1962), paid little attention to the moral dilemmas of war. As Brodie (1974: 438) put it, such strategists were 'preoccupied almost exclusively with the winning of wars, as though the latter were to be conceived as something comparable to athletic contests'. Nevertheless, the attitude of many realists to war came very close to the Just War tradition's view. Their position was neatly summed up by Brodie (1974: 3):

[T]he decision to go to war has not always in retrospect appeared wrong, the alternative in some instances being submission to unmitigated lawlessness, tyranny, and other evils. Those to whom Hitler is a live memory cannot be in doubt about that. On the other hand, it is right to cultivate skepticism, because this is an area of consideration too much cluttered with obsessive symbols, and clear thinking does not flourish in it. Men have fought and bled for values held too sacred to question and yet in fact juvenile.

In the remainder of this section I will outline some of the key ideas of two of the leading proponents of this new type of realism – Hans Morgenthau and Reinhold Niebuhr.

Morgenthau's approach to war was based on the observation that positive international law had failed both to prevent war and to moderate its conduct. The reason for this failure was not law's *inherent* inability to constrain international behaviour but rather the lack of correspondence between positive law and the nature of international politics at the time. Morgenthau argued that law could play a role in moderating behaviour in international societies where key actors believed themselves bound to a wider community. He argued that between the end of the Thirty Years' War and the French Revolution, for instance, the Just War tradition succeeded in moderating the conduct of war but that its ability to do so had been eroded by two factors: the decline of aristocratic responsibility for foreign affairs, which had destroyed the international community of aristocrats that had given values associated with chivalry and honour their moral weight; and the rise of nationalism and 'total wars' (Morgenthau 1948: 87, 89). If, as John Westlake argued (1894: 267), restraints on war depended on the parties feeling that they belonged to a whole larger than their 'respective tribes', it stood to reason that nationalist-, fascist- or communist-minded states would not be constrained in their engagements with others. Much of Morgenthau's writing about war can be understood as an attempt to reconcile this reality with a desire to prevent and limit violent conflict.

Morgenthau believed that the lack of constraint on the exercise of state power was the defining characteristic of the twentieth century (see Lebow 2003: 222). He argued that although political leaders should be constrained by their own morals and those of their society, they should not rely solely on morality or law to protect the state. Instead, political leaders needed to maximize their country's military power and should be prepared to use that power, in an unconstrained manner if necessary. Morgenthau worried that this middle way had been jettisoned by American policy-makers, who had switched from naïve Wilsonian idealism to an equally problematic European *realpolitik* (Lebow 2003: 240). Whilst his 'tragic vision' of politics insisted that the best a political leader could achieve was the 'lesser evil', he did not believe that unrestrained warfare was an essential part of international life. Instead, through his many and varied works, Morgenthau outlined at least two ways in which political leaders could work towards 'realistic' restraints on war.

First, political leaders ought to give weight to moral considerations when deciding how to act. Echoing Deutsch, Morgenthau argued that hegemonic peace was easier to maintain in an anarchic world when others believed that the hegemon acted legitimately. Thus, for instance, Morgenthau (1969: 134–8) believed that the US could not win the Vietnam War because the majority of Vietnamese and world opinion believed the Vietnamese cause to be just. Waging such wars would prove too costly, Morgenthau argued, because it would incite moral opprobrium, making it more difficult for the US to secure its vital national interests in other arenas. Second, although he argued that positive law did not restrain states, he did not argue that it *could* not. Morgenthau conceded that law could influence behaviour within communities and allowed for the possibility of international communities. Much as Kant had done, Morgenthau lamented the blind faith placed in positive law and the lack of inquiry into the conditions that made rule-following more likely. In its place, he proposed a functionalist international law based on the idea that 'a rule, be it legal, moral or conventional, is valid when its violation is likely to be followed by an unfavourable reaction, that is, a sanction against its violator' (Morgenthau 1940: 276). In short, Morgenthau argued that we needed not only to create rules about war but also structures for their enforcement.

Reinhold Niebuhr was less pessimistic than Morgenthau about the potential for morality in politics, but agreed that political problems comprised elements of morality, power and prudence that had to be balanced (McKeogh 1997: 12). However, he went one step further than Morgenthau by arguing that self-interest and morality were not separate realms. Niebuhr (1959: 30–1) suggested that no area of politics was ever immune from moral claims, but, on the other hand, no moral action could escape the pull of parochial self-interest. Niebuhr, like Morgenthau, perceived his own position as a *via media* between an irresponsible pacifism that refused to oppose fascism and communism and an unbridled realism that countenanced nuclear first-strike.

Niebuhr (1932: 174) rejected traditional Just War criteria, insisting that no moral values were absolute and that all could be sacrificed in order to protect other values. Moral judgements should be reserved for specific cases and should be consequentialist. Niebuhr adopted this position because he was dissatisfied with at least two aspects of traditional Just War thinking. First, he believed that Just War criteria could be abused, making it dangerous to value ideas like 'just cause' (Niebuhr 1936: 76–7). Much better, thought Niebuhr, to deny absolute values and evaluate each case on its merits. Second, he argued that the Just War tradition's criteria were indeterminate and could not, therefore, constrain action (in Davis and Good 1960: 168).

Niebuhr argued that political leaders should pursue the national interest, however defined, but wherever possible align it with considerations of international justice. Where such alignment was not possible, leaders were obliged to weigh up the competing moral demands. According to Niebuhr, this qualification of the pursuit of self-interest was vital as failure to qualify self-interest with higher shared notions of justice would lead to conflict caused by the narrow-minded pursuit of self-gratification or conquest. On the other hand, failure to accommodate self-interest also contained the seeds for destruction (Niebuhr 1953: 136–7).

Both Morgenthau and Niebuhr acknowledged that moral and legal considerations should be factored into decision-making. Having lived through the Second World War and the onset of the Cold War, however, both were concerned about the dangers of over-reliance on morality and law and therefore insisted that they play a secondary role to power and prudence. In so doing, they made important and lasting contributions to the Just War tradition. Not least, they prompted subsequent Just War writers to take more seriously the ethical dilemmas confronted by political leaders. Advocates of the Just War tradition needed to understand that there were sometimes good reasons for rule-breaking behaviour and that decision-makers were often confronted by a range of competing values. Unfortunately, it was only very recently that scholars and political leaders alike began to take these principled realists more seriously, at least in part because later realists misappropriated these thinkers to defend the claim that morality and law should play *no* part in foreign policy (see Williams, M. C. 2005).

Legalism

After the Second World War, legalists continued to build a body of positive law aimed at restricting both the state's right to wage war and its conduct. The failure to prevent Germany and Japan's aggressive wars was seen not as a failure of positive law *per se*, but as evidence that the law needed strengthening (Smith, H. A. 1947). The United Nations Charter, promulgated in 1945, went further than the League Covenant by expressly prohibiting the threat or use of force (Article 2(4)). All international force was outlawed except when used in self-defence (Article 51) or when authorized by the UN's Security Council for the purpose of maintaining international peace and security (the Chapter VII mechanism). The Charter thereby tightened the principle that sovereigns had an obligation to justify themselves to their peers whenever they decided to use force and delimited the types of justification that would be acceptable to international society. In essence, 'aggressive war' for whatever purpose was deemed illegal, so states using force would have to prove either that they acted in self-defence or with the approval of the host government. More recently, some states have preferred to use the second type of permissible justification by claiming that their recourse to force was implicitly authorized by the Security Council (see Byers 2005: 40–50).

Contemporary Just War writers have tended to criticize the UN Charter system for forbidding aggressive war and downplaying the role of justice in determining a war's legitimacy. As Johnson (1999: 57) has argued, labelling a war as 'aggressive' does not resolve the question of whether or not it is just, yet the UN Charter makes precisely that presumption. The Charter's drafters chose this highly restrictive model to counter the problem of 'abuse'. It was widely believed that Germany, Japan and Italy had 'abused' the Covenant's indeterminacy to avoid opprobrium. The key to solving the problem of abuse was to remove the ambiguities by building into the Charter a 'presumption against aggressive war'. This presumption may have contributed towards the steady decline of inter-state war since 1945. It has also produced some perverse effects, however. In 1979, Vietnam invaded Cambodia to remove Pol Pot, a genocidal dictator whose regime murdered at least two million Cambodians. The presumption against aggressive war forced Vietnam to justify its invasion by claiming that it was acting in self-defence, a claim that was rejected by many states, who imposed sanctions on Vietnam, demanded its immediate withdrawal from Cambodia, and even offered indirect support to the *génocidaires* (Wheeler, N. J. 2000: 78–110). This tension between positive law's presumption against aggressive war and natural law's 'presumption against injustice' (Johnson's term) is arguably the central dilemma of *jus ad bellum* today.

Positive law in relation to *jus in bello* developed more cautiously but has evolved into a system of detailed and comprehensive rules. Moreover, since the creation of the International Criminal Court (ICC) in 2002, 'widespread and systematic' breaches of those rules have become almost universally punishable. Since 1945, developments in the laws of war have run alongside the evolution of international human rights law, centred on the Universal Declaration of Human Rights. That declaration put forward the basic idea that humans must not be mistreated without good reason. Although the laws of war developed somewhat separately from human rights law, the latter created basic principles based on supposedly inalienable human rights (such as the right to life) that should not be violated, even in war (Best 1994: 70–2).

International society's first attempt to grapple with *jus in bello* issues after the Second World War came in the form of the four Geneva Conventions of 1949. The ICRC convened a meeting of experts in 1947, which produced a draft convention that was then put to states at a conference in Geneva in 1949. Although there was considerable agreement on the fundamentals, such as the need to afford further protection to non-combatants and prisoners of war and the need for some sort of oversight, a number of issues proved contentious. The ICRC's draft had envisaged a convention that applied to all forms of armed conflict, but many states – particularly newly decolonized states and colonial powers – did not want protection afforded to rioters, guerrillas and terrorists (see Yingling and Ginnance 1952: 395). On the other hand, countries that had been recently occupied by the fascists worried that a rule giving states a free hand to suppress local insurgents could be used by unjust aggressors to justify brutality towards the host population and insisted that the convention recognize that partisans had liberated parts of Europe. The result was a compromise. Common Article 3 committed parties in 'non-international' wars to respect human rights without specifying any particular privileges for insurgents, and the Convention on the Protection of Civilians (Convention IV) offered legal protection to non-combatants in occupied territories (see Freeman 1947: 581). The upshot, however, was that the victims of international wars received more protection from the laws of war than did the victims of civil wars (Durr 1987: 268).

The second major dispute concerned oversight. The ICRC argued that positive law could moderate behaviour only if it was enforced (Pictet 1951: 469). Delegates considered the creation of a permanent war crimes tribunal on the Nuremberg model but this proved to be a political non-starter. The eventual solution was a twofold system of monitoring and punishment. Monitoring was covered by the 'protecting power' procedure, whereby a belligerent could invite a third party to monitor its enemy's compliance with the Geneva Conventions. In cases where the enemy state refused to give its consent to the protecting power, the ICRC was obliged to fulfil that role (see Levie 1961: 386). The concept was stillborn. Most of the conflicts after 1949 were non-international and the protecting power system did not apply to these cases. Furthermore, even in international wars, states seldom accepted a third party as a protecting power. Vietnam, for example, refused the ICRC access to its camps, insisting that American prisoners were war criminals, not prisoners of war (Aldrich 1981: 766). Enforcement of the Geneva Conventions would depend on either UN Security Council action or the evolution of some kind of permanent international tribunal. Neither innovation came to fruition until the 1990s.

The Geneva Conventions comprised a comprehensive code of *jus in bello*, granting wide protection to non-combatants, the wounded and sick and prisoners of war (Miller, R. I. 1975: 35–65). By the 1980s, it was widely held that the Conventions had the status of customary law binding on all. Consequently, grave breaches of the Conventions were universally punishable, though there remained no instrument for punishing perpetrators (Meron 1987). Moreover, within a decade or so of their enactment, it became clear that there were significant gaps in the Conventions. Not least, there was no prohibition on indiscriminate bombardment and no proportionality clause in the four Conventions (Best 1994: 106–7). Furthermore, decolonization and the overwhelming preponderance of internal wars created an impetus for extending the protections afforded in international wars to internal conflicts. Between 1974 and 1977, states returned to Geneva to negotiate additions to the Conventions.

The first Geneva Protocol significantly extended the protection afforded to non-combatants. It insisted that attacks be strictly limited to military objectives, defining these as 'those objects which by their nature, location, purpose or use make an effective contribution to military action and whose total or partial destruction, capture or neutralization, in the circumstances ruling at the time, offers a definite military advantage' (Article 52, Protocol I). In other words, soldiers were forbidden from attacking non-combatants or their property, though so-called 'dual use' facilities remained lawful targets. Soldiers were also obliged to evaluate the proportionality of their attacks, with Article 51(5) outlawing attacks on military objects which 'may be expected to cause' excessive civilian casualties. The Protocol also forbade the indirect targeting of non-combatants through attacks calculated to destroy vital civilian infrastructure and cause starvation. In short, the first Geneva Protocol created a system of positive law analogous to the Just War tradition's prohibition of attacks against non-combatants. The Protocol's principle of discrimination also provided the catalyst for conventions banning weapons considered inherently indiscriminate (Doswald-Beck 1987: 253). For example, the 1980 Convention on Conventional Weapons and subsequent amendments banned booby traps, lasers and weapons that injure by creating fire and heat, on the grounds of inherent indiscriminacy. The 2000 Convention prohibiting the manufacture, sale and use of land-mines was also justified on this basis. Of course, the question of discrimination made it problematic for the nuclear powers to adopt the Protocol because it is very difficult to see how nuclear weapons could be used discriminately. Despite the non-signature of states such as the US, UK and Russia owing to concerns about the legality of their nuclear arsenals, all three have indicated that they believe the Protocol to be binding and that the legality of the use of nuclear weapons is indeterminate (see Aldrich 1991: 19), a position confirmed by the International Court of Justice (ICJ) in the *Legality of Nuclear Weapons* case (1996).

Protocol II regulated how states might respond to internal insurgents. Above all, it reinforced the basic idea behind human rights law, that states were not free to treat their own citizens however they liked, though it afforded states considerable latitude in deciding whether or not a particular insurgency could be labelled an 'armed conflict', thereby bringing the Protocol into play (Forsythe 1978). Nevertheless, some states – particularly the US – complained that Protocol II gave too many rights to 'terrorists' and tied the hands of states combating them (Gasser 1987).

Through the Geneva Conventions and Protocols and other instruments such as the Genocide Convention, a comprehensive system of positive law designed to moderate the use of force and protect non-combatants has been created. The system did little, however, to deter despots such as Pol Pot and Idi Amin from systematically massacring non-combatants. Furthermore, in the so-called 'new wars' of the 1990s, the direct targeting of non-combatants once again became a war strategy. As a result of this seemingly growing impunity towards the law, the question of enforcement was raised once again, culminating in the creation of the International Criminal Court (ICC) in 2002.

Attempts to enforce the law through judicial proceedings were not entirely new. Before the Tokyo and Nuremberg tribunals after the end of the Second World War, states had attempted to deal with the vanquished Napoleon and the defeated German Kaiser through judicial processes (Bass

2000). The Nuremberg and Tokyo trials proved more successful, though they had an air of 'victor's justice' about them (see Minnear 1971). In the wake of these trials, the UN established an International Legal Commission (ILC) with the task of creating a global war crimes court. This lack of progress contributed to the culture of impunity evident in Yugoslavia, Rwanda and elsewhere in the 1990s. Having failed to halt or ameliorate the bloodshed, the Security Council sought to punish the perpetrators by creating *ad hoc* war crimes tribunals for Yugoslavia and Rwanda.

In 1998, 161 states sent representatives to Rome to negotiate the creation of a permanent ICC (Ball, H. 1999: 192). Broadly speaking, states divided into three groups. The 'like-minded' group included over sixty states such as Canada, New Zealand, Argentina, South Korea, Singapore and South Africa, as well as the entire European Union with the exception of France. This group favoured a strong and independent court. The 'Security Council' group comprised the other permanent members of the Security Council and argued that the ICC should be controlled by that body. In the end, Russia and France were suitably satisfied with the Rome Statute to vote in favour, whilst the US and China opposed it. Finally, some states such as Iran, Iraq and Libya opposed the very idea of an ICC. In a final vote at the end of the summit, 121 states voted in favour of the Statute and only seven voted against (including the US, Israel, China, Iran, Iraq and Libya).

Under the Statute, the ICC has jurisdiction to prosecute individuals for committing genocide, crimes against humanity, war crimes or crimes of aggression. The delegates at Rome could not reach agreement on what constituted a crime of aggression, even though war crimes tribunals after both world wars had executed people for that very crime. It was agreed, therefore, that no one would be indicted for 'crimes of aggression' until consensus emerged about what constituted such a crime. There was no problem reaching a consensus on what constituted genocide. Here, the Rome Statute adopted the wording of the 1948 Genocide Convention, which had been used to prosecute individuals in both the International Criminal Tribunal for the Former Yugoslavia and the International Criminal Tribunal for Rwanda. There was much less agreement about the specificities of war crimes and crimes against humanity. The bases for the definition of war crimes were the four 1949 Geneva Conventions and the two additional Protocols. Syria insisted that war crimes should only apply in inter-state wars and not internal conflicts, arguing that restricting a state's right to use force against insurgents breached sovereignty and encouraged terrorism. This motion was opposed by Germany and Canada, and ultimately defeated by a more than two-thirds majority (Economides 2002: 116–19). The Statute therefore followed the Geneva Conventions and referred to 'grave breaches' of the laws of war set down in the Conventions and additional Protocols.

The definition of crimes against humanity proved thornier. Unlike war crimes, crimes against humanity were not gathered in already well-established treaties. The Rome Statute was therefore obliged to offer an original and authoritative definition. It identifies crimes such as the traditionally recognized crime of murder and others that have emerged as a result of recent experience, including rape and other forms of sexual enslavement, 'forcible population transfer' (ethnic cleansing), enforced disappearances (drawn from the Latin American experience), enforced sterilization (opposed by China) and apartheid (Robertson 1999: 335). The key question was: when did a crime become significant enough in its scale to constitute a crime against humanity? There was widespread agreement that credibility depended on setting a high threshold. Thus, in order to breach Article 7 of the Statute, the acts listed above had to be committed 'as part of a *widespread or systematic* attack directed against any civilian population' (Article 7, emphasis added). Many non-governmental agencies at Rome were unhappy at the narrowness of this definition, believing that it set the threshold too high.

Arguably the most controversial aspect of the ICC's Statute was its relationship with domestic law and the Security Council. The US argued that domestic jurisdiction should have primacy and there were no notable dissenters. Thus, under the Statute, the state whose citizen is accused has primary responsibility for investigating the allegations and prosecuting the alleged perpetrator if it sees fit. Only if the relevant state is unwilling or unable to investigate the complaint would the matter fall under the ICC's jurisdiction. However, the US was not satisfied with this safeguard and wanted the Security Council to decide when a prosecution would be launched. It argued that the Statute's high thresholds would be irrelevant if the prosecutor was able to launch investigations independently of the Security Council. If the Security Council did not wield control, it argued, the prosecutor's office would become an overly powerful and politicized body. Such a body would in all likelihood try to force trumped-up charges against US personnel (Graff 2002).

The 'like-minded' group argued that a strong, credible and universal court needed an independent prosecutor who was free to initiate investigations. In contrast, the US, France and China insisted that the prosecutor should investigate only those cases referred to it by the Security Council. The problem with this formulation was that it could not overcome the problem of selectivity and perception of 'victor's justice' that accompanied earlier efforts to prosecute war criminals. Of the permanent members, only the UK was opposed to this proposition. The vast majority of other states also opposed this idea and used the voting procedure to block it.

Since 1945, therefore, the positive laws of war have developed into a comprehensive system of rules comprising a presumption against aggressive war, rules governing the principle of non-combatant immunity and legitimate conduct in war, and a system, albeit partial, for prosecuting those accused of grave breaches. As the debates about the 1977 Protocol and ICC demonstrate, however, the development of legal rules has been heavily constrained by realist considerations. Whilst not entirely ruling out the possibility of legal restraint, the persistence of realist thinking is evident in many states' approach to negotiating on the basis of perceived 'national interest' and reluctance to rely on the 'paper screen' of law to provide security. However, both legalism and realism have been unable to provide definitive answers to a number of moral dilemmas related to modern war. Since at least the 1970s, therefore, there has been a resurgence of natural law-type thinking. This gathered further momentum after the 11 September 2001 attacks on New York and Washington. Thus, for instance, Oliver O'Donovan (2003: 23) argued that the legalism predominant in *jus ad bellum* should be replaced by a 'praxis of judgment' that would permit war to end or prevent grave injustice regardless of its legal status, granting the Just War tradition a 'natural law rather than positive law orientation'. More pointedly, Elshtain (2003) called for a revived Augustinian account of the Just War which permits the punishment (by war) of wrongdoers and sees the question of just cause in more or less objective terms.

Thus, moralists and politicians continue to utilize natural law's basic proposition: that some things are by nature right or wrong. Such arguments are used to fill the gaps in positive law, to interpret positive law in particular cases, or to justify overriding the law. There are at least three reasons for the resurgence of natural law thinking as a counter-point to legal positivism. First, there is growing recognition that international law is indeterminate. Its decentralized nature makes it difficult to achieve definitive judgements about what the law has to say about specific issues. In such cases, actors often use moral judgement to unravel complicated claims. Natural law provides moral foundations on which to base such judgements. Second, positive law does not yield much insight into some of the most pressing moral issues of our time. For instance, the ICJ's ruling on nuclear weapons left their legitimacy open to question. Positive law deals with actions, not intentions, and whilst it can provide guidance about the use of nuclear weapons, it could not furnish much insight into the morality of purchasing security by threatening to annihilate a significant portion of the world's population through deterrence (see Johnson 2004: 79). As a result, several ethicists framed their discussion of the legitimacy of nuclear deterrence in natural law terms (e.g. Roszak 1963: 100–9; Russett 1984; Tucker 1985). Finally, positive law can produce counter-intuitive conclusions by elevating the principle of non-aggression above the principle of fighting injustice or maintaining the peace, though it is worth noting that the UN system is flexible enough in theory to accommodate both ideas through its Chapter VII mechanism (see above).

Conclusion

Just as the holy wars of the seventeenth century produced realist and legalist reactions, so too the mechanized wars of the nineteenth century encouraged legalists to explore methods of restraining the conduct of war. Although they attempted to limit the conduct of war through humanitarian activism and the creation of new law, they conceded – and indeed legitimized – the state's legal right to wage war. The two world wars, however, had a profound effect on understandings of *jus ad bellum*. The sovereigns' right to wage war was replaced by the condition that they had to persuade their peers of the legitimacy of the case for war. Under the UN system, sovereigns were obliged to justify their decision to wage war before the Security Council. In doing so, they were confined to two types of permissible argument: self-defence and the prior authorization of the Security Council. However, since the early 1990s some moralists and political leaders have invoked arguments similar to those of earlier natural law theorists to argue that in certain circumstances concerns about justice should override positive law (see Chapters 8 and 10).

Progress in the sphere of *jus in bello* has been more pronounced. Today, there is a comprehensive system of laws governing the conduct of war. These laws not only proscribe certain types of actions, they include provision for the supervision of belligerents by third parties and a judicial system for the punishment of perpetrators. Today's realists tend not to argue that *jus in bello* principles be overruled when necessity seems to dictate. Instead, as the US argued in the ICC negotiations, they worry about 'politicized' international justice and insist that domestic law take priority over international prohibitions. However, the principled realism of Morgenthau and Niebuhr still influences political leaders inasmuch as leaders must constantly balance that which is 'right' with that which is 'necessary' or 'effective' in cases where the two collide.

PART II

CONTEMPORARY ISSUES

6

The Just War Tradition Today

This chapter introduces the second part of the book. It details the three main sub-traditions (realism, positive law, natural law) identified in the introduction and charted in the previous five chapters. It then briefly summarizes the Just War tradition's main rules and different ways of interpreting them. This section defends the proposition that two of the rules ought to be understood as absolute requirements: the idea that actors are obliged to provide good reasons when they decide to wage war and the principle of non-combatant immunity. The third part explores how we can use the tradition to make normative judgements about contemporary war, focusing on three key challenges that confront the tradition: the relationship between *jus ad bellum* and *jus in bello*; the question of whether perceived necessity permits either rule-breaking or a permissive interpretation of the rules; and the question of how rules change.

The Three Sub-Traditions

Realism

The account of realism adopted in this book is in the tradition of the 'tragic vision' (Lebow 2003) evident in the work of Machiavelli, Hobbes, Morgenthau and Niebuhr. Typically, realism is viewed as antithetical to Just War thinking (e.g. Johnson 1999: 19–21; Walzer 1977: 3–20), but there are good grounds for maintaining a realist strand within an account of the Just War tradition. First, many realists do not hold the view commonly ascribed to them that 'moral restraints have no validity in . . . international politics' (Forde 1993: 64). Second, some realists have consistently reflected on normative matters relating to war (see Chapter 5). Third, realism focuses on the pivotal role played by politics, power and interests in shaping judgements about the legitimacy of war.

Realist insights draw our attention to 'lesser evil' issues and force us to confront the basic proposition that abstract moral principles influence behaviour only when actors use them to guide their actions. If moral and legal rules become alienated from their social context, they cease to play a significant role in constraining behaviour. They must therefore engage in constant conversation with political realities. Doing so confronts us with the idea that universal morality is at best 'thin' compared to the 'thick' moral relations *within* political communities (see Walzer 1994). In other words, the moral and legal predilections that shape decision-making about war derive more from the decision-maker's own community than from a sense of universal obligation. Moreover, the primary responsibility owed by political leaders is to their own citizens. Leaders have a duty to protect the physical security, material wealth and common life of their citizens, and these obligations override other obligations to law and morality (Hendrickson 1997: 23; Kennan 1985). For most leaders, most of the time, there are no radical disputes between these two sets of duties. However, when the state's survival or vital interests are at stake, political leaders are duty-bound to do whatever necessary to protect them, even if that means violating the Just War tradition's rules.

The realist insistence that political leaders give priority to the interests of their own citizens leads to national partiality. Because they are morally obliged to place the interests and welfare of their citizens above those of the enemy's, political leaders will value their own citizens' lives (even if those citizens are soldiers) more than those of other states' citizens (see Linklater 1990; McMahan and McKim 1993). Although national partiality does not necessarily challenge Just War's rules, it contributes to the general realist argument that the rules can be overridden when necessary and changes how the rules are applied. Most obviously, national partiality shifts the balance of proportionality. Proportionality requires that politicians and soldiers weigh the likely good to be achieved by a particular war or military action against all the likely costs: friendly and enemy deaths, non-combatant deaths, damage to property, and wider indirect costs. According to the doctrine of national partiality, these costs should not be weighed equally. Costs to friendly forces and interests should be valued more highly than costs borne by others (McMahan 1996, 1997). National partiality is also manifested in calculations about how much risk friendly soldiers should expose themselves to in order to protect enemy non-combatants. Whilst, at face value, the Just War tradition would seem to suggest that the lives of non-combatants be privileged, in practice states are likely to value the lives of their combatants more highly than that of enemy or neutral non-combatants. This is typically justified by the argument that because friendly forces are engaged in a Just War, the greater good is served by them prevailing, the likelihood of which would be reduced if the lives of enemy non-combatants were afforded a status equal to or greater than the lives of friendly forces.

A moral purist would reject national partiality on the grounds that it is indefensible in terms of the Just War tradition. Intellectually, this is compelling given the weight of argument in the first five chapters. However, it runs up against the empirical observation that not only do political and military leaders consistently display national partiality, more often that not their societies *expect* them to do so. Societies tend to expect their governments to expend more energy protecting fellow citizens, even members of the armed forces, than protecting foreign non-combatants.

A further contribution made by realism is its focus on prudence and a general scepticism towards moralism. One of the core criticisms of the Just War tradition as a whole is that by convincing political leaders of the justice of their cause, it contributes to moralism, which, as Tony Coady argues (2005: 21), 'can distort practical thinking ... by treating complex matters of moral opinion as though they were matters of moral certainty'. Just War principles, the argument goes, can so convince a political leader of war's justice and the certainty of victory that he or she becomes blinded to the practical difficulties associated with using war to enforce what may be a more marginal and disputable moral case. Therefore, realists tend to be sceptical of moral certainties (e.g. Carr 1960; Waltz 1979: 201). In place of moralism, realists council prudence. Prudence is a consequentialist ethic, which holds that the normative quality of an act is shaped by its consequences.

Echoes of realism can be heard in the Just War tradition. Scepticism towards moralism lies at the heart of Vitoria's insistence that judgements about just cause can never be made with certainty. Likewise, prudential calculations are related to criteria of proportionality and reasonable chance of success. Moreover, the two elements of realism that stand in sharpest contrast to traditional understandings of the Just War (national partiality and the idea that international morality is 'thin' at best) alert us to some of the ways in which moral and legal principles are interpreted in practice.

Positive Law and Natural Law

Most contemporary scholarship tends to separate positive law and natural law into two distinct modes of reasoning: legal and ethical (e.g. Byers 2005: 2; Kratochwil 1989: 42). By contrast, I view them as two elements of a common Just War tradition. There are three reasons for this. First, legal arguments provide only part of the broader justifications for recourse to war or conduct in war and of its normative evaluation. Second, separating positive law and natural law does a historical disservice to the Just War tradition. From Cicero until the twentieth century, the 'law' of war comprised both positive law *and* natural law. Indeed, the Martens clause explicitly states a linkage between natural law and contemporary positive law. To look at it another way, were Grotius and Vattel ethicists or jurists? Both gave natural law a place in their systems of international law, especially in sectors where positive law was either absent or incomplete, but both also stressed the centrality of positive law. Finally, states provided justifications for war long before they were legally required to; they violate the positive laws of war at least as often as they do the precepts of natural law; and, as the Afghanistan case shows (see Chapter 8), they sometimes feel obliged to offer moral justifications for war even when the legal case is widely accepted. The approach taken in this book, therefore, is not to separate the Just War tradition and positive international law, but to view the latter as a component of the former alongside the other two components of realism and natural law.

Today, the overwhelming majority of normative thinking about war takes place within the framework of positive law. For the purposes of this book, positive law is understood as having three primary sources: written treaties endorsed by states (such as the 1949 Geneva Conventions), customary practice and *opinio juris* – the judgments of authoritative bodies like the International Court of Justice, the International Criminal Court and *ad hoc* tribunals (Shaw, M. N. 2003: 65–88). There are many different ways of 'reading' positive international law. Legal positivists argue that the law should be interpreted in its own terms, shorn of ambiguous, imprecise and indeterminate ethical considerations. For them, the task of adjudication involves finding the appropriate rule and applying it to the facts of the case in order to determine whether or not the rule has been violated and to what extent (see Higgins 1994: 4–5). An alternative, constructivist, view insists that 'decision-makers are faced with making choices between competing legal claims, each of which could, depending on context, be valid' (Wheeler, N. J. 2004b: 194). Viewing positive law as a process rather than rules does not grant political leaders a licence to interpret the law however they see fit, as realists claim, though it is hard to deny that this does happen (see Krasner 1999). Instead, as outlined in the introduction, different actors serve as 'judges and juries', testing the validity of legal claims and framing their political behaviour accordingly (Higgins 1994: 7).

Until approximately 150 years ago, international law was framed by the natural law tradition. From Aquinas to Grotius, texts on the law of nations held that proper behaviour in international relations was governed by certain natural rights and intuitions that accrued simply from being human, or sovereign, and were knowable to all through the exercise of moral reasoning (Hall 2001). There are broadly two sources of natural law: theological and secular. The theological account holds that humans are bestowed with certain natural predispositions, intuitions and interests by God. These give humans certain rights and responsibilities. The secular account produces many of the same principles but from a very different source. It holds that as rational beings with the capability for reason, individuals have certain inherent rights. This makes some types of action right or wrong in themselves. An alternative holds that humans all have certain needs (food, shelter, recognition) and that these needs create rights and duties (Caney 2005: 72–7).

Nowadays, writers and politicians tend not to invoke natural law. It became unfashionable in the twentieth century for at least four reasons. First, jurists argued that natural law provided sovereigns a *carte blanche* to wage war whenever they saw fit. Second, as Kant noted, the appeal to natural law did not constrain leaders in practice. Third, natural law is too vague and ambiguous to serve as a useful guide for action. Finally, some multiculturalists have argued that what is often considered to be 'natural' law is actually a form of liberalism (Parekh 1997). For these reasons, it is necessary that positive law temper natural law. It is important not to discard natural law completely, however, because it points towards common, over-lapping, moral values (see introduction). Although natural law itself is seldom invoked, political leaders commonly use natural-law type arguments. Whether it be condemning terrorists or justifying humanitarian intervention, political leaders and publics often refer to fundamental moral intuitions that are derived, essentially, from natural law.

Natural law and positive law are therefore closely interrelated. Without natural law, positive international law potentially boils down to the preferences of the powerful. It loses a connection with both conceptions of justice and the moral consensus of the society of states as a whole. Moreover, positive law without the natural law injunction stipulated in the Martens clause would remain forever partial. However, natural law without positive law is a licence for war. It is too vague and ambiguous to guide our normative judgements. A comprehensive account of the Just War tradition cannot, therefore, avoid the interdependence between these two types of law. Neither can be persistently privileged over the other, nor can they be conflated.

The Just War Criteria

This section details the Just War tradition's key rules and illustrates the different ways of reading those rules from the perspective of the three sub-traditions: positive law, natural law and realism. Just War rules are commonly divided into two lists: those governing the decision to wage war (*jus ad bellum*) and those governing its conduct (*jus in bello*). Recently, a third set of rules has been developed, governing how the victors should conduct themselves after the war (*jus post bellum*). This is discussed in greater detail in Chapter 10. *Jus ad bellum* comprises three types of criteria: substantive, prudential and procedural. Some writers argue that the first two types are more important than the third in framing judgements about the legitimacy of decisions to wage war (Johnson 1999: 32–3). Of course, the Just War tradition insists that *all* the criteria be satisfied, but in practice there is little doubt that actors afford differing weight to the criteria when making legitimacy judgements. Moreover, the question of whether particular criteria are satisfied in specific cases is often hotly contested.

Jus ad bellum contains four substantive criteria. The first is right intention: individuals must wage war for the common good, not for self-aggrandizement or because of hatred of the enemy. Right intention is seldom discussed nowadays and it has recently been suggested that it should be eschewed because it is not at all clear why actors must have right intentions when they wage war (Brown, C. 2002: 108–9; Moellendorf 2002: esp. 120–58). This argument overlooks the role that right intentions play. As we saw in Chapters 1 and 2, right intention stands at the very heart of the Just War tradition's justification for killing. Killing for personal gain or through hatred or envy is wrong. When a soldier kills another, therefore, he must do so only because it is the only way of defending the common good or righting a wrong (see Nagel 1972; Norman 1995: 180). Eschewing right intention begs the question of how we justify killing in war at all. There are three possible avenues. The first would be to argue that as all individuals have a right to defend themselves – including their access to goods like food, fuel and shelter – all political communities have a right to defend themselves because they are cooperative amalgams of individuals. The problem with this argument, as David Rodin (2004a) has demonstrated only too well, is that the individual analogy quickly breaks down. Unless one is invaded by a genocidal state intent on killing every member of its target society, an invading army does not threaten everyone, not even every soldier. Therefore not all individuals in the attacked state enjoy a right to self-defence since they are not all under threat. The second avenue would be an act-utilitarian justification which holds that it is legitimate to kill if it leads to the greatest happiness of the greatest number. The problem with this approach is that it undermines other rules. If it is permissible to kill in general to serve the greater good, why limit killing only to combatants? Why not serve the common good more quickly by killing non-combatants? The third proposition would be to argue that killing requires no special justification, but this is rejected by domestic law and runs counter to everything the Just War tradition attempts to accomplish. In short, therefore, the principle of right intention remains the most plausible defence of killing in war.

The second substantive rule is that war may only be waged for a just cause. This is usually limited to self-defence, defence of others, restoration of peace, defence of rights and the punishment of wrongdoers. Just cause is often viewed in absolute terms: a combatant either has a just cause or does not. Today, this tendency is supported by legal positivism, which holds that actors either comply with the law or violate it (Walzer 1977: 59). However, from Vitoria onwards, most Just War writers separated objective or true justice (knowable to God) from subjective justice (knowable to humans). A war can certainly appear just on both sides and humans cannot break this veil of ignorance. There are two ways of coping with this. First, as Vitoria argued, princes should show due care before they wage war. They should seek advice from learned people and listen to the opponent's arguments. Second, the just cause rule should be understood in relative terms. It is a matter not of either having or not having a just cause, but of having more or less of one. Sometimes this is labelled 'sufficient cause': do we have a sufficiently just cause to legitimize the actions we plan to take? This, of course, requires an assessment of two factors: the reason for war and the intended strategy.

This leads us to the third criterion: proportionality of ends. This asks whether the overall harm likely to be caused by the war is less than that caused by the wrong that is being righted. Vitoria suggested that proportionality played a significant role in judgements about the legitimacy of war. Whilst war was legitimate to right wrongs, not all wrongs legitimized war. Some wrongs were neither grievous nor widespread enough to legitimize the inevitable evils that war entailed. On this view, proportionality is more than a prudential calculation. After all, prudence is always viewed from the eye of the beholder. A prudential account of proportionality would ask only whether the likely costs to *us* are greater than the likely benefits. Proportionality in the Vitorian sense requires a calculation of *all* the likely costs.

The final substantive test is last resort: is the use of force the only, or most proportionate, way that the wrong is likely to be righted? Last resort does not require the exhaustion of every means short of force. If it did, force would never be licit because one can always continue to negotiate. Instead, last resort demands that actors carefully evaluate all the different strategies that might bring about the desired ends, selecting force if it appears to be the only feasible strategy for securing those ends. In some ways, this formulation eases the epistemological problem associated with last resort. As popularly conceived, it is almost impossible to ascertain when the last resort has been reached because non-violent alternatives are always available, at least theoretically. The view of last resort offered here eases (but does not overcome) this problem by simply requiring evidence that decision-makers have seriously considered the alternatives to war and inviting other actors to consider the non-violent alternatives in their adjudication of the legitimacy of war.

Prudential criteria impose important checks on decisions to wage what would otherwise be justifiable wars. The principal prudential check is reasonable chance of success. This criterion holds that as war always entails some degree of evil and endangers non-combatants, it is wrong to wage war for a justifiable purpose unless those instigating it can reasonably expect to prevail. From a realist perspective, prudence includes both the overall likelihood of success and calculations about the costs of success. In other words, a state may be able to prevail but the cost of prevailing may be higher than it wishes to pay to satisfy a particular just cause. Because, from a realist perspective, political leaders have a primary moral responsibility to the welfare of their own citizens, they may not sacrifice that welfare unless their *vital* interests are at stake.

The third type of constraints are the procedural requirements of right authority and proper declaration. Canon lawyers and scholastic intellectuals resolved the first question in favour of sovereign princes. Only those leaders with no clear superior could legitimately authorize war. In the modern era this translated into sovereign states, and from the eighteenth until the mid-twentieth century, states were effectively given a free hand to authorize war whenever they saw fit. This right was heavily restricted, however, by the 1945 UN Charter. The question of who has the right to authorize war remains a moot point today. Positive law suggests that only states under attack and the UN Security Council have this right. On the other hand, natural law and realism hold that individual states and coalitions may legitimately wage war in other instances. Furthermore, it is widely accepted today that other actors may also legitimately wage war in some circumstances.

The requirement for proper declaration had its origins in the Roman fetial system, which prescribed procedures for declaring war. During the Middle Ages, the declaration requirement supported the right authority test because only those princes with the authority to declare war and not be removed from power had the right to wage war. The requirement also forced those about to embark on war clearly to state their case, providing an opportunity for peaceful restitution. Nowadays, the declaration can serve a third purpose: it clearly marks the transition from peace to war and hence the type of legal rules that ought to be applied.

Jus in bello regulates the conduct of war. It contains three basic rules. First, it incorporates the principle of discrimination: non-combatants must never be deliberately attacked. I argue below that this rule should be understood as an absolute prohibition. Second, it comprises the principle of proportionality: military targets may only be attacked when their military value outweighs the foreseeable destruction that will result. Third, combatants must not use prohibited weapons or conduct themselves in ways that violate the laws of war.

Underpinning *jus in bello* is the doctrine of double-effect, first articulated by Thomas Aquinas. According to Aquinas, the doctrine holds that any act may have two consequences: one that is intended and one that is not. Even if we intend good, our actions might cause unintended negative consequences. According to the doctrine of double-effect, unintended negative consequences are excusable if four conditions are satisfied:

1 The desired end must be good in itself.
2 Only the good effect is intended.
3 The good effect must not be produced by means of the evil effect.
4 The good of the good effect must outweigh the evil of the evil effect (proportionality) (Ramsey 1961: 43 and 48–9).

There is a major flaw with this rendition, and double-effect injunctions ought to be treated sceptically. It is worth quoting Walzer (1977: 156) at length here:

Simply not to intend the death of civilians is too easy. . . . What we look for in such cases is some sign of a positive commitment to save civilian lives. Not merely to apply the proportionality rule and kill no more civilians than is militarily necessary. . . . Civilians have a right to something more. And if saving civilian lives means risking soldiers' lives, the risk must be accepted.

The idea that it is possible to separate intent and act, particularly when referring to individuals in combat, has often been criticized. Critics argue that there is no practical difference between *intending* the deaths of non-combatants near military targets and merely *foreseeing* it (McKeogh 2002). According to Walzer and the contemporary laws of war, although we can never fully know an actor's intentions, we can ascertain something approximating intentions by focusing on actions. To display an intention not to harm non-combatants, combatants must demonstrate both that they did not deliberately seek to kill non-combatants and that they have taken every reasonable precaution to minimize the likelihood of harming non-combatants (due care). However, whilst combatants must accept marginally higher risks in order to reduce the risk to non-combatants, there is a limit to how much risk they are obliged to accept. To return to Walzer (1977: 156):

[T]here is a limit to the risks that we require. These are, after all, unintended deaths and legitimate military operations, and the absolute rule against attacking civilians does not apply. War necessarily places civilians in danger; that is another aspect of its hellishness. We can only ask soldiers to minimize the dangers they impose.

In practice, the question of where the limit of acceptable risk lies is hotly contested. Realists insist that military commanders should at all times prioritize the lives of their combatants (Hendrickson 1997: 37–8). Those informed by positive law and natural law find this position objectionable. They tend to follow Walzer in arguing that combatants ought to place themselves in harm's way to reduce the risks to non-combatants. Even accepting this view, however, there remain significant differences over *how much* additional risk should be accepted. These debates cannot be resolved in the abstract, but only through empirical assessments of individual cases. Even then, in marginal cases the degree of acceptable risk is indeterminate and open to political contestation (see Chapter 9).

The Just War tradition therefore comprises a body of rules that govern the decision to wage war (*jus ad bellum*) and the conduct of war (*jus in bello*). The tradition itself comprises three sub-traditions (realism, positive law, natural law). Each of these sub-traditions offers a different interpretation of the rules and affords them different weight. This is illustrated in Table 1, which is illustrative and certainly not definitive. Judgements about whether particular wars or military actions are legitimate depend upon the relevant balance between the three sub-traditions. This raises a number of problems beyond that of simply unravelling the different interpretations. How are *jus ad bellum* and *jus in bello* related? Can some of the rules be broken or stretched in emergency situations? How do the rules change? Because the second part of the book is primarily concerned with how these questions play out in normative debates about contemporary war, the following section will briefly sketch out my approach to them.

The Just War in Practice

The Just War tradition comprises both a set of rules and three major sub-traditions. The sub-traditions differ on at least three counts. First, they offer different interpretations of the Just War criteria. Second, they afford different weight to the criteria. Whilst natural law is particularly concerned with the deontological rules and generally sceptical about consequentialism, realism insists that consequences are paramount. Third, they offer different modes of reasoning. It is not only positive law that has procedures governing how successful arguments ought to be made. Just as a realist argument is unlikely to sway a court of law, so legal arguments are unlikely to sway the opinion of those who think that necessity demands certain courses of action.

Because the Just War framework is a composite of the three sub-traditions, it stands apart from them (see Figure 1, introduction). No single mode of reasoning or method of interpreting the criteria can consistently prevail over the other two. Neither should one set of arguments be ignored. How, then, are we to make judgements about the legitimacy of particular wars and military actions? In the introduction, I argued that legitimacy is shaped by a balance between the three sub-traditions. When 'judges' and 'juries' in international society and world society make and contest normative judgements about war, they tend to draw upon these three sub-traditions, placing different weight upon them.

Of course, there are no actual juries or judges, so legitimacy judgements are always to some degree indeterminate. The level of indeterminacy can vary considerably. Everyone (individuals, organizations, states) can and ought to be members of the global jury by evaluating legitimacy claims and deciding whether to validate them or not. Such judgements ought to attempt to balance the insights of the three sub-traditions, but that is not necessarily how members of the global jury operate. Sometimes the global jury passes a clear judgement: the tens of millions who protested against the wars in Iraq and Vietnam spoke for a larger body of world opinion. The judgement

Table 1: Just War and the three sub-traditions

Rule	Realism	Positive law	Natural law
Jus ad bellum			
Right intention	*Raison d'état* National interest	Uphold the law	Right a wrong Maintain peace Love of neighbour Common good
Just cause	*Raison d'état* Self-defence National interest	Self-defence Collective enforcement under Chapter VII of the UN Charter	Self-defence Enforce a legal right Enforce and defend natural law and punish violators
Right authority	State	State Anti-colonial non-state actor	State Defined political community
Proportionality of ends	Favourable balance of costs and benefits for the state	No prescription	Anticipated overall evils of war must be less than overall good likely to be achieved
Last resort	Unfavourable shift in the balance of power Emergence of threat to national interests	When a threat is imminent, overwhelming, leaving no alternative	When force is the least worst option
Declaration	None necessary	Useful in determining which rules to apply UN Security Council authorization	Statement of cause for war Opportunity for peaceful restitution
Jus in bello			
Discrimination	May be overridden when necessary	Non-combatant immunity Double-effect Due care	Non-combatant immunity Double-effect Due care [Walzer's supreme emergency]
Proportionality	Balance of costs to the state, society and the military Prudential considerations	Attack must not be likely to cause disproportionate harm	Attack must not be likely to cause disproportionate harm
Abiding by conventions	Useful for reciprocal purposes Can be overridden if necessity dictates	Positivism: obligation to follow law Constructivism: suspected violations open to political contestation	Obligation to obey law No obligation to obey unjust law [Utilitarianism: no obligation to obey unjust laws that produce bad consequences]

is never unanimous, however. Tens of millions supported those same wars on moral, legal and prudential grounds. Moreover, no matter how much influence one thinks global civil society has on world politics, the best the global jury can hope to achieve is to help influence the judges' decisions. Ultimately, powerful states determine whether or not rule-breakers will be punished. Their judgements are likewise premised on a mixture of natural law, positive law and realism – with the latter undoubtedly weighing more heavily for judges than it does for jury members. My point here is twofold. First, normative judgements about war are framed by the interrelationship between the three sub-traditions. Second, such judgements take place within a political context.

The second part of the book highlights three different types of dilemma: the difficult relationship between *jus ad bellum* and *jus in bello*; the question of whether perceived necessity permits either rule-breaking behaviour or a permissive interpretation of the rules; and the question of how rules change.

The Relationship between Jus ad Bellum *and* Jus in Bello

Since the early twentieth century, a consensus has developed which holds that *jus ad bellum* and *jus in bello* are logically separate (Vanderpol 1919). According to Walzer (1977: 21), 'war is always judged twice', and the two judgements are 'logically independent'. *Jus ad bellum* asks questions of political leaders; *jus in bello* holds soldiers accountable. Thus, a justifiable war might be waged unjustly; an unjust war may be waged justly. However, this is not how classic Just War writers saw it. For Augustine, Aquinas and the canon lawyers, a war was judged once by reference to *both* sets of issues. If a belligerent failed the *jus ad bellum* test, every act of violence it unleashed – whether against combatants or non-combatants – had to be considered unjust because those who ordered the violence had no licence for doing so. 'Logically' speaking – to paraphrase Walzer – therefore, *jus ad bellum* and *jus in bello* are not independent; they are arranged in a hierarchical relationship (one must satisfy *jus ad bellum* in order to be even considered to have satisfied the *jus in bello*). This view has a certain appeal. Why should soldiers who launch unjust aggression or defend a genocidal regime enjoy the same rights as those who fight for a justifiable cause? The grounds for separating the two cannot be 'logical', as Walzer suggests, or 'historical', because the earliest Just War writers did not separate them. The best grounds for separating *jus ad bellum* and *jus in bello* are pragmatic, consequential and intimately related to the overarching aim of the Just War tradition: the limitation of warfare.

If every violent act in an unjust war was considered unlawful and immoral, every member of the aggressor's army could be justifiably seen as a criminal, subject to punishment. If all participants in an unjust war are culpable, the victorious defenders might be acting justly if they summarily killed all of their enemies once the fighting was over. In the past, such killings were frequent and justified precisely on these grounds. However, if combatants know that they will be killed if they surrender, they are more likely to (1) fight to the death and (2) use whatever means available to prevail. This would make war bloodier and less rule-governed. Thus, restraining the actual conduct of war requires that combatants and non-combatants be granted certain rights regardless of whether the cause they are fighting for is justifiable. There is a further consideration here. The soldiers charged with fighting a war are seldom the people responsible for initiating it, and we cannot presume that the soldiers agree with what they are being asked to do. Some armies are conscript armies that force individuals to fight. Finally, if every act of violence in an unjust war were considered equally wrong, it would be impossible to encourage restraint in the unjust side's conduct. There are therefore sound act-utilitarian and rule-utilitarian grounds for separating *jus ad bellum* and *jus in bello*. For the former, the separation reduces the level of killing necessary to prevail; for the latter, it creates an incentive for combatants to abide by the rules, thus limiting war. Although philosophically problematic, the principle of moral symmetry limits the scope of justifiable killing to that which is necessary to prevail.

Defending the separation of *jus ad bellum* and *jus in bello* on pragmatic rather than principled grounds enables us to reconsider cases that call the separation into doubt: an unjust war fought justly, and a just war fought unjustly. I will focus on the latter rather than the former but it is worth noting that where people believe a war to be unjust, they will tend to argue that any use of force by the unjust party is wrong. Does a justifiable war fought unjustly remain justifiable? This question is especially significant in relation to terrorism and humanitarian intervention and is discussed in detail in Chapters 7 and 10. It is incongruous to argue that one's conduct can never undermine one's reason for acting. Echoing Aquinas, Vitoria and Grotius, I argue that unjust war conduct can undermine the *jus ad bellum* case for war. Recall that Vitoria argued that one may not wage war to right all wrongs, but only if the evil of war itself is less than the evil that is being countered. To make judgements about relative evils, we need to know two things: first, the nature and extent of the evil that the war intends to prevent, halt or punish; second, the intended means of countering the evil. If the chosen means are such that the cumulative evil unleashed by the war surpasses the cumulative good that can be reasonably expected to accrue from a successful outcome, the proposed war would fail the proportionality of ends test. In this case, the means chosen would undermine the *jus ad bellum* justification for war. It may also have a corrosive effect on perceptions of just cause. Recall that earlier I argued that just cause is relative and that the idea of 'sufficient cause' relates the reason for fighting to the methods used.

In short, therefore, I argue that *jus ad bellum* and *jus in bello* are related inasmuch as the selection of unjust ways of fighting can undermine an actor's *jus ad bellum* case.

Emergencies and Necessities

The second critical question is whether the Just War tradition's rules can be legitimately overridden in times of dire necessity. This question is particularly pertinent to the so-called 'war on terror', where some states have argued that the threat of terrorism demands that rules governing matters like detention, torture and self-defence be overridden. There are broadly four ways of responding to this problem: realism, invoking a supreme emergency exception, pleading mitigation and changing the rules. The fourth response will be considered in the following section. What the realist, supreme emergency and mitigation approaches have in common is the idea that the rules can sometimes be overridden without being changed. However, they have very different ways of approaching the problem. Realists argue that when necessity dictates, political leaders are obliged to override the rules. The supreme emergency position holds that whilst the rules cannot be lightly overridden, there are situations where the danger is so great that it requires measures that are expressly forbidden (Walzer 1977: 251). Nations only face a supreme emergency when the costs of losing are catastrophic. Although they differ on the threshold for overriding the rules, realist and supreme emergency arguments both insist that in some circumstances consequences should override the rules. They disagree, however, on the status of those rules. For the realist, rule-breaking in times of necessity is not wrong; indeed, it is morally required. For the advocate of the supreme emergency exception, the rule-breaking behaviour itself remains wrong but is excused because of the circumstances.

The third position is mitigation. A mitigation argument holds that actors may act in ways forbidden by the rules but seek to excuse their behaviour by pointing to mitigating circumstances. Other actors will assess the facts of the case and choose whether to legitimate the mitigating argument by deciding whether to condemn the act and punish the perpetrators, remain ambivalent or offer praise and support. The act remains wrong, but other actors agree to excuse it because of the exceptional circumstances (Chesterman 2003: 53).

There are (at least) two important limits to the use of supreme emergency and mitigation arguments: the first involves their place within the broader Just War framework; the second refers to their relationship with particular rules. A mitigation argument typically involves three moves: an admission of guilt; an appeal to common principles embedded in either positive law, natural law or realism; and judgement by third parties. Mitigation arguments can either involve the use of natural law to mitigate violations of positive law, or use one moral rule to justify breaking another, presumably lesser, moral rule. Mitigation may alter either the balance between Just War's constitutive sub-traditions in a particular case (where natural law or realism is successfully invoked to mitigate positive law violations) or the balance of reasoning within one of the sub-traditions (natural law or positive law). In other words, mitigation operates at the level of the secondary norms, not at the level of legitimacy. If a mitigation argument succeeded at the legitimacy level (see Figure 1), it would no longer be a mitigation argument, because the rule itself would need to have changed for the argument to succeed (Clark, I. 2005: 24). In short, mitigation legitimizes rule-breaking only if it is permitted by the other sub-traditions.

This brings us to the question of whether the violation of *any* rules can be legitimized through mitigation. I argue that the Just War tradition contains two moral absolutes, which may never be overridden: the duty to provide good reasons for the use of force and the principle of non-combatant immunity. The first absolute rule is that political leaders may only wage war if they offer good reasons for doing so. There are at least two grounds for this.

First, international society rests on the mutual recognition by states that they are bound by a common set of rules (Bull, H. 1977: 9–10). Order in such a society rests on the mutual recognition of sovereignty and the principle of non-intervention (Bull, H. 1977; Vincent 1974, 1986). As such, all states have an interest in maintaining the international society that partly constitutes them. Of course, the principle of non-intervention has been repeatedly broken, but when states or other actors do so they feel obliged to offer special justifications. It is necessary that they do, because failure to do so could undermine the legitimacy principles that together constitute international society.

Second, the obligation to give good reasons constrains recourse to war. In an argument echoed by many liberals after the First World War, Jeremy Bentham (1962: 546–60) insisted that if political leaders were obliged to publicize their reasons for war, making them available for domestic and international scrutiny, they would be less able to wage patently unjust wars. Likewise, 'democratic peace' theorists argue that democratic states are less likely to fight unjust wars partly because their governments are obliged to build a domestic political consensus for war and are constrained by legal rules (e.g. Doyle 1997; Russett 1993).

The *jus ad bellum* criteria afford considerable latitude to political leaders and have often been criticized as too permissive (e.g. Myers, R. J. 1996). Critics insist that whilst the Just War inhibits actions that cannot be justified by reference to it, the *jus ad bellum* in particular is quite elastic, to the extent that almost anything can be justified by reference to it (see Tucker 1960: 13). This claim is more apposite in relation to *jus ad bellum* than it is in relation to *jus in bello*, where the rules are somewhat more precise. However, as I argued in the introduction, the primary function of the Just War's rules is to provide a framework for meaningful normative discussion about war. So, whilst states and other combatants are free to draw long bows in their *jus ad bellum* arguments, members of international society and world society will evaluate those claims by reference to the Just War framework and the perceived facts of the case. To recall the language of judges and juries used earlier, history is littered with judges imposing harsh sentences on those they deem to have been rather too elastic in their justifications: Iraq when it invaded Kuwait in 1990, Germany when it invaded Poland in 1939. Such judgements are, of course, mediated by politics. Powerful and legitimate states enjoy a wider degree of elasticity than do weaker and/or less legitimate states. Nevertheless, none can escape the requirement to offer good reasons for their decision to wage war.

The second absolute rule is non-combatant immunity. The idea that non-combatants should be immune from direct targeting is one of the fundamental elements of the 'war convention', however conceived. As was noted in Chapter 1, Sun Tzu in fifth-century China, as well as the ancient Hindu, Egyptian and Hebrew civilizations, believed that prisoners of war and non-combatants should be treated with respect, whilst, in the Western tradition, Plato insisted that armies refrain from burning habitations and killing the civilian population of the enemy state. Although Augustine was ambivalent about the treatment of non-combatants, virtually every other key member of the Just War tradition forbade killing them directly. Medieval canon law prohibited the use of force against certain classes of people who performed important peacetime roles and played no role in hostilities (clerics, farmers, merchants), whilst the chivalric tradition forbade violence against the weak. The principle of non-combatant immunity is arguably the most clearly understood and widely accepted element of the contemporary laws of war. It is enshrined in all four of the Geneva Conventions concluded on 12 August 1949 and is central to the Rome Statute of the International Criminal Court (see Chapter 5). According to Colm McKeogh (2002: 7–11), the principle of non-combatant immunity is important for seven reasons. First, non-combatants have committed no wrong and therefore they may not have war waged upon them. Second, they are not participating in the fighting. Third, they are unable to defend themselves. Fourth, killing non-combatants is militarily unnecessary. Fifth, maintaining non-combatant immunity reduces the casualties of war. Sixth, sparing women, children and those who perform essential peacetime functions is essential for species survival. Seventh, killing non-combatants is contrary to the laws of war.

Why should non-combatant immunity be granted absolute status? Michael Walzer provides the answer. 'A legitimate act of war', Walzer (1977: 135) concludes, 'is one that does not violate the rights of the people against whom it is directed.' Moreover, 'no one can be threatened with war or warred against, unless *through some act of his own* he has surrendered or lost his rights' to life and liberty. By becoming soldiers, individuals tacitly permit themselves to be warred against in return for a right to wage war on enemy soldiers. This distinction lies at the heart of the justification of war itself. It is this distinction that differentiates war from brute force. Actions that break this rule cannot be excused without undermining the broader legitimacy framework provided by the Just War tradition. In other words, it would be difficult – if not impossible – to distinguish meaningfully between war as a social practice and mass murder/brute force if it were considered permissible to kill non-combatants deliberately in some circumstances.

To summarize, politicians and soldiers may sometimes break the rules legitimately if they are able successfully to develop a mitigating argument. However, mitigation operates amongst and within the Just War tradition's secondary norms (positive law, natural law, realism) and shapes rather than determines judgements about the legitimacy of particular acts. Moreover, the Just War tradition contains two absolute rules which cannot be overridden or open to mitigation: actors remain obliged to provide good reasons for waging war, and combatants must never deliberately target non-combatants.

Rules Change

One of the central points of the first part of the book was the claim that the Just War tradition's rules are not static. They are open to sometimes wildly different interpretation, their meaning can change, their relative importance alters, old rules can die and new ones appear. Since the September 11 terrorist attacks there has been an outpouring of arguments for rules change. Some argue that the Just War tradition is an unsuitable normative framework for evaluating terrorism (Goodin 2005). Others insist that the rules governing self-defence are anachronistic. The question of how rules change is therefore significant. Rule-breakers could, for instance, choose not to mitigate their arguments but insist instead that they are creating new rules (e.g. Byers 2003a). How should we decide whether to accept these claims? Legal rules change through either the conclusion of new treaties or the evolution of customary practice. The first is relatively self-evident. Customary change is more difficult to chart. At the legal level, customary laws require a mixture of consent, consistent practice and positive legal opinion (*opinio juris*). In other words, states must consistently act as if they were bound by the new rule and argue that they are acting in that way *because* the rule stipulates such action. The rule must also be endorsed by authoritative voices in international law such as the International Court of Justice.

Changes to the law do not, however, directly equate with changes in what is regarded as legitimate behaviour. Changes to the Just War tradition's fundamental rules only come about if all three of the sub-traditions move into agreement and a broad consensus emerges. Given the plurality of views, values and interests encompassed in the sub-traditions, such change is rare and proposed adjustments are usually hotly contested. As a rule of thumb, therefore, when assessing proposed changes and proposing my own changes I utilize two basic propositions. First, consistency is important. Proposed changes must apply equally to all unless grounds for treating like cases differently are proffered and generally accepted. Second, Kant's first categorical imperative provides a useful benchmark. Just War rules must be generalizable and must be cognizant with the other rules. That is, a proposed rule can be adopted only if it is accepted as universal and does not produce counter-intuitive outcomes. If the proposed rule cannot be generalized without producing counter-intuitive outcomes, we should resist it. Undoubtedly, 'judges' play the most significant role in this regard, but 'juries' can help influence their decision-making.

The second part of the book locates these four issues (conflict between the sub-traditions, the relationship between *jus ad bellum* and *jus in bello*, the question of emergency ethics and rules change) within debates about contemporary war related to terrorism, pre-emption, aerial bombardment and humanitarian intervention.

7

Terrorism

Since 11 September 2001 terrorism has been widely identified in the Western world as the primary threat to world peace (e.g. Gunaratna 2004: 2–3; Heisbourg 2004: 3–18). This chapter asks whether terrorism is ever justifiable. As the answer to that question depends on how we define terrorism, the first part develops a moral definition, which attempts to elucidate 'the features of acknowledged core instances of terrorism which merit and explain the moral reaction which most of us have toward them' (Rodin 2004b: 753). I follow Tony Coady (1985) in defining terrorism as the deliberate targeting of non-combatants for political purposes. It is this character, I argue, that marks terrorism out from other types of violence in contemporary normative debates.

Defining terrorism as the deliberate targeting of non-combatants for political purposes leaves two questions unanswered. First is the question of *jus ad bellum*. Terrorism can be committed by both states and non-state actors and sometimes in campaigns that satisfy the *jus ad bellum*. Therefore, we need a revised understanding of 'right authority' in order to apply a meaningful test to non-state actors. Second, my definition raises the question of the point at which the use of terrorist tactics undermines what may otherwise be the justifiable recourse to violence. It is important here to distinguish between *acts of terrorism* and *terrorist organizations*. The latter, I suggest, are those organizations that either make widespread and systematic use of terrorist tactics or persistently refuse to attack military targets (Lackey 1989: 85). When their terrorist tactics cause greater harm than the likely good that would be brought about by victory, such organizations violate the proportionality of ends principle and undermine their *jus ad bellum* case.

The second section discusses four ways in which terrorism has been justified and argues that each is flawed in important respects. The final part of the chapter applies a moral framework that builds on these insights via three cases of terrorism. Although my framework permits states to be labelled 'terrorist' and it is important to acknowledge that state terrorism has killed vastly more people than non-state terrorism (Rummel 1994), all three of my cases focus primarily on non-state actors. There are two reasons for this. First, the current debate about terrorism is focused entirely on the non-state variety. Second, I have selected the cases in order to demonstrate three distinct moral types of terrorism: Al-Qaeda is a case of *clear-cut terrorism*; Israeli and Palestinian violence is *grey-area terrorism*; and the African National Congress' struggle against apartheid is a case of *partial terrorism*. Terrorism as defined here is always wrong and its perpetrators should always be condemned and, where appropriate, punished. What is variable, I argue, is the impact that terrorist acts have on the overall legitimacy of either an organization or a political cause.

What is Terrorism and Why is it Wrong?

Although the term 'terrorism' is frequently used, there is little agreement about its definition. Even the mood of consensus that swept international society after September 11 did not produce agreement about what terrorism was. Jeremy Greenstock, chair of the UN Security Council's committee on terrorism, conceded that 'it might be easier to define terrorist acts than terrorism generally' (in Abi-Hashem 2004: 71). As pure description, the cliché that one man's terrorist is another man's freedom fighter is apt. In the late 1980s, the Reagan administration insisted that the Nicaraguan Contras were freedom fighters combating communism. Gerald Kaufman, the British Labour Party's Foreign Affairs spokesman, disagreed. Pointing to the Contras' many atrocities against non-combatants, Kaufman labelled them terrorists (Jenkins 2003: 26). The cliché does not get us very far towards a moral understanding of terrorism but is a useful starting point for it reminds us that 'terrorism' is not a purely descriptive term. As Martha Crenshaw (2003: 11) put it, 'when people choose to call the actions of others "terrorist" or to label others as "terrorists", this choice often has a prescriptive policy relevance as well as a moral connotation'.

Our starting point for a moral definition of terrorism should be the everyday usage of the word. In common usage today, 'terrorism' is a label one attaches to particular acts of political violence to delegitimize them. The question then is: what is it that makes terrorism immoral? Most definitions of terrorism point to one or more of four characteristics:

1   Terrorism is politically motivated violence (Anderson and Sloan 1995).
2   It is conducted by non-state actors (Tilly 2002).
3   It intentionally targets non-combatants (Weiss, P. 2002: 12).
4   It achieves its aims by creating fear within societies (Goodin 2005).

Not all of these characteristics are morally reprehensible and not all acts or campaigns commonly labelled 'terrorist' reflect all these elements. To build a moral definition of terrorism, we need to ascertain which of these characteristics are unjust and why.

The idea that terrorism is *politically motivated* violence distinguishes it from criminal violence and violence caused by mental illness. In the 1960s and 1970s, these two types of violence were often considered core categories of terrorism (e.g. Hacker 1976). Though less prevalent, these ideas persist today (e.g. Laqueur 2001: 80). There are at least two problems with this view. First, psychological studies suggest that most convicted terrorists are not mentally ill (Silke 2003: 32). Second, neither lone mentally ill terrorists nor groups that use terrorism for criminal purposes raise serious moral dilemmas. They are either simply mentally ill or criminal: they make no serious claims on our understanding of the legitimacy of violence (Hudson 2000: 40–8). Therefore, most contemporary writers associate terrorism with political violence. However, identifying terrorism as politically motivated violence does not help us explain why it is condemned because political violence may be justified by recourse to *jus ad bellum* criteria.

The second element of many definitions of terrorism, especially favoured among governments, is that it is conducted by *non-state actors*. The 1937 Convention on Terrorism defined terrorism as violence against the state (see Bassiouni 2001: 71–8). Some US government agencies continue to regard terrorists as non-state actors and this view is widespread in the literature (e.g. Coates 1997: 123–7; Whittaker 2002: 10). As I demonstrated in Part I, there is a widespread presumption that the sovereign state is the only authority capable of authorizing legitimate political violence. Indeed, this presumption was embedded in the positive law of war, which did not, until 1977, grant rights to 'irregular' combatants. The claim that terrorism is something waged by non-state actors therefore appears to render it unjust.

However, there are at least two possible ways of justifying the use of force by non-state actors. First, many actors have recognized a right for citizens or subjects to rebel against oppressive governments, and the liberal idea that sovereignty is bestowed not by God but by the will of the people has found its way into positive international law. If that is the case, a people must have the right to use political violence in order to overthrow an oppressive government (Mill 1867: 153–78). In the twentieth century, these ideas prompted positive international law to take an ambiguous position on the question of whether peoples had a legal right to revolt against oppressive rulers (Andreopoulos 1994: 211). Second, it is widely recognized that the use of force by non-state actors may be justified in cases where the sovereign either has dissolved (as in Somalia and Yugoslavia in the 1990s) or has been unjustly overrun by a foreign power (wartime France).

It is not therefore the fact that terrorists can be defined as non-state actors that provides the basis for a moral definition, for there are many cases of non-state actors using force legitimately. However, it is important that we do not absolve non-state actors of their responsibility to satisfy the *jus ad bellum* criteria (Hyams 1975: 15). In particular, non-state actors who engage in violence must demonstrate that they are a rightful authority. This requires three tests. First, non-state actors must demonstrate that they enjoy high levels of support within a readily identifiable political community. Second, they must demonstrate that their constituents share their political aspirations and endorse the strategy of violence (see Wilkinson 1983: 344). Finally, they must pass an instrumental test by showing that they are capable of controlling their members and making and upholding agreements with others (Thompson, J. 2002: 92–3). If these three criteria are satisfied, a non-state actor may claim the mantle of rightful authority. Before choosing violence, however, they must still satisfy the other *jus ad bellum* criteria.

It is the third element of most definitions of terrorism that renders it unjust: the intentional targeting of non-combatants. Any act of war that intends to kill non-combatants or that uses non-combatants as means to an end is unjust. There are a number of compelling moral, prudential and legal arguments to support an absolutist position on the principal of non-combatant immunity, as I outlined in Chapter 6. In short, we believe terrorism to be wrong because it entails deliberately killing those who ought not to be killed (see Coady 2002).

The final element common to many definitions of terrorism is its ambition to spread fear. The aim is to create a general context of societal fear that will coerce those in authority to accede to the terrorists' demands. It is the spread of fear, Jean Bethke Elshtain (2001a: 264) argues, that makes terrorism particularly dangerous because 'none of the goods human beings cherish – including politics itself – can flourish absent a measure of civic peace and security'. Likewise, Robert Goodin (2005) insists that the use of violence to create fear for political purposes is terrorism's distinctive feature. There are two principal reasons why this makes terrorism immoral. First, it breaches the Kantian injunction that humans should not be used as means. Second, it threatens the welfare of civil society as a whole and therefore indirectly breaches the discrimination principle. However, it would be perverse to suggest that pursuing policy change through the *threat* of violence was less justifiable than actually using violence. States often use 'coercive diplomacy', using the threat of force to persuade others to change their course of action. The consequences that Elshtain mentions above may also be foreseen consequences of justifiable wars. Furthermore, it is not at all clear that all terrorist organizations use violence to create generalized fear, as Goodin suggests. Some target specific individuals whilst some others pursue more genocidal agendas. The spread of fear is pernicious only to the extent that it is a consequence of an unjust war or the intentional targeting of non-combatants.

A Moral Definition of Terrorism

Once we break down our understanding of terrorism to its core components, it becomes clear that not all of its features are distinctive or give rise to 'the moral reaction most of us have' towards it. The only element of terrorism that marks it out in this way is its intentional targeting of non-combatants. Hence, I offer a moral definition of terrorism as the deliberate targeting of non-combatants for political purposes. Before I elaborate on how this moral definition can provide us with a framework for evaluating terrorism, it is important to note briefly some of the potential problems with it. First, some reject the moral absolutism at its heart. Second, some complain that the definition produces counter-intuitive outcomes. Third, some challenge the distinction between combatant and non-combatant.

Gerry Wallace (1991: 129) rejects the 'absolutist' view that it is always wrong to kill non-combatants, arguing that 'in certain circumstances there are equally powerful and accessible intuitions which support the opposite view'. In circumstances where killing the innocent is the only way to prosecute a justifiable war, Wallace argues that the distinction between combatants and non-combatants can be put aside. This leads Khatchadourian (1998: 75–6) to suggest that the prohibition on killing innocent people can be 'restricted' if it is the only means of self-defence. Thus, Wallace and Khatchadourian argue that the principle of non-combatant immunity itself should be restricted on consequentialist grounds. The question ultimately boils down to whether or not one accepts the view that there are, or should be, such restrictions. As I demonstrated in Chapters 5 and 6 especially, both natural law and positive law reject this position and neither Wallace nor Khatchadourian gives us good reason to doubt the validity of this view.

The second type of argument against the moral definition of terrorism offered here is that it produces counter-intuitive outcomes. That is, the definition forces us to label some acts as 'terrorist' that we would not normally choose to label so; and to label others that most agree are terrorism as something else. As an example of the first type of problem, Robert Young (2002: 24–5) points to the 1978 kidnapping of former Italian Prime Minister Aldo Moro by the Red Brigades and the 1984 Brighton bombing where the IRA attempted to blow up Margaret Thatcher and other members of the British cabinet. He claims that in neither case could the intended target be usefully defined as 'innocent' yet both attacks were labelled terrorist. However, if the intended victims were not non-combatants (I am not convinced by this conflation of innocence and combatancy), there seem to be no good grounds for inciting public moral outrage by labelling these acts 'terrorism'. If the perpetrators did not satisfy the *jus ad bellum* criteria, then both acts are simply cases of unlawful and immoral violence. If they did satisfy the criteria, both must be interpreted as legitimate acts of war.

As an example of a case where a terrorist act does not deliberately target non-combatants, Virginia Held (1991: 62) points to Hizbollah's 1983 attack on the US Marine barracks in Lebanon, which killed 241 people, mostly Marines. Judged by the moral definition offered here, this attack would not be considered 'terrorist' because the targets were military personnel. According to Held, such a judgment 'seems arbitrary'. However, the crucial moral judgement in this case is a *jus ad bellum* decision, not a *jus in bello* one. We would not condemn a French resistance fighter for driving a truck-load of explosives into a German military barracks in 1942 France. We condemn the Lebanon attack not because of the nature of the attack itself, but because it targeted American Marines who we believed were justly stationed in Lebanon. If it is to make moral sense, 'terrorism' must refer to types of action, not to particular groups irrespective of their behaviour. The danger of labelling everything as 'terrorism' is moral inconsistency, which ultimately breeds moral relativism.

The third type of criticism holds that it is not as easy to draw a distinction between combatant and non-combatant as the moral definition offered here suggests (Held 1991: 63). This is a criticism often levelled at the Just War tradition as a whole. There are certainly grey areas. Are civilians who work in dual-use plants (such as an engine factory that makes engines for cars and tanks) legitimate targets? Are *all* members of an oppressive regime or occupying power combatants, or only those directly involved in fighting? Are policemen combatants? Are off-duty soldiers? These are grey-area questions that can be evaluated only on a case-by-case basis. However, they do not undermine the idea of a distinction between combatants and non-combatants because, firstly, they are a minority of cases and, secondly, the very fact that they are considered grey areas is a product of the combatant/non-combatant distinction. Removing or downplaying the distinction simply removes the dilemma and lessens the normative significance of these questions. Moreover, eroding the centrality of the combatant/non-combatant distinction plays into the hands of one of the central justifications of terrorism: that there are no non-combatants.

Acts of terrorism, therefore, are always wrong because they involve the deliberate targeting of non-combatants. The broader question is whether individual acts of terrorism fundamentally undermine the legitimacy of a group's recourse to force. At what point do the perpetrators of terrorism become terrorists? Is the Royal Air Force a terrorist organization because it launched a campaign of terror over German cities during the Second World War? Are the state of Israel and Palestinian authority illegitimate because they are founded on the back of terrorist campaigns? Are we hypocrites if we welcome the political outcomes that terrorism may produce (for instance, the capitulation of Japan in 1945) but denounce the means that were used?

To answer these questions, it is useful to distinguish between *acts of terrorism* and *terrorist organizations*. The first hurdles that any state or non-state actor wishing to use political violence has to cross are the *jus ad bellum* tests. Whatever we label it, political violence that does not satisfy these hurdles is always immoral. Let us assume that in a given case the *jus ad bellum* test has been satisfied. Acts of terrorism are individual acts that are part of a wider struggle. Individual transgressions of the *jus in bello*, which acts of terrorism undoubtedly are, whilst always wrong in themselves, do not undermine the legitimacy of the overall struggle until the total harm inflicted exceeds the likely good to be obtained by victory. Nevertheless, perpetrators of such acts should always be condemned and, where appropriate, punished. Acts of terrorism cross the threshold into a campaign of terror where the organization committing the campaign can be properly labelled 'terrorist' when either of two conditions are met. First, the commission of terrorist acts is 'widespread and systematic'. Second, the combatants involved display a persistent refusal to attack military objectives. The commission of terrorism undermines a cause's *jus ad bellum* case when it fails the proportionality test. When a state or non-state actor crosses either of these thresholds, it properly earns the label 'terrorist'. However, whilst an organization or state may be delegitimized when it crosses either of these thresholds, the overall justification for the use of force *per se* is only delegitimized if it fails the proportionality test. Nevertheless, there are a number of ways of justifying the direct targeting of non-combatants. The following section briefly charts four such arguments.

Justifications of Terrorism

This section critically discusses four types of justification for terrorism. This being so, it is important to note at the outset that all four endorse actions that are forbidden by the positive laws of war. As such, to provide a plausible exception to the prohibition on killing, each justification would need to present a convincing case predicated on either natural law or realism. None of them accomplish this task. Moreover, all except the divine mandate justification ignore *jus ad bellum*.

Consequentialism

Consequentialists insist that we should judge an act by its outcomes. Violent means employed to achieve worthwhile ends are considered legitimate if they accomplish their aim even if the means are morally or legally proscribed (see Whittaker 2004: 108–9). There are broadly two types of consequentialist justifications of terrorism: utilitarianism and what may be described as the 'anti-oppression exception' (by Smilansky 2004: 791).

The utilitarian argument holds that terrorism may be preferable to conventional war because it is less costly. This argument was employed by the US to justify the atomic terror attacks on Hiroshima and Nagasaki. Although horrific, the argument goes, far fewer people died as a result of the atomic attacks than would have died as a result of a conventional invasion of Japan (see Goodin 1995: 3–28, 265–88). There are a number of problems with this position. First, it is always an uncertain calculus (Walzer 1977: 262). Historians remain bitterly divided on the claim that the atomic attacks on Japan reduced the overall amount of bloodshed (see Rhodes 1995; Walker, W. 1997). Second, it fails to justify why non-combatants should forgo their rights in order to protect the lives of combatants. The utilitarian argument requires us to accept the murder of non-combatants in order (possibly) to save some other combatants and non-combatants. Such a proposition is unacceptable to both natural law and positive law.

The 'anti-oppression exception' holds that terrorism is justified when it is a weapon of the weak wielded against oppressors. It is widely acknowledged that if we obliged the weak to follow the same rules as the strong, they would, almost by definition, never prevail (French 2003: 33–5; Young 2002: 27). What Kai Nielsen terms 'revolutionary terrorism' (1981: 435–49) is justifiable when terrorists have good reason to believe that their violent acts might be effective and that the suffering caused by terrorism is lower overall than the suffering inflicted by the prevailing order (see Santoni 2003: 60, 117–27). There are at least three problems with this position. First, if a terrorist can justly ignore non-combatants' rights, it follows that its victims may also ignore the rights of those whom the terrorists claim to represent, as the victims may also legitimately claim to be 'oppressed'. Second, providing an 'anti-oppression exception' to non-combatant immunity creates the potential for abuse, ultimately undermining the values that terrorists claim to be defending. Third, the idea that terrorism is a form of 'self-defence' overlooks its nature. Targeting non-combatants does nothing to directly protect the would-be terrorist or his/her constituents from imminent or actual attack.

Collective Responsibility

Many terrorist organizations, apologists and a handful of scholars argue that non-combatants who benefit materially from an oppressive regime lose their 'innocence' and become legitimate targets (see Ignatieff 1998: 1147). Referring to the terror bombing of Nazi Germany, Burleigh Wilkins (1992: 25) argues that only those Germans who actively resisted the Nazis and renounced all the benefits that accrued from membership of the Nazi state should have been immune from attack. According to Wilkins (1992: 29), it is legitimate to target non-combatants provided all political and legal avenues have been exhausted and the violence is 'directed against members of a community or group which is collectively guilty of violence'. Wilkins (1992: 31) admits that this means legitimizing violence 'upon those who in their individual capacity may have done or intended no harm to the would-be terrorists or to the community or group to which they belong', a view supported by Frantz Fanon (1965: 34–7). Terrorist organizations themselves frequently invoke the collective responsibility argument to justify targeting non-combatants. For instance, Al-Qaeda insisted that Americans – 'civilians and military' – were collectively responsible for the US military presence in the Middle East and its support for Israel (see Pojman 2003: 142).

Most troublingly, this position equates non-combatancy with 'innocence' and combatancy with 'guilt' and removes important constraints on war. Many Just War theorists and canon lawyers did likewise until it became clear that this reasoning provided a rationale for mass slaughter. If communities could be held collectively responsible for crimes, why not slaughter the whole community? The Just War tradition developed the distinction between combatants and non-combatants as a way of prohibiting mass slaughter. Furthermore, collective responsibility erodes the very rights that terrorists claim for themselves. A justifiable violent struggle against oppression is a struggle for the preservation of human rights, the most basic being the right to life. There are only two circumstances in which an individual loses that right – both by his or her own volition: by joining the armed forces or by being found guilty by an authoritative court of a crime punishable by death. The doctrine of collective responsibility removes the fundamental right to life and makes it conditional on an individual's relationship to perceived oppression. The right to life thus made conditional, the terrorist organization loses one of its central means of justification. In addition, there is an empirical problem. Wilkins, Fanon and others all argue that terrorism against oppression produces a more just social order. Unfortunately, there is little empirical evidence to support this claim (Khatchadourian 1998: 84–5). Finally, there is a question of moral consistency. If communities can be collectively judged for their wrongdoing, why cannot the victims of terrorism collectively judge the terrorists and their constituent communities and use that judgement to justify oppression?

Supreme Emergency

According to Walzer (1977: 251), there are situations where the danger confronted is so great and the options so limited that they require the use of measures expressly barred by natural and positive law. The supreme emergency doctrine implies an important but subtle modification of the 'anti-oppression exception'. In a supreme emergency, the rule of non-combatant immunity remains intact but is temporarily overridden. This position was expressed by Sheikh Fadlallah, one of Hizbollah's spiritual guides in the 1980s. Fadlallah, like many Palestinians, believed that the Palestinians faced a 'supreme emergency'. Forced by the thousand to leave their lands and live in refugee camps, Palestinians, he believed, were the victims of slow-motion genocide. Fadlallah thus justified the use of 'unconventional' means by reference to the Palestinians' right to self-defence and the imbalance of power. This alone, however, was not enough to justify the direct targeting of non-combatants. Fadlallah insisted that such attacks were only justifiable 'on an enemy whom it is impossible to fight by conventional means' (in Kramer 2002: 145). Thus, he argued that Hizbollah could temporarily override the principle of non-combatant immunity because Palestinians confronted a supreme emergency and had no alternative means of fighting.

The supreme emergency argument encounters many of the same problems as consequentialism and collective responsibility. I have argued elsewhere (Bellamy 2004) that it: contradicts the rest of Walzer's rights-based Just War theory; undermines the principle of non-combatant immunity and opens the door to abuse; is predicated on the fallacious assumption that there are sometimes no alternatives to killing non-combatants; and draws on a misplaced strategic belief that targeting non-combatants can defend a group facing a supreme emergency. On top of that, Walzer (2004a: 54) himself has since argued vigorously against terrorism, insisting that it cannot be justified in supreme emergency terms unless 'the oppression to which the terrorists claimed to be responding was genocidal in character'. There are few such cases, Walzer argued, because terrorism is used more as a tool for securing political success than for avoiding disastrous defeat.

Divine Mandate

The final type of justification is divine mandate. Many contemporary terrorists claim that they have been authorized by God to launch terrorist attacks. Yitzhak Rabin's assassin claimed a divine mandate, as have many Christian anti-abortion terrorists in the US (Bandura 2004: 125–6). In recent years, figures in most major religions have endorsed divinely sanctioned terrorism. One of the main problems with the divine mandate is that it is impossible to disprove, it can be claimed by almost anyone, and it can be used to justify anything. There is no limit whatsoever on what God can 'command'.

The question of divine mandate created problems for Just War thinkers precisely because it could be invoked to justify anything. Vitoria argued against it on the grounds that there was no precedent and no direct proof that God commanded war in particular cases. He left open the possibility that God *could* issue a mandate for war but insisted that those claiming such a mandate provide evidence of its existence (see Chapter 3). We could say much the same today in response to terrorists who claim a divine mandate. Religious believers must accept the theoretical possibility that God could issue a mandate for war, but those invoking such a mandate are required to prove its existence by more than faith. Given that today, as in Vitoria's time, there remains no precedent for such a mandate, it must be admitted that the likelihood of a terrorist group furnishing compelling evidence to support its claim to a divine mandate is very slim at best.

There are therefore at least four ways of justifying the direct killing of non-combatants by terrorists. All are flawed in important respects. In particular, they all threaten to undermine the rules of war by making them conditional on political preferences. Furthermore, all four approaches fail the consistency test. Those making consequentialist, collective responsibility, supreme emergency and divine mandate claims do not permit others to make similar claims against them. This implies an objective account of justice that has long been unsustainable. The final section of this chapter explores three brief case studies to illustrate how the account of terrorism offered here can shape our evaluation of different types of terrorism.

Three Types of Terrorism

According to the moral schema offered in this chapter there are three potential types of terrorism. The first is *clear-cut terrorism*. In these cases, state or non-state actors make widespread and systematic use of terrorism and/or persistently refuse to attack military targets. This persistent breaching of *jus in bello* undermines any *jus ad bellum* case that the terrorists might articulate. The second type of terrorism is *grey-area terrorism*. In these cases, terrorist tactics are part of a wider political, social and military struggle. Whilst there are certainly *acts* of terrorism, which ought to be condemned, it is not clearly apparent whether there is a systematic and widespread *campaign* of terrorism or whether the actors involved persistently refuse to target the enemy's military. The third type of terrorism is *partial terrorism*. In these cases, states or non-state actors commit acts of terrorism that fall short of the two thresholds (widespread and systematic, and persistent refusal to attack military targets). As a result, if the actor satisfies the requirements of *jus ad bellum*, the commission of terrorist acts does not undermine the overall legitimacy of the campaign though the individual acts of terrorism should be condemned.

Clear-Cut Terrorism: Al-Qaeda

Al-Qaeda is a clear-cut terrorist organization. Although it has occasionally attacked military targets (most notably the USS *Cole* on 12 October 2000 and the Pentagon on 11 September 2001), it has made widespread and systematic use of terrorism. As well as the USS *Cole* attack, Al-Qaeda is responsible for the World Trade Centre bombing in 1993, the bombing of a Philippine airlines flight in 1994, the murder of two German nationals in Libya in 1994, a plan to simultaneously destroy eleven US aircraft over the Pacific and assassinate the pope, the 1998 bombing of the US embassies in Nairobi and Dar es Salaam, and the September 11 attacks on New York and Washington (Burke 2003: 7–22).

Does Al-Qaeda have good grounds for its resort to force? It has two principal objectives. First, it seeks to remove all governments within the lands of Islam that do not rule according to its fundamentalist interpretation of the faith. According to Osama bin Laden, Western influence in the Islamic world has corrupted and divided the region's governments, making Muslims subservient to the West (Alexander and Swetnam 2001: 2). Al-Qaeda aims to overthrow these corrupt governments and replace them with a unified Islamic caliphate (Jacquard 2002: 93–8). Second, Al-Qaeda wishes to end what it sees as the American oppression of Muslims worldwide. According to bin Laden, 'America and its allies are massacring us in Palestine, Chechnya, Kashmir and Iraq. The Muslims have a right to attack America in reprisal.' He continued, 'for over half a century, Muslims in Palestine have been slaughtered and assaulted and robbed of their honour and of their property' (in Esposito 2002: 22–3).

These aims do not satisfy the principles of either just cause, right intent or proportionality of ends. The desire to establish a united Islamic caliphate would be justifiable only if it was the express wish of the overwhelming majority of people concerned. By all accounts, though, it enjoys the support of a small minority in the Islamic world, and the Taliban experience suggests that the proposed caliphate would be much *more* oppressive than the prevailing status quo. Importantly, neither the Just War tradition nor Islamic teaching permits the use of force to convert non-believers or enforce a particular brand of fundamentalism (Silverman 2002: 78). Al-Qaeda's first ambition therefore falls at the initial hurdle. The second ambition could be a just cause for war if Al-Qaeda could demonstrate that the US was responsible for the unjust killing of Muslims. In particular, the cases of Palestine and Iraq stand out. In both cases, there may be a just cause for armed resistance. Nevertheless, Al-Qaeda would still have to satisfy the requirements for 'right intention' and 'legitimate authority'. Given its first ambition, it is clear that Al-Qaeda does not intend simply to support the liberation of Palestine and Iraq. Having 'liberated' these countries, it would attempt forcibly to establish a particular type of regime regardless of whether the overwhelming majority of people in Palestine and Iraq supported it. Furthermore, in neither Palestine nor Iraq does Al-Qaeda satisfy the rightful authority test. Thus, Al-Qaeda does not have a credible *jus ad bellum* case.

In the absence of a *jus ad bellum* case, there is little reason to assess Al-Qaeda's conduct in relation to *jus in bello*. However, it is worth briefly considering Al-Qaeda's justification of violence against non-combatants because it makes consistent use of three of the justifications identified in the previous section: collective responsibility, consequentialism and divine mandate. Bin Laden has repeatedly argued that the American people are collectively responsible for the Israeli occupation of Palestine and the suffering of Iraqis and other Muslims. The American government, he argues, manufactures arms and gives them to Israelis who use them to massacre Palestinians. Because Americans elect their government, it stands to reason for bin Laden that all Americans are responsible for Muslim suffering (in Esposito 2002: 23–4).

Al-Qaeda also makes use of consequentialist arguments (specifically the 'anti-oppression exception'). Drawing a distinction between 'commendable' and 'reprehensible' terrorism, bin Laden insisted that Al-Qaeda's struggle falls into the 'commendable' bracket because 'it is directed at the tyrants, the traitors who commit acts of treason against their own countries and their own faith. . . . Terrorizing those and punishing them are necessary measures to straighten things and make them right' (in Esposito 2002: 24–5). Finally, all of this is supported by the claim that Al-Qaeda terrorism enjoys a divine mandate. Bin Laden reportedly told an ABC reporter that 'Allah is the one who created us and blessed us with this religion, and orders [us] to carry out our holy struggle – jihad – to raise the word of Allah above all the words of unbelievers' (in Williams, P. L. 2002: 135).

By invoking collective responsibility, consequentialism and divine mandate, Al-Qaeda has attempted to legitimize its terrorist campaign against the West and other Muslims. Excluding its role in the Iraqi insurgency, of fourteen major terrorist incidents related to Al-Qaeda since the early 1990s, only five were directed against military targets. Six – with the September 11 atrocity counted only once – were either directed against non-combatant targets or (in the case of the Pentagon attack) used the killing of non-combatants as a means to an end. Three (the Nairobi and Dar es Salaam embassy bombings and a plot to destroy a third US embassy) are of questionable status. The casualty figures are more striking. In total, Al-Qaeda has been directly responsible for fewer than two hundred US combatant deaths and over 3,500 non-combatant casualties. These figures suggest that Al-Qaeda fails both *jus in bello* tests. As such, it is an excellent case of clear-cut terrorism. It uses terrorism on a widespread and systematic scale and clearly fails the *jus ad bellum* test. Not all cases are so clear, however, as the next section will demonstrate.

Grey-Area Terrorism: Israel and Palestine

The dispute between Israel and Palestine is particularly complicated because both sides have committed acts of terrorism and both can sustain plausible *jus ad bellum* cases. The key question is whether those instances of terrorism undermine the legitimacy of their case for violence. I will begin by briefly discussing the Zionist campaign for an independent Jewish homeland before moving on to focus on Palestinian terrorism since the 1987 *Intifada*.

After the First World War, Britain was given a League of Nations mandate to govern Palestine. In 1917, the so-called 'Balfour declaration' stated that Britain intended to create a Jewish state on the territory of Palestine (Groisser 1982: 117–18). This eventually sparked a full-scale Arab rebellion between 1936 and 1939. As well as targeting the British, Arabs also attacked Jewish settlements (Hoffman 1998: 48). In 1935, Vladimir Jabotinsky's 'Revisionist Party' established a militia wing known as *Irgun Zwei Leumi* (Irgun), which conducted violent reprisals against Palestinians. Jabotinksy used a consequentialist argument to justify terrorism, arguing that the use of 'military might' against Arabs was legitimate because the Zionist cause was moral (Schechtman 1961: 474). As the attacks were widened to include Arabs unconnected with attacks on Jews, Irgun insisted that the Arabs bore collective responsibility for attacks on Jews (Lustick 1995: 525).

In 1939, the British, keen to end the Arab revolt before the outbreak of the impending war with Germany, issued a white paper rejecting the idea of a Jewish state in Palestine and imposing severe restrictions on Jewish immigration to the region. Irgun responded with a short-lived rebellion that was formally suspended when Britain declared war on Nazi Germany (Hoffman 1998: 48–9). Others, including the notorious Joseph Stern, continued to attack British targets in Palestine, killing two policemen in 1941 in retaliation for the use of torture by the British. When the two policemen turned out to be Jewish themselves, Stern was permanently discredited.

The violent campaign for a Jewish state began again in 1943–4. In 1943, Yitzhak Shamir, a future Prime Minister of Israel, publicly defended the use of terrorism. He insisted that

neither Jewish ethics nor Jewish tradition can disqualify terrorism as a means of combat. We are very far from having any moral qualms as far as our national war goes. . . . Terrorism is for us a part of the political battle . . . and it has a great part to play: speaking in a clear voice to the whole world . . . it proclaims our war against the occupier. (In Lustick 1995: 527)

In 1944, once it became clear that the Allies were likely to prevail over the Nazis, Irgun's new leader, Menachem Begin, declared that in the light of Britain's refusal to withdraw from Palestine or create a Jewish state, the armistice between the Jews and British was over. Begin (1977: 45) also condemned Britain for not doing more to protect European Jews and for blocking the migration of Jewish refugees to Palestine. Irgun launched a campaign of violence that focused on killing British soldiers and police and destroying public buildings.

Once the Second World War ended, Irgun launched a more widespread campaign of terrorism, first against the British and then against Arabs. Although many more Arab non-combatants than British combatants or non-combatants were killed during Irgun's bloody campaign, the most notorious incident was the July 1946 bombing of the King David Hotel, which killed ninety-one people. Irgun's target was hotel rooms used by the British administration, but its tactic was to place a large bomb in the kitchen. Thus, even if the attack was not indiscriminate, it was certainly disproportionate. Despite Begin's protestations to the contrary, there is no evidence that Irgun took measures to reduce the risks to non-combatants.

The terrorist campaign persuaded Britain to hand over the Palestinian mandate to the UN. Now intent on creating a Zionist state with a Jewish majority, Irgun turned on the Arabs. Begin threatened to 'turn Palestine into a bloodbath' as Irgun adopted a strategy that became known in the 1990s as 'ethnic cleansing'. The strategy comprised a series of highly publicized massacres designed to terrorize Palestinians into flight. The most notorious of these was the April 1948 massacre in Deir Yassin, where approximately 300 Palestinian non-combatants were killed. Hundreds of thousands of Palestinians fled their homes, allowing the Jews to claim a majority in the lands that would be called Israel. Begin (1977: 164) proudly reflected that: 'Of the about 800,000 Arabs who lived on the present territory of the State of Israel, only some 165,000 are still there. The political and economic significance of this development can hardly be overestimated.' The strategy succeeded, and under immense pressure from the US, the UN conceded to the creation of an independent State of Israel on more than two-thirds of the territory of the Palestine mandate.

There is no doubt that terrorism played an important part in the birth of Israel. Even if attacks on the British are not properly labelled terrorist, the ethnic cleansing of Arabs certainly is. We need to begin by asking whether Irgun satisfied the *jus ad bellum*. The Jewish nationalists had no *prima facie* just cause. The Jews had neither a legal nor a moral right to an exclusive homeland. *Prima facie*, an independent Palestine should have been a secular state comprising Arab and Jewish populations – a view that both the British and UN held after the Second World War. However, three factors support the Jewish claim. First, in the 1917 Balfour declaration, Britain promised the Jews a homeland on the territory of Palestine. The declaration certainly gave Britain a moral obligation to create a Jewish homeland, but it could be objected that Britain had neither a moral nor a legal right (the latter residing with the League of Nations) to determine

Palestine's future status, and that the Balfour declaration was superseded by the 1939 white paper.

The second factor was the Holocaust and the fact that Britain prevented the migration of European Jews to safety in Israel. Britain's failure to protect European Jews during the Holocaust certainly creates a powerful moral case for the creation of a strong Jewish state. On the other hand, before and during the war itself Britain had good strategic reasons for denying Jewish migration: migration risked a further Arab rebellion and, worse, an Arab alliance with the Nazis. This strategic concern created a moral imperative because an Arab rebellion and German alliance could have prolonged the war. Nevertheless, it is not clear that this utilitarian consideration justifies the failure to help Jews fleeing Europe, much less the British practice of turning around ships containing Jewish refugees (see Hyams 1975: 154). Britain had a moral obligation to protect European Jews, but there was disagreement about the best way to do that: assist Jewish migration and therefore save as many Jews as could escape Hitler's clutches, or pacify the Arabs, thus helping to shorten the war. What condemns Britain is not so much that it refused to accommodate Jews in Palestine, but that it also refused to make alternative arrangements to protect them.

The third factor was that in the 1930s and 1940s, the British cracked down on Jewish political activism, killing and torturing many Jews. This, Jewish nationalists argue, qualifies British rule as an oppressive regime, justifying armed rebellion against it. From the British point of view, however, such measures were a justifiable response to Jewish terrorism. From this perspective it was Jewish terrorism that provoked the British response.

Thus, the Jewish nationalists had a plausible if not entirely convincing just cause for rebellion against the British. However, the case for establishing a Jewish state by expelling the majority Arabs was weak. The Arabs had formed the majority for a millennium. Although the anti-Jewish violence that accompanied the 1930s rebellion certainly gave the Jews a right of self-defence, it did not give them a right to seize an exclusive Jewish homeland.

The Jewish case is not helped by the other *jus ad bellum* criteria. It is not clear that Irgun and the Stern gang acted with right intention by aiming to promote peace and right a wrong. Given Palestinian demographics, the creation of a Jewish state was hardly likely to contribute to the peace. Moreover, although Britain undoubtedly committed wrongs, it is not clear that Jewish violence was directed at righting those wrongs. Irgun's claim to be a legitimate authority is perhaps less questionable (by 1942 at least, the Stern gang had no case to make), though its significance is more doubtful. For the most part, Irgun satisfied the three rightful authority criteria identified earlier. The problem, however, is that whilst it could certainly claim to represent a distinctive political community, it was a *minority* community. Irgun could not claim to speak for Palestine as a whole. To assess appropriately the Jewish nationalists' case in relation to the *jus ad bellum*, therefore, we need to separate out its campaign against the British and its subsequent campaign against the Arabs. The former is a case of simultaneous ostensible justice where both sides made plausible claims. The latter is less so. Irgun and others had very little justification for the campaign of terror against the Arabs.

The same distinction needs to be made when interrogating the Jewish campaign's adherence to *jus in bello*. In its campaign against the British, Irgun was relatively discriminate. It primarily targeted soldiers, policemen and other government officials. Given its use as a centre of administration, the King David Hotel bombing is condemned not because it was indiscriminate but because it was disproportionate. If we were to take the campaign against the British alone, therefore, we would not be justified in labelling Irgun 'terrorists'. Its post-war campaign against the Arabs, however, was quite different. Here, Irgun targeted non-combatants in order to terrorize other Arabs into fleeing their homes. Its campaign against the Arabs was certainly terrorist, and for an unjust cause at that.

In rejecting the consequentialist argument that terrorism can be justified because it works, Walzer (2004a: 56) argued that 'no nation I know of owes its freedom to a campaign of random murder'. Israel may owe its freedom to a campaign of limited violence against the British, but it owes its identity to a campaign of random murder against Arabs. Without the anti-British campaign the mandate would not have been quickly passed to the UN; without the anti-Arab campaign a viable *Jewish* state could not have been created. It is placing the two campaigns together that makes Jewish terrorism a hard case. There were some good grounds for rebellion and statehood, there was also evidence of discriminate targeting. Nevertheless, there is little justification for using violence to create a homogeneous state, and Irgun used widespread and systematic violence against Arab non-combatants to do just that. Moreover, far from distancing itself from terrorist attacks, the Israeli state elevated its terrorists to the most senior positions. No fewer than four advocates (if not perpetrators) of terrorism (Begin, Shamir, Ben Gurion and Sharon) subsequently became Prime Minister of Israel. Thus, whilst the use of terror tactics did not necessarily undermine the cause of freedom from British rule, the terrorist campaign against the Arabs crossed the proportionality threshold beyond which terrorist violence undermines the *jus ad bellum* case for war.

For much of its existence, Israel has been the target of political violence. One of the main instigators of that violence, the Palestine Liberation Organization (PLO), was formed in 1964. Prior to the 1967 Arab–Israeli war, one of the PLO's factions – Fatah – spearheaded the military struggle against Israel by launching guerrilla attacks against Israeli forces (Wieviorka 1988: 225). These operations were one of the reasons cited for Israel's pre-emptive invasion of Egypt in 1967. In that war, Israel seized control of Gaza, the West Bank and Sinai. Fatah continued to wage what it described as an insurgent campaign against Israel, comprising guerrilla operations against Israeli forces launched from Jordan, the bombing of military and non-military targets and the shelling of Jewish settlements. It also attempted to internationalize the struggle through a campaign of air-craft hijacking. In 1987 the Palestinians launched an uprising – the *Intifada* – in Gaza and the West Bank and a new Palestinian organization, Hamas, burst onto the scene.

Hamas is an offshoot of the Palestinian Muslim Brotherhood, which prior to 1987 had played a non-violent role in the occupied territories (Esposito 2002: 94–101). The Brotherhood ran schools and youth camps, and provided health services. When the *Intifada* erupted, it formed a mili-tary wing, 'Hamas', to carry the fight to the Israelis. Between 1987 and 1994, Hamas launched guerrilla attacks against Israeli military and police units. When Israel and the US condemned them as terrorists, Hamas insisted that it was legitimate to target the occupiers, insisting that it only attacked Israeli combatants. These tactics changed in 1994 after a Jewish settler opened fire in a Hebron Mosque, killing twenty-nine worshippers. Hamas responded with suicide bomb attacks against non-combatants. Since 1994, Hamas, Islamic Jihad and other organizations have consistently used suicide and non-suicide bomb attacks against Israeli non-combatants. Between 1994 and 2001, approximately 341 Israelis were killed in this campaign, almost all of them non-combatants, and the killing has continued since (Pape 2003: 357–60). In 2003, Hamas announced a unilateral ceasefire, though sporadic attacks continued. After boycotting the Palestinian politi-cal process, it fielded candidates in the 2006 elections, winning a majority and forming the new government.

There was wide debate within Hamas about the decision to shift from targeting combatants to non-combatants. Some Hamas leaders argued that targeting non-combatants contradicted the Qur'an's teaching and delegiti-mized the Palestinian cause. Others, including Sheikh Yassin, Hamas' former spiritual leader, who was assassinated by the Israelis in 2004, argued that suicide bombing was the only effective weapon that remained to the Palestinians and defended it on the grounds that Israelis were collectively responsible for the oppression of Palestinians (Shahid 2001: 124).

Abdul Aziz Rantisi, Yassin's successor as Hamas leader until his own assassination by the Israelis the same year, defended the suicide attacks on two grounds (see Juergensmeyer 2001: 73–5). First, he argued that they were reprisals for similar Jewish actions. Rantisi claimed that in its early years, Hamas only targeted combatants and 'took every measure' to prevent attacks on non-combatants. He argued that the Israeli government was complicit in an attack on Palestinian demonstrators at the al-Aqsa Mosque in 1990 as well as in the 1994 Hebron massacre mentioned earlier. Rantisi therefore claimed that Hamas' switch to suicide attacks against non-combatants was necessary for Palestinian self-defence: 'if we did not respond this way, Israelis would keep doing the same thing'. Second, Rantisi argued that Israelis were collectively responsible for the wrong being committed against Palestinians (both in Juergensmeyer 2001: 74).

Are these Palestinian organizations terrorist organizations or legitimate rebels using illegitimate tactics? Organizations like Hamas and Fatah have reasonably strong cases in *jus ad bellum* terms. There is a good case for armed Palestinian resistance to Israel. That case clearly extends back to the 1940s, but we do not need to go that far back to find a just cause. Israel's occupation of Gaza and the West Bank is widely recognized as illegal. Given Israel's failure to comply with international law, the use of force by Palestinians could be considered a legitimate way of satisfying their rights. In principle, Palestinian violence would satisfy the condition of right intent so long as it was directed at righting the wrong of Israeli occupation. It would also be proportionate, unless the Palestinians unleashed genocide, ethnic cleansing or weapons of mass destruction. Finally, it seems relatively clear that although Palestinian politics is deeply divided, armed organizations struggling to free the occupied territories from Israeli rule broadly satisfy the three 'legitimate authority' rules identified earlier.

However, we cannot divorce these considerations from the fact that the armed Palestinian struggle has been characterized by widespread and systematic violence against non-combatants. In recent years, the number of Israeli non-combatant deaths has greatly exceeded the number of combatant deaths. That said, we also cannot ignore the fact that in their early years both Hamas and Fatah directed their violence against Israeli security personnel. Nor can we overlook the fact that both organizations have non-military wings and provide social services. Taking all of this, and the *jus ad bellum* case, into account, it seems that these organizations have not crossed two of the three criteria. They have not persistently refused to engage Israeli forces, and although each terrorist attack is immoral, their cumulative evil is not self-evidently greater than the evil that they are trying to undo. However, both Hamas and Fatah have committed 'widespread and systematic' acts of terrorism, so their military wings at least deserve the title of terrorist. Thus, although the organizations have undoubtedly discredited themselves, they have not yet discredited the wider *jus ad bellum* case because it is not clear that they have acted disproportionately. They are, however, both perilously close to doing so, and many plausibly argue that they have already done so. Should they undermine the post-Arafat peace process through bomb attacks on non-combatants, for instance, the case for arguing that they had crossed the final threshold would be quite strong.

The Israel/Palestine case therefore provides an excellent example of grey-area terrorism. In these cases, definitive judgements are almost impossible and judgements about whether particular groups have crossed the threshold from *acts of terrorism* to becoming *terrorist organizations* are marginal. In both cases, there are elements of the armed struggle that are justifiable and others that are less so. The critical question is: what impact do the unjustifiable elements have on the justifiable ones? In the case of Jewish terrorism, whilst the idea of an Israeli state may be legitimate, there are doubts about its legitimacy as a Jewish rather than secular state and about the legitimacy of its borders. In the case of Palestinian terrorism, whilst there are fewer doubts about the *prima facie jus ad bellum* case, suicide attacks against non-combatants cannot continue indefinitely without at some point undermining that case, if they have not already done so.

Partial Terrorism: The African National Congress

The African National Congress (ANC) provides a seminal case of *partial terrorism*. Although the ANC committed individual acts of terrorism, it did not cross either of the three thresholds ('widespread and systematic', 'persistent refusal to attack military targets', 'proportionality'). Furthermore, the ANC's terrorist attacks formed only a small part of its wider campaign of violence against the apartheid regime in South Africa. In turn, the campaign of violence was only a small and mainly symbolic part of the overall struggle against apartheid. Arguably the most critical elements of the struggle were the non-violent ones, particularly the withdrawal of black labour and efforts to make South Africa 'ungovernable' during the 1980s (Zunes 1999). Although we cannot excuse the individual acts of terrorism, those acts undermined neither the legitimacy of the struggle against apartheid nor the ANC's position within that struggle.

South Africa's apartheid system was based on the idea that the country's racial groups should develop separately. The whites, who comprise about one-quarter of the population, occupied 87 per cent of the land, condemning many blacks to life either in shanty towns on the edges of cities or in the so-called 'bantustans' in the country. Among other things, apartheid involved a system of racially organized economic exploitation. The South African economy, and white wealth, was based on cheap black labourers, many of whom came from the southern Africa region. The system was maintained by a policy of strict segregation that placed limits on where blacks could live and work. They could not travel without the authorities' permission. Black workers were forced to live in dormitories, separated from their families. Political dissent was harshly repressed. Arbitrary arrests were commonplace, as were torture and killings (Marx, A. W. 1992: 4–7).

From the outset, the ANC's political aim, set out in the 1955 'Freedom Charter', was the restoration of equal rights to blacks. It argued that blacks, like whites, should have the right to vote, own and trade land, own businesses and travel freely. They should have access to a similar standard of social welfare as whites, adequate schools and hospital facilities. Finally, the ANC argued that everyone should have the right not to be arbitrarily arrested, beaten or killed by government authorities. It wanted to establish a liberal democracy, not simply replace white domination with black domination. In its 1949 programme, the ANC declared that it would accomplish these goals through non-violent means (Kuper 1958: 43).

Although key figures in the ANC never lost their ideological commitment to non-violence, the strategy became harder to maintain in the face of state violence. Non-violent protest became perilous because strikes were forbidden and freedom of speech was highly restricted. The turning point came in March 1960 when the police massacred sixty-nine peaceful protesters in Sharpeville. Black leaders were interned and imprisoned, and the ANC itself was banned. According to Nelson Mandela, non-violent protest had placed blacks in harm's way without delivering tangible progress. Some in the ANC, Mandela tells us, continued to argue the case for non-violence on ethical grounds. Others, however, 'said that we should approach this issue not from the point of view of principles, but of tactics, and that we should employ the method demanded by the conditions. If a particular method or tactic enabled us to defeat the enemy, then it should be used' (Mandela in Whittaker 2003: 240). Mandela initially argued that non-violence was the most appropriate tactic because 'the state was far more powerful than we, and any attempts at violence by us would be devastatingly crushed'. However, as it became clear that even non-violent protest would be crushed, he shifted ground, insisting that 'violence was the only weapon that would destroy apartheid' (in Whittaker 2003: 241).

After a protracted debate, the ANC leadership agreed to use violence. A splinter organization, *Umkhonto we Sizwe* (Spear of the Nation – MK), was created and Mandela placed at its head. The bulk of MK's operations comprised guerrilla attacks against South African police and military targets. It also launched a bombing campaign against vital infrastructure, such as electricity cables and power stations. In these operations, MK was generally careful to issue warnings and ensure as far as possible that non-combatants were not injured. The ANC even went as far as to declare itself bound by the 1949 Geneva Conventions and 1977 Protocol (Jenkins 2003: 23).

However, throughout the 1970s there were cases of MK operatives bombing the houses of pro-government blacks and other opponents of the ANC (Zunes 1999: 140). The most controversial attacks came in 1986 when MK launched several attacks on non-combatants. Two Durban bars frequented by whites were bombed. The bombers had intended to kill as many people as possible and the bomb was packed with bullets and metal scraps. Three women were killed and over seventy people injured (Jenkins 2003: 27–9). In 1985 MK bombed the South African air force headquarters in Pretoria, killing nineteen non-combatants.

There can be little doubt that the ANC had a sound case in relation to *jus ad bellum*. Its opposition to the South African regime aimed to right the very widely acknowledged wrong of apartheid. The ANC's stated policy was one of equal rights not black overlordship, suggesting that it acted with right intention. A limited and carefully calibrated guerrilla struggle was a proportionate response to apartheid. Finally, the ANC's electoral success after apartheid suggests that it can stake a powerful claim to have met the three criteria for legitimate authority.

The Durban attacks and recurrent attacks against black opponents were acts of terrorism, however. Their perpetrators should be condemned and punished. Moreover, like the King David Hotel bombing, the bombing of the South African air force headquarters raises serious concerns about pro-portionality and due care (were appropriate measures taken to minimize non-combatant casualties?). These attacks do not, however, come close to satisfying any of the three thresholds for judging when *acts of terrorism* earn an organization the label *terrorist*, let alone the proportionality thresh-old needed to undermine the initially just cause. There are at least three good reasons for this. First, attacks on non-combatants were sporadic, not widespread, suggesting that they were not systematic. Second, with the exception of the Pretoria bombing, there is little evidence that these attacks were ordered by the ANC leadership. Moreover, there is evidence that MK training specifically focused on the destruction of property key to the regime, not the killing of non-combatants. Third, the terrorist attacks described here constituted a small part of a much wider guerrilla struggle against the South African armed forces that was waged throughout much of southern Africa.

The final consideration in the ANC case is that it has done more than any of the other state or non-state actors discussed in this chapter to disclose its activities. The ANC submitted itself to South Africa's post-apartheid Truth and Reconciliation Commission. Though it did not always support the Commission's findings, particularly when it was criticized, the ANC's disclosure before the Commission signalled an attempt to distance itself from some of the worst acts of terrorism committed in its name (Boraine 2000: 300–39).

Conclusion

This chapter has explored the question of whether terrorism is ever justifi-able. Because the answer to that question depends very much on what is meant by 'terrorism', it began by offering and defending a moral definition of terrorism as the intentional targeting of non-combatants for political purposes. Considering, and rejecting, four potential justifications for killing non-combatants, I argued that terrorism is never justifiable. Its perpetrators should always be condemned and punished by the appropriate authorities. However, if we are to apply this idea consistently, there is a need to distinguish between *acts of terrorism* and *terrorist organizations*. Failure to distinguish between the two forces us either to withdraw from moral consistency or to make counter-intuitive moral judgements. In particular, it would make many of us hypocrites for welcoming political ends brought about by immoral means (victory over Japan in the Second World War, for instance). I have suggested that there are three levels of moral culpability for terrorism: *partial*, *grey area* and *clear-cut*.

This approach provides a framework for interrogating the morality of the different types of violence often labelled 'terrorist' by reference to the Just War tradition. It insists that actors are always required to put forward a plausible *jus ad bellum* justification. If the actor fails to do so, every act of violence that it unleashes is immoral. Once violence is engaged, it is important to place limits on its conduct. At the heart of those limits are the twin principles of non-combatant immunity and proportionality. What is suggested here is that there is not only a point where the breaching of those principles delegitimizes the organization responsible, but also a point at which violating them on a large scale undermines the legitimacy of the wider struggle. In short, there are important limits on what may be done for any political cause without undermining the cause itself.

8

Pre-emption

The right of self-defence has been described as a 'fundamental principle' of international law and is also the bedrock of the natural law tradition's just causes for war (Schwarzenberger 1955). Traditionally, scholars have admitted that the right comprises permission to respond with force to both actual and imminent attacks (e.g. Arend and Beck 1993: 72; Kegley and Raymond 2003). However, the ambiguous place of pre-emptive self-defence in Article 51 of the UN Charter gave rise to a debate between restrictionists, who called for a literal interpretation (ruling out pre-emption), and counter-restrictionists, who argued that the UN Charter did not replace the customary right of pre-emption. Since the September 11 attacks on New York and Washington, these debates have become more pointed. Many scholars and policy-makers insisted that the ability of terrorists and 'rogue states' to inflict mass casualties at short notice required a less restrictive way of thinking about self-defence. The so-called 'Bush doctrine', promulgated in 2002, claimed a right for the US to act pre-emptively against terrorists, states harbouring terrorists and other 'rogue' regimes (NSS 2002).

This chapter accepts the view that self-defence needs to be rethought to take account of the fact that massive threats may emerge more rapidly and quietly than anticipated by the UN Charter's drafters. It aims to develop a new way of thinking about pre-emption that addresses the threat of terrorism. At the outset, it is important to recognize that I am only discussing pre-emption in relation to terrorism, defined in Chapter 7 as the deliberate targeting of non-combatants for political purposes. As understood here, a terrorist threat may emerge from either a non-state terrorist organization or a state ('rogue' or otherwise), so theoretically the expanded right to pre-emption could be used to justify attacks on states. The first section outlines the traditional view of self-defence in both natural law and positive international law. It shows that both permit a limited right of pre-emption where such acts are justified by necessity, the temporal imminence of the threat and proportionality. The second section details recent American attempts to redesign the right of self-defence. It identifies three broad schools of thought ('new liberals', 'new realists' and the exceptionalist view signalled by the 2002 *National Security Strategy* – hereafter labelled *Strategy*). The first two approaches, I argue, are flawed in important respects – not least because they eschew the traditional concepts of imminence, necessity and proportionality. The third approach points towards a way of rethinking pre-emption without rejecting the traditional concept. Developing this, I articulate an approach that permits the pre-emptive use of force against terrorists and those who harbour them whilst guarding against the perils of an overly permissive regime. The final part of chapter will apply this approach to three post-September 11 cases: Operation *Enduring Freedom* in Afghanistan, the 2002 missile attack in Yemen and the 2003 invasion of Iraq.

Self-Defence in the Just War Tradition

All the various elements of the Just War tradition recognized self-defence as a just cause for war. For many writers, sovereigns had not only a right but a *duty* to defend their communities (e.g. Vattel 1916: 246; Wolff 1934: 804). This obligation derived from the sovereign's responsibility to protect his or her subjects. On the whole, writers tended to permit a limited right of pre-emption in the face of an imminent threat but expressly rejected preventive war, viewing it as tantamount to aggression. Grotius listed as the first 'just cause' of war 'an injury not yet done which menaces body or goods'. In cases where 'an attack by violence is made on one's person, endangering life, and no other way of escape is open, under such circumstances war is permissible, even though it involve the slaying of the assailant' (Grotius 1925: 172). This right, however, was limited to cases where the threat was 'immediate and imminent' (Grotius 1925: 173). Lest there be any doubt, Grotius (1925: 549) went on specifically to identify preventive war (war born of fear of future threat) as an unjust cause of war. He argued that unjust parties to a conflict had no right to self-defence, though his conception of justice in war meant that sovereigns almost always had a degree of justice on their side affording them a legal right of self-defence at least (see Chapter 4).

Samuel Pufendorf (1994: 264) agreed that a man may kill an aggressor once 'the aggressor, showing clearly his desire to take my life, and equipped with the capacity and the weapons for his purpose, . . . has gotten into the position where he can in fact hurt me'. Like Grotius, though, Pufendorf also sought to limit the right, insisting that force could be used only in the absence of viable alternatives (such as escape) (see Sofaer 2000: 216, n. 25). Vattel (1916: 248–50) was a little more permissive than the others, arguing that sovereigns might act even when they were not absolutely certain about the imminent danger. However, he insisted that if there were reasonable doubts, states should take care to avoid becoming an aggressor and must have good grounds for believing themselves threatened (Vattel 1916: 130).

This view found its way into positive international law. In the 1928 Kellogg–Briand Pact, states reserved the right to use force in self-defence, including pre-emption. Pre-emption was apparently forbidden, however, in Article 51 of the UN Charter, which declared that 'nothing in the present Charter shall impair the inherent right of individual or collective self-defence if an armed attack occurs'. It is worth noting that in the French version of this article, the phrase 'inherent right' is rendered *'droit naturel'* (natural right), a clear indication of the close links between positive law and natural law (Dinstein 1988: 169). Since 1945, interpretations of Article 51 have tended to fall into one of two camps, restrictionists and counter-restrictionists, separated by two issues in particular: the nature of an 'armed attack' and the question of pre-emption.

Restrictionists argue for a narrow interpretation on both counts (e.g. Combacu 1986; Delbrück 2002). They claim that an 'armed attack' refers only to large-scale invasion. This view was supported by the ICJ in its judgment in the *Nicaragua v. United States* case (1986). Whilst finding that the sending of armed bands into another state may constitute an armed attack, the Court insisted that it was 'necessary to distinguish the most grave forms of the use of force (those constituting an armed attack) from other less grave forms' (ICJ 1986: 103). Restrictionists therefore insist that cases of sabotage or state-sponsored terrorism do not give the victim state a right to use force in self-defence against the host state (e.g. Brownlie 1963: 275–80).

Restrictionists also insist that Article 51 expressly rules out pre-emption, arguing that states have a right to use force in self-defence only *after* an armed attack has occurred, a view supported by the ICJ in the *Nicaragua v. United States* case (Kelsen 1948: 792). They argue that if these limits were loosened, states would be encouraged to abuse the right to self-defence, eroding the distinction between aggression and defence (Cassese 1986: 515–16). Although there is evidence that the Charter's drafters intended Article 51 to provide only a limited right of self-defence, the idea that a state should wait to be attacked before taking measures to defend its citizens has been widely criticized. Sir Humphrey Waldock described it as 'a travesty of the purposes of the Charter' (in Roberts, G. 1999: 483), whilst Myers McDougal (1963: 599) insisted that there was no evidence in the Charter's *travaux préparatoires* that the drafters intended to place new limits on states' pre-Charter right to self-defence. As a result, counter-restrictionists insist that Article 51 did not override the customary rights that states enjoyed prior to the Charter.

On the first issue, counter-restrictionists insist that if the phrase 'armed attack' means what it says, it must mean all 'armed attacks' regardless of scale (Kunz 1947: 878). They disagreed with the ICJ's view on the matter in 1986, and international reactions to the US intervention in Afghanistan (see below) seem to support the claim that the law may have changed in relation to this question. For counter-restrictionists, state support for terrorism constitutes an armed attack so long as the level of violence is sufficiently grave (Cassim et al. 1975: 607–8). Counter-restrictionists also argue that Article 51 does not diminish a state's inherent right to pre-emptive self-defence. There are at least two justifications for this view. First, it is implied in the Charter's language. Article 51 explicitly endorses a state's *inherent* or *natural* right to self-defence. That inherent right clearly includes a right of pre-emption. Moreover, if Article 51 is read as permitting the use of force against breaches of Article 2(4), then this also permits pre-emption because Article 2(4) prohibits both the 'threat' and the 'use' of force (Bowett 1958: 191–2).

The second justification for a broader reading of Article 51 is customary practice. Since 1945, states have tended to judge pre-emption on the merits of each case (Arend 2003; Franck 2002). When the threat is demonstrably imminent, international society has shown itself willing to tolerate pre-emption. The paradigmatic case of this was the world's reaction to Israel's 1967 pre-emptive attack on Egypt. Although some states condemned Israel, many others accepted that an invasion was imminent and chose not to do so (Gray 2000: 112–13). In other cases, however, states criticized as precipitate the use of force for ostensibly pre-emptive purposes. For example, the 1981 Israeli air strike on the Osirak nuclear reactor in Iraq was 'strongly condemned' by the UN Security Council (Res. 487), though several counter-restrictionist lawyers supported Israel's case (e.g. D'Amato 1996: 262–3; McCormack 1996: 297–302). States found that the reactor did not pose an imminent threat and that Israel had used force as a first not last resort (Yoo 2004: 765). This demonstrates that states and scholars are prepared to make judgements about the legitimacy of pre-emption on a case-by-case basis, lending support to the counter-restrictionist claim that there is a theoretical right of pre-emption.

It seems clear from this that – restrictionist concerns notwithstanding – the right of self-defence permits pre-emption in some cases but forbids 'preventive' attacks. The questions now are: (1) in what situations is pre-emption justifiable? And (2) where do we draw the line between pre-emption and prevention? We can begin to answer these questions by considering the exchange of diplomatic notes between the UK and US concerning the sinking of the *Caroline* in 1837. Although relatively insignificant as a case in its own right, the *Caroline* case is important as a basis for understanding when the right of pre-emption can be invoked, for at least two reasons. First, the fact that the wording of the right to pre-emption in US Secretary of State Daniel Webster's communication with the British was accepted without question by both sides and has not been challenged by states since suggests that it is an accurate reflection of the consensus on this matter (see

Alexandrov 1996: 20). Second, Webster's formula is often cited in legal cases. For example, it was cited in the Nuremberg trials to reject German claims that the invasion of Norway was legitimate self-defence (Dinstein 1988: 228).

In 1837, the UK and US were in a state of peace but there was an armed insurrection against British rule in Canada. The rebels began using an American-owned ship, the *Caroline*, to transport supplies from the American side of the Niagara River. On 29 December 1837, Canadian troops loyal to Britain boarded the ship, killed several Americans, set the ship alight and allowed it to drift over the Niagara Falls. At the time of the attack the *Caroline* was docked on the American side of the border, not in its usual port on the Canadian side. The US protested against the attack, claiming that it violated its sovereignty, but the British insisted that they were exercising their right to self-defence.

The debate began with a note from US Secretary of State John Forsyth to the British Minister in Washington on 5 January 1838. Forsyth demanded a full explanation and labelled the attack an 'extraordinary outrage'. The British Minister responded by blaming the Americans for failing to prevent the use of its territory by the Canadian rebels and justified the attack as 'a necessity of self-defence and self-preservation' (Stevens 2004: 24–5). Not surprisingly, the US rejected this argument, disputing Britain's claim to a right of 'hot pursuit', arguing that the level of threat that could justify 'hot pursuit' must be 'imminent, and extreme, and involving impending destruction' (Stevens 2004: 35).

The debate was revived in late 1840 when a former British soldier was arrested in New York and charged with arson and murder in relation to the *Caroline*. The US government invited the British government to apologize for the incident and pay compensation in return for the dismissal of charges against the soldier. The British Minister agreed immediately and despatched an apologetic note to the US government. In a 1842 reply to the British, the American Secretary of State, Daniel Webster, explained that for the claim of self-defence to be justifiable, Britain was required to 'show a necessity of self-defence, instant, overwhelming, leaving no choice of means, and no moment for deliberation'. The action taken must also involve 'nothing unreasonable or excessive; since the act, justified by the necessity of self-defence, must be limited by that necessity and kept clearly within it' (letter from Mr Webster to Mr Fox [24 April 1841], British and Foreign State Papers 1129, 1138). In order to invoke a right of pre-emption, therefore, a state has to demonstrate the imminence of an attack, the necessity of pre-emption and the proportionality of its intended response.

In the light of Article 51, state practice since 1945 and the ICJ's position, the three cornerstones of Webster's doctrine – imminence, necessity and proportionality – at best constitute a limited right of pre-emption (see Detter 2000: 86). There are therefore good grounds for arguing that contemporary positive international law permits a limited right of pre-emption that extends beyond Article 51 but is nevertheless limited by customary international law owing to the *Caroline* case and state practice since.

Between them, natural law and positive international law appear to grant states a limited right of pre-emption in cases that satisfy the usual *jus ad bellum* criteria plus the criteria of imminence and necessity. Jurists worry, with good reason, that expanding the right beyond the *Caroline* formula would increase the likelihood of abuse and make it harder for observers to evaluate the legitimacy of a state's claims. The problem comes in defining what 'imminence' means in relation to terrorism. As George W. Bush (2002b) put it, 'we cannot wait for the final proof – the smoking gun – that could come in the form of a mushroom cloud'. It is for this reason that three revisionist schools of thought have come to the fore calling for a change to the way that pre-emption is conceived. The following section evaluates these claims.

Revisionist Arguments

The idea that self-defence needs rethinking in the wake of September 11 is widely accepted (e.g. Buchanan and Keohane 2004; Gow 2005). In light of what we now know about terrorism's destructive potential, there are at least four good reasons for rethinking pre-emption. It is important to stress that these four reasons provide a case for rethinking pre-emption in relation to *terrorism*: that is, the threat of direct attacks against non-combatants in countries other than those that host the terrorists (see Chapter 7). These reasons do not constitute a case for rethinking pre-emption in relation to traditional threats posed by national militaries.

First, there is a sound prudential argument that prevention is better than cure. In hindsight, Clinton's decision not to take firmer action against Osama bin Laden between 1996 and 1998 was a bad misjudgement (see Clarke, R. A. 2004: 101–204). By this logic, the norm of pre-emption must be refashioned to place fewer costs on political leaders who wish to take earlier action against would-be terrorists. Second, whereas conventional wars are preceded by clear warnings, most obviously troop deployments, such clear indicators do not usually precede mass-casualty terrorist attacks (Daalder 2002). It is virtually impossible for a liberal democracy to guard against terrorism at all times and in all places. There is widespread agreement, therefore, that the best way to reduce the threat of terrorism is to adopt a proactive strategy (see Betts 2002: 33; David 2003: 119). Third, the potential for mass-casualty terrorism renders a reactive strategy imprudent at best and potentially immoral. Finally, although deterrence still has an important role to play in world politics – particularly in relation to so-called 'rogue states' – its ability to constrain the type of terrorism witnessed on September 11 in the short term is limited (see Freedman 2004: 121–3).

The challenge to rethink the concept of pre-emption has been taken up by at least three groups. The first are 'new liberals'. 'New liberals' argue that the world can be refashioned through law (and force) into a stable and orderly society that guarantees the rights of individuals. They insist that liberal states are more likely to resolve their disputes peacefully through legal mechanisms than are non-liberal ones (Slaughter 1995: 503). As such, they are committed to spreading democracy, protecting democracies threatened by anti-democratic forces, and creating robust forms of international law enforcement. Some, such as Fernando Tesón (1998: 62–3), insist that liberal states may use war against illiberal states as a means of realizing this ambition, whilst others argue that the process of liberalization should be slower and predominantly non-violent (e.g. Slaughter 1995: 240). Such debates aside, 'new liberals' agree that international law should be changed to make the world safer for liberal democracies.

The starting point for the 'new liberal' call to reform pre-emption is a recognition that international law is a vital tool for regulating behaviour but that it must be refashioned (Slaughter 2003a: 37–44). Feinstein and Slaughter (2004) therefore suggest a new principle to guide law: 'the duty to prevent'. This, they argue, is warranted by the fact that 'we live in a world of old rules and new threats' (Feinstein and Slaughter 2004: 138). Although the Security Council is the most appropriate forum for dealing with these new threats, the burden of proof needs to be shifted from democracies that fear that they might be attacked to nations suspected of weapons of mass destruction (WMD) proliferation and collusion with terrorists. Against such threats, waiting for traditionally understood pre-emption 'is usually impractical because suspected facilities are often difficult to spot or hit' (Feinstein and Slaughter 2004: 147). Feinstein and Slaughter (2004: 148–9) continue, 'this is not to suggest that the use of [pre-emptive] force should be discounted as ineffective but that the most effective action is preventive', namely action taken before the perceived threat materializes. Preventive action may involve the use of force, which may be conducted unilaterally so long as the intervener attempts multilateral avenues first.

There are a number of problems with this proposal. First, it conflates the threat of terrorism with that of WMD proliferation by states. Whilst there are good grounds for rethinking pre-emption in response to terrorism, there is little evidence to suggest that by itself WMD proliferation by states poses a new type of threat. WMD-armed states have refrained from supplying terrorists to date, principally because they fear escalation from potential victims (Byman 2005: 303). Of course, the 'nightmare scenario' involves a rogue state passing WMDs on to non-state terrorists. Although this is a possibility, and one that must potentially trigger any right of pre-emption, it is inaccurate to argue that WMD proliferation by 'rogue states' constitutes a *prima facie* terrorism threat because it has not done so in the past and there is no evidence that it will do so in the future. Second, the right of prevention it seeks to create would blur the distinction between aggression and defence. Third, if a 'threat' is to be used as a justification for war, it must be demonstrable (see Chapter 6). Preventive wars are launched before a threat has fully emerged and it is therefore not demonstrable. Fourth, a doctrine of prevention can lead to empire when potential future threats are removed and the obligations of governance fall on those who have effected 'regime change' (see Snyder 2003: 31–5). Finally, given the widespread consensus that preventive war is both immoral and illegal, recourse to prevention absent a global consensus risks undermining the *rule of law*, which the 'new liberals' insist is imperative in the struggle against tyranny.

By contrast, 'new realists' insist that international law on self-defence is simply irrelevant and that states, particularly the US, should be guided by their own interests in deciding whether or not to use pre-emptive or preventive force. According to two Republican hawks, the US should not bind itself to either positive or natural law by restricting its pre-emptive activities to cases of demonstrable imminent threat. Instead, 'where intelligence is uncertain, prudent leaders will inevitably minimize risks by erring on the side of the worst plausible assumption. And rightly so' (Frum and Perle 2003: 27). This assertion of America's right to decide for itself when and where it will act pre-emptively is based on a three-pronged critique of the rules governing self-defence.

The first is a denunciation of Article 51. 'New realists' argue that Article 51 is redundant because it does not permit the use of force against those who aid and abet terrorists; it rules out forcible 'regime change' when governments provide safe havens for terrorists; and it does not permit pre-emptive or preventive self-defence (Glennon 2002: 541–9). The second is a rejection of the Security Council's ability to protect states from attack. 'New realists' point to the Security Council's 'paralysis' during the Cold War and its 'failure' to sanction military force in Kosovo (1999) and Iraq (2003) as proof of its inability to protect international peace and security (Glennon 2003; Yoo 2004: 742). The third line of argument insists that the UN Charter's rules regulating the use of force have been broken so many times that they are no longer law. As Glennon (2002: 540) put it, 'between 1945 and 1999, two-thirds of the members of the United Nations – 126 out of 189 – fought 291 interstate conflicts in which over 22 million people were killed'. The 'upshot' of all this, Glennon (2002: 540) concludes, is that the Charter regime governing the use of force has 'all but collapsed' and that the Just War alternatives are little more than 'archaic notions of universal truth' (Glennon 2003: 19). Thus, the US should make its own decisions about how best to defend itself.

'New realism' is problematic, for a number of reasons. First, the claim that the UN Charter's rules on the use of force are defunct is not credible.

Rule-breaking has the effect of altering the law only if the rule-breakers justify their actions by articulating a new principle and other states validate that justification. In the cases of NATO's intervention in Kosovo and the US-led invasion of Iraq, states did not consistently claim a new right and there is certainly no indication that other states recognized a change in the law (see Byers 2003a). Second, Glennon's claim that the Security Council is irrelevant and ineffectual is not supported by the Iraq case, where the Council was the hub of global debate about using force (see Slaughter 2003b: 204). Third, 'new realism' fails the consistency test without offering good grounds for exceptionalism as it is highly unlikely that any US government would tolerate others having the freedom of manoeuvre that the 'new realists' claim for the US. Finally, 'new realists' mistakenly equate US interests with the universal good (e.g. Rice 2000: 49).

In its 2002 *Strategy*, the US government offered a third way of rethinking pre-emption which does not try to rewrite the rules. According to Donald Rumsfeld (2001a), 'the problem with terrorism is that there is no way to defend against the terrorists at every place and every time against every conceivable technique. Therefore, the only way to deal with the terrorist network is to take the battle to them.' The *Strategy* insisted that,

given the goals of rogue states and terrorists, the United States can no longer solely rely on a reactive posture as we have in the past. The inability to deter a potential attacker, the immediacy of today's threat, and the magnitude of potential harm that could be caused by our adversaries' choice of weapons, do not permit that option. We cannot let our enemies strike first. (NSS 2002: 15)

The *Strategy* held that 'imminence' should permit action 'even if uncertainty remains as to the time and place of the enemy's attack' (NSS 2002: 15). The US, it argued, could not wait until a terrorist threat was 'fully-formed' before acting. For some, this represented an attempt to change the law, along 'new liberal' lines (see Byers 2003b); for others, an attempt to claim an exceptional right of preventive war (e.g. Wheeler, N.J. 2003: 191). However, in the *Strategy*, at least, the American argument was not that 'imminence' should be abandoned or rethought, or that fear alone was enough to constitute just cause for war, but that its meaning in the face of a terrorist threat was quite different to its meaning in relation to traditional threats from states. Being smaller in scale, covert in nature and requiring less planning and logistics than traditional threats, a terrorist threat could be imminent even if the time and place of the attack remained unclear. In other words, the *Strategy* replaces a strictly temporal understanding of imminence with a view, widely accepted by international lawyers, that imminence should be understood qualitatively as requiring 'that it is believed that any further delay in countering the intended attack will result in the inability of the defending state to effectively defend itself against the attack'

(Wilmhurst 2005: 9). Unlike the 'new liberals' and 'new realists', therefore, the *Strategy* advocated neither a radical reformulation of the law nor rule-breaking behaviour. Instead, it situated the new doctrine firmly within customary international law and argued for a revised interpretation of the imminence requirement.

The *Strategy* has been widely criticized for stretching the concept of 'armed attack' and for being deliberately misleading in labelling what is in essence a strategy of *prevention* as pre-emption (Johnstone, I. 2004: 832). The problem, though, is not so much with the *Strategy* but with the Bush administration's rhetoric and actions. Indeed, a few states, including Russia and India, responded favourably to the *Strategy* (Byers 2004: 541). There is, however, an important disjuncture between the *Strategy* and US rhetoric (see Brown 2003a). Recall that that the *Strategy* permits doubt only about the time and place of the attack; the enemy target must still be shown to have both the *intent* and the *means* to attack. However, in a speech to the German parliament in May 2002, Bush stated that the US was prepared to use force against 'rogues' *before* they acquired the means of terrorism and irrespective of whether or not they had displayed a specific intent to attack (in Halper and Clarke 2004: 140). A month later, he told a West Point graduation ceremony that 'we must take the battle to the enemy and confront the worst threats *before they emerge*' (Bush 2002a, my emphasis). Thus, in its public statements, the US administration has implied that it claims an exclusive right of preventive war, not the more limited right of expanded pre-emption claimed in the *Strategy*. According to the rhetoric, a potential target need possess neither an intention nor the means of attacking the US and its allies.

The Bush administration's efforts partly to justify the 2003 invasion of Iraq as an act of pre-emption add weight to the argument that the US has actually adopted a strategy of prevention, mislabelled as pre-emption. The administration itself was clearly divided on the issue. When asked whether Iraq was an example of the *Strategy* in practice, Secretary of State Colin Powell emphatically replied 'no, no, no' (Weisman 2003). Instead, he argued that the war was an act of enforcement in accordance with past UN Security Council resolutions. However, Vice-President Dick Cheney consistently justified the war in terms of the need to *prevent* Iraq acquiring WMD, and since the war Bush himself has fallen back on the argument that 'America is safer' as a consequence (in Daalder and Lindsay 2003: 127).

How, then, should pre-emption be reconceptualized to meet the threat of terrorism? There are two important caveats to begin with. First, states that act pre-emptively must satisfy all the *jus ad bellum* criteria. What is offered here is a framework for assessing whether claims to pre-emptive force might sometimes count as a 'just cause'. If the other criteria are not satisfied, especially proportionality of ends, the resort to force cannot be legitimate. Second, the expanded concept of pre-emption offered here applies only to the threat of terrorism as defined in Chapter 7. If the nature of the threat is non-terrorist, the *Caroline* criteria continue to apply.

The central concepts of pre-emption are imminence, necessity and proportionality. According to the *Strategy*, it is only imminence that needs reinterpreting. Traditionally, both positive law and natural law have defined 'imminence' in temporal terms. A threat is imminent only immediately before the hammer is about to fall: when the enemy has displayed an intention to attack, has armed itself, has deployed its forces into an offensive formation and is about to strike. The problem, of course, is that if the planned attack is a mass-casualty terrorist attack, it is usually too late to respond at this point. We cannot overlook the fact that the existence of such a tight definition of imminence, derived from the *Caroline* case, may be due, at least in part, to the fact that the two parties to that dispute were states with relatively good relations (Sofaer 2003: 219). In cases where mutual mistrust is higher, and doubt and mistrust are seldom higher than when confronting terrorism, a wider concept of imminence ought to be conceded to provide states with realistic means of preventing attacks.

The need for a more flexible concept of imminence has been recognized by the ICJ, which ruled in 1997 that

'[i]mminence' is synonymous with 'immediacy' or 'proximity' and goes far beyond the concept of 'possibility' . . . the 'extremely grave and imminent peril' must 'have been a threat to the interest at the time'. That does not exclude, in the view of the Court, that a 'peril' appearing in the long term might be held to be 'imminent' as soon as it is established, at the relevant point in time, that the realization of that peril, however far off it might be, is not thereby any less certain and inevitable. (In Yoo 2004: 752)

Thus, the ICJ recognized that an imminent threat could be temporally distant yet nevertheless imminent depending on the likelihood of realization and the gravity of the peril. In situations where a state can demonstrate that an actor has the intention and means to launch terrorist attacks against it or its allies, it is reasonable to suggest that the 'imminence' test is satisfied even if it is unsure of the precise time and target of the anticipated attack. However, it is important to insist that this slight reinterpretation of imminence be carefully limited, because imminence remains pivotal to any justification of self-defence itself (Rodin forthcoming). The *demonstrability* of the intent and means is critical. It is not enough for a government to convince itself of the threat. It must present reliable and accurate evidence both to its own citizens and to other states and global civil society (see Roberts, B. 1998: 103–4). Judges and juries (see Chapter 6) will evaluate the evidence to decide whether, on a case-by-case basis, the pre-emptive attack was legitimate by reference to the demonstrable gravity of the threat, the known intentions of the potential terrorists and their ability to satisfy those intentions. The more actors that validate the action, the more legitimate it can be considered. In some cases it is not always appropriate for a state to reveal what it knows *before* it launches a pre-emptive attack, because doing so risks informing the terrorists of what it knows and losing the opportunity to strike them, but the burden of proof falls squarely on those that use pre-emptive force to demonstrate their case either before or immediately afterwards (Charney 2001: 835).

The second criterion is necessity. According to Webster, necessity required that the threat be 'instant, overwhelming, leaving no choice of means, and no moment for deliberation'. State practice itself has recognized that this sets the bar too high. Neither Israel's 1967 attack on Egypt nor the 2001 invasion of Afghanistan by the US and its allies would satisfy these criteria. Writing in 1961, McDougal and Feliciano (1961: 231) offered a more appropriate understanding of necessity. For them, the necessity criterion is satisfied when the degree of imminence is 'so high as to preclude effective resort by the intended victim to non-violent modalities of response'. Pre-emption is warranted when the use of force is the only reasonable way in which the threat can be averted. It does not require that all other means be exhausted first, but we are entitled to ask whether those that use pre-emptive force had reasonable alternatives. At the very least, we would expect a government using pre-emptive force in this way to be able to demonstrate that it seriously considered other, non-violent, options and to explain its reasons for not choosing these other courses of action.

This leaves the thorny question of whether it is only the intended victim who enjoys a right to act pre-emptively. I suggested that it was not necessary to know with certainty either the target or time of the intended terrorist attack. This approach permits states that are not the intended target to use force pre-emptively if the twin conditions of imminence and necessity, as well as the other *jus ad bellum* conditions, are satisfied. This can be justified on three grounds. First, such acts could be interpreted as collective self-defence. Second, given my definition (see Chapter 7), terrorism can be viewed as a universal crime with a global jurisdiction. As such, states have a legal right to apprehend terrorists globally. Finally, mass-casualty terrorism represents such an affront to natural law that it grants states a moral right to use force to prevent it everywhere.

Although this expanded concept of pre-emption helps to meet the strategic challenge posed by terrorism, it creates three potential problems that positive law attempted to overcome by setting such a high threshold. The first is the problem of abuse. Making pre-emption more flexible blurs important moral and legal distinctions and creates avenues for political leaders to justify aggressive wars in terms of pre-emption. The principal barrier to abuse is accountability. In the schema offered here, governments are obliged to demonstrate their case to their own citizens, other states and global civil society, making it very difficult for them to abuse pre-emption justifications.

The second problem is that by adding further ambiguity to the right of pre-emption, this revised doctrine places greater emphasis on the factual elements of each case. Assessments of factual evidence are never free of values and politics, giving the powerful an opportunity to sway others by bringing financial, military and political pressure to bear. As Byers argues (2003a: 182), this means that 'it is more likely that the criterion of imminence would be regarded satisfied when the United States wished to act militarily than when others wished to do the same'. It is certainly the case that weak states and those out of favour in the West would have a much more difficult time persuading the most powerful members of international society of their cause than the US and its allies. That is not to say that the US' claims will always be generally accepted, as the Iraq case demonstrates. Moreover, the fact that the powerful have much more room for manoeuvre than the weak pervades the application of normative constraints on war. Perceived rule-breaking always imposes costs, but the powerful are better able to bear those costs than the weak, at least in the short term.

The third problem is that a more permissive doctrine of self-defence may increase the potential for error (see Crawford 2003: 35). States may be encouraged to use force precipitately, based on flawed intelligence or misperceptions of threat. There are no sure ways of eliminating this problem. It stands to reason that the earlier a state acts, the more likely the chances for error and misperception, and vice versa: a state that waits longer will be more certain of its case but risks waiting too long. The problem can be moderated but not resolved by the due care requirement: a government must demonstrate that it has taken every reasonable step to verify its evidence. If it fails to do so, it acts unjustly.

It is therefore important to limit this expanded right of pre-emption in several ways. The expanded right of pre-emption still poses three tests: imminence, necessity and proportionality. To satisfy the first test, those invoking the expanded right must demonstrate that a group or state has both the intention and the means to conduct terrorist attacks. However, unlike under the traditional concept, under the expanded concept it is not necessary to know with certainty when or where the terrorists will strike. To satisfy the second, it must demonstrate that the use of force is necessary. To satisfy the third, the military response must be proportionate to the evil being prevented. The final section will consider how this framework works in practice by applying it to three recent cases, all of which have been justified – among other things – as pre-emptive self-defence: Operation *Enduring Freedom* in Afghanistan, the 2002 missile attack on Al-Qaeda suspects in Yemen, and the 2003 invasion of Iraq.

Cases

Afghanistan

The US began planning an attack on Afghanistan in the immediate after-math of the September 11 attacks. British Prime Minister Tony Blair sup-ported the idea of military action against Afghanistan so long as the US published its evidence against Al-Qaeda and gave the Taliban government in Afghanistan an opportunity to hand over Al-Qaeda suspects for trial (Daalder and Lindsay 2003: 102–3). The US accepted both of Blair's sug-gestions and both states published detailed evidence identifying Al-Qaeda's responsibility for the September 11 attacks. Moreover, they demonstrated that September 11 was part of an ongoing campaign of terrorism against the US and its allies. Having presented its case, the US then embarked on two weeks of coercive diplomacy to persuade the Taliban to hand over Al-Qaeda suspects. Only when it became clear that the Taliban would not cooperate did the US and its allies use force, on 7 October 2001. In its explanation to the Security Council, the US insisted that it was exercising its inherent right to self-defence and that it also planned to attack 'military installations of the Taliban regime' (S/2001/946, 7 October).

For much of October 2001, the CIA led military operations in Afghani-stan. US strategy involved Special Forces and air strikes against Al-Qaeda and a simultaneous push by Afghanistan's 'Northern Alliance' against the Taliban. By late October, however, it had become clear that this strategy was not working. The Northern Alliance was not making headway against the Taliban, and although US forces were striking Al-Qaeda targets, most had already been abandoned and little progress was being made on killing or capturing key Al-Qaeda leaders. In early November, therefore, the US changed its strategy. Control was passed to the Pentagon and the US began directly supporting the Northern Alliance by engaging Taliban forces from the air and with Special Forces and a limited number of ground forces. The effects of this shift were rapid and decisive. Mazar-e-Sharif fell to the Northern Alliance on 10 November and Kabul fell a day later.

By publishing detailed evidence of Al-Qaeda's guilt and demonstrating the Taliban's refusal to suppress the terrorists, the US and its allies satisfied the imminence and necessity conditions set out in the *expanded* concept of pre-emption outlined above. Importantly, they did not satisfy the tradi-tional criteria because the US knew neither the time nor the place of Al-Qaeda's next strike and the organization was not involved in an on-going attack on the country. Nevertheless, the US' right to invoke self-defence to justify its use of force in Afghanistan was recognized by a large majority of states (Fitzpatrick 2002). In Resolutions 1368 and 1373, the UN Security Council affirmed the US' 'inherent' right of self-defence; both NATO and the Organization of American States identified September 11 as an 'armed attack' entitling the US to respond with military force; on 7 October itself, the President of the Security Council reaffirmed the Council's support for the US; and many states and organizations usually hostile to the use of US military power chose not to condemn its use in Afghanistan (Johnstone, I. 2004: 828–9).

Despite this, a number of doubts were expressed about whether the war was a legitimate act of self-defence. First, some restrictionists argued that the use of force in self-defence is only legitimate during the attack itself. To accept this argument, however, we must accept an untenably rigid interpretation of Article 51 that is inconsistent with both positive and natural law (see Franck 2001: 839).

Second, and more plausibly, some critics complained that the right of self-defence only extended to Al-Qaeda and that therefore the use of force against the Taliban was illegitimate. Jordan Paust (2001–2: 540), for example, argued that 'unless the state is organizing, fomenting, directing or otherwise directly participating in armed attacks by non-state terrorists, the use of military force against the state, as opposed to only the non-state terrorists, is impermissible'. According to this logic, Operation *Enduring Freedom* was unlawful and immoral because the Taliban had not attacked the US and had shown no intention of doing so. Moreover, the loose relationship between the Taliban and Al-Qaeda was not enough to establish Afghanistan's responsibility for the attacks on the US (Myjer and White 2002: 7). Paust argued that the US should have used judicial means to apprehend Al-Qaeda suspects. He admits that the US had a right to use force against Al-Qaeda and that US forces could have legitimately targeted Taliban forces in self-defence, but insists that the use of force to effect regime change went beyond that permitted by self-defence.

This argument, however, is based on a narrow reading of the law that overlooks contextual factors. Operation *Enduring Freedom* was at least in part an act of pre-emptive self-defence against an enemy who had a clearly expressed intention and the means to launch terrorist attacks against the US and its allies. The US and its allies could not remove the very real threat posed by Al-Qaeda without also removing the Taliban, which had both formally (by refusing to cooperate with the US and its allies) and informally (by actively cooperating with Al-Qaeda on the ground) provided direct assistance to the organization.

A third critical argument suggested that the intervention into Afghanistan was a disproportionate response to the September 11 attacks. Myjer and White (2002: 8) asked whether 'an attack against a small part of the United States' justified 'an armed response against a whole country', whilst others asserted that the intervention looked more like a violent reprisal than an act of self-defence (see Simpson 2004: 334). However, proportionality does not require that the level of force used in self-defence be comparable to the threat. Rather, it insists that the level of force be limited to that which is necessary to remove the threat. Given conditions in Afghanistan and the relationship between the Taliban and Al-Qaeda, it is reasonable to suggest that the threat of future Septembers 11, could only be lessened by regime change. Moreover, both prior to the war and in its early phases, the US gave the Taliban ample opportunity to save itself by assisting in the apprehension of Al-Qaeda terrorists.

In sum, Operation *Enduring Freedom* was a widely supported act of an albeit somewhat broader understanding of self-defence. It shows that when a state is able to demonstrate the imminence of a threat and necessity for action, others are willing to accept a broader right of self-defence even when the time and place of purported further terrorist attacks are unknown (see Cassese 2001: 996–7). This is particularly clear given that Operation *Enduring Freedom* and its international reception slightly amended the customary view of self-defence in at least two ways. First, the US employed a broad definition of 'armed attack' that incorporated relatively isolated incidents separated by considerable periods of time and this was generally accepted. Second, it insisted that states be held accountable for harbouring terrorists and most of the world agreed (see Simpson 2004: 338–40).

Yemen

On 3 November 2002, a Predator drone belonging to the CIA launched two Hellfire missiles and destroyed a car travelling along a desert road in Yemen, close to the border with Saudi Arabia (Thomas, E. and Hosenball 2002: 48). The Pentagon claimed that the target was Qaed Salim Sinan al-Harethi, the head of Al-Qaeda's operations in Yemen and thought to be the master-mind behind the 2000 attack on the USS *Cole* (Johnstone, D. and Sanger 2002).

The US used three justifications for the attack. First, it argued that the attack did not raise *jus ad bellum* issues because it was simply a further element of the global 'war on terror' (Aldicott 2002). As Condoleezza Rice explained, 'we're in a new kind of war, and we've made very clear that it is important that this new kind of war be fought on different battlefields' (in O'Connell 2003: 454). There are many problems with this position. Taken literally, a war on terror is a war on a tactic. It is the equivalent of respond-ing to Pearl Harbor by waging a war on surprise attacks rather than on Japan. That aside, if we understand the war on terror as a war on Al-Qaeda and its allies, Rice's argument becomes more persuasive. Be that as it may, the fact that the US took its campaign to another state, endangering Yemeni non-combatants, means that we are entitled to explore the *jus ad bellum* question of whether it was a legitimate act of pre-emption. Not least, as O'Connell (2003: 454) argues, we are entitled to ask these questions because at the time of the attack Yemen was not itself engaged in an armed conflict.

Finally, there is a real danger that granting the US a right to strike any-where, at any time, in the name of the 'war on terror' risks undermining the *jus ad bellum* constraints on the recourse to force.

The second justification was that the attack was conducted with the consent of the Yemeni government. According to some reports, Yemeni authorities provided the US with the necessary intelligence to enable the strike (Lumpkin 2002). This claim certainly covers potential legal concerns about the strike, because the right of a state to request assistance from other states to suppress terrorist groups is widely recognized (Byers 2002: 403–4). However, it does not resolve the moral questions because of the possibility that Yemen's consent may have been coerced and the different standards used by natural law and positive law.

The third justification engages directly with *jus ad bellum*. It insists that the strike was an act of pre-emption against a known Al-Qaeda leader who had targeted the US before and was, in all probability, planning to do so once again. Deputy Defence Secretary Paul Wolfowitz described the attack as a successful tactical operation that had removed a danger to the US (in Kolff 2003). Likewise, Aldicott (2002) insisted that the attack was a legiti-mate act of self-defence against enemy combatants.

In order to evaluate these claims we need to apply the *expanded* concept of pre-emptive self-defence outlined in the previous section, because the perceived threat was terrorist. We need to ask whether the threat was immi-nent in the expanded sense of the term, whether the use of force was neces-sary, and whether the US acted proportionately and with due care. The answer to the first question is relatively straightforward. The intended target, Harethi, was believed to be a leading member of the Al-Qaeda cell that attacked the USS *Cole* in 2000. If that is the case, we can consider the imminence test satisfied because Harethi had a clearly expressed intention to strike the US and the means to do so once again at some point. The ques-tion, however, is how sure are we that Harethi *was* in fact who the US claimed he was; after all, in the light of the Iraqi WMD issue there are good reasons for not taking US intelligence at face value. This in turn raises the question of what standard of proof we require. Some of the attack's critics complained that the US was acting as judge, jury and executioner and that by taking pre-emptive action rather than arresting and trying the suspects it failed to prove Harethi's guilt 'beyond reasonable doubt' (Calhoun 2003). This formula sets the threshold too high because it is difficult to know with certainty precisely when and where a terrorist will strike. Moreover, Geneva Protocol I (1977) insists that the principle of due care only requires combatants to take 'every feasible precaution' to minimize harm to non-combatants. Given the evidence supplied by the US, apparently corrobor-ated by Yemen, and the fact that no plausible counter-evidence has emerged, it is fair to conclude that Harethi did pose a threat and that measures against him were therefore justified.

The second element of the expanded concept of self-defence is necessity. To satisfy this criterion, the US needs to demonstrate that there were no reasonable alternatives to force. Some of the attack's critics, including Amnesty International (see Kolff 2003: 241), focused on the question of whether the US and Yemen could have arrested the suspects and subjected them to due process. Since the attack, no evidence has emerged to suggest that either Yemen or the US seriously contemplated arresting the suspects immediately prior to the missile strike. However, in December 2001, thirteen Yemeni soldiers had been killed in an operation aimed at arresting Harethi and destroying Al-Qaeda cells near the Saudi border (Thomas, E. and Hosenball 2002: 48). Although the US strike came almost one year later, it is at least plausible to argue that it was part of an on-going campaign against Al-Qaeda in Yemen. Having failed to arrest Harethi, this line of argument goes, the Yemeni government and the US were entitled to utilize alternative strategies. This is a plausible justification because law enforcement officers, like soldiers, are not required to increase danger to themselves in order to lower the risks to enemy combatants/criminals.

On balance, although doubts remain about whether the use of force was the only reasonable way of removing the terrorist threat, the Yemen missile strike can be considered a (barely) legitimate act of pre-emption. It is important, however, that we do not simply ignore these concerns and that governments are held to account, for at least two reasons. Governments can and do provide misleading information either deliberately or unintentionally. Going to war on the basis of misperceptions about an imminent threat caused by intelligence failures and/or a lack of due care is immoral, illegal and imprudent. The Yemen attack was the thin end of the wedge. The US did not provide the necessary evidence and information, but on the balance of probabilities its missile attack in Yemen can be viewed as justifiable.

Iraq

The US and its allies used three arguments to justify their decision to invade Iraq in 2003. The formal legal case rested on the argument that Iraq's persistent breach of Security Council Resolution 687, which had brought the 1991 Gulf War to an end, invalidated the ceasefire. These ceasefire violations revived Resolution 678 authorizing the use of force to remove Iraqi forces from Kuwait and restore 'regional peace and security' (see Murphy 2003: 427–8). The UK emphasized the humanitarian imperative for removing Saddam's regime, which was one of the world's worst human rights abusers (see Wheeler, N. J. and Morris forthcoming). In its public justifications, the US administration sometimes argued that the war was justified because it had made America more secure (Clarke 2004: 266). According to the Bush administration, Iraq under Saddam posed a possible if not actual threat to the US because of the potential for it to pass WMD to terrorists and its ability to provide a safe harbour for them. In this brief discussion, I will focus on this self-defence justification.

During the protracted Security Council debate that preceded the invasion, US Ambassador John Negroponte insisted that 'if the Security Council fails to act decisively in the event of further Iraqi violations, this resolution does not constrain any member state from acting to defend itself against the threat posed by Iraq' (S/PV.4644). Negroponte's reference to 'self-defence' clearly alluded to the US doctrine of pre-emption. Indeed, the idea that a right of pre-emption might be used to legitimize an invasion of Iraq had been floated as early as June 2002 (see Pilger 2002). Speaking shortly after the war, Bush told an ABC journalist that 'I made my decision [to go to war] based upon enough intelligence to tell me this country was threatened with Saddam Hussein in power'; he continued, 'America is a safer country' (in Clarke 2004: 266).

Did the US satisfy the imminence and necessity tests required to justify the invasion of Iraq as an act of pre-emption? The first question is which standard of pre-emption should apply? The US administration clearly believed that the wider interpretation intimated by the 2002 *Strategy* should apply because Iraq posed an indirect terrorist threat through its desire to acquire WMD and its purported link with Al-Qaeda. Immediately after September 11, Paul Wolfowitz – the neo-conservative Deputy Secretary for Defence – argued that there was between a ten and fifty per cent chance that Iraq was involved in the terrorist attacks (Daalder and Lindsay 2003: 104). The administration then persistently claimed that there was 'some' link between Iraq and September 11, or, at the very least, a link between Iraq and Al-Qaeda (Bush 2002b). By this logic, Iraq could decide at a moment's notice to provide Al-Qaeda with chemical or biological weapons to use against the US (Dorman 2004: 148). On 5 February 2003, Colin Powell told the Security Council that since 1996, the Iraqi regime had expressed an interest in supporting Al-Qaeda and that it therefore constituted a direct threat to American security (S/PV.4701). He concluded that the only way to meet the danger that potential Iraqi WMD might find their way into Al-Qaeda's hands was to endorse the use of force since 'the United States will not and cannot run that risk to the American people'.

This argument was fundamentally flawed. There was only 'tenuous' evidence of links between Iraq and Al-Qaeda (see Record 2004). Indeed, there is reason to think that even US intelligence agencies believed there was nothing in the claim. The closest the US got to evidence was a memo leaked by Under-Secretary of Defence Doug Feith purporting to contain intelligence demonstrating such a link. In fact, the data simply showed that Iraqi officials had occasionally met Al-Qaeda operatives and some of the intelligence reports even suggested that Iraq and Al-Qaeda had failed to reach an understanding. The Pentagon swiftly announced that the memo did not constitute evidence of a link between Iraq and Al-Qaeda. As for the fact that officials had held meetings, Richard Clarke (2004: 270) – the United States' former counter-terrorism chief – argues that it would have been surprising had Iraqi officials not met Al-Qaeda officials at some point. This assessment was confirmed by the Butler committee's report on British intelligence and Iraq. Butler concluded that British intelligence had advised the government that although there were contacts between the Iraqi regime and Al-Qaeda, 'there was no evidence of cooperation' (Butler 2004: 120). After the collapse of the Taliban in Afghanistan, Afghan refugees had established a terrorist training camp in northern Iraq, but that was in Kurdish-controlled territory beyond the reach of Saddam's forces (Butler 2004: 119). In September 2003, Dick Cheney admitted that there was no link between Iraq and September 11, and in 2004 the administration admitted that there probably was no cooperative relationship between Iraq and Al-Qaeda either.

We can draw two conclusions from this. First, we can reject the claim that the expanded right of pre-emption should be applied in the Iraq case. The US failed to demonstrate that an imminent terrorist threat emanated either from Iraq itself or from its alleged relationship with Al-Qaeda. Second, more worryingly, contrary to Bush's claim, there is little evidence to suggest that US intelligence agencies advised that Iraq and Al-Qaeda enjoyed a cooperative relationship that might constitute a threat. According to the British Butler report, as early as late 2001 the British Joint Intelligence Committee had concluded that there was no practical cooperation between Iraq and Al-Qaeda, and the prospect of Iraq training Al-Qaeda in chemical weaponry – directly referred to by Bush – was not even alluded to (Butler 2004: 119). If this is the case, the claim that there was a link was disingenuous.

There could still be a case for justifying the invasion of Iraq in pre-emptive terms if it could be demonstrated that Iraq itself posed an imminent threat. Powell made this move when he argued that Iraq was deliberately concealing its WMD and missile technologies and might therefore constitute a threat to its neighbours and US interests (S/PV.4701). Even if those claims could have been sustained, it would not have been enough to justify pre-emptive war. The US would still have had to demonstrate that force was the only reasonable way in which the threat could have been removed and it would have had to demonstrate that at the time of the invasion Iraq *intended* to attack another country. In the event, it failed to do either.

Since the invasion, it has become evident that many of Powell's claims were inaccurate. The Iraq Survey Group (2004), created by the US government to investigate Iraq's WMD failed to find WMDs or evidence of an active WMD programme. It concluded that Iraq had no missiles capable of delivering nuclear, chemical or biological weapons, that it had unilaterally destroyed its undeclared chemical stockpiles in 1991, and that it had abandoned its biological warfare programme in 1995.

Is Iraq therefore a case of invincible ignorance? On reflection, this is the most generous interpretation of the self-defence argument as there is little evidence that US intelligence agencies advised that Iraq and Al-Qaeda had a cooperative relationship that posed an imminent threat. More worryingly, there is evidence that the administration did not show due care in reaching its decision that Iraq posed a threat. Prior to the war, there was evidence that Iraq did not pose a threat. As well as the intelligence reports discussed above, Hans Blix, the UN's chief weapons inspector in Iraq, also insisted that Iraq did not pose an immediate threat. On 10 February 2003, he presented a report to the Security Council which identified a heightened level of Iraqi cooperation and openly contradicted some of Powell's earlier claims about Iraq's WMD capabilities (S/PV. 4707). In particular, Blix argued that although the Iraqi government had still not provided full disclosure, the UN weapons inspectors had failed to find any evidence of either Iraqi WMD or on-going WMD programmes. Meanwhile, France and Germany presented an alternative proposal for strengthening the inspections regime. Powell rejected the proposal, insisting that continued inspections would not bring about disarmament (S/PV. 4707). However, the increasingly positive tone of Blix's reports and the existence of a seemingly viable alternative path to disarmament make the US arguments appear implausible.

Given all this, it seems clear that in 2003 Iraq did not satisfy any of the conditions necessary to justify pre-emption. Iraq did not pose an imminent threat, and, given the balance of evidence, even accepting imperfect knowledge, there were not many reasonable grounds at the time for believing that it did. Moreover, the use of force was not necessary because other courses of action remained available. Some realists, for instance, argued that containment was proving effective (Mearsheimer and Walt 2003).

Conclusion

Terrorist threats materialize quickly. It is virtually impossible for any state other than totalitarian dictatorships to defend against terrorism at all times and in all places. If a state waits until it knows precisely when and where the terrorists intend to strike before using force to prevent them, it has probably waited too long. For Just War writers, the state not only has a right to defend its citizens, it has a moral obligation to do so. The problem is that defeating terrorist organizations requires an offensive strategy. That is, the intended victim state must take the initiative and destroy the terrorists' training network, arms supplies, leadership structure and financial security. Although defeating terrorism requires non-military strategies too, it may also involve using force overseas to forestall imminent attacks. However, it is difficult, if not impossible, to know exactly when and where a terrorist is going to strike. Indeed, concealing these facts is central to the terrorists' *modus operandi.* Traditionally, both positive law and natural law have imposed tight limits on pre-emption. The threat must be temporally imminent, sufficiently grave, leave no time for deliberation, and force must be the only way of removing the threat.

This traditional concept of pre-emption does not adequately meet the strategic demands created by the need to combat mass-casualty terrorism because it fails to distinguish between terrorist and traditional threats. The concept of pre-emption detailed here involves reinterpreting imminence. Rather than temporal imminence, I suggested that a terrorist threat is imminent when a group expresses a clear intention to use terrorism and begins acquiring the means to do so. In such cases, states may act pre-emptively even if they are unsure about when and where terrorist attacks will fall.

The three cases highlighted different aspects of this expanded concept of pre-emption. In Operation *Enduring Freedom*, the US put forward a pre-emptive justification that was widely endorsed even though it was unable to satisfy the traditional criteria by identifying when and where the perceived Al-Qaeda threat was going to manifest itself. The 2002 missile strike on Yemen raised some difficult issues in relation to necessity, but it too was widely seen as a legitimate act of self-defence, though there was more dissent in this case than in relation to Afghanistan. Attempts to justify the 2003 invasion of Iraq by reference to self-defence demonstrate two important limits on pre-emption and the consequences of exceeding those limits. On occasions, senior US figures tried to argue that Iraq constituted a terrorist threat, either because its WMD capabilities posed an immediate threat to the US and its allies or because of the danger that Iraq would pass its WMD material to Al-Qaeda. Both claims proved inaccurate. The very best that can be said about the US administration's decision-making in this case is that it failed the due care test. That is, it assumed that its own intelligence was correct and that the UN's was incorrect and therefore failed to verify its own evidence. More worrying is the evidence that flawed arguments were sometimes deliberately used by political leaders.

The problem with stretching an expanded right of pre-emption is that it risks undermining the right and more besides. Today, pre-emption is associated with Iraq, and the global consensus that legitimated *Enduring Freedom* and the Yemeni missile strike has all but eroded. This will make it harder for the US and its allies to combat Al-Qaeda without undermining international order. This has both moral and prudential ramifications. If states and peoples choose to reject the idea of an expanded right of pre-emption in response to the threat of terrorism, pre-emptive attacks against terrorists are more likely to be seen as unjust, thereby increasing the risk of future terrorism. In turn, the political and material costs associated with such actions will increase, making it harder, not easier, to win the war on Al-Qaeda.

9

Aerial Bombing

This chapter explores some of the ethical dilemmas associated with aerial bombing, particularly as they relate to the so-called 'war on terror'. Waging a war on insurgents, terrorists and their allies raises particular dilemmas because terrorists are often indistinguishable from non-combatants. Terrorists and their supporters conceal themselves among the civilian population, manipulating the moral and legal restraints observed by their enemies to further their cause. This is aided by the fact that today's liberal societies expect their leaders and militaries to follow basic moral and legal rules even when their adversaries do not (Beier 2003: 411–12). Often, military targets are not easily identified. Threats can emerge rapidly from ostensibly civilian sources. In this environment it is hard to distinguish combatant from non-combatant, and the costs of failing to destroy potential combatants can be high.

Focusing on Operation *Enduring Freedom* in Afghanistan, this chapter addresses the dilemma of distinguishing between combatants and non-combatants when conducting aerial bombing. Given this problem, there is a temptation to revert to Sherman's logic and insist that as the terrorists and their supporters caused the war, the blame for all its destruction must lie with them, a temptation to which US Secretary of Defence Donald Rumsfeld (2001b) has occasionally succumbed. But this logic runs counter to the Just War tradition. Not least, moral consistency means that we cannot decry terrorism whilst also denying moral responsibility for non-combatant casualties that result from our military operations. The issue becomes more complicated still when we consider 'dual-use' targets. When terrorists and their allies hide amidst the civilian population, military commanders are presented with two dilemmas: is discrimination possible, and is the likely damage to non-combatant lives and property proportionate to the military significance of the target? The issue is further muddied by the question of where moral responsibility lies. That is, whilst we can accept responsibility for the foreseen but unintended *direct* negative consequences of our actions, who is responsible for the *indirect* consequences, that is, those consequences that come to fruition because of another's actions? For example, if non-combatants are used as 'human shields', if command posts are situated in housing areas, if terrorists and insurgents base themselves in a mosque, who is responsible for the non-combatant casualties that result from ostensibly legitimate attacks on those terrorists?

For many Just War writers, the responsibility for non-combatant deaths in such cases lies with the terrorists and insurgents who place non-combatants in harm's way. Reflecting on the Vietnam War, Paul Ramsey (2002: 435–6) insisted that 'in devising a military riposte [to guerrillas], it will not be those who are directing the counter-insurgency who illicitly enlarged the target and chose to fight the war indiscriminately. Instead, the tragedy is that they *have* an enlarged legitimate target because of the decision of the insurgency to fight the war by means of peasants.' William O'Brien (1981: 100) concurred, arguing that 'it seems fair to assign the major responsibility to the Communist forces for the civilian losses, destruction and displacement caused by turning the population centres into battle-fields'. Referring to Palestine, Johnson (1984: 59) argued that the Israeli Defence Force was not primarily responsible for non-combatant deaths. Responsibility lay with 'those who use them [non-combatants] as involuntary shields'.

The main problem with this view is that it relies on an overly permissive interpretation of the doctrine of double-effect. According to these writers, it is enough to insist that as we are not deliberately targeting non-combatants, we are not responsible for their deaths (see Hurka 2005: 47–50). Following Walzer, I adopt a more restrictive doctrine, which holds that it is not enough simply not to intend the deaths of non-combatants (see Chapter 6). Instead, combatants are required to do everything possible to minimize the likelihood that non-combatants will be harmed.

A balance has to be struck between rigid adherence to the rules and the instrumental requirements of waging successful wars. There are, nevertheless, some moral absolutes that are fundamental to the Just War tradition and can never be breached. The most fundamental of these is the commitment not to deliberately kill, maim or otherwise harm non-combatants and the additional requirement to take active steps to minimize potential harm to them. This in itself raises a practical dilemma: how to balance the military's responsibility to prevail with its responsibility for minimizing the harm suffered by enemy non-combatants? The challenge here is to avoid the moral tragedy of fighting terrorism effectively at the expense of the very values that we are fighting for (Niebuhr 1932). My primary purpose in this chapter is to show how the Just War tradition can frame judgements about the legitimacy of the minutiae of war, helping us to avoid this tragedy.

This chapter proceeds in four parts. The first discusses the principles of discrimination and proportionality in relation to aerial bombing. The second provides an overview of the strategy and targeting process used in Operation *Enduring Freedom*. The third and fourth sections address the issues of targeting mistakes and weapons selection, respectively.

Discrimination and Proportionality

The key problem facing those charged with directing aerial bombing campaigns is that terrorists and insurgents make themselves virtually indistinguishable from non-combatants: they launch operations from civilian areas, they are physically indistinguishable from non-combatants and they use human shields. These tactics give rise to pressing dilemmas relating to discrimination and proportionality. How are commanders, planners and pilots to discriminate between combatants and non-combatants in this context? What level of risk should they accept in order to increase the chances of distinguishing between combatants and non-combatants? How is the danger of collateral damage to be balanced against the military advantage gained by attacking particular targets?

It is worth briefly recapping what the Just War tradition has to say about discrimination and proportionality. There is a close relationship between natural law and positive law on these questions. In many ways, the former provides the basic principles, whilst the latter offers specific prohibitions and criteria. The clearest explication of positive law's position on discrimination and proportionality is contained in the 1977 Geneva Protocol I. Article 52(2) codifies the principle of discrimination by insisting that militaries may only attack 'objects which by their nature, location, purpose or use make an effective contribution to military action'. This article draws the distinction between combatant people and facilities (those making 'an effective contribution to military action') and non-combatants, not between soldiers and civilians. However, it leaves considerable room for manoeuvre with regard to dual-use facilities. The logic of Article 52(2) strongly suggests that any facility that makes an effective contribution to the military campaign is a legitimate target, so long as the proportionality criteria are satisfied (see Shue 2003: 101; cf. Shue and Wippman 2002).

In cases where there is doubt about whether a potential target is making an effective contribution to the enemy's military campaign, to what extent is a commander responsible for ensuring that the intended target is indeed a military one? The close interrelationship between military and civilian objects in operations against terrorists and insurgents makes it difficult for military commanders to be certain that a potential target is making an effective contribution to the enemy's military efforts as required by Protocol I. On the one hand, insisting that commanders not strike unless they are absolutely certain that at the specific time of the attack a particular facility is making an effective military contribution to the terrorist or insurgent campaign places too great a restriction on targeting and risks undermining the military effort. On the other hand, a completely permissive interpretation would not satisfy the doctrine of double-effect and would be tantamount to licensing indiscrimination. Article 57 of Protocol I offers a useful formulation to guide our judgements on this. It holds that 'those who plan or decide on an attack shall do everything feasible to verify that the objectives to be attacked are neither civilians nor civilian objects'. The phrase 'everything feasible' provides a useful sliding scale. At one end of the scale, when the target is a fixed object permanently used for a military purpose it is reasonable to expect that the target selection process will use a variety of different methods to ascertain and verify the nature of the target. At the other end of the scale, however, pilots striking targets of opportunity or engaged in tactical air support may rely on only one or two sources of evidence: their own vision (does the facility, vehicle or individual *look* like it is making an effective military contribution) and/or an immediate external verification (preferably from a forward spotter on the ground, an unmanned drone or, less preferably, a very recent satellite image).

The proportionality principle is enshrined in Article 57(2)(iii) of Protocol I, which prohibits attacks 'which may be expected to cause incidental loss of civilian life, injury to civilians, damage to civilian objects, or a combination thereof, which would be excessive in relation to the concrete and direct military advantage anticipated'. This is supported by Article 57(a)(i), which insists that combatants 'take all feasible precautions in the choice of means and methods of attack with a view to avoiding, and in any event to minimizing, incidental loss of civilian life'. The problem here, as Nicholas Wheeler (2002: 209) has noted, is that positive law's rendering of the proportionality principle is just as vague as natural law's – it offers no guidance or method for deciding when the threat of collateral damage is 'excessive'. This leaves us with at least three dilemmas.

First, how are we to balance force protection with the protection of enemy non-combatants from unintended harm? Walzer's position – which I endorse – is that we should be prepared to place combatants in harm's way in order to reduce the risks to enemy non-combatants (Walzer 1977: 156). But how much danger is acceptable? Military commanders are also legally responsible for the welfare of soldiers under their command. A commander may not recklessly place subordinates in harm's way, or jeopardize the mission by prioritizing the protection of enemy non-combatants over force protection (see Carlino 2002: 16–19). A particular problem with military targets situated in urban environments is that it is often difficult to distinguish a dire threat from normal civilian activity and there is sometimes a direct trade-off between protecting enemy non-combatants and force protection: the earlier one acts to meet a potential threat, the lower the risk to the military, but the higher the peril faced by non-combatants. Here, the doctrine of double-effect – and Walzer's (1977: 152–9) reformulation of it in particular – provides a useful rule of thumb. We should expect soldiers and aircrew to take positive steps to reduce the threat to non-combatants as far as possible, even if that means accepting a marginal increase of risk to their own lives. However, they should not go beyond the point at which the risk they expose themselves to becomes so catastrophic that it endangers the overall mission. Moreover, it is important to recognize that political leaders, military commanders and the wider public will tend to display national partiality. That is, they will value their own citizens' lives (even if those citizens are soldiers) more than those of other states' citizens, particularly citizens of enemy states (McMahan and McKim 1993). In a sense, national partiality is a moral requirement in the realist tradition and certainly has an important part to play in the practical ethics of war. It strengthens the idea that there are powerful limits on the degree of peril to which a state can subject its soldiers in order to protect enemy non-combatants.

The second dilemma prompted by proportionality is: how are we to balance the relative value of a military objective and the lives of non-combatants? For some consequentialist pacifists, the death of a single non-combatant is enough to render an attack disproportionate (Holmes 1989: 15). This is not a position endorsed by either positive law or natural law. According to these approaches, actors are required to make judgements based on the merits of each case. In the case of air strikes against fixed targets where there is usually time for planning and deliberation, decision-makers must assess the value of the intended target and the likely collateral costs of attacking the target in a particular way at a particular time. Where the decision-maker is satisfied that attacking the intended target would produce a demonstrably advantageous military effect, he or she must choose the means and time of attack calculated to cause the least amount of collateral damage. In short, there must be a system of ethical and legal evaluation prior to targets being approved for attack. Most Western militaries have such systems (Roblyer 2004: 16–18). In air strikes on moving targets or so-called 'targets of opportunity', the time frame for making these types of judgements is dramatically shortened (Air Land Sea Application Center 1997). Nevertheless, the proportionality principle requires combatants in these situations to make the same calculations, though our *post-facto* judgements in these cases have to take into account the significant time constraints and the fact of imperfect knowledge and vision. Whilst proportionality assessments are subjective, unfavourable assessments by third parties can have a number of negative effects on the campaign: they can strain alliance relations, weaken the perceived justice of the campaign and erode domestic support (Schmitt 1999: 118).

The third dilemma associated with proportionality is the relative moral quality of direct and indirect harm. Are combatants morally responsible for indirect harm to non-combatants caused by the combination of an air strike and an intervening act by a second party? For example, if enemy combatants hide their vehicles in a residential area and those vehicles are attacked and local non-combatants killed, who has primary responsibility for the non-combatant deaths? Who is responsible for the death of non-combatants if they are used as human shields? The suggestion here is that those who launch the attack do have a degree of responsibility, shared with those who place non-combatants in harm's way, which may be primary or secondary depending on the case in question. The responsibility for indirect harm is less than responsibility for direct harm, but foreseeable indirect harm should nevertheless be counted in proportionality calculations (Hurka 2005: 50). This position is reflected in Protocol I. On the one hand, Article 58(b) demands that military and civilian objects be kept separate as far as possible and forbids their deliberate intermingling, whilst Article 57(5) recognizes that no circumstances waive a belligerent's duty to abide by the principles of discrimination and proportionality.

Operation *Enduring Freedom*

Since the end of the Cold War, the use of air power for strategic effect has become the weapon of choice for the US and its allies. Although ground troops, especially Special Forces, played a pivotal role, the bulk of the US contribution to the overthrow of the Taliban regime in Afghanistan came in the form of aerial bombardment. According to some strategic thinkers, the advent of precision-guided munitions (PGMs), which permit the US to strike targets accurately from a great distance, constitutes a revolution in military affairs whereby the US and its allies can destroy an enemy's military capabilities without exposing either their own military or enemy non-combatants to significant levels of harm (Friedman and Friedman 1996: xi). Ward Thomas (2001: 169), for example, demonstrates that aerial bombardment by the US and its allies today kills far fewer non-combatants per bomb than it did in the past. Thomas' central thesis is that norms become stronger when powerful states have the wherewithal to satisfy their requirements. Consequently, the advent of PGM warfare has significantly increased societal expectations about the minimization of non-combatant casualties. Not only do Western societies today expect virtually 'casualty-free' warfare in relation to their own armed forces, they expect war to be more or less casualty-free from the perspective of enemy non-combatants as well (McInnes 2003).

The airpower strategy adopted by the US Air Force in Afghanistan is best described as 'effects-based' (Arkin 2000: 49). According to the influential air strategist John Warden (1988), a state's ability to wage war derives from its vital networks, which he depicts as concentric circles. The aim of aerial bombardment is not straightforward destruction, but the disruption and destruction of those networks, reducing an enemy's capacity to wage war (Lambeth 2000: 101). On the face of it, this strategy sits well with the Geneva Protocol because it selects targets on the basis of their contribution to the enemy's military mission. On closer inspection, however, the strategy gives rise to serious concerns. In most societies, the military and civilian infrastructures are interrelated: power stations, roads, bridges, water pumps, and the like, serve both. Not only does Warden's strategy encourage the targeting of dual-use facilities to disrupt a state's vital infrastructure and hence its military capability, it could also give rise to targeting facilities that are not making a direct military contribution but which are, nevertheless, part of a *network* that is. For example, television studios may not be directly broadcasting military messages but may be part of a wider communications network that is integral to the enemy's military effectiveness.

At the outset of Operation *Enduring Freedom* in early October 2001, US officials and politicians insisted that every step would be taken to minimize non-combatant casualties (see Bush 2001; Myers, R. 2001). To accomplish this aim, the US developed a sophisticated target-approval system. The cycle began with the commander's statement of objectives and guidance, usually framed in terms of the enemy's critical military networks and the rules of engagement, which are set by the Secretary of Defence and approved by the President. From there, the process began of selecting targets and deciding when and with what weapons each target should be hit. Legal advisers provided on-going counsel about whether specific targets were prohibited and oversaw every stage of this process (Roblyer 2004: 17). In practice, the role of the legal adviser was limited by the fact that most contentious targets were contentious not because of the discrimination principle, but because of proportionality concerns. As such, they involved subjective judgements, and insiders reported that in such cases *political* considerations tended to be more restrictive than *legal* ones (Roblyer 2004: 16–17). Wherever possible, once a target had been selected, computer modelling was used to predict the collateral consequences of striking particular targets with particular types of weapon in order to determine which weapon should be used in order to maximize effectiveness whilst minimizing potential harm to non-combatants (Roblyer 2004: 17–18).

There is ample evidence to suggest that these strategies had a profound effect on targeting in Afghanistan. As one air force commander put it, 'there's been a decision by the people running this war to rely on the advice of lawyers to a greater extent than they have before' (in Wheeler, N. J. 2002: 211). These controls often frustrated pilots and planners, who were widely cited complaining that the tight restrictions on targeting hampered their ability to fight the war. According to one officer, 'we knew we had some of the big boys, but the process [of target approval] is so slow that by the time we got the clearances, and everybody had put in their two cents, we called it off' (in Ricks 2002: 109). On another occasion, Central Command refused to approve the targeting of what appeared to be a military convoy because legal advisers believed that it might be a trick and that the convoy might contain children and other non-combatants. The same legal adviser was also criticized for insisting that those seeking clearance for attacks be 'sure' about the military nature of the target, forcing target planners to verify intelligence, sometimes causing significant delays in the target-approval process (Ricks 2002: 111). The result, the complainants insisted, was that 'we end up not bombing the bad guys' because of concerns about non-combatant casualties (Arkin 2002). As one officer summed up: 'the whole issue of collateral damage pervaded every level of the operation. It is shocking, the degree to which collateral damage hamstrung the campaign' (in Ricks 2002: 111). Inadvertently, these complaints suggest that the US attempted to follow the guidelines set out by the principles of discrimination and proportionality. It is only right and proper that in cases where the nature of the target is uncertain or the danger of non-combatant harm is great, the protection of non-combatants takes precedence over targeting something of dubious military value (see Westhusing 2002).

Despite this evidence, there are a number of significant concerns relating to both discrimination and proportionality. According to Carl Conetta (2002), although a higher proportion of PGMs were used in Afghanistan than in Kosovo (60 per cent compared to 30 per cent), there was a significantly higher rate of civilian casualties in Afghanistan. Conetta estimated that between 1,000 and 1,300 non-combatants had been killed by January 2002. Marc Herold (2002: 17) puts that figure even higher, at around 2,700. It is worth noting that the number of non-combatant deaths in Iraq was slightly higher again. One account suggests that between 5,500 and 7,500 non-combatants were killed by coalition forces, the majority by aerial bombardment, whilst another put that figure at approximately 3,750 (see Shaw, M. 2005: 115–23). These figures alone prompt important questions about the conduct of the air campaign. In particular, they raise questions about how targets were selected and verified and about the use of particular types of weapons such as 'cluster bombs', which are considered by some to be inherently indiscriminate (e.g. Human Rights Watch 2002). The following sections will address these two issues in detail.

Target Selection and Verification

Mistakes in targeting result from one of two causes: human error and technological failure (Shaw, P. M. 1997: 29–30). To satisfy the principles of discrimination and proportionality, it is necessary to minimize mistakes as far as possible and demonstrate due care. In relation to target identification, Protocol I (Article 52(2)) insists that in doubtful cases the commander should assume that a potential target is a civilian object and hence immune from attack, unless it can be proven to be making an effective contribution to the enemy's military campaign. According to Conetta (2002), there were three main causes of non-combatant casualties in Operation *Enduring Freedom*. First, there was the use of weapons guided by Global Positioning Satellite rather than laser-guided weapons (the former are cheaper and less accurate). Second, Taliban and Al-Qaeda forces sought refuge in residential areas. Third, owing to decades of civil war, Afghanistan's vital networks were largely inoperable, forcing the US Air Force to focus on moving targets and targets of opportunity, which are more difficult to strike accurately and which present a much smaller time-window for deliberation about potential collateral damage.

Most targeting mistakes in Afghanistan had their roots in intelligence and information-sharing failures. Although technological failure results in a weapon missing its target in approximately 5 to 10 per cent of cases, the vast majority of these cases did not produce significant collateral damage. A weapon is considered to have missed its target if it does not land on the precise location it was aimed at. Most 'misses' land within thirty metres of their target and in most cases this disables the intended target and has minimal collateral effect (Eason 2001). For example, if the target is a weapons dump and the target coordinates are fixed somewhere in the middle of the facility, a weapon that lands thirty metres from the target still hits the dump. For this reason, technological failure cannot be directly equated with collateral damage. That is not to say that weapons failure did not cause civilian casualties, but that on most occasions some form of human error was involved.

Given this, it seems that most non-combatant casualties were caused by one of two factors: first, intelligence and information-sharing errors. That is, the bombs hit the target they were supposed to hit but it transpired that the target was incorrectly identified. Second, non-combatant casualties were collateral damage caused by attempts to strike moving objects and the propensity for Al-Qaeda and the Taliban to use non-combatants as human shields and civilian structures for cover. According to US officers, most of the air strikes conducted in Afghanistan were directed at 'emerging' targets, in other words targets that did not appear on maps and for which the danger of collateral damage cannot be accurately predicted (Sewall 2002: 7).

The first problem, intelligence failure, has two components. The first is the misidentification of targets by intelligence-gathering agencies. This was a particular problem in Afghanistan because the US did not have a well-established intelligence network there and depended on intelligence from local Afghans, which was far from reliable and frequently malicious and politically motivated, as well as other sources such as British intelligence (Cryer 2002: 52). In order to protect its own forces, the US Air Force occasionally short-cut the targeting process described above and relied on unverified intelligence provided by Afghans for the identification and location of mobile targets, rather than placing American troops on the ground to search for and verify military targets. As a result of the flawed and unverified intelligence provided by Afghans, the US launched a number of attacks against civilian targets. Most famously, this included the bombing of a wedding party in June 2002. Initially, the US denied that it had bombed the party and then claimed that it was in fact a meeting of Taliban officials. The US insisted that its aircraft had received anti-aircraft fire from the area and that the target was only engaged after it had been positively identified as the source of the ground fire. On the same day as the attack, a US A-10 aircraft had elected not to strike its assigned target in the same area as the wedding party because of the lack of military activity in the area (US Central Command 2003). After considerable media scrutiny, however, it was admitted that the target had been a wedding party and that the decision to attack it had been based on flawed and unverified intelligence provided by Afghans (Harding 2002). The most likely explanation appears to be that the A-10s, having been despatched to the area to strike what they believed to be a Taliban headquarters on the basis of erroneous Afghan information, mistook gunfire into the air – a common practice at Afghan weddings – for anti-aircraft fire. This was an easy mistake to make given that the pilots believed their target to be a military one.

The second type of intelligence failure stemmed from a combination of the misidentification of targets and the failure of different government agencies to share relevant information about the location of protected and politically sensitive buildings. This problem first became apparent during Operation *Allied Force* in 1999. On 7 May 1999, B-2 bombers dropped three bombs on the Chinese Embassy in Belgrade, killing four people. The cause of this catastrophic mistake, which temporarily threatened to undermine the entire operation, was bureaucratic in origin. The map used by the CIA to identify targets in Belgrade was an outdated 1992 'city plan of Belgrade' which did not show the Chinese Embassy, which was built in 1997. The agency updated the map in 1998, but failed to indicate the embassy's move across Belgrade's river. At the same time, as part of a cost-cutting exercise, the CIA's imagery intelligence and human intelligence components were separated. The imagery, maps and coordinates for target acquisition in Serbia came from the National Imagery and Mapping Agency. The confusion was caused by the fact that the Yugoslav Federal Directorate, the intended target of the attack, was in the same vicinity as the Chinese Embassy and both buildings looked alike in satellite imagery because they had similar roofs. Upon finding a building that looked like the Directorate, in the vicinity of the Directorate, the Imagery and Mapping Agency incorrectly identified the Chinese Embassy as the Directorate and scheduled it for attack. The problem was exacerbated by the fact that NATO was fast running out of fixed targets to strike, so the agency was required to find new targets quickly. Thus, there was no time to verify the target by, for instance, cross-checking it with human intelligence. Scores of people in the Defence Department and State Department would have known the location of both the Directorate and the Embassy. Moreover, a simple check of Belgrade's telephone book would have exposed the error (see Clark, W. K. 2001: 291). The Chinese Embassy bombing was therefore a product of bureaucratic failure caused in part by the lack of a system for verifying intelligence, in part by the paucity of accurate data about Belgrade, and in part by the severe time constraints imposed on the process of target identification.

Similar mistakes occurred during Operation *Enduring Freedom*. The case that stands out in this regard is the repeated bombing of an ICRC warehouse in Kabul in October 2001 (Roberts, A. 2002: 18). The ICRC warehouse was attacked by the US on both 16 and 26 October. On neither occasion was there any suggestion of weapons malfunction. The ICRC insisted that at the outset of the war it had informed the US about the location of its facilities in Afghanistan and that the warehouse was clearly marked with a red cross on its roof. Thus, even had the target planners incorrectly identified the ICRC building as an enemy target, its identity as a protected building should have become apparent to the pilot before the bombing. In such cases, the pilot is legally and morally obliged to call off the attack. In this case, however, there was evidently a failure of information-sharing and target verification. Those in the Defence Department who received the ICRC's information about the location of its warehouse either failed to pass that information on, or failed to ensure that the information was acted upon. The circumstances of the 16 October bombing suggest that the warehouse was attacked with 'stand-off' weapons launched from a high altitude and/or from a distance, meaning that the pilot was unable to verify the target visually.

After the 16 October attack, the ICRC again informed the US of the location of its facilities in Afghanistan (ICRC 2001). When coupled with the public reporting of the first strike, it could be expected that the US would have taken measures to avoid attacking the warehouse again. However, on 26 October a B-52 bomber attacked the warehouse. The US reported human error in the targeting process (BBC World News 2001a). Once again, the attack raises significant questions about information-sharing and target verification both during the planning process and during the actual mission. The ICRC (2001) claimed that the attack occurred near midday and was launched from an aircraft that was nearby and flying slowly at low altitude.

Do the intelligence failures associated with this and other mistaken attacks breach the principle of discrimination? Recall that there are two levels of responsibility. The first asks whether non-combatants were deliberately attacked. The evidence suggests that they were not. Clearly, US strategy focused on attacking combatants, though it must be conceded that, assuming the ICRC's report to be accurate, the second strike on the ICRC compound could be interpreted as an intentional strike on a civilian target. In the absence of a detailed account of the mission from the US Air Force, it is impossible to know for sure what happened, but it is incumbent on the US Air Force to provide a full account and take measures against those who failed to pass on or act on the necessary information. With this case as a partial exception, however, we can conclude that the US did not intentionally target non-combatants.

The second level of responsibility relates to the question of due care. It is not enough simply not to intend to kill non-combatants. Combatants must take positive steps to minimize the risk to non-combatants. The US Air Force has a targeting process designed to minimize risk, and evidence suggests that this played a crucial role in US strategy. However, collateral damage could have been lower still had the US taken all feasible precautions to minimize harm to non-combatants. First, the US displayed national partiality in prioritizing the protection of its own forces over that of Afghan non-combatants. In the early stages of the war, Rumsfeld himself tacitly admitted that the US did not have sufficient human intelligence on which to base its target selection when he announced that he would deploy more ground troops into Afghanistan to assist with target selection and approval (BBC World News 2001b). It could be argued that due care only requires practicable action, not actions that could jeopardize the military mission, and that the US did not have troops on the ground for sound prudential reasons (see Cryer 2002: 50). This is a partially persuasive argument, as the Taliban continued to hold much of Afghanistan's territory until its collapse in the first weeks of November. However, the due care principle insists that in cases where the target's identity is in doubt owing to incomplete or unverified intelligence, the potential attacker should refrain from striking unless necessity (such as the protection of ground forces or non-combatants from an imminent attack) dictates otherwise. Military advantage alone cannot justify taking a gamble on a target proving, *post facto*, to be military. As Cryer (2002: 50) argues, such strikes are essentially 'blind' and hence indiscriminate.

This judgement only holds if the US knew at the time that the information it was getting from Afghans was faulty. Rumsfeld's claim that by the end of October the US was trying to improve its intelligence-gathering capabilities suggests that it became aware of the problem only once the war had begun, and that once it did so, it took measures to remedy the fault. However, even after Rumsfeld's statement, the US refused to place significant numbers of troops on the ground in Afghanistan and targeting mistakes continued. For the world's only remaining superpower with a military budget dwarfing that of all its nearest competitors combined, this effort does not satisfy the due care test or seriously challenge the claim that the US valued force protection more than the protection of Afghan non-combatants.

Weapons Selection

The second set of concerns relates to the use of particular types of weapons. Whilst weapons such as the BLU-82 (the so-called 'daisy cutters') and depleted uranium raised important questions about proportionality, one type of bomb favoured by the US and UK, so-called 'cluster bombs', has, as noted, been described in some quarters as inherently indiscriminate (e.g. MacAskill et al. 2001; Norton-Taylor and Ward 2001; Weibe 2000). Cluster bombs are designed to deliver a large amount of smaller submunitions over a significant area, increasing the overall radius of destruction that a bomb can achieve. They are generally meant for use against troop concentrations, airfields – especially runways – and air defence units (Leggette 1986). Even when targeted at military objects, cluster bombs present two sets of problems that cast doubt on their discriminacy and proportionality: first, because the submunitions are not individually targeted, there is a high chance that the bomb attack itself could cause casualties among non-combatants; second, unexploded submunitions effectively become anti-personnel landmines (Herby and Nuiten 2001).

The key question here is whether the inability to direct each submunition and the threat that unexploded submunitions pose to non-combatants make the weapon inherently indiscriminate. Again, Protocol I provides guidance. The Protocol prohibits attacks 'which employ a method or means of combat which cannot be directed at a specific military target' (Article 51(4)(b)) and forbids bombings that treat 'separate and distinct' military targets as one (Article 51(5)(a)). At very least, this suggests that cluster bombs can be discriminately used only against military targets that are well away from civilian areas. Even if this condition is satisfied, however, cluster bombs may still have an indiscriminate *effect.* Protocol I defines indiscriminate attacks as including those 'which employ a method or means of combat the effects of which cannot be limited as required by this Protocol' (Article 51(4)(c)). Coupled with the requirement to take 'all feasible precautions' to protect non-combatants, it is difficult to see how one could consider as discriminate an attack in an area likely to be frequented by non-combatants before those who launched the attack have had the opportunity to remove unexploded submunitions (Cryer 2002: 61 and n. 137). In the brief discussion that follows I will focus on these two problems.

The US made widespread use of cluster bombs against front-line targets in Afghanistan. Cluster bombs were used extensively against the Taliban's regional headquarters near Herat and in northern Afghanistan. Investigators commented that, in general, cluster bombs were used accurately against clear military targets. Reporting on one strike, the de-mining action group the HALO Trust commented that the US Air Force delivered cluster bombs 'right next to' Taliban trenches that had the effect of destroying both the trenches and Taliban vehicles parked nearby without causing collateral damage (in Human Rights Watch 2002: 20). According to Human Rights Watch, the military bases targeted around Herat were large enough to absorb the cluster bomb's 'footprint' without collateral damage.

There were, however, cases where cluster bombs were used in areas adjacent to those occupied by non-combatants, and in three cases that it investigated in detail, Human Rights Watch (2002: 21–3) found that cluster bombs had been responsible for the death of some twenty-five non-combatants. It is worth briefly exploring those three cases:

1 *Ainger.* On 17 November, three cluster bombs hit the village of Ainger (a fourth landed in a dry canal nearby) killing five non-combatants, including three children. Reports suggest that although there were no Taliban based in the village, Taliban were on the move nearby. There was no clear evidence that the Taliban had actually passed through the village, but it is possible that they had done so prior to the bomb attack. It is likely therefore that the bombs missed their moving Taliban targets.

2 *Ishaq Suleiman.* Over the course of six days from 31 October 2001, Ishaq Suleiman was hit by five cluster bombs, killing eight non-combatants. A further four non-combatants were later killed by unexploded submunitions. Taliban were present in the village during all five strikes, having fled from their nearby headquarters which had been heavily damaged by cluster bombs. After the first two attacks, villagers tried to force the Taliban to leave, which they did after the fifth attack. Although witness reports suggested that the attacks were discriminately aimed at the Taliban, with one bomb landing very near to where the Taliban hid some of their vehicles, Human Rights Watch interviews with US Air Force officials suggest that the bombs actually missed their intended target, which was the nearby headquarters. This seemed to be corroborated by the fact that villagers reported that the Taliban would enter the village at night whilst all five strikes were during the day.

3 *Qala Shater.* On 22 October, a cluster bomb fell on Qala Shater, a suburb of Herat, killing eleven and injuring thirteen non-combatants. Although a small number of Taliban had entered Qala Shater to pray at the mosque on the day of the attack, their small number and the fact that they were not occupying the suburb suggests that they were not the intended target. The likely target, according to Human Rights Watch, was probably a heavily fortified military facility almost one mile away.

The first observation to make is that in the latter two cases, the Taliban placed non-combatants in harm's way. In Ishaq Suleiman, Taliban fighters attempted to hide amid the civilian population and in Qala Shater they placed a military facility in a civilian area. These acts were both illegal and immoral. For several Just War writers, this alone would be enough to place the blame for non-combatant casualties solely on the Taliban. However, both the revised doctrine of double-effect and Protocol I place a heavier burden on the US and its allies, for they are required to show due care and take 'all feasible precautions' to protect non-combatants – even those placed in harm's way by the enemy. In all three cases, it seems that the bombs missed their intended target, though there is room for doubt about that in the Ishaq Suleiman case. Nevertheless, according to Human Rights Watch, the choice of cluster bombs to strike targets relatively close to residential areas constitutes a failure to take 'all feasible precautions'. Indeed, it argues that the use of cluster bombs near residential areas should be presumed indiscriminate (Human Rights Watch 2002: 24). Although I broadly agree with the latter proposition, I am not entirely convinced that the three cases cited above fall foul of this prohibition precisely because in all three cases there was evidence to suggest that the bombs missed their intended target. The element of indiscrimination comes into play when a cluster bomb hits its intended target but some of its submunitions nevertheless harm non-combatants. However, in these three cases the non-combatant casualties may have been the result of bombs *missing* their target. In order to claim that the use of cluster bombs was indiscriminate in these cases, we would need to model the likely impact that the submunitions would have had on non-combatants had they hit their intended target. This, in turn, raises the question of how much distance there should be between the military objective and residential areas. In the two cases where the intended target was a fixed object, there was around one mile between the target and where the bombs actually landed. This is well beyond the 'normal' distance that a failed US bomb lands from its target, suggesting that the non-combatant casualties were caused by targeting error rather than the reputedly indiscriminate nature of the cluster bombs.

Given the fact that the carnage wreaked was caused by the bombs *missing* their target, it is worth posing the proportionality question of whether the danger posed by large numbers of small munitions is greater or less than that posed by the alternative – a single unitary bomb. The US Defence Department, for instance, is on the record as arguing that unitary bombs cause more collateral damage than cluster bombs because they have a larger blast range (Human Rights Watch 2001: 10, n. 33). It argues that whilst the submunitions damaged civilian buildings, unitary bombs would have flattened them. This is certainly a plausible argument, but in the absence of a comprehensive comparative study it is impossible to draw any definitive conclusions.

Of the three cases of direct harm to non-combatants caused by cluster bombs, the Ainger case is most troubling. In that case, it appears that US forces belatedly targeted moving objects without verifying whether the military objects were actually present at the time of the attack or what the likely collateral damage would be. The other two cases present another thorny question: if there is to be a general moral prohibition on the use of cluster bombs close to residential areas, how far apart do the military objectives and non-combatant areas need to be? I propose that the limit be drawn by combining the outer limit of the cluster bomb's blast range (458 metres maximum on the largest type, the CBU-87) (see Lennox 1999: 87) with the expected outer limit of the margin of error (30 metres) of a bomb dropped by the US Air Force. According to this calculation, military targets that are located more than 500 metres away from residential areas may be hit with cluster bombs without causing collateral damage unless the margin of error is greater than what is normally expected. Within these limits, sustaining the argument that cluster bombs are indiscriminate would require (1) evidence that they are less accurate than other types of munitions and (2) evidence that when they inadvertently land in residential areas they can be expected to cause more damage than other types of munitions. To date, neither type of evidence has emerged.

In the Ainger case it is fair to conclude that whilst the US certainly did not deliberately act indiscriminately, it did fail the due care test because it did not take 'all feasible precautions' to minimize civilian casualties. That was more a result of the types of information/verification failure in a context of severe time restraints discussed above than the type of weapon. In the other two cases, however, it is difficult to sustain the case that the US failed the due care test in attacking the targets it did because the evidence seems to suggest that had the bombs struck their intended targets, the non-combatant victims would have been spared (by virtue of the fact that they were more than 500 metres away from the intended targets).

The much more problematic issue in relation to cluster bombs is their indiscriminate *effects*. Each submunition that fails to explode on impact effectively becomes a landmine: a type of weapon commonly believed to be inherently indiscriminate because it detonates irrespective of whether it is touched by a combatant or non-combatant and has no means of discriminating between the two. According to Human Rights Watch (2002: 25), by December 2002 unexploded submunitions had killed 127 non-combatants in Afghanistan, the majority of them children. As well as posing a direct threat, unexploded submunitions also have a number of indirect consequences for non-combatants. They make the collection of wood and water dangerous in some parts of the country and have a negative impact on agriculture by making some areas too dangerous to work on.

Do these ostensibly indiscriminate effects mean that the use of cluster bombs themselves should be deemed indiscriminate? It seems fairly evident that the US is not being directly indiscriminate. There are no credible reports of US forces deliberately using cluster bombs against civilian objects or non-combatants. Indeed, one could argue that cluster bombs are much like any other weapon in that all weapons pose an indiscriminate threat when they malfunction. The question of whether the US has taken every feasible precaution to minimize the damage that unexploded ordinance causes to non-combatants and civilian property poses a more difficult test.

Such precautions would include taking measures to reduce the proportion of failed submunitions and doing everything feasible to remove unexploded submunitions from the battlefield.

There is considerable debate about the failure rate of submunitions in Afghanistan. According to the US Air Force, the failure rate was 5 per cent, whereas the HALO Trust estimated the failure rate to be between 15 and 22 per cent (Fassihi 2001). The US reported to the UN Mine Action Group that seventy-eight targets were struck by a total of 1,120 cluster bombs, comprising 244,420 submunitions (Conetta 2002: n. 11). What this means is that at war's end there were between 12,221 and 53,772 unexploded submunitions in Afghanistan. Even at the lower end, this poses a significant threat to non-combatants. The first way to reduce this threat would be to lower the failure rate. In 2001, the US Secretary of Defence, William Cohen, announced that weapons manufacturers should aim to produce cluster weapons with a failure rate of 1 per cent or less and that future weapons procurement would be guided by this expectation (Human Rights Watch 2002: 30). As a result, the failure rate of newer weapons is considerably lower than that of older weapons. However, Cohen permitted the military to stockpile older submunitions, with the result that over a billion submunitions with a failure rate of between 5 and 22 per cent are currently stockpiled. There are reports that the US made extensive use of such 'legacy' weapons in Afghanistan. In late November, two non-combatant casualties – one a farmer in Kalakan and the other a boy near Herat – were blamed on unexploded submunitions from CBU-87s. CBU-87s were developed in 1983, and according to one report their failure rate was 'at least' 5 per cent (Watson and Getter 2001).

It is impossible to know precisely how many of the newer types of cluster bombs the US has in its possession and therefore it is difficult to make judgements about weapons selection. However, given that the CBU-87 is both an old weapon with a relatively high failure rate and the largest variant of cluster bomb, it is reasonable to expect the US not to use these weapons unless it is militarily necessary (not merely useful). Even then, the weapon should not to be used close to civilian areas. Given the high failure rate, the 500-metre separation suggested above offers scant protection from the long-term effects of these weapons. The use of such weapons in any other than remote areas would therefore fail the due care test. At very least, due care requires the use of the type of cluster bombs least likely to contain failing submunitions whenever they are used in areas likely to be traversed by non-combatants before they can be cleared of unexploded ordnance.

Because unexploded submunitions pose a continuing threat to non-combatants after the cessation of hostilities, those who delivered them have a responsibility to do everything feasible to remove them. Anything short of this breaches the principle of due care. Although de-mining and the removal of unexploded munitions have progressed apace in Afghanistan,

the overwhelming bulk of the effort was conducted by the UN Mine Action Programme and NGOs such as HALO (ICBL 2002: 593–5). The HALO Trust alone has dedicated twelve teams to clearing the unexploded submunitions from fifty-two places where cluster bombs were used. By the end of 2002, 111 cluster bomb sites had been cleared out of an estimated total of 227, with much of the remainder being cleared in 2003–4 (Human Rights Watch 2002: 33; ICBL 2004). The clearance of unexploded submunitions progressed well, and de-miners reported it had proven much less problematic than the removal of landmines (Sampson 2002). The most troubling issue was the very limited role played by the US government, the actor with the primary moral responsibility for removing the weapons. Most de-mining agencies in Afghanistan told Human Rights Watch that the US government provided little or no help, and that it had not even provided accurate information about the location and type of cluster bomb attacks, information considered crucial for the swift removal of unexploded submunitions. The US directly provided only eleven privately contracted de-miners and in the first eight months after the war donated only $7 million in cash and equipment to the de-mining effort (Human Rights Watch 2002: 37–8). To put this in perspective, the HALO programme in Afghanistan comprised up to 2,000 local and international de-miners and the Afghan government estimated that around $40 million was needed for de-mining (Afghanistan Ministry of Foreign Affairs 2002; ICBL 2004).

On two counts, therefore, the US failed the due care test. First, it used old weapons with relatively high failure rates in close proximity to residential areas. The decision to use such weapons in any other than the most remote regions, when other – more reliable – weapons were available, effectively placed non-combatants at greater risk in return for unknown benefits presumably linked to the relative cost and availability of newer weapons and the CBU-87's larger footprint. Second, having dropped cluster bombs, the US and its allies had a special responsibility to remove the threat to non-combatants posed by unexploded submunitions. Although the clearance of submunitions has progressed well in Afghanistan, the US government's contribution to that effort was not indicative of it doing everything feasible to protect non-combatants. Those responsible for delivering cluster bombs are primarily responsible for their clearance. Failure to assume this primary responsibility is a breach of due care.

Conclusion

Was the aerial bombardment of Afghanistan during Operation *Enduring Freedom* legitimate? It seems fairly clear that the air campaign was discriminate. The US stated its intention not to target non-combatants and utilized a targeting process designed to ensure this. As a result, the overall campaign

was remarkably accurate. The key problems were associated with the second test, that of due care.

Did the US and its allies take 'all feasible precautions' to protect non-combatants? The answer to that question must be tempered by acknowledging that the Taliban and Al-Qaeda attempted to erode the distinction between combatants and non-combatants by locating military facilities in residential areas and hiding themselves among the civilian population. The Taliban and Al-Qaeda bear at least part of the responsibility, and in several of the cases described above the primary responsibility, for non-combatant deaths. Nevertheless, in at least two respects the conduct of the air war by the US and its allies failed the due care test due in large part to national partiality.

First, it did not always do everything feasible to verify intelligence about targets, resulting in erroneous target selection. The US displayed national partiality by prioritizing the safety of its military personnel over that of Afghan non-combatants. It chose not to deploy significant numbers of ground forces or forward air controllers to identify and verify targets, presumably because of the attendant risks of doing so. As a consequence, it sometimes relied on unverified intelligence provided by Afghan sources that often proved unreliable. There is also evidence, from the first ICRC compound bombing for instance, that pilots were protected by altitude and the use of stand-off weapons. Though there were cases of pilots making visual contact with a target and choosing not to strike because of the lack of military activity, the ICRC case is a clear example of a pilot not making visual contact with a target clearly marked as a protected building.

Second, practices associated with the use of cluster bombs also demonstrated a failure of due care. The US and its allies failed to take all feasible precautions to minimize the harm to non-combatants caused by unexploded submunitions. The US used older weapons with higher failure rates to strike targets close to civilian areas and made a meagre contribution to clearing unexploded submunitions. Although there may be good operational reasons for the former, there are no good reasons for the latter. In sum, therefore, the US conducted the air war with a high degree of respect for discrimination and proportionality but tended to transfer risk (see Shaw, M. 2005: 86) from US forces to Afghan non-combatants – a morally (though not necessarily legally and politically) problematic strategy.

10

Humanitarian Intervention

The most violent conflicts in the world today are civil wars, often involving government-sponsored atrocities against non-combatants. In the 1990s, genocide in Rwanda killed at least 800,000, war in the former Yugoslavia killed at least 250,000 and forced thousands more to flee, and protracted conflicts in Sierra Leone, Haiti, Somalia, Sudan, Liberia, East Timor, the Democratic Republic of Congo (DRC) and elsewhere killed millions more. Approximately 90 per cent of these victims were non-combatants. In the twentieth century around 40 million people were killed in wars between states, whilst 170 million were killed by their own governments (Rummel 1994: 21). This raises important questions about when, if ever, outsiders are entitled to use force to protect non-combatants from their own governments. Do states have a legal or moral right to intervene in such cases? Do they have a *duty* to do so? The first part of this chapter briefly charts contemporary controversies about humanitarian intervention. The second outlines the evolution of thinking about humanitarian intervention within the Just War tradition. The third offers a framework for evaluating the legitimacy of humanitarian intervention. The final part investigates how this approach can shape our understanding of the ethics of humanitarian intervention by applying it to three recent cases: Kosovo, Iraq and Darfur.

The Contemporary Debate

The debate about the legitimacy of humanitarian intervention hinges on the relative value afforded to sovereignty, self-determination and the ban on the use of force, on the one hand, and universal human rights, on the other. It is possible to identify four broad positions according to whether they prioritize natural law or positive law and offer a permissive or restrictive account of humanitarian intervention. This section briefly outlines each of these positions.

Communitarianism

Communitarians argue that communities or nations have value in themselves. They claim that nations enjoy a 'common life' and should be free to determine their own system of governance. There is a 'fit', they argue, between the political community and the state, and it should be assumed that the latter enables the former to develop and protect its own ideas about how its members ought to live. Michael Walzer (1977: 87) argues that governments forfeit their sovereignty only when they enslave and massacre their own people, whereas John Stuart Mill (1973: 368–84) maintained that oppressed people themselves should overthrow their oppressors. The communitarian case has been widely criticized. Critics insist that there is no neat fit between nations and states, that it should not be assumed that states protect the common good, and that individuals are not parcelled into incommensurate groups (e.g. Doppelt 1978; Parekh 1997: 60).

Legal-Positivist: Restrictionist

Restrictionists hold that that the common good is best preserved by maintaining a ban on force not authorized by the UN Security Council. They assume that international society comprises a plurality of diverse communities each with different ideas about the best way to live (Rengger 2000: 105). International society is based on rules that permit communities to pursue their own conceptions of the good without infringing on others' right to do likewise (see Linklater 1998: 59). At the heart of this system are the UN Charter's rules governing the use of force. In a world characterized by radical disagreements about how societies should govern themselves, humanitarian intervention would create disorder as states waged wars to protect their own way of life and force others to live by their ethical preferences (Jackson, R. 2000: 291). Moreover, states have shown a distinct predilection towards 'abusing' humanitarian justifications to legitimize wars that were anything but humanitarian. Most notoriously, Hitler insisted that the 1939 invasion of Czechoslovakia was inspired by a desire to protect Czechoslovak citizens whose 'life and liberty' were threatened by their own government (in Brownlie 1974: 217–21). For these reasons, the argument follows, states developed a framework of positive law comprising a comprehensive ban on the use of force except in self-defence or when authorized by the Security Council. Without this general ban there would be *more war* in international society but not necessarily more genuine humanitarian interventions (Chesterman 2001: 231).

This position has been criticized on a number of grounds. First, Fernando Tesón (1997) argues that it is predicated on a partial reading of Grotius and

Vattel, who insisted that natural law imposed limits on how a sovereign may behave towards his own citizens, and overlooks the wealth of customary practice suggesting that sovereignty carries responsibilities as well as rights. Second, Thomas Weiss (2004: 135) claims that the fear of abuse is exaggerated. Third, some positive lawyers suggest that restrictionists overlook the body of international law relating to human rights (e.g. Mertus 2000; Scheffer 1992).

Legal-Positivist: Counter-Restrictionism

The counter-restrictionist perspective holds that diverse communities can and do reach agreement about substantive moral standards and that states have the authority to uphold those standards (Linklater 1998: 166–7). They argue that there is a customary right (but not duty) of intervention in what Nicholas Wheeler (2000: 13) describes as 'supreme humanitarian emergencies'. Counter-restrictionists claim that there is agreement in international society that cases of genocide, mass killing and ethnic cleansing constitute grave humanitarian crises warranting intervention (e.g. Arend and Beck 1993; Tesón 1997). Some lawyers go as far as to read a humanitarian exception to the ban on force into the text of the UN Charter. W. Michael Reisman (1985: 279–80) argued that had the Security Council functioned as originally intended, it would have enforced a basic minimum of human rights and taken action against states that committed genocide, mass murder or ethnic cleansing. Because the Council failed to do this, he argued, part of the justification for the ban on force was eroded, creating a right for states to take unilateral humanitarian action when necessary. Lori Fisler Damrosch (1991: 219) claimed that humanitarian intervention is not forbidden because it violates neither a state's 'territorial integrity' nor its 'political independence', the two conditions set out in Article 2(4) of the UN Charter.

There are a number of problems with this approach. In particular, it exaggerates the extent of consensus about the use of force to protect human rights, epitomized by Richard Falk's description of the 1990s as 'undoubtedly the golden age of humanitarian diplomacy' and Thomas Weiss' claim that 'the notion that human beings matter more than sovereignty radiated brightly, albeit briefly, across the international political horizon of the 1990s' (Falk 2003; Weiss, T. G. 2004: 136). This putative 'golden age' included the world's failure to halt the Rwandan genocide, the UN's failure to protect civilians sheltering in its 'safe areas' in Bosnia, the failure to prevent the widely predicted mass murder that followed East Timor's vote for independence in 1999, and massacres in both Burundi and Sudan. Moreover, the Security Council has yet to authorize intervention against a fully functioning sovereign state.

Liberal Cosmopolitanism

The final approach places less emphasis on the importance of inter-state consensus and focuses instead on the natural law idea that individuals have certain inalienable rights. It differs from counter-restrictionism because it insists that external actors have a duty as well as a right to intervene in supreme humanitarian emergencies (Rawls 1999: 119). Sovereignty should be understood as an instrumental value because it derives from a state's responsibility to protect the welfare of its citizens, and when a state fails in this duty, it loses its sovereign rights (Tesón 2003: 93). There are a variety of ways of arriving at this conclusion. Some draw on Kant's concept of the rational individual to insist that all individuals have certain pre-political rights (Caney 1997: 34). Others argue that today's globalized world is so integrated that massive human rights violations in one part of the world have an effect on every other part, creating moral obligations (Blair 1999). Some Just War writers use Augustine's insistence that force be used to defend public order to argue that intervention to end injustice is 'among the rights and duties of states until and unless supplanted by superior government' (Ramsey 2002: 20). The Christian duty to offer charity to those in need, Paul Ramsey (2002: 35–6) argues, is universal.

The liberal cosmopolitan approach is also problematic. First, there are good reasons to doubt the empirical validity of the claim that all individuals have intrinsic rights, particularly because liberalism (the source of most of the rights) is rejected in many parts of the world (Parekh 1997: 54–5). Others such as Chris Brown (2002) and Christian Reus-Smit (1999) contend that it makes no sense to talk of pre-political rights because rights are meaningful only when there are institutions bearing requisite duties. Tesón (2004: 100) counters by arguing that there is widespread consensus about 'basic rights' amongst the world's major ethical systems, whilst Charles Beitz (1979: 422) argues that the communitarian case against intervention also lacks empirical support. Second, there is a strong likelihood that a norm endorsing the use of force to protect individual rights would be abused, taking us back to the restrictionist case against intervention.

In sum, almost every aspect of humanitarian intervention is contested. One cannot argue that ethical principles should always override the law in cases where the two collide because (1) legal rules protect important values and (2) there is no consensus within natural law. On the other hand, those who find simple answers in a restrictive reading of the legal ban on force must also confront the moral consequences of their choice. As Ramsey (2002: 23) puts it, 'anyone who is impressed only by the immorality and probable ineffectiveness of interventionary action should sensitize his conscience to the immorality and probable ineffectiveness of non-intervention'. In order to untie this Gordian knot, we need to begin by understanding the context in which these different perspectives arose and their historical relationship to one another.

Humanitarian Intervention in Natural and Positive Law

The evolution of Just War thinking about humanitarian intervention can be divided into three epochs. In the first, from Augustine to the early Middle Ages, Christendom was formally (if not physically) united in a common political and ethical space. There was a broad consensus that political leaders had a universal duty to uphold justice. Secular rulers had a responsibility to uphold the law throughout Christendom and a divine duty to protect the innocent (Elshtain 2001b: 8). Sovereignty provided no barrier against action, nor did it limit the geographical extent of a ruler's obligations, because the extent of a ruler's domain was not geographically settled, the divinely constituted natural law was considered binding on all Christians and most political entities were not wholly sovereign.

During the second epoch, which ran from the end of the Middle Ages until 1945, the moral and legal consensus held that there was a right but not a duty to wage war to protect the innocent. There was a consistent trend towards restricting that right until by the eighteenth and nineteenth centuries many liberals were arguing against a right of humanitarian intervention, whilst many states defended their right to intervene. There were two pivotal changes during this epoch: first, rights and duties were decoupled; second, the idea of a common Christian space was gradually replaced with the idea of separate and incommensurate political communities.

Vitoria replaced the 'duty' to intervene with a 'permission' to do so, and placed important limits on how the right could be invoked and on the scope of permissible action. Whilst he shared the view that humanity was a 'universal community' governed by natural law, he argued that the prosecution of war to protect the innocent be constrained (Vitoria 1991a: 288). Given that all humans were 'neighbours' in God's eyes, Vitoria (1991a: 288) argued that 'anyone, and especially princes may defend them from such tyranny and oppression'. He singled out cannibalism and human sacrifice as providing just cause for war, but insisted that intervening princes should not continue to prosecute the war once the violations cease, may not use natural law as a pretext for seizing land or goods, conducting forcible conversions or despoiling Indians of wealth and gold, and must make provisions to protect and increase their temporal goods, pass good laws, and ensure that they are enforced (Vitoria 1991c: 223–7).

Grotius argued that, *in extremis*, sovereigns had a limited right but no duty to aid the subjects of other states. He maintained that all persons and states enjoyed pre-social rights under natural law. Natural law prohibited certain acts but did not demand that individuals aid one another (see Nardin

2002: 61–2). Grotius (1925: 584) placed important limits on when sovereigns may wage war to aid others and remained deeply concerned about the potential for abuse. He insisted that subjects had a responsibility to obey the law, and were wrong to rebel in cases where their ruler was not obviously tyrannical. Even where rule was obviously tyrannical, Grotius refused to endorse a right of rebellion, though he did endorse the right of other sovereigns to intervene (see Nardin 2002: 62).

The two chief concerns evident in this work – that a state is based on the assumed consent of its citizens and the danger of abuse – coupled with the rise of the idea of simultaneous ostensible justice, continued to erode the consensus on the right to defend foreigners against extreme violations of natural law. Pufendorf (1934) insisted that sovereigns did not have a right to punish others for violations of the natural law and might only help third parties when invited to do so. Wolff (1934) removed even this caveat and imposed an absolute ban on 'punitive war'. John Stuart Mill endorsed this position, insisting that free governments could be established only through a domestic struggle for liberty. Mill shared Kant's view that a rule of non-intervention was a necessary prerequisite for free, republican government, though he argued that only 'civilized' peoples could exercise this right and that 'barbarians' were rightly subjected to foreign rule (Mill 1973: 377–8; cf. Bain 2003: 2, 143 and Doyle 2001: 214). The pre-eminent jurist of the eighteenth century, Vattel, endorsed the general principle of non-intervention on the grounds that each state had the right to govern itself as it saw fit (Vattel 1916: 131) and states had a right to punish only crimes that affected their safety or that of their citizens (Vattel 1916: 116). However, he accepted Pufendorf's view that intervention was permissible if a sovereign's rule was so tyrannical that it caused a legitimate revolt and the rebels requested aid (Vattel 1916: 131), a view partially accepted by Mill, who admitted a right of intervention in cases where civilized peoples were oppressed by foreign nations (Mill 1973: 176).

It is important to place these arguments in context. The overriding concern for many of these writers was to avoid repetition of the disastrous wars that had engulfed Europe for much of the seventeenth century. The post-Grotian writers mentioned above were galvanized by a mixture of concerns, but two stand out. First, there was a clear belief in the value of order predicated on a system of equal sovereigns, within Europe at least. Second, liberals such as Pufendorf, Wolff and Mill were only too aware that a right of intervention could be used by absolutist monarchies to crush more liberal regimes. Given this, it is not surprising that an intellectual consensus emerged in favour of either a complete ban on intervention or else a very limited right, whilst European states themselves often justified the use of force in humanitarian terms throughout the eighteenth and nineteenth centuries (see Chesterman 2001: 35).

Positive law caught up with the emerging consensus among natural lawyers in 1945, at the beginning of the third epoch. At least three considerations helped to galvanize states into agreeing a complete ban on the use of force. First, Hitler's use of humanitarian justifications to legitimize the invasion of Czechoslovakia demonstrated the danger of abuse all too clearly. Second, there was a widespread consensus that order could be maintained only by outlawing force. Third, the anti-colonial movement insisted that foreign interference in the government of other nations was morally wrong. The new positive legal order was predicated on a clear ban on the use of force set out in Article 2(4) of the UN Charter but contained a mechanism for authorizing humanitarian intervention: Chapter VII of the UN Charter entitled the Security Council to authorize collective enforcement action wherever it identified a threat to international peace and security (see Chapter 5).

However, the Security Council did not function as intended, and its permanent members failed to assume their responsibilities as millions were killed in Biafra, Cambodia, Uganda, East Pakistan, Latin America, Zaïre/Democratic Republic of Congo, Rwanda, Sudan, the Balkans, Afghanistan, East Timor and elsewhere. In relation to humanitarian intervention, sovereignty often came to be understood as something like an absolute value. During the Cold War, states remained reluctant to justify interventions on humanitarian grounds and international society steadfastly refused to legitimate such actions. In the most extreme case, the US and some of its allies imposed economic sanctions on Vietnam as punishment for its 1978 invasion of Cambodia which ousted Pol Pot's regime, responsible for the butchery of around two million Cambodians. Although there was progress towards a weak norm of authorized intervention in the 1990s (see Wheeler, N. J. 2000), the Security Council took four years to reach a consensus over Bosnia, failed altogether to do so over Kosovo, Iraq and Darfur, and stood aside during the 1994 Rwandan genocide.

This litany of failure created a 'chasm' between the Security Council's record and the professed normative aspirations of most of the world's peoples (Brunee and Toope 2004: 800). As a result there have been numerous attempts to articulate alternatives. The Catholic Church, for instance, insists that individuals are members of both their state and the global 'human family' (John Paul II 1992: 37–9). According to John Paul II (1993: 587), 'the principles of sovereignty of states and of non-interference in their internal affairs – which retain all their value – cannot constitute a screen behind which torture and murder can be carried out'. From this perspective, sovereignty is seen as an instrumental value that enables governments to establish orderly and just societies, but when governments fail to fulfil sovereignty's purpose, their legitimacy is diminished. Because humanity is a unified whole, the use of force against sovereigns who abuse their citizens is justified 'as an exercise of cosmopolitan justice or global solidarity' (Miller, R. B. 1991: 57).

This view of sovereignty is common today. In the mid-1990s, Francis Deng and his collaborators (1996) put forward the idea of 'sovereignty as responsibility'. Echoing John Paul II, UN Secretary-General Kofi Annan (2001) used the 2001 Nobel Lecture to argue that 'the sovereignty of states must no longer be used as a shield for gross violations of human rights'. Many liberal states have echoed these views in recent years. The US government has labelled as 'rogues' those states that 'brutalize their own people and squander their natural resources for the personal gain of their rulers' (NSS 2002). The British government pledged itself to use military force to prevent and halt future genocides (Blair 2001). Even non-liberal states have joined the chorus, rhetorically at least. The African Union's Constitutive Act, signed on 11 July 2000, awarded the new organization a right to intervene in member states to halt war crimes and crimes against humanity (Article 4(h)). In practice, however, these ideas continue to crash against a persistent tendency among many, if not most, of the world's states to privilege non-intervention over human rights.

It is important to understand the natural law and positive law components of the humanitarian intervention debate as intersecting streams rather than isolated traditions. They prioritize different values for different reasons. It is worth briefly summarizing their position on four pivotal questions.

Sovereignty as an absolute or instrumental value. There is a surprisingly broad consensus that sovereignty is instrumental. It is to be valued because of what it *does* not what it *is*. Critically, anti-interventionists agree that sovereignty is valuable only because it helps to satisfy other social goods.

The idea of common rights. There appears to be a wider consensus about common rights than suggested by the debate as outlined in the first part of the chapter. In natural law, the debate boils down to the instrumental question of whether outsiders can help realize those rights. The question of whether there are common rights is more divisive among positive lawyers. Restrictionists argue that there is no consensus on the enforcement of basic human rights law, whilst counter-restrictionists dispute this. On balance, it is a long time since political actors believed that genocide, mass murder and ethnic cleansing were justifiable, suggesting a broad consensus that these acts are wrong because they violate rights common to all.

Who has a right to intervene? Some communitarians accepted the idea that intervention is permissible if invited by those struggling to liberate themselves or if the intervener is in some way affected by the armed struggle. Those who accepted the view that outsiders could play a role in assisting people to realize their rights suggested that any legitimate state could use force to help others achieve those rights. The main problem with this perspective is the danger of abuse. This is the primary reason why restrictionists endorse a comprehensive prohibition on force. The UN Charter system offers a theoretical mid-point between total prohibition and an entirely permissive order by granting the Security Council the legal authority to authorize enforcement action. Sadly, the Council has not functioned as intended.

Is there a duty to intervene? According to the earliest Just War writers, the natural rights that all men enjoyed translated into universal duties. However, they were writing in a period where there was a common system of laws and institutions grounded in *ius gentium* and canon law. As this hierarchical system was gradually replaced by a system of territorial sovereigns, the idea that natural rights entitled universal duties was eroded. In some respects, divorcing the right to intervene from a duty to do so exacerbates the problem of abuse by providing states with a high degree of discretion to determine when they will and will not use force to prevent and punish violations of natural law (Himes 1994: 89).

With these four sets of issues in mind, the next part of the chapter attempts to articulate a Just War approach to humanitarian intervention that charts a path through these competing ideals.

Just War and Humanitarian Intervention

In 2001, the Canadian government gave the high-profile International Commission on Intervention and State Sovereignty (ICISS) the task of untying the Gordian knot of humanitarian intervention (ICISS 2001: viii). The ICISS (2001: 17) insisted that the primary responsibility for protecting civilians lay with the host state and that outside intervention could be contemplated only if the state proved either unwilling or unable to fulfil its responsibilities. On the question of when to intervene, the ICISS (2001: para. 4.19) adopted the commonly held view that intervention should be limited to 'extreme' cases where there was large-scale or imminently threatened loss of life or ethnic cleansing, whether deliberately caused by the state or facilitated by neglect or incapacity. The question of authority proved thornier. The ICISS proposed a three-layered distribution of responsibility. Primary responsibility lay with the host state. Secondary responsibility lay with the domestic authorities working in partnership with outside agencies. If the primary and secondary levels failed to ameliorate the humanitarian emergency, international organizations would assume responsibility (ICISS 2001: para. 6.11). At this third level of responsibility, the ICISS accepted the view that primary legal authority was vested in the Security Council.

If the Security Council was deadlocked, it argued that potential interveners should approach the General Assembly under the Uniting for Peace mechanism and, if that failed, work through regional organizations (ICISS 2001: paras 6.29–6.40). To improve the likelihood of consensus in the Council, the ICISS recommended that its permanent members commit themselves to criteria relating to the use of force in humanitarian emergencies. It was suggested that states always seek Security Council authorization before using force; that the Council commit itself to dealing promptly with humanitarian emergencies involving large-scale loss of life; that the permanent members commit themselves to not casting a veto to obstruct humanitarian action unless their vital national interests are involved; and that Security Council members recognize that if they fail to fulfil their responsibility, other states and organizations may take it upon themselves to act – undermining the Council's standing in the world (ICISS 2001: xii–xiii). The Commission insisted that the question of military intervention be placed firmly on the global agenda if two 'just cause thresholds' (large-scale loss of life and ethnic cleansing) and four 'precautionary principles' (right intention, last resort, proportional means, reasonable prospects) were satisfied (ICISS 2001: xii).

The search for a legitimating framework is not entirely novel. Earlier attempts have been deeply influenced by Just War thinking (e.g. Fisher 1994: 51–9; Phillips and Cady 1996). All too often these approaches focused on the tradition's natural law defence of intervention at the expense of engagement with either natural or positive law's opposition to intervention. Taking positive law seriously places important constraints on the application of criteria. In the framework that follows I attempt to balance these competing sets of values.

Primary Consideration: Right Authority and Just Cause

In order to constrain 'abusive' humanitarian interventionism whilst enabling the genuine variety, it is important to recognize a profound connection between right authority and the just cause threshold. Most Just War approaches to humanitarian intervention begin with just cause. Were it not for the need to restrain abuse, enable genuine action and demonstrate respect for anti-interventionist arguments it would certainly be most appropriate to begin with the just cause – the nature and scale of the problem at hand – and to look at the issue from the victim's perspective, as the ICISS insists. To do that, however, would require either setting a low just cause threshold that may invite abuse or setting a high threshold to avoid abuse, as the ICISS did. The problem with the ICISS threshold (mass murder and large-scale ethnic cleansing) is that it sets the threshold higher than necessary. In theory, the Security Council may legitimately identify emergencies as threats to international peace and security, even where there is no pattern of mass killing or ethnic cleansing. In practice, it has been reluctant to do so, though it could be plausibly argued that, although bad, the situations in Haiti in 1994 and Côte d'Ivoire in 2002 did not satisfy these criteria, yet in both cases the Security Council passed Chapter VII (enforcement) resolutions.

This raises two questions: why is authorized intervention legitimate in lesser cases? And, if authorized intervention is legitimate in those cases, why not unauthorized intervention? Recall that communitarians argue that conceptions of the good are constituted within political communities but they admit that political communities may agree about a thin layer of common principles to govern relations between them. A key part of that legal framework is the Security Council's right to identify threats to international peace and security and authorize collective enforcement. The assumption underpinning this piece of law is that the Council acts for the common good. Thus, if it authorizes humanitarian intervention it presumably does so because *common* values have been violated. It follows from this that it cannot be assumed that unauthorized interveners are defending common values. It may well be that a plausible defence along these lines can be put forward in individual cases, but unauthorized intervention begs the question of why, if the values at stake were common ones, intervention was not authorized. This places a further burden of justification on the interveners, requiring them to sustain a more compelling case in relation to the other criteria than is required for authorized interventions.

There are at least four potential sources of authority: the invitation of the host government, the UN Security Council, regional organizations and individual states. As I noted earlier, the ICISS helpfully placed these four sources in a hierarchical relationship (host state, UN, regional organizations, individual states). This begs two important questions. First, how much value should be attached to host government consent? Second, is the relationship between the four levels sequential?

Not only does host government consent ease legal concerns about intervention, it also helps satisfy communitarian concerns by permitting the assumption that external intervention is requested by the target population. However, there are at least two problems with affording primacy to host state consent. First, if consent is given, are the interveners entitled to act in ways only consented to, for instance delivering aid but not using force to halt genocide? In most cases today, the government is at very least a party to the conflict and in many cases it is the primary cause of the humanitarian emergency. Ideally, therefore, an intervention force should be able to defend its legitimacy even if the host government withdraws its consent. The second problem with privileging host state consent lies in its motives for requesting assistance. If the government is a party to the conflict, it may be tempted to offer consent to further its own interests. In the early 1990s, the Yugoslav government requested that an arms embargo be placed on it. At the time, the Security Council welcomed the request as evidence of Yugoslavia's commitment to preventing the war. After the war broke out, however, the motives behind that request became all too evident. The overwhelming majority of former Yugoslav military hardware fell into the hands of the Serbian government whilst the arms embargo denied the new governments of Slovenia, Croatia and Bosnia-Hercegovina the means of effectively defending themselves.

Whilst host government consent may confer legal legitimacy, it does not provide the moral authority that some suggest. A humanitarian intervention is not legitimate simply because it has host government consent. It is important to ask questions about the nature of the government's consent, its role in the humanitarian catastrophe, and its potential motives before placing too much faith in it. Government consent should not, therefore, be viewed as prior to the other forms of authority.

The ICISS argued that the relationship between the different types of authority for humanitarian intervention ought to be sequential. There are two practical problems with this. First, it significantly increases the potential political costs of intervention. Consider a hypothetical situation where the British government was committed to acting to stop ethnic cleansing in Kosovo but other NATO members were not. The sequential model would have required Blair to ask Milošević for permission to intervene; present a draft Security Council resolution and have it rejected; approach the General Assembly and fail to acquire a two-thirds majority; and then fail to persuade all the members of the EU or NATO to act, before taking unilateral action. It is highly unlikely that in such a case Britain would intervene, having faced so many political setbacks. The legitimacy costs, both domestically and internationally, would simply be too high. Second, moving through the levels of responsibility sequentially imposes significant delays. Suppose the Security Council agrees to launch a diplomatic mission or to impose travel bans on suspected war criminals, or calls for militia to be disarmed. How long should potential interveners wait to see if these measures work before acting outside the Council? Given that rapid deployment is widely understood to be a key determinant of success in humanitarian intervention (e.g. Brahimi et al. 2000), we should not endorse an ethic of intervention that precludes it in the worst cases. Although there is a clear hierarchy of preferable authority (UN Security Council, UN General Assembly, appropriate regional organization, individual states), we should not in all cases require states to pursue authorization in each venue before acting.

To summarize, the Security Council has the authority to sanction intervention in cases where it believes that violations of common values constitute a just cause. The legitimacy of the Security Council's decision to authorize force remains conditional on it satisfying the other *jus ad bellum* criteria, but it is important to note that force may be a proportionate response to many injustices below the threshold of mass killing and ethnic cleansing. In 'extraordinary' cases that satisfy the ICISS' just cause threshold, regional organizations, coalitions of the willing or individual states may act outside the Council. Although they have a responsibility to gauge the will of the Security Council, in cases where there is on-going mass killing and large-scale ethnic cleansing, they are not obliged to engage in protracted negotiations, pursue non-forcible policies through the Council, or table draft resolutions that are likely to be vetoed. The primary obligation in these cases is to stop the killing and ethnic cleansing. In short, there is a sliding scale between the level of authority and the just cause threshold. All other things being equal, the higher the level of authority, the lower the just cause threshold, and vice versa. This is both constraining and enabling. It guards against abuse by requiring Security Council authorization in contentious cases, but it enables action when the crimes are worst by permitting a larger number of actors to authorize intervention.

Other Criteria

The relationship between authority and just cause does not complete the moral interrogation of humanitarian intervention. Like all decisions to wage war, humanitarian intervention must satisfy the other *jus ad bellum* criteria: right intention, proportionality, prudence and last resort. In addition, humanitarian interveners have two special responsibilities not necessarily incumbent on those who use force for other justifiable purposes such as self-defence: they must calibrate their choice of military means to the intended humanitarian ends and make a long-term commitment to reconstruction (*jus post bellum*).

Right intention and the duty to intervene

One of the most significant contemporary debates concerns the question of whether it is the humanitarian *motive* of the intervener or the humanitarian *outcome* that is produced by the intervention that is most significant in ascertaining its legitimacy (cf. Verwey 1998; Wheeler, N. J. 2000). Both positions misconstrue the Just War tradition by overlooking the important difference between an actor's *motives* and its *intentions*. A state may launch a humanitarian intervention for self-interested reasons (motives) but its *intention* may still be humanitarian: it may be calculated, for instance, that regional order is best accomplished by protecting human rights and democracy. The Just War tradition requires that those embarking on humanitarian intervention have a primarily humanitarian *intent*. Although it is always difficult to determine an actor's intentions, it can be approximated by focusing on four issues: (1) whether the actor acknowledges a duty to prevent and halt supreme humanitarian emergencies; (2) the justifications the actor offers to legitimize the intervention; (3) the calibration of means and ends; and (4) a long-term commitment to post-war reconstruction.

The first requirement is potentially the most controversial. States do not often openly accept that they have a duty to intervene, though it is tacitly acknowledged when they concede 'failures' in Rwanda, Srebrenica and elsewhere (Glanville 2005). When states admonish themselves for not acting, they are implying that inaction was wrong. Recognizing a duty to contemplate intervention is important, for two reasons. First, rights always entail duties. With universal rights come universal duties. Rights without duties are hollow, and since there is broad agreement that there are *some* universal rights (such as the right not be killed in a genocide), it follows that there must be some universal duties, including a duty to enable others to enjoy fundamental rights. Because it would be unrealistic to expect every individual to take action to enable every other individual to enjoy these rights, duties are mediated by political institutions (Shue 1988: 698). That is not to say that states have a duty to wage humanitarian war whenever there is just cause, but that the reasons for not intervening in particular cases ought to be normative, based on proportionality and prudential concerns. Second, acknowledging a right but not a duty to intervene creates the potential for abuse. The key then is to acknowledge that not every state has a duty to contemplate intervening in supreme humanitarian emergencies. When states intervene for ostensibly humanitarian purposes, making use of a permissive moral right of intervention, they acknowledge the existence of universal rights and duties, and therefore become obligated to contemplate action in other similar crises. Acknowledging this duty involves two tests. First, in any given case, it is fair to expect potential interveners to acknowledge their sense of *obligation* to act, otherwise humanitarian language becomes a mere rhetorical tool. A good indicator of this may be the political risks that a leader is prepared to accept in order to act. In Germany, Joschka Fischer risked his political future over Kosovo and Gerhard Schroeder likewise over Afghanistan. The second test is to assess how those same states reacted to other humanitarian emergencies. States are not required to intervene in every case, but a state that uses humanitarian justifications in one case ought to recognize a duty to uphold universal rights by exploring options in other like cases.

Proportionality and prudence

Humanitarian interventions must be proportionate and prudent. That is, they must be calculated to cause more good than harm. A government that controls the media but does not murder its citizens may not be the subject of intervention because it would be disproportionate. The lower end of the just cause scale may encompass states like Afghanistan in 2001, Iraq in early

2003, Burma, North Korea, Zimbabwe and Uzbekistan. These are/were states that torture, murder and unjustly imprison thousands of their citizens each year. If an authorized intervention could be conducted in these states in a way that minimized harm to civilians, it could be legitimate, though it is hard to see how casualties could be kept to such low levels as to be proportionate.

Prudence places a further limit on the extent of the humanitarian duties described above, and, as we saw in Chapter 6, it should be part of any Just War conversation. In most cases, proportionality and prudence dictate the same policy. For instance, Western intervention to halt the Russian assault on Chechnya would have been both imprudent (Western forces would have suffered heavy casualties, Europe would have been destabilized, conflict might have been protracted) and disproportionate (it is likely that more Russians and Chechens would have died as a result). However, it is possible to envisage instances where humanitarian intervention may be proportionate but imprudent because of the potential costs to the intervener. A state may not sacrifice large numbers of its citizens for uncertain humanitarian outcomes in foreign countries. Although states owe duties to foreigners, they owe their primary duty of care to their own citizens (see Chapter 6).

Calibrate ends and means

Interveners should select strategies that enable them to prevail without undermining humanitarian outcomes. This may require more than abiding by *jus in bello* principles, placing two additional burdens on political leaders and military commanders. First, military planners should pay particular attention to due care in selecting targets and weapons. In humanitarian interventions, failure to exhibit due care casts serious doubt on the legitimacy of the operation as a whole. Second, political and military leaders should select the military strategy calculated to achieve the best humanitarian outcome in the shortest amount of time and with the least danger to non-combatants. This requirement raises important questions about the relative value afforded to force protection and protection of non-combatants. In Chapter 9, I argued that whilst military commanders are required to accept higher risks to their soldiers if doing so reduces the danger to non-combatants, there are important limits on how much risk they are obliged to accept. There is no reason to think that the relationship between force protection and the protection of non-combatants should be different in humanitarian interventions. The key difference is that in humanitarian interventions the persistent prioritization of force protection or failure to demonstrate due care has a more readily apparent negative impact on the perceived justice of the war as a whole (*jus ad bellum*) than in other types of justifiable war.

Jus post bellum

The second additional moral requirement for those embarking on humanitarian intervention is an obligation to rebuild the target country afterwards. In some sense, all participants in war have this obligation and there are good reasons to argue for the inclusion of *jus post bellum* as a third plank of the Just War tradition, though this is premature at present (see Orend 2000b, 2002; Walzer 2004b). Under *jus post bellum*, states that embark on humanitarian interventions are required to assist the host population in rebuilding their country, though they must not impose their own blueprint for reconstruction on unwilling peoples. Commitment to *jus post bellum* is therefore an important indicator of the intervener's humanitarian purposes. The failure to demonstrate commitment in this area casts serious doubt on an intervener's humanitarian intent and, where this was the principal justification for going to war, the legitimacy of the intervention itself.

This framework is predicated on the idea that there are certain universal moral rights that cross cultural boundaries. However, it rejects the idea that states can decide for themselves when and where they use force in order to protect those rights. The framework begins with the claim that there is an intimate relationship between the scale of the just cause and the intervention's source of authority. States may act unilaterally in relatively clear-cut cases of genocide, mass murder and large-scale ethnic cleansing so long as the other Just War criteria are satisfied. In more ambiguous cases, however, they are obliged to act collectively. Collective action guards against abuse (which becomes less important as the magnitude of the humanitarian crisis increases) and ensures that force is used only to protect *common* values. Humanitarian interventions must be conducted with humanitarian intent, which can be evaluated by four tests: do the interveners appear to recognize a duty to act in other like cases? What justifications do they offer? Have they carefully calibrated the military means with the humanitarian ends? Do they make a commitment to *jus post bellum*? Finally, humanitarian intervention, like all wars, must satisfy the other *jus ad bellum* and *jus in bello* criteria. In particular, all of the above considerations are dependent on calculations of proportionality and prudence. The challenge now is to apply this framework to case studies focusing on hard cases where the Security Council refused to authorize action.

Cases

Kosovo 1999

On 24 March 1999, NATO launched Operation *Allied Force* to prevent a humanitarian catastrophe in Kosovo. The intervention was not authorized by the Security Council. NATO chose not to present a draft resolution because Russia threatened to veto any resolution authorizing force (Wheeler, N. J. 2000: 261). NATO's intervention in Kosovo is therefore a significant test of the legitimacy of humanitarian intervention because it involved a group of states stepping outside the UN framework and using force to end a humanitarian emergency. A commission of experts found the intervention to be 'illegal but legitimate' (IICK 2000: 4), meaning that whilst it did not satisfy the strictures of positive law, there was at least a partial consensus that it was 'sanctioned by its compelling moral purpose' (Clark, I. 2005: 212). In other words, there was a tension between positive law and natural law, with NATO and its supporters arguing that the compelling nature of the moral case overrode the legal rules. Most NATO members chose not to defend the intervention on legal grounds, arguing instead that the ethnic cleansing of Kosovar Albanians created a moral imperative for action. A Russian draft Security Council resolution (see S/PV.3989) condemning the intervention was rejected by twelve votes to three (Russia, China, Namibia). Whilst the failure of the Russian draft did not constitute retrospective authorization (see Wheeler, N. J. 2001: 156), it adds credence to the counter-restrictionist claim that there is a moral consensus among liberal states and some others about the necessity of sometimes unauthorized intervention in supreme humanitarian emergencies (see Wheeler, N. J. 2004a: 44–5). It should not be overlooked, however, that many, if not most, of the world's states opposed intervention (see Schnabel and Thakur 2000).

Judgements about the legitimacy of NATO's intervention in Kosovo revolve around two questions. The first is the all-important question of the relationship between right authority and just cause. Immediately before the war, Clinton (in Anon. 1999) argued that 'I think that whatever threshold they [the Serbs] need to cross has been crossed'. NATO's position was that ethnic cleansing in Kosovo constituted a grave affront to Europe's core values and that, as Blair put it, 'we cannot allow war to devastate part of our continent, bringing untold death, homelessness and suffering' (in Wheeler, N. J. 2000: 265–6). Opponents of the war disputed NATO's claim that the crisis in Kosovo had crossed the just cause threshold. To counter the argument that the threshold had been crossed, Russian diplomats pointed to the legitimacy of Serbia's cause (preserving Yugoslavia's territorial integrity), war crimes committed by the Kosovo Liberation Army, and the relatively low casualty figures. They questioned whether the use of force was proportionate and argued that the most prudent way to proceed was in collaboration with the Yugoslav government (see Lynch 2001).

Where on the sliding scale of right authority and just cause did Kosovo sit? Some of NATO's critics insisted that the alliance acted precipitately, sharing Russia's assessment that the crisis was not serious enough to warrant intervention (e.g. Chomsky 1999; Walker, H. 2005: 36–7). The pivotal retrospective question, often overlooked, is: what triggered the decision to begin the bombing? The popular version of events holds that NATO had decided to intervene in the event of Milošević refusing to accept the Rambouillet settlement proposed by NATO and Russia (see Chomsky 1999: 107; McGwire 2000). When Milošević did just that, ostensibly because the proposed settlement granted NATO forces freedom of movement throughout Yugoslavia, NATO began its bombing campaign. In actuality, many NATO members believed that failure to sign the deal alone could not trigger intervention. The US argued that there were two triggers: non-acceptance of the proposed settlement *and* ceasefire violations. On 18 March, it insisted that the Yugoslav government had triggered both of them (in Weller 1999: 491). However, some European allies (France, Italy and Greece in particular) were not convinced that either of the thresholds had been crossed in the immediate aftermath of Rambouillet. They believed that there remained scope for negotiation and that the escalating violence in Kosovo was not indicative of a general breakdown of the ceasefire. The decision to bomb was not a foregone conclusion. On 20 March, reports of a new wave of systematic ethnic cleansing began to emerge, but even then some European allies remained reluctant to intervene. Richard Holbrooke was despatched to Belgrade to seek a political settlement. When the North Atlantic Council met on 22 March, Holbrooke reported that no progress with Milošević was likely. Crucially, the number of Kosovar Albanians ethnically cleansed in the preceding days had climbed to 60,000 and reports of mass murders were emerging (see US Department of State 1999a, 1999b). In the face of this rapidly escalating humanitarian crisis, Italy, Greece and France withdrew their opposition to immediate airstrikes (see Clark, W. K. 2001: Ch. 6). The important point here is that although the failed negotiations brought NATO leaders to the table, it was the perception of an *immediate* humanitarian crisis that forced reluctant states to agree to the bombing campaign.

It is reasonable therefore to conclude that the humanitarian crisis in Kosovo was dire enough to warrant unauthorized intervention, though this case is more marginal than the Darfur case discussed below. The intervention's legitimacy, however, depends on whether NATO satisfied the other criteria. Here there are two significant problems. First, there is considerable doubt about whether NATO properly calibrated its means (airstrikes) and ends (protecting Kosovar Albanians). Second, there are some doubts as to whether NATO's targeting satisfied the proportionality and discrimination principles. In what follows, I will focus on the first set of issues because the targeting issues in relation to Kosovo are very similar to those explored in Chapter 9. Moreover, the International Criminal Tribunal for the Former Yugoslavia (ICTY 2000) explored these complaints and concluded that NATO did not have a legal case to answer.

Did NATO fail to calibrate means and ends and contribute, indirectly, to the humanitarian catastrophe? NATO's strategy involved missile strikes from ships and airstrikes from aircraft mostly flying at over 15,000 feet, ostensibly to avoid anti-aircraft fire. According to NATO's critics, the lack of a ground component or low-level bombing raids denied NATO the means of systematically targeting active Serb forces on the ground without significantly increasing the risk of collateral damage by attempting to bomb moving targets. NATO did target Serb forces in Kosovo throughout the campaign but this proved much less effective than had been hoped (Posen 2000). During the war, NATO switched its emphasis to attacking Serbia's military, economic and governance infrastructure. The argument follows that the decision to restrict the war to bombing from 15,000 feet and not contemplate a credible ground alternative left NATO incapable of preventing ethnic cleansing and mass murder and provided a convenient cover for Serbian forces to escalate their actions against the Kosovar Albanian population. During the first few weeks of the intervention, Serb forces ethnically cleansed more than a million Kosovar Albanians, apparently uninhibited by NATO.

The most common explanation for this is that NATO valued the lives of its pilots and soldiers more than those of the Kosovar Albanians it was purportedly saving. The UN Human Rights Commissioner, Mary Robinson, argued that reliance on airstrikes demonstrated a lack of 'moral courage' on NATO's part (in Wheeler, N. J. 2000: 272). Others argued that NATO could have targeted Serb forces in Kosovo more effectively by placing its aircrews in harm's way by permitting them to fly lower. It is undeniable that concern about sustaining casualties played an important role in shaping NATO's strategy, particularly in the US. There are, however, good grounds for arguing that this was not the only consideration and that there was a sound prudential case for limiting the intervention to airstrikes. When Clinton (1999) told the American people at the outset of the war that 'I do not intend to put our troops in Kosovo to fight a war', he was speaking to three audiences. First, and most obviously, he was attempting to allay domestic fears about potential American casualties. Second, he was attempting to forestall opposition in the Republican-controlled Congress and Senate. Finally, Clinton was speaking to reluctant allies such as France, Italy and Greece that were deeply concerned about the legality of intervention. Had a possible ground invasion been touted, these three states would have probably vetoed the aerial campaign. Thus, a more significant than hitherto recognized role was played by alliance concerns about the legality of unauthorized intervention. These concerns militated against a ground invasion and 'regime change'. In short, the choice facing political leaders in March 1999 was one not between different types of intervention, but between an air campaign and no intervention at all.

There was also a good moral case for limiting the intervention to airstrikes. We should be sceptical about the claim that NATO aircraft should have flown at lower altitudes. Precision-guided bombs need a glidescope of about 12,000 feet to lock onto their target properly, and flying fast jets at lower altitude does not improve a pilot's visual perspective of the battle-field (see Lambeth 2001). Moreover, attempting to strike moving targets in close proximity to non-combatants, as opposed to fixed targets, dra-matically increases the likelihood of collateral damage and targeting errors (see Chapter 9). The argument that NATO should have accompanied its aerial bombardment with a ground invasion also runs up against calcula-tions of proportionality and prudence. As Afghanistan and Iraq demon-strate, the risks to non-combatants in ground invasions are much higher than in aerial campaigns. At least 3,750 non-combatants were killed during the initial phases of the American-led invasion of Iraq, compared to fewer than 500 non-combatants during the whole of the Kosovo campaign. Given the marginal nature of the judgement that the just cause crossed the threshold legitimizing unauthorized intervention, it could be argued that NATO had little room for manoeuvre without drifting into dispropor-tionate force.

This begs the question of whether NATO would have done better if it had chosen not to use force. It is undeniable that as many Kosovar Albanians were killed and ethnically cleansed during the seventy-eight days of NATO's campaign as in the preceding twelve months. Primary respon-sibility for the mass murder and ethnic cleansing lies with the Serb perpe-trators, but NATO was morally obliged to take every reasonable step to minimize indirect harm. Once the decision to intervene had been taken, NATO's duty of care extended to doing everything possible within the boundaries of prudence, proportionality and discrimination to prevent mass murder and ethnic cleansing, and ensuring, as far as possible, the security of those forced to flee their homes. By and large, NATO satisfied this duty of care. It maintained a permanent presence in Kosovo's skies and attacked Serb forces on the ground whenever it could. NATO also made a significant contribution to efforts to house Kosovar Albanian refugees (Wheeler, N. J. 2000: 268–9). That still leaves us with the question of whether it would have been better not to act at all. The answer to this ques-tion brings us full circle and is based on a judgement about how bad the situation in Kosovo would have got without intervention. There are two crucial points. First, any political progress that was made prior to March 1999 was made because NATO threatened Yugoslavia with force. Given Yugoslav non-compliance in early 1999, the failure to use force would have undermined NATO's credibility and significantly reduced the likelihood of future coercive diplomacy altering Serb behaviour. Second, and this is absolutely crucial, the wave of mass murder and ethnic cleansing that accompanied the airstrikes began at least four days (and according to some sources as many as six days) *before* NATO intervened (Gellman 1999). As I argued earlier, there are good grounds for believing that had Milošević not unleashed another wave of ethnic cleansing, the North Atlantic Council would not have reached a consensus about airstrikes. In other words, the reign of terror in Kosovo would have happened irrespective of whether NATO had intervened or not.

The Kosovo case demonstrates that the relationship between right authority and just cause is central to debates about the legitimacy of humanitarian intervention. NATO and Russia failed to agree on whether the scale of the crisis in Kosovo created just cause for intervention. In my view, Milošević's forces had crossed the threshold by launching a campaign of mass murder and ethnic cleansing that could be ended only by force. Important doubts remain, however, as to whether NATO properly calibrated its ends and means. There is no doubt that NATO members displayed national partiality in the strategy they chose, which was at least partly geared towards preserving allied lives, but the strategy also kept inadvertent non-combatant casualties to a minimum. That the strategy also minimized direct risks to non-combatants may have been a happy coincidence, but it is a morally significant one. On the other hand, the strategy limited the extent to which NATO could protect Kosovar Albanians against some of the indirect consequences of its intervention. Such concerns need to be balanced against NATO's clearly humanitarian intention in Kosovo, demonstrated by its justifications and commitment to post-conflict reconstruction. Moreover, it should be recalled that at least some of NATO's reticence, particularly on the part of states such as Italy, France and Greece, stemmed more from grave misgivings about the legal basis for war than from national partiality.

Iraq 2003

To date, the debate about whether the 2003 invasion of Iraq can be legitimated as a humanitarian intervention has focused on the question of whether the allies were motivated by humanitarian concerns. Kenneth Roth (2004) argues that the Iraq war cannot be considered a humanitarian intervention because the humanitarian impulse had not been a primary motivation. As a result, the allies chose strategies that harmed the civilian population and failed to plan for post-war reconstruction, thereby undermining the likelihood of positive humanitarian outcomes. Nicholas Wheeler and Justin Morris (forthcoming) reject this view. They argue that although states never act for purely humanitarian reasons, Bush, Blair and Australia's John Howard were at least partly motivated by such concerns. That they acted in the face of stern global opposition and bungled their planning by assuming that Iraqis would greet them as liberators certainly undermines the war's legitimacy, but the humanitarian argument should not be ruled out of hand. The approach taken here has a different starting point. According to the framework outlined in the previous section, the question of motives and intentions is secondary to the question of authority and just cause. The problem with viewing Iraq as a humanitarian intervention is not so much the interveners' motives as the difficulty of arguing that humanitarian conditions in early 2003 were so bad as to warrant unauthorized intervention.

Bush, Blair and Howard all argued at one time or another that Saddam's record of human rights abuse warranted intervention to remove him. The British Foreign and Commonwealth Office released a short report in November 2002 documenting the decades of human rights abuse in Iraq. The Iraqi regime, the report pointed out, was guilty of torture, abusing women, abusing prisoners, conducting summary executions, persecuting Kurdish and Shi'ite minorities and gassing its own people (Foreign and Commonwealth Office 2002: 2). Shortly before the war, Blair (2003) responded to the huge anti-war demonstrations by insisting that

if the result of peace is Saddam staying in power . . . then I tell you there are consequences paid in blood for that decision too. But these victims will never be seen. They will never feature on our TV screens or inspire millions to take to the streets. But they will exist nonetheless. Ridding the world of Saddam would be an act of humanity. It is leaving him there that is in truth inhumane.

Similar sentiments were echoed by Bush (2003) and John Howard (2003).

There is little doubt that Saddam's regime had a terrible human rights record. In 1988, Iraqi forces crushed a Kurdish rebellion with chemical and conventional weapons, killing an estimated 100,000 people (Stromseth 1993: 81). Immediately after the 1990–1 Gulf War, Iraqi forces again went into action to suppress rebellion. This time, the Kurds and Shi'ites rebelled at the instigation of George Bush Sr and were brutally crushed. By the end of April 1991 tens of thousands of civilians had been killed and over two million refugees had fled Iraq (Freedman and Karsh 1993: 419–20). There is little doubt that in both 1988 and 1991 the Iraqi government committed acts of mass murder, crossing the just cause threshold. At that time, unauthorized intervention would have been legitimate had the other conditions been satisfied. This raises two important questions about the humanitarian credentials of the 2003 Iraq war: was the humanitarian emergency in Iraq on-going? And, if the answer to that question is negative, is it legitimate to intervene more than a decade after the killings to remove the government responsible?

It is uncontroversial to suggest that the level of government killing in Iraq eased after 1992 and did not worsen immediately before the war. This is not to excuse the Iraqi regime, but it does call into question the necessity of unauthorized force for humanitarian purposes in 2003. To recapitulate, the relationship between right authority and just cause permits unauthorized interventions only in the most severe cases. The Security Council would have been entitled to authorize enforcement action on humanitarian grounds in 2003 had a consensus emerged to this effect. However, the absence of reference to a 'current, growing or imminent' humanitarian emergency in Iraq within Security Council resolutions is evidence that 'the Security Council, as a whole, did not consider the situation in Iraq to be a threat to international peace and security *for humanitarian reasons*' (Vesel 2004: 56, my emphasis). The unauthorized use of force against Iraq in either 1988 or 1991 would have been a legitimate response to on-going mass murder. For the use of force to count as a last resort in 2003, however, there would have had to be an escalation of human rights abuse in Iraq, including mass killing and/or ethnic cleansing.

The question of timing is fundamental, for whilst there may be agreement that common values are violated by a state's repression of its people, both classical Just War thinking and contemporary scholarship place a considerable weight on the immediacy of the problem. In 1999, Iraq ranked only thirteenth on a list of government human rights abusers (*Observer* 1999). Whatever else the Iraqi regime was guilty of, it was not guilty of mass killing and ethnic cleansing at the beginning of 2003.

The claim that the Iraq war was a legitimate humanitarian intervention is more persuasive than the claim that it was an act of either pre-emption or collective law enforcement. Had the claim been levelled during Saddam's brutal crackdowns in 1988 or 1991, and had the other conditions been satisfied, the unauthorized overthrow of Saddam's regime might have been legitimate. When the coalition did invade, however, Iraqi forces were not committing mass murder and ethnic cleansing, the just cause threshold had not been crossed and therefore individual states were not entitled to intervene without authorization. The pay-off is that, rightly or wrongly, a large majority of the world's states believe that the coalition abused humanitarian justifications to suit their own purposes. This will set back attempts to galvanize a global consensus on the necessity of action when basic rights are violated on a massive scale. It is too early to draw clear conclusions, but this widespread perception is likely to make it harder in future to forge a Security Council consensus about humanitarian intervention in all but the very worst of cases because many states will be highly sceptical about humanitarian claims levelled by Western governments.

Darfur 2003–

The first two case studies have tested the limits of the permissive right to intervene. As I noted earlier, humanitarian intervention is generally understood as an imperfect duty: actors may intervene to prevent and halt supreme humanitarian emergencies, but no one actor is obliged to do so (Walzer 2000: xiii). The lack of correspondence between right and duty encourages abuse by granting states a wide latitude to choose not to intervene. The key question is: which states – if any – have a responsibility to advocate and conduct humanitarian interventions? I argued that states that invoke a right to intervene in one case have a responsibility to protect threatened populations elsewhere. Failure to accept this duty casts serious doubt on the credibility of actors who put forward a humanitarian case to justify their interventions in other cases. This is not an argument against all forms of selectivity, however. A state's responsibility to protect others must be balanced against two considerations. First, there are prudential calculations. Military intervention may sometimes be imprudent because it exposes the intervener's forces to unacceptable levels of risk or endangers stability. Prudence may dictate that there are some wrongs that simply cannot be righted by military force, though other policy options may be available (Brown, C. 2003b: 45). The second limitation is proportionality: it may be calculated that a potential intervention is likely to cause more harm than good. In such cases, intervention would be unjust. In this final case study I will explore which agents have a responsibility to act, and in what circumstances, by reference to an on-going humanitarian emergency.

Since 2003, the Sudanese government and *Janjaweed* militia have conducted a brutal campaign of mass killing and ethnic cleansing in response to an uprising in Darfur (de Waal 2005: 129). Recent surveys place the number of deaths caused by direct violence between 73,700 and 172,154. Deaths from malnutrition and preventable disease in internally displaced persons (IDP) camps stood at 108,588 in January 2005, with approximately 25,000 more having died in inaccessible regions (Coebergh 2005). The British House of Commons International Development Committee (2005) put the total casualty figure at approximately 300,000. At least 1.8 million more had been forced to flee their homes (Anon. 2004b). Following a unanimous vote by the US Congress, Colin Powell took the unprecedented step of labelling the violence 'genocide' (BBC World News 2004a).

The world's response to the Darfur crisis has been muted. At the time of writing, a small under-funded and under-staffed African Union mission (AMIS) was deployed there but it had proven unable to halt sporadic escalations of violence or prevent the humanitarian situation deteriorating (Deen 2005). The UN Security Council took an ambivalent position. On the one hand it failed to impose serious sanctions on Sudanese officials and did not contemplate using force to protect civilians or humanitarian aid. On the other hand it has placed limited sanctions on specific individuals and in 2005 took the momentous step of referring the Darfur case to the International Criminal Court (ICC) (Res. 1590 (24 March 2005), 1593 (31 March 2005)).

The first question is: where on the sliding scale of just cause and right authority does the Darfur crisis sit? It is not unreasonable to argue that Darfur is a clearer case than either Kosovo or Iraq. In early 2004, Jan Pronk, the UN's representative in Sudan, accused the government-backed Arab militia of 'ethnic cleansing' and warned that, left unchecked, the humanitarian catastrophe in Darfur would be comparable to Rwanda (in BBC World News 2004b). In April 2004, the UN Human Rights Commission despatched a fact-finding team which found 'a disturbing pattern of disregard for basic principles of human rights and humanitarian law is taking place in Darfur, for which both the armed forces of Sudan and its proxy militia . . . are responsible' (UNHCHR 2004: 8). It concluded that 'there is a reign of terror in Darfur' and that the government and its proxies were almost certainly guilty of widespread crimes (UNHCR 2004: 15). On 25 January 2005, a UN Commission of Inquiry created by the Security Council to investigate allegations of grave crimes in Darfur concluded that whilst the Sudanese government did not have a policy of genocide, it was implicated in numerous war crimes and crimes against humanity. Moreover, 'in some instances individuals, including government officials, may commit acts with genocidal intent' (International Commission of Inquiry on Darfur 2005: 4).

Given all this, it is clear that the crisis in Darfur has crossed the just cause threshold. Thus, according to the schema offered here, regional organizations, coalitions of the willing and individual states are entitled to intervene to protect Darfur's civilians without either Security Council authorization or the Sudanese government's consent. Along with the permissive right, however, comes a moral duty to act that is limited only by prudence and proportionality. The question now is which agents have a duty to act? Or, is Walzer (2000: xiii) right to insist that the obligation to intervene falls on no particular state or group of states?

The question of who had a duty to intervene was the nub of the global debate about how best to respond to the crisis. Generally speaking, three alternatives were suggested: the Sudanese government; the African Union in cooperation with the government; or the UN. Many traditional opponents of intervention expressed the first position, arguing that sovereignty granted Sudan the primary responsibility, and primary right, to care for its citizens in Darfur. Thus, Pakistan, China and Russia argued that the scale of human suffering in Darfur was insufficient to provoke serious reflection on whether Sudan was fulfilling its responsibilities to its citizens (S/PV.4988). Similar arguments were later expressed by traditional supporters of humanitarian intervention. Unlike that of Pakistan, China and Russia, which based their arguments on a near absolutist conception of sovereignty, UK and UN opposition to intervention was ostensibly prudential. A senior British Foreign Office official told reporters that the UK had two problems with coercive measures against Sudan. First, the UK was 'wary of giving the impression that the international community is beating up on the government of Sudan'. Second, invoking the 'responsibility to protect', the UK believed that 'the best way to deliver security to the people of Darfur is to get those with primary responsibility for it to do it . . . the government of Sudan' (Anon. 2004a). British officials apparently worried that coercion could inflame the situation in Sudan without delivering security, owing to the logistical difficulties that a Darfur deployment would entail. On 2 September 2004, Jan Pronk endorsed the idea that the Sudanese government had primary responsibility for ending the crisis (S/PV.5027).

A second position suggested that the African Union (AU) had a responsibility to assist the government of Sudan. In July 2004, the AU began the deployment of a small force to protect its civilian monitors in Darfur who were observing the El Fashir ceasefire agreement of 9 June 2004. Initially, an AU force of approximately 3,000 troops drawn from nine states was envisaged (Anon. 2004c, 2004d). In mid-August, Rwanda deployed an advance party of 154 troops and its president insisted that his troops would use force to protect civilians if necessary (Human Rights Watch 2004a). Although the AU indicated that its troops would indeed fulfil this role, in a communiqué to the Security Council some AU members expressed reservations. When Nigeria deployed the first 153 of an intended 1,500 troops, its president insisted that his forces would only protect AU observers and operate with the consent of the Sudanese government (Human Rights Watch 2004b). With Sudan refusing to consent to a broad civilian protection mandate, a compromise was found whereby AMIS troops would only protect vulnerable civilians in their vicinity (AU 2004: 6).

It soon became clear that the AU lacked the necessary financial and logistical resources to deploy even the modest 3,000 peacekeepers originally intended and was unable to protect Darfur's civilians (UN News 2004). On 20 December 2004, a senior AU monitor reported that government forces had attacked villages using aircraft (Anon. 2004e). Days later, Annan complained that the world's peacekeeping strategy in Darfur was 'not working' and that AMIS had failed to protect civilians or prevent the crisis from deteriorating. In February 2005, Pronk complained that AMIS was too small and its deployment too slow to afford real protection to Darfur's civilians (both in Deen 2005). Others complained that the AMIS deployment was 'chaotic', characterized by 'poor logistical planning' and 'lack of trained personnel, funds and experience in intervening to protect civilians' (in Moni 2005).

The AU's inability to protect Darfur's civilians raises the question of whether the Security Council should have assumed primary responsibility. This argument was expressed in the Council by the Philippines and Romania, but importantly not by some of the Council's permanent members that had supported one or both of the interventions in Kosovo and Iraq (see S/PV.5015, S/PV.5040). Despite clear evidence of mass killing and ethnic cleansing, both Russia and China threatened to veto any resolution authorizing enforcement action in Darfur. Whilst it must be conceded that their opposition to enforcement might partially stem from genuine concerns about the erosion of sovereignty, it is also important to note that both states have significant economic interests in Sudan (Peterson 2004).

With the Security Council blocked, the AU's mission proving ineffective and the just cause threshold so evidently crossed, other states and organizations had both a right and a duty to act. Nevertheless, states who acted outside the Council in Kosovo and Iraq did not contemplate doing likewise in this case. Whilst some of them – particularly the US and UK – may have had good prudential reasons for not deploying significant numbers of troops in Darfur owing to military overstretch caused by their commitments in Iraq, Afghanistan, the Balkans and elsewhere, those reasons did not preclude these states from persuading others (such as other European allies) to intervene or providing financial and logistical support to an intervening force.

The duty to intervene that falls upon those who invoke a right to do so in other cases is not a blind obligation; it is dependent on calculations of prudence and proportionality. We are entitled to expect advocates of humanitarian intervention in one case seriously to contemplate acting outside the Security Council when humanitarian catastrophes cross the just cause threshold. Off the record, British officials commented that military intervention in Darfur was impractical because of the region's inaccessibility, making it impossible to deploy vehicles to the region. This claim stands in stark contrast to the insistence of the British Chief of Staff, General Mike Jackson, that Britain could rapidly deploy 5,000 peacekeepers to Darfur if necessary (BBC World News 2004c). Moreover, Darfur is relatively flat, open terrain and the majority of civilians are already housed in IDP camps. Air power and light infantry could be effectively utilized to protect the camps from *Janjaweed* attacks. Finally, whilst it is true that Darfur lacks either a coastline or a proper runway, neighbouring Chad houses French military bases equipped with runways that could act as ideal staging posts (UNHCR 2004). This is not the place to discuss the pros and cons of potential intervention in detail. My point is that if the UK's central claim for not considering intervention in Darfur – when by its previous actions it had acknowledged a duty to do so – is prudential, it is obliged to offer a detailed account of its calculations.

The stronger prudential case against American or British intervention lies outside Darfur. Both the American and British militaries are seriously overstretched. Having badly miscalculated both the challenges of rebuilding Iraq and the lifespan of the Taliban sympathies in Afghanistan, at the time the US had around 150,000 troops in the former and 16,000 in the latter. The UK maintained a force of around 8,000 in Iraq (BBC World News 2005). Allowing for troop rotations, these commitments alone account for significant portions of the US and UK's deployable forces. Furthermore, there are genuine prudential concerns about the best way to achieve peace in the whole of Sudan. Over the past decade, the civil war waged by the Sudanese People's Liberation Movement/Army in the south and the Sudanese government has cost approximately two million lives. A peace agreement concluded in 2005 brought this war to an end. The UK was deeply concerned that if the

Security Council applied too much pressure on Khartoum, the Sudanese government might walk away from the peace agreement. The first argument provides a compelling reason why the US and UK may be unable to lead an intervention into Darfur. It suggests that unless they too can find a compelling prudential argument, the burden of intervention should fall on states such as France, Germany, Spain and the Scandinavian countries, which supported intervention in Kosovo. The second argument provides a slightly less compelling case. If the world's most powerful states were committed to both the peace agreement and Darfur, it is not inconceivable that they could create a balance of incentives and punishments that would enable intervention in Darfur whilst forcing the Khartoum government to abide by the Comprehensive Peace Agreement. Moreover, these states could have made troop contributions to the UN force deployed in the south of Sudan and encouraged that mission gradually to spread into Darfur.

To reiterate, the concern with Darfur is not so much that the US and UK have not intervened but that neither these states nor their allies seem to have accepted their duty to protect Darfurians. A responsibility to protect does not demand military intervention in every case but it does oblige states that have claimed a moral right to intervene on humanitarian grounds in other cases genuinely to explore the possibilities for action. States that invoked a broad right of intervention in the Kosovo and/or Iraq cases cannot avoid a duty to act in a case like Darfur without undermining future claims for a permissive right of intervention. These states are obliged to explore the possibilities of collective action through the Security Council and, if that route is not open and if the just cause is sufficiently great, seriously to contemplate unauthorized action.

Because the duty to intervene is conditional on calculations of prudence and proportionality, it does not directly follow that the failure to intervene in Darfur violates that duty. Although I have yet to see convincing arguments that military intervention would be disproportionate, the US and UK at least have good prudential grounds for not committing large numbers of their own troops. However, these states can be criticized for not trying harder to forge a global consensus on enforcement action or offering material support to the AU or other potential interveners. The same cannot be said for states such as France and Germany that are not heavily involved in Iraq, certainly have some capability to act (particularly France), and offered similarly strong moral justifications for their intervention in Kosovo. These states should not escape criticism for failing to act in Darfur.

Conclusion

Humanitarian intervention is arguably the most hotly contested type of contemporary warfare. The different sub-traditions within the Just War tradition are themselves deeply divided. The main purpose of this chapter is to explore whether it was possible to develop an approach that remained sensitive to these different perspectives. It needs to be recognized that there are some crimes that are such an affront to natural law that they must be halted and the perpetrators punished. However, arguments that international order rests on sovereignty, that conceptions of the good tend to be constructed within political communities, and that the danger of abuse is very real, ought to be taken seriously. Theoretically, the UN Charter provides an ideal mechanism for resolving these claims. The Security Council has the legal authority to authorize collective enforcement action in response to grave breaches of natural law and provides a bulwark against abuse by ensuring that action is limited to cases of grave breaches of common values.

Unfortunately, Security Council members place their own interests before the collective good, as the American attitude towards Iraq and the Russian and Chinese attitude towards Darfur demonstrate only too well. As a result, the Security Council has a history of failing to authorize timely intervention against genocidal regimes: Idi Amin, Pol Pot, Slobodan Milošević, the Hutu *Interahamwe* and now Sudan's *Janjaweed* all escaped timely authorized enforcement action. However, because positive law and natural law are part of a common Just War tradition, an approach to humanitarian intervention needs to balance the requirements of both. The approach adopted here attempted to do just that by developing a relationship between just cause and right authority, and articulating a number of subsequent conditions. When all these conditions are met, I argued, intervention is not only permissible but morally required – subject to calculations of prudence and proportionality.

The tensions and dilemmas that this produces were clearly demonstrated in the three cases. Kosovo demonstrated the difficulty of ascertaining the relationship between just cause and right authority in less than clear-cut cases and raised important questions about the relationship between means and ends and the depth of an intervener's commitment to the humanitarian cause. Although justifiable, I argued that the intervention raised some difficult questions. In the Iraq case, the scale of human rights abuse at the time of the invasion was not sufficient to justify unauthorized intervention. Whilst Saddam's regime was certainly guilty of mass murder, especially in 1988 and 1991, it was not conducting a programme of murder and ethnic cleansing when the allies invaded in 2003. Unauthorized intervention for humanitarian purposes in this case was therefore unjust. The Darfur case provides a useful test for the question of who bears the duty to intervene in humanitarian crises. I argued that those states that invoked a right to intervene in other cases were encumbered with a responsibility to protect in this case. Failure to satisfy that duty should give us cause for grave doubts in future cases where those same states invoke a right to intervene for humanitarian purposes. Whilst the US and UK had sound prudential reasons for not committing large numbers of their own troops, their failure to mobilize support or contemplate acting outside the Security Council was morally troubling. Moreover, serious questions must be asked of states such as France and Germany that acted outside the Council in 1999 in relation to Kosovo but have to date refused to contemplate doing so in Darfur.

Conclusion

In the preceding pages, I have made three key claims about the Just War tradition. The first is that, rather than being a theory or a checklist used to determine whether a particular war is just or unjust, the Just War tradition offers a framework that diverse communities use to debate the legitimacy of wars. Without a common language, it would be impossible to have meaningful debate because the different positions articulated by actors would be incommensurable. The Just War tradition permits actors to justify themselves in a meaningful way. Others evaluate those justifications and decide whether or not to legitimate them. In turn, such decisions play an important role in determining their practical responses. The tradition itself contains many competing ethical theories, each of which offers a different way of interpreting the legitimacy framework. The Just War tradition provides that language by pointing to an overlapping consensus that has emerged over centuries about the causes for which war might be waged, the intentions and prudential considerations that lie behind the decision to fight, and expectations about how wars might be justly conducted. Viewed this way, the tradition poses a series of questions but provides few authoritative answers itself. From this perspective, it makes little sense to claim authority through the 'faithfulness' of our understanding of the tradition in the past (cf. Johnson 2005: 28).

Secondly, borrowing from Ian Clark's account of legitimacy (2005), I argued that the Just War tradition is comprised of three primary sub-traditions, labelled here as natural law, positive law and realism. What is considered just in relation to war in any given circumstance depends on the interrelationship between these three secondary norms. This view is not one widely shared by contemporary Just War thinkers, who tend to suggest that the Just War offers a countervailing – moral – perspective to that offered by international law. For example, James Turner Johnson (1999, 2005) rails against international law's 'presumption against aggressive war', insisting that the law can be overridden when necessary by the 'presumption against injustice' that underpins the Just War tradition. I outlined my objections to this separation of law and ethics in Chapter 6.

Here, I will limit my comments to the problematic *effects* of this argument, of which I think there are at least two. First, divorcing law and Just War risks undermining the vitality of the latter. Just War thinking without law is theologically oriented, ethnocentric and lacking in authority. Although it might exercise ethicists, it is questionable whether, absent its connection with the laws of war, the Just War tradition would have the effect that it does in shaping debate about the legitimacy of war. Second, overriding the law in favour of Just War thinking would, in all likelihood, help produce a more disorderly but not necessarily more just world order. As I observed in the previous chapter, not only does the prevailing legal order permit collectively authorized aggressive wars against injustice (the 'Chapter VII' mechanism), there is also no evidence that states have refrained from acting to uphold justice unilaterally *because* of the legal ban on force (see Chesterman 2001). Legal rules governing recourse to force reflect political agreement around the idea that it is not enough for a state to wage war to defend its own parochial understanding of justice; to permit that would allow states to wage war for almost any reason. Incorporating the law within our conception of Just War means that states must persuade others of their just cause, reducing the likelihood of abuse. Allied to the idea of three sub-traditions is the claim that there should be a place for classical realism within the Just War tradition. I outlined my reasons for this in Chapter 6, but in short if the Just War tradition is to provide a common language for decision-makers, soldiers and bystanders it must incorporate elements of language relating to prudence and necessity.

Finally, in the second part of the book I demonstrated ways in which changing world events are putting pressure on different parts of the Just War tradition. The problem of terrorism raised questions about the tradition's suitability as a legitimacy framework for conflicts comprising non-state actors and less than all-out violence. What I suggested there was that the tradition raised important questions about the legitimacy of terrorism which could be addressed through a long-overdue reassessment of the nature of rightful authority. The study of aerial bombing in Afghanistan demonstrated not only the remarkable similarity between ethical and legal requirements but their adaptability to cover new forms of technology and methods of fighting. Finally, the discussion of pre-emption and humanitarian intervention considered, in detail, the relationship between law and ethics in cases where the apparent ethical requirement to fight is balanced by the legal prohibition. In both chapters, I demonstrated that the law is restrictive for good reasons but that is indeterminate enough to allow flexibility when there is a compelling prudential or moral case for action.

What I have tried to offer in this book is a holistic account of the Just War that takes into account the myriad factors that shape an actor's judgements about the legitimacy of war. The tradition that emerges from this is pluralist and indeterminate, but it is precisely its pluralism and indeterminacy that give the tradition its centrality as a common framework, and it is the conversation itself, and the recognition that normative constraints are partly constitutive of war as a distinct social practice, that plays the key role in mitigating the evils of war.

Bibliography

Abi-Hashem, P. (2004), 'Peace and War in the Middle East: A Psychopolitical and Sociocultural Perspective', in F. M. Moghaddam and A. J. Marsella (eds), *Understanding Terrorism: Psychosocial Roots, Consequences and Interventions* (Washington, DC: American Psychological Association).

Adams, R. M. (1962), *The Better Part of Valor: More, Erasmus, Colet and Vives on Humanism, War and Peace 1496–1535* (Seattle: University of Washington Press).

Afghanistan Ministry of Foreign Affairs (2002), 'Project Document for Mine Action for Peace/DDR', AFG/04401.

African Union (AU) Peace and Security Council (2004), Communiqué PSC/PR/Comm.(XVII), 17th meeting, 20 October.

Air Land Sea Application Center (1997), 'Targeting: The Joint Targeting Process and Procedures for Targeting Time-Critical Targets', FM 90-36/MCRP 3-16 1F/NWP 2-01.11/AFJPAM 10-225.

Akashi, K. (1988), *Cornelius van Bynkershoek: His Role in the History of International Law* (The Hague: Kluwer International).

Aldicott, J. (2002), 'The Yemen Attack: Illegal Assassination or Lawful Killing?', at http://jurist.law.pitt.edu/forum/forumnew68.php, accessed 22 March 2006.

Aldrich, G. H. (1981), 'New Life for the Laws of War', *American Journal of International Law*, 75 (4).

Aldrich, G. H. (1991), 'Prospects for United States Ratification of Additional Protocol I to the 1949 Geneva Convention', *American Journal of International Law*, 85 (1).

Aldrich, G. H. (2000), 'The Laws of War on Land', *American Journal of International Law*, 94 (1).

Aldrich, G. H. and C. M. Chinkin (2000), 'A Century of Achievement and Unfinished Work', *American Journal of International Law*, 94 (1).

Alexander, Y. and M. S. Swetnam (2001), *Usama bin Laden's al-Qaida: Profile of a Terrorist Network* (New York: Transnational Publishers).

Alexandrov, S. (1996), *Self-Defense Against the Use of Force in International Law* (The Hague: Kluwer Law International).

Ambrose (1896), 'Of the Duties of the Clergy', in P. Schaff and H. Wace (eds), *A Select Library of Nicene and Post-Nicene Fathers* (London: Parker & Co.).

Anderson, S. and S. Sloan (1995), *Historical Dictionary of Terrorism* (Metuchen, NJ: Scarecrow Press).

Andreopoulos, G. J. (1994), 'The Age of National Liberation Movements', in M. Howard, G. J. Andreopoulos and M. R. Shulman (eds), *The Laws of War: Constraints on Warfare in the Western World* (New Haven: Yale University Press).

Angell, N. (1972), *The Great Illusion: A Study of the Relation of Military Power to National Advantage*, 4th edition (London: Garland).

Anglo, S. (1969), *Machiavelli: A Dissection* (London: Paladin).

Annan, K. (2001), 'Nobel Lecture', 10 December 2001, at http://www.nobel.se/peace/laureates/2001/annan-lecture.html, accessed 18 March 2004.

Anon. (1999), 'Ethnic Cleansing Reaches New Heights', *The Times*, 21 March.

Anon. (2004a), 'Security Council Disagrees Over Sudan Sanctions', *Sunday Standard* (Nairobi), 22 August.

Anon. (2004b), 'UN Refugee Agency Withdraws Staff from South Darfur Over Sudanese Restrictions', UN News Service, New York, 11 November.

Anon. (2004c), 'African Union Sending Military Force to Darfur', CBS News, 6 July.

Anon. (2004d), 'African Union to Send Troops to Darfur', Reuters, 5 July 2004.

Anon. (2004e), 'Troops Attack in Darfur as a Deadline Passes', Reuters, 20 December.

Aquinas, T. (1998), *Selected Philosophical Writings*, ed. and trans. T. McDermott (Oxford: Oxford University Press).

Aquinas, T. (2002), *Political Writings*, trans. R. W. Dyson (Cambridge: Cambridge University Press).

Arend, A. C. (2003), 'International Law and the Pre-emptive Use of Military Force', *The Washington Quarterly*, 26 (2).

Arend, A. C. and R. J. Beck (1993), *International Law and the Use of Force: Beyond the UN Charter Paradigm* (London: Routledge).

Arendt, H. (1964), *Eichmann in Jerusalem: A Report on the Banality of Evil* (London: Penguin).

Aristotle (1998), *The Politics*, trans. E. Baker, ed. R. F. Stalley (Oxford: Oxford Paperbacks).

Aristotle (2004), *The Nicomachean Ethics*, trans. J. A. K. Thomson, ed. Hugh Tredennick (London: Penguin).

Arkin, W. M. (2000), 'Smart Bombs, Dumb Targeting?', *Bulletin of the Atomic Scientists*, 56 (3).

Arkin, W. M. (2002), 'Fear of Civilian Deaths May Have Undermined Effort', *Los Angeles Times*, 16 January.

Armstrong, A. C. (1931), 'Kant's Philosophy of Peace and War', *Journal of Philosophy*, 28 (8).

Armstrong, A. C. (1933), 'Hegel's Attitude on War and Peace', *Journal of Philosophy*, 30 (25).

Art, R. J. and K. N. Waltz (1983), 'Technology, Strategy and the Use of Force', in R. J. Art and K. N. Waltz (eds), *The Use of Force: International Politics and Foreign Policy*, 2nd edition (Lanham, MD: University Press of America).

Ashworth, L. (1996), 'Cities, Ethnicity and Insurgent Warfare in the Hellenic World', *War & Society*, 14 (2).

Augustine (1876), 'Contra Faustum', in M. Dods (ed.), *The Works of Aurelius Augustine* (Edinburgh: T. and C. Clark).

Augustine (1955a), *The Problem of Free Choice*, annotated and trans. D. M. Pontifex (London: Longmans).

Augustine (1955b), 'Letter to Count Boniface', in W. Parsons (ed.), *Saint Augustine Letters Vol. IV (165–203)* (New York: Fathers of the Church Inc.).

Augustine (1972), *The City of God*, trans. H. Bettenson (London: Penguin).

Bachrach, B. S. (1994), 'Medieval Siege Warfare: A Reconnaissance', *Journal of Military History*, 58 (1).

Bailey, S. D. (1972), *Prohibitions and Restraints in War* (London: Oxford University Press for the Royal Institute of International Affairs).

Bain, W. (2003), *Between Anarchy and Society: Trusteeship and the Obligation of Power* (Oxford: Oxford University Press).

Bainton, R. H. (1960), *Christian Attitudes Toward War and Peace: A Historical Survey and Critical Re-evaluation* (Nashville, TN: Abingdon Press).

Ball, H. (1999), *Prosecuting War Crimes and Genocide: The Twentieth-Century Experience* (Lawrence: University Press of Kansas).

Ball, T. (1984), 'The Picaresque Prince: Reflections of Machiavelli and Moral Change', *Political Theory*, 12 (4).

Ballis, W. (1937), *The Legal Position of War: Changes in its Practice and Theory from Plato to Vattel* (The Hague: Martinus Nijhoff).

Bandura, A. (2004), 'The Role of Selective Moral Disengagement in Terrorism and Counterterrorism', in F. M. Moghaddam and A. J. Marsella (eds), *Understanding Terrorism: Psychosocial Roots, Consequences and Interventions* (Washington, DC: American Psychological Association).

Barber, R. (1995), *The Knight and Chivalry*, revised edition (Woodbridge: Boydell Press).

Bass, G. J. (2000), *Stay the Hand of Vengeance: The Politics of War Crimes Tribunals* (Princeton: Princeton University Press).

Bassiouni, M. C. (2001), *International Terrorism: Multilateral Conventions (1937–2001)* (New York: Transnational Publishers).

BBC World News (2001a), 'US Admits Second Bombing Error', 27 October.

BBC World News (2001b), 'Rumsfeld Defends Bombing Campaign', 5 November.

BBC World News (2004a), 'Powell Declares Genocide in Sudan', 9 September.

BBC World News (2004b), 'Mass Rape Atrocity in West Sudan', 19 March 2004.

BBC World News (2004c), 'EU Steps up Pressure Over Darfur', 24 July.

BBC World News (2005), 'Italy Plans Iraq Troop Pull-Out', 15 March 2005.

Bederman, D. J. (2001), *International Law in Antiquity* (Cambridge: Cambridge University Press).

Begin, M. (1977), *The Revolt*, revised edition (New York: Nash Publishing).

Beier, J. M. (2003), 'Discriminating Tastes: "Smart" Bombs, Non-Combatants, and Notions of Legitimacy in Warfare', *Security Dialogue*, 34 (4).

Beitz, C. (1979), 'Bounded Morality: Justice and the State in World Politics', *International Organization*, 33 (3).

Bellamy, A. J. (2004), 'Supreme Emergencies and the Protection of Non-Combatants in War', *International Affairs*, 80 (5).

Bellamy, A. J. and P. D. Williams (2005), 'Who's Keeping the Peace? Regionalization and Contemporary Peace Operations', *International Security*, 29 (4).

Bennett, A. L. (1984), *International Organisations*, 3rd edition (London: Prentice Hall).

Bentham, J. (1962), 'A Plan for An Universal and Perpetual Peace', in J. Bowring (ed.), *The Works of Jeremy Bentham: Volume II* (New York: Russell and Russell).

Berman, H. J. (1983), *Law and Revolution: The Formation of the Western Legal Tradition* (Cambridge, MA: Harvard University Press).

Best, G. (1994), *War and Law Since 1945* (Oxford: Clarendon Press).

Betts, R. K. (2002), 'The Soft Underbelly of American Primacy: Tactical Advantages of Terror', *Political Science Quarterly*, 117 (1).

Bien, J. (1981), 'Politics of the Present: Machiavellian Humanism', *Philosophy and Phenomenological Research*, 42 (2).

Black, J. (1998), *War and the World: Military Power and the Fate of Continents 1450–2000* (New Haven: Yale University Press).

Blair, T. (1999), Speech by the Prime Minister, Tony Blair, to the Economic Club of Chicago, Hilton Hotel, Chicago, USA, Thursday, 22 April 1999, at http://www.globalpolicy.org/globaliz/politics/blair.htm, accessed 22 March 2006.

Blair, T. (2001), 'Speech to the Labour Party Conference', 2 October 2001, at http://www.australianpolitics.com/news/2001/01-10-02b.shtml, accessed 22 March 2006.

Blair, T. (2003), Speech at the Labour Party Conference on Local Government, Women and Youth, Glasgow, 15 February 2003, at http://www.scottishlabour.org.uk/tbiraq/, accessed 22 March 2006.

Bobbitt, P. (2002), *The Shield of Achilles: War, Peace and the Course of History* (London: Penguin).

Bonanate, L. (1995), *Ethics and International Politics* (Columbia: University of South Carolina Press).

Bond, B. (1996), *The Pursuit of Victory: From Napoleon to Saddam Hussein* (Oxford: Oxford University Press).

Bonet, H. (1949), *The Tree of Battles of Honoré Bonet*, trans. and ed. G. W. Coopland (Cambridge, MA: Harvard University Press).

Bonney, R. (1991), *The European Dynastic States 1494–1660* (Oxford: Oxford University Press).

Booth, K. (2001), 'Ten Flaws of Just War', in K. Booth (ed.), *The Kosovo Tragedy: The Human Rights Dimensions* (London: Frank Cass).

Boraine, A. (2000), *A Country Unmasked* (Oxford: Oxford University Press).

Borgwardt, E. (2005), *A New Deal for the World: America's Vision for Human Rights* (Cambridge, MA: The Belknap Press of Harvard University Press).

Bornstein, D. (1975), *Mirrors of Courtesy* (Hamden, CT: Archon Books).

Boucher, D. (1994), 'British Idealism, the State, and International Relations', *Journal of the History of Ideas*, 55 (4).

Boukema, H. J. M. (1983), 'Grotius' Concept of Law', *Archive für Rechts- und Sozialphilosophie*, 1.

Bower, S. E. (2000), 'The Theology of the Battlefield: William Tecumseh Sherman and the US Civil War', *Journal of Military History*, 64 (4).

Bowett, D. (1958), *Self-Defence in International Law* (Manchester: Manchester University Press).

Boyle, F. A. (1999), *Foundations of World Order* (Durham, NC: Duke University Press).

Brahimi, L. et al. (2000), *Report of the Panel on United Nations Peace Operations*, UN General Assembly, A/55/305S/2000/809.

Brailey, N. J. (2002), 'Sir Ernest Satow and the 1907 Second Hague Peace Conference', *Diplomacy and Statecraft*, 13 (2).

Brodie, B. (1974), *War and Politics* (New York: Macmillan).

Brooke, C. (1969), *The Twelfth Century Renaissance* (London: Thames and Hudson).

Brown, C. (2002), *Sovereignty, Rights and Justice: International Political Theory Today* (Cambridge: Polity).

Brown, C. (2003a), 'Self-Defense in an Imperfect World', *Ethics and International Affairs*, 17 (1).

Brown, C. (2003b), 'In Defense of Inconsistency', in D. K. Chatterjee and D. E. Scheid (eds), *Ethics and Foreign Intervention* (Cambridge: Cambridge University Press).

Brown, P. R. L. (1995), *Authority and the Sacred: Aspects of the Christianisation of the Roman World* (Cambridge: Cambridge University Press).

Brownlie, I. (1963), *International Law and the Use of Force by States* (Oxford: Clarendon Press).

Brownlie, I. (1974), 'Humanitarian Intervention', in J. N. Moore (ed.), *Law and Civil War in the Modern World* (Baltimore: Johns Hopkins University Press).

Brunee, J. and S. J. Toope (2004), 'The Use of Force: International Law After Iraq', *International and Comparative Law Quarterly*, 53 (3).

Buchanan, A. and R. O. Keohane (2004), 'The Preventive Use of Force: A Cosmopolitan Institutional Proposal', *Ethics and International Affairs*, 18 (1).

Bull, H. (1977), *The Anarchical Society: A Study of Order in World Politics* (London: Macmillan).

Bull, H. (1979), 'Review Article: Recapturing the Just War for Political Theory', *World Politics*, 31 (4).

Bull, M. (2002), 'The Roots of Lay Enthusiasm for the First Crusade', in T. Madden (ed.), *The Crusades: The Essential Readings* (Oxford: Blackwell).

Bullinger, H. (1849), *The Decades*, ed. Thomas Harding (Cambridge: Cambridge University Press).

Bumke, J. (1977), *The Concept of Knighthood in the Middle Ages*, trans. W. T. H. and E. Jackson (New York: AMS Press).

Burke, J. (2003), *Al-Qaeda: Casting a Shadow of Terror* (London: I. B. Tauris).

Burnell, P. (1993), 'The Problem of Service to Unjust Regimes in Augustine's City of God', *Journal of the History of Ideas*, 54 (2).

Bury, J. B., S. A. Cook and F. E. Adcock (1927), *The Cambridge Ancient History: Volume V, Athens 478–401 BC* (Cambridge: Cambridge University Press).

Bush, G. W. (2001), 'Address to the UN General Assembly', 10 November.

Bush, G. W. (2002a), Speech at the West Point Graduation ceremony, 1 June 2002, at http://www.whitehouse.gov/news/releases/2002/06/20020601-3.html, accessed 22 March 2006.

Bush, G. W. (2002b), Speech at Cincinnati, 7 October 2002, at http://www.whitehouse.gov/news/releases/2002/10/20021007-8.html, accessed 2 February 2005.

Bush, G. W. (2003), Remarks by the President in Address to the Nation, 17 March 2003, at http://www.whitehouse.gov/news/releases/2003/03/20030317-7.html, accessed 12 May 2005.

Butler, Lord, of Brockwell (2004), *Review of Intelligence on Weapons of Mass Destruction* (London: Her Majesty's Stationery Office), 14 July.

Byers, M. (2002), 'Terrorism, the Use of Force and International Law after 11 September', *International and Comparative Law Quarterly*, 51 (2).

Byers, M. (2003a), 'Pre-emptive Self-Defence: Hegemony, Equality and Strategies of Legal Change', *Journal of Political Philosophy*, 11 (2).

Byers, M. (2003b), 'Letting the Exception Prove the Rule', *Ethics and International Affairs*, 17 (1).

Byers, M. (2004), 'Policing the High Seas: The Proliferation Security Initiative', *American Journal of International Law*, 98 (3).

Byers, M. (2005), *War Law: International Law and Armed Conflict* (London: Atlantic Books).

Byman, D. (2005), *Deadly Connections: States that Sponsor Terrorism* (Cambridge: Cambridge University Press).

Cadoux, C. J. (1919), *The Early Christian Attitude to War* (London: Headley Bros.).

Cahn, S. (ed.) (1997), *Classics of Modern Political Theory: Machiavelli to Mill* (Oxford: Oxford University Press).

Calhoun, L. (2003), 'The Strange Case of Summary Execution by Predator Drone', *Peace Review*, 15 (2).

Caney, S. (1997), 'Human Rights and the Rights of States: Terry Nardin on Non-Intervention', *International Political Science Review*, 18 (1).

Caney, S. (2005), *Justice Beyond Borders: A Global Political Theory* (Oxford: Oxford University Press).

Carlino, M. A. (2002), 'The Moral Limits of Strategic Attack', *Parameters*, 32 (1).

Carnahan, B. H. (1998), 'Lincoln, Lieber and the Laws of War: The Origins and Limits of the Principle of Military Necessity', *American Journal of International Law*, 92 (2).

Caron, D. D. (2000), 'War and International Adjudication: Reflections on the 1899 Peace Conference', *American Journal of International Law*, 94 (1).

Carr, E. H. (1960), *The Twenty Years Crisis 1919–1939: An Introduction to the Study of International Relations* (London: Macmillan).

Cassese, A. (1986), 'Return to Westphalia? Considerations in the Gradual Erosion of the Charter System', in A. Cassese (ed.), *The Current Legal Regulation of the Use of Force* (Dordrecht: Martinus Nijhoff).

Cassese, A. (2001), 'Terrorism is also Disrupting Some Crucial Legal Categories of International Law', *European Journal of International Law*, 12 (5).

Cassim, V., W. Debevoise, H. Kailes and T. W. Thompson (1975), 'The Definition of Aggression', *Harvard International Law Journal*, 16 (1).

Chadwick, E. (1999), 'Gone with the War? Neutral State Responsibility and the Geneva Arbitration of 1872', *Leiden Journal of International Law*, 12 (4).

Charney, J. I. (2001), 'The Use of Force against Terrorism and International Law', *American Journal of International Law*, 95 (4).

Chesterman, S. (2001), *Just War or Just Peace? Humanitarian Intervention and International Law* (Oxford: Oxford University Press).

Chesterman, S. (2003), 'Hard Cases Make Bad Law: Law, Ethics and Politics in Humanitarian Intervention', in A. F. Lang, Jr (ed.), *Just Intervention* (Washington, DC: Georgetown University Press).

Chomsky, N. (1999), *The New Military Humanism: Lessons from Kosovo* (Monroe, ME: Common Courage Press).

Christopher, P. (1994), *The Ethics of War and Peace: An Introduction to Legal and Moral Issues* (Englewood Cliffs, NJ: Prentice Hall).

Chroust, A.-H. (1941–2), 'The *Ius Gentium* in the Philosophy of Law of St Thomas Aquinas', *Notre Dame Lawyer*, 22 (2).

Cicero (1928), *De Re Publica III*, trans. C. Keyes (New York: G. P. Putnam's Sons).

Cicero (1961), *De Officiis*, trans. W. Miller (Cambridge, MA: Harvard University Press).

Clark, I. (2003), 'Legitimacy in a Global Order', *Review of International Studies*, 29 (S1).

Clark, I. (2005), *Legitimacy in International Society* (Oxford: Oxford University Press).

Clark, W. K. (2001), *Waging Modern War* (New York: Public Affairs).

Clarke, R. A. (2004), *Against all Enemies: Inside America's War on Terror* (New York: Free Press).

Claude, I. (1964), *Swords into Plowshares*, 4th edition (New York: McGraw Hill).

Clausewitz, C. von (1993), *On War*, ed. and trans. M. Howard and P. Paret (London: Everyman's Library).

Clinton, W. (1999), 'Address to the Nation', 24 March 1999, at http://www.pbs.org/newshour/bb/europe/jan-june99/address_3-24.html, accessed 25 May 2005.

Coady, T. (1985), 'The Morality of Terrorism', *Philosophy*, 60 (1).

Coady, T. (2002), 'Terrorism, Just War and Supreme Emergency', in T. Coady and M. O'Keefe (eds), *Terrorism and Justice: Moral Argument in a Threatened World* (Melbourne: Melbourne University Press).

Coady, T. (2005), 'Intervention, Political Realism and the Ideal of Peace', in T. Coady and M. O'Keefe (eds), *Righteous Violence: The Ethics and Politics of Military Intervention* (Melbourne: Melbourne University Press).

Coates, A. J. (1997), *The Ethics of War* (Manchester: Manchester University Press).

Coebergh, J. (2005), 'Sudan: The Genocide has Killed More than the Tsunami', *Parliamentary Brief*, 7 (9) February.

Combacu, J. (1986), 'The Exception of Self-Defence in UN Practice', in A. Cassese (ed.), *The Current Legal Regulation of the Use of Force* (Dordrecht: Martinus Nijhoff).

Conetta, C. (2002), 'Operation Enduring Freedom: Why a Higher Rate of Civilian Bombing Casualties?', Project on Defense Alternatives, briefing report No. 11, 24 January.

Corbett, P. E. (1951), *Law and Society in the Relations of States* (New York: Harcourt, Brace and Co.).

Coriden, J. A. (1990), *An Introduction to Canon Law* (London: Cassell).

Covell, C. (1998), *Kant and the Law of Peace: A Study in the Philosophy of International Law and International Relations* (New York: St Martin's Press).

Craig, C. (1992), 'The New Meaning of Modern War in the Thought of Reinhold Niebuhr', *Journal of the History of Ideas*, 53 (4).

Crawford, N. C. (2003), 'The Slippery Slope to Preventive War', *Ethics and International Affairs*, 17 (1).

Crenshaw, M. (2003), 'The Problem of Objectivity in Definition', in D. J. Whittaker (ed.), *The Terrorism Reader*, 2nd edition (London: Routledge).

Cryer, R. (2002), 'The Fine Art of Friendship: *Jus in Bello* in Afghanistan', *Journal of Conflict and Security Law*, 7 (1).

D'Amato, A. (1996), 'Israel's Air Strike Against the Osiraq Reactor: A Retrospective', *Temple International and Comparative Law Journal*, 10 (2).

D'Arcy, M. C. (1930), *Thomas Aquinas* (London: Edward Benn).

D'Entrèves, A. P. (1951), *Natural Law: An Introduction to Legal Philosophy* (London: Hutchinson University Library).

D'Entrèves, A. P. (1959), *The Medieval Contribution to Political Thought* (New York: The Humanities Press).

Daalder, I. (2002), *The Use of Force in a Changing World: US and European Perspectives* (Washington, DC: Brookings Institution).

Daalder, I. and J. M. Lindsay (2003), *America Unbound: The Bush Revolution in Foreign Policy* (Washington, DC: Brookings Institution).

Damrosch, L. F. (1991), 'Commentary on Collective Military Intervention to Enforce Human Rights', in L. F. Damrosch and D. J. Scheffer (eds), *Law and Force in the New International Order* (Boulder, CO: Westview).

David, S. R. (2003), 'Israel's Policy of Targeted Killing', *Ethics and International Affairs*, 17 (1).

Davie, M. R. (1929), *The Evolution of War* (New Haven: Yale University Press).

Davis, H. R. and R. C. Good (eds) (1960), *Reinhold Neibuhr on Politics: His Political Philosophy and its Application to Our Age as Expressed in His Writings* (New York: Charles Scribner's Sons).

de Waal, A. (2005), 'Briefing: Darfur, Sudan: Prospects for Peace', *African Affairs*, 104 (414).

Deane, H. A. (1963), *The Political and Social Ideas of St Augustine* (New York: Columbia University Press).

Deen, T. (2005), 'New UN Force for Sudan Will Skirt Darfur Crisis', Inter Press Service, 9 February.

Delbrück, J. (2002), 'The Fight Against Global Terrorism: Self-Defense or Collective Security as International Police Action? Some Comments on the International Legal Implications of the "War Against Terrorism"', *German Yearbook of International Law*, 44.

Delos, J. T. (1950), 'The Dialectics of War and Peace: Part II', *The Thomist*, 13 (4).

Deng, F., S. Kimaro, T. Lyons, D. Rothchild and I. W. Zartman (1996), *Sovereignty as Responsibility: Conflict Management in Africa* (Washington, DC: Brookings Institution).

Detter, I. (2000), *The Law of War*, 2nd edition (Cambridge: Cambridge University Press).

Dinstein, Y. (1988), *War, Aggression and Self-Defence* (Cambridge: Grotius Publications).

Donagan, A. (1977), *The Theory of Morality* (Chicago: University of Chicago Press).

Donnelly, J. (1989), *Universal Human Rights in Theory and Practice* (Ithaca, NY: Cornell University Press).

Doppelt, G. (1978), 'Walzer's Theory of Morality in International Relations', *Philosophy and Public Affairs*, 8 (1).

Dorman, A. (2004), 'The United States and the War in Iraq', in P. Cornish (ed.), *The Conflict in Iraq, 2003* (London: Palgrave Macmillan).

Doswald-Beck, L. (1987), 'The Civilian in the Crossfire', *Journal of Peace Research*, 24 (3).

Doyle, M. W. (1997), *Ways of War and Peace: Realism, Liberalism and Socialism* (London: W. W. Norton).

Doyle, M. W. (2001), 'The New Interventionism', *Metaphilosophy*, 32 (1/2).

Draper, G. I. A. D. (1992), 'Grotius' Place in the Development of Legal Ideas about War', in H. Bull, B. Kingsbury and A. Roberts (eds), *Hugo Grotius and International Relations* (Oxford: Clarendon Press).

Duchhardt, H. (2000), 'War and International Law in Europe: Sixteenth to Eighteenth Centuries', in P. Contamine (ed.), *War and Competition Between States* (Oxford: Clarendon Press).

Dunant, H. (1959), *A Memory of Solferino*, English edition (Geneva: International Committee of the Red Cross).

Durr, O. (1987), 'Humanitarian Law of Armed Conflict: Problems of Applicability', *Journal of Peace Research*, 24 (3).

Eason, G. (2001), 'Why Bombing Can Go Wrong', BBC World News, 16 December.

Economides, S. (2002), 'The International Criminal Court', in M. Light and K. Smith (eds), *Ethics and Foreign Policy* (Cambridge: Cambridge University Press).

Edwards, C. S. (1981), *Hugo Grotius, the Miracle of Holland: A Study in Political and Legal Thought* (Chicago: Nelson Hall).

Elshtain, J. B. (1985), 'Reflections on War and Political Discourse: Realism, Just War and Feminism in a Nuclear Age', *Political Theory*, 13 (1).

Elshtain, J. B. (ed.) (1992), *Just War Theory* (New York: State University of New York Press).

Elshtain, J. B. (2001a), 'How to Fight a Just War', *Blueprint Magazine*, 15 November, at http://www.dlc.org/ndol_ci.cfm?&kaid=124&subid=307&contentid=39 18, accessed 22 March 2006.

Elshtain, J. B. (2001b), 'Just War and Humanitarian Intervention', *Ideas: From the National Humanities Centre*, 8 (2).

Elshtain, J. B. (2003), *Just War against Terror: The Burden of American Power in a Violent World* (New York: Basic Books).

Erasmus, D. (1907), *Erasmus Against War*, trans. and ed. J. W. Mackail (Boston: Merrymount Press).

Erasmus, D. (1962), *Bellum*, trans. W. R. Tyler (Barre, MA: Imprint Society).

Erasmus, D. (1964), 'The Complaint of Peace', in J. P. Dolan (ed.), *The Essential Erasmus* (New York: Plume Books).

Erasmus, D. (1968), *The Education of a Christian Prince*, trans. L. K. Born (New York: Columbia University Press).

Erdmann, C. (1977), *The Origin of the Idea of the Crusade*, trans. M. W. Baldwin and W. Goffart (Princeton: Princeton University Press).

Esposito, J. L. (2002), *Unholy War: Terror in the Name of Islam* (Oxford: Oxford University Press).

Evans, M. (ed.) (2005), *Just War Theory: A Reappraisal* (Edinburgh: Edinburgh University Press).

Falk, R. (2003), 'Humanitarian Intervention: A Forum', *Nation*, 14 July.

Fanon, F. (1965), *The Wretched of the Earth* (London: Grove Press).

Fassihi, F. (2001), 'Death Lurks Underfoot', *Star-Ledger*, 23 December.

Feinstein, L. and A.-M. Slaughter (2004), 'A Duty to Prevent', *Foreign Affairs*, 83 (1).

Fernandez, J. A. (1973), 'Erasmus on the Just War', *Journal of the History of Ideas*, 34 (2).

Finnemore, M. (1996), *National Interests in International Society* (Ithaca, NY: Cornell University Press).

Finnis, J. (1998), *Aquinas: Moral Political and Legal Theory* (Oxford: Oxford University Press).

Finucane, R. C. (1983), *Soldiers of the Faith: Crusaders and Moslems at War* (London: J. M. Dent and Sons).

Fisher, D. (1994), 'The Ethics of Intervention', *Survival*, 36 (1).

Fitzpatrick, J. (2002), 'Sovereignty, Territoriality and the Rule of Law', *Hastings Comparative and International Law Review*, 25 (2).

Fleiss, P. J. (1960), 'War Guilt in the History of Thucydides', *Traditio: Studies in Ancient and Medieval History, Thought and Religion*, 16 (4).

Forde, S. (1993), 'Classical Realism', in T. Nardin and D. R. Mapel (eds), *Traditions of International Ethics* (Cambridge: Cambridge University Press).

Forde, S. (1998), 'Hugo Grotius on Ethics and War', *American Political Science Review*, 92 (3).

Foreign and Commonwealth Office (2002), *Saddam Hussein: Crimes and Human Rights Abuse: A Report on the Human Costs of Saddam's Policies by the Foreign and Commonwealth Office* (London: HMSO, 2002).

Forsythe, D. P. (1978), 'Legal Management of Internal War: The 1977 Protocol on Non-International Armed Conflict', *American Journal of International Law*, 72 (2).

Forsythe, D. P. (2005), *The Humanitarians: The International Committee of the Red Cross* (Cambridge: Cambridge University Press).

France, J. (1994), *Victory in the East: A Military History of the First Crusade* (Cambridge: Cambridge University Press).

France, J. (1999), *Western Warfare in the Age of the Crusades, 1000–1300* (Ithaca, NY: Cornell University Press).

Franck, T. M. (2001), 'Terrorism and the Right of Self-Defense', *American Journal of International Law*, 95 (4).

Franck, T. M. (2002), *Recourse to Force: State Action against Threats and Armed Attacks* (Cambridge: Cambridge University Press).

Freedman, L. (2004) *Deterrence* (Cambridge: Polity).

Freedman, L. and E. Karsh (1993), *The Gulf Conflict* (London: Faber and Faber).

Freeman, A. V. (1947), 'War Crimes by Enemy Nationals Administering Justice in Occupied Territory', *American Journal of International Law*, 41 (3).

French, S. E. (2003), 'Murderers not Warriors: The Moral Distinction Between Terrorists and Legitimate Fighters in Asymmetric Conflicts', in J. Sterba (ed.), *Terrorism and International Justice* (New York: Oxford University Press).

French, S. E. (2005), *The Code of the Warrior: Exploring Warrior Values Past and Present* (Lanham, MD: Rowman and Littlefield).

Friedman, G. and M. Friedman (1996), *The Future of War* (New York: Crown).

Frum, D. and R. Perle (2003), *An End to Evil: How to Win the War on Terror* (New York: Random House).

Fulcher of Chartres (1941), *Chronicle of the First Crusade*, trans. M. E. McGinty (Philadelphia: University of Pennsylvania Press).

Gallagher, C. (2002), *Church Law and Church Order in Rome and Byzantium* (Aldershot: Ashgate).

Gallie, W. B. (1978), *Philosophers of War and Peace* (Cambridge: Cambridge University Press).

Garner, J. W. (1915), 'Some Questions of International Law in the European War', *American Journal of International Law*, 9 (1).

Garnett, J. (1975), 'Limited War', in J. Baylis, K. Booth, J. Garnett and P. Williams (eds), *Contemporary Strategy: Theory and Policies* (London: Croom Helm).

Gasser, H.-P. (1987), 'An Appeal for Ratification by the United States', *American Journal of International Law*, 81 (4).

Gautier, L. (1959), *Chivalry*, trans. D. C. Dunning, ed. J. Levron (London: Phoenix House).

Gellman, B. (1999), 'The Path to Crisis: How the United States and its Allies Went to War', *New York Times*, 18 April.

Gentili, A. (1933), *De Jure Belli Libri Tres*, trans. J. C. Rolfe (Oxford: Clarendon Press for the Carnegie Endowment for International Peace).

Gilbert, A. (1986), 'Moral Realism, Individuality, and Justice in War', *Political Theory*, 14 (1).

Gilpin, R. G. (1981), *War and Change in World Politics* (Cambridge: Cambridge University Press).

Gilpin, R. G. (1984), 'The Richness of the Tradition of Political Realism', *International Organization*, 38 (2).

Glanville, L. (2005), *Norms, Interests and Humanitarian Intervention* (MA (Research) thesis, Macquarie University).

Glennon, M. J. (2002), 'The Fog of Law: Self-Defense, Inherence, and Incoherence in Article 51 of the United Nations Charter', *Harvard Journal of International Law and Public Policy*, 25 (2).

Glennon, M. J. (2003), 'Why the Security Council Failed', *Foreign Affairs*, 82 (3).

Goodin, R. E. (2005), *What's Wrong with Terrorism?* (Cambridge: Polity).

Gow, J. (2005), *Defending the West* (Cambridge: Polity).

Grabmann, M. (1928), *Thomas Aquinas: His Personality and Thought*, authorized by Virgil Michel (New York: Longmans, Green and Co.).

Graff, J. (2002), 'America is not Pleased', *Time*, 8 July, at http://www.time.com/time/europe/magazine/printout/0,13155,901020708-267731-1,00.html, accessed 29 March 2006.

Gray, C. (2000), *International Law and the Use of Force* (Oxford: Oxford University Press).

Gregor, D. B. (1953), 'Athenian Imperialism', *Greece & Rome*, 22 (1).

Griffith, S. H. (1993), 'St. Augustine', in E. Ferguson (ed.), *Personalities of the Early Church*, Vol. I (New York: Garland Publishing).

Groisser, P. L. (1982), *The United States and the Middle East* (New York: State University of New York Press).

Grotius, H. (1925), *De Jure Belli ac Pacis Libri Tres*, trans. F. W. Kelsey (Washington, DC: Carnegie Council).

Gunaratna, R. (2004), 'Introduction', in R. Gunaratna (ed.), *The Changing Face of Terrorism* (Singapore: Marshall Cavendish).

Haakonssen, K. (1985), 'Hugo Grotius and the History of Political Thought', *Political Theory*, 13 (2).

Habermas, J. (1997), 'Kant's Idea of Perpetual Peace with the Benefit of Two Hundred Years' Hindsight', in J. Bohman and M. Lutz-Bachmann (eds), *Perpetual Peace: Essays on Kant's Cosmopolitan Idea* (Cambridge, MA: MIT Press).

Hacker, F. J. (1976), *Crusaders, Criminals, Crazies: Terror and Terrorism in Our Time* (New York: W. W. Norton and Company).

Hale, J. R. (1962), 'War and Opinion: War and Public Opinion in the Fifteenth and Sixteenth Centuries', *Past and Present*, 22 (2).

Hale, J. R. (1983), *Renaissance War Studies* (London: Hambledon).

Hale, J. R. (1985), *War and Society in Renaissance Europe: 1450–1620* (London: Leicester University Press in Association with Fontana Paperbacks).

Hall, S. (2001), 'The Persistent Spectre: Natural Law, International Order and the Limits of Legal Positivism', *European Journal of International Law*, 12 (2).

Halliday, W. R. (1922), *Lectures on the History of Roman Religion: From Numa to Augustus* (London: Hodder & Stoughton).

Halper, S. and J. Clarke (2004), *America Alone: The Neo-Conservatives and the Global Order* (Cambridge: Cambridge University Press).

Hamburger, M. (1951), *Morals and Law: The Growth of Aristotle's Legal Theory* (New Haven: Yale University Press).

Hancock, C. L. (1994), 'Cicero Versus Machiavelli: Does the End Justify the Means?', *Contemporary Philosophy*, 16 (6).

Hanson, V. D. (1999), 'Sherman's War', *American Heritage*, 50 (7).

Harding, L. (2002), 'No US Apology Over Wedding Party', *The Guardian*, 3 July.

Harris, W. V. (1979), *War and Imperialism in Republican Rome: 327–70 BC* (Oxford: Clarendon Press).

Hartigan, R. S. (1966), 'Saint Augustine on War and Killing: The Problem of the Innocent', *Journal of the History of Ideas*, 27 (2).

Hartigan, R. S. (1983), *Lieber's Code and the Law of War* (Chicago: Precedent).

Hashimi, S. and S. Lee (eds) (2004), *Ethics and Weapons of Mass Destruction: Religious and Secular Perspectives* (Cambridge: Cambridge University Press).

Haslam, J. (2002), *No Virtue Like Necessity: Realist Thought in International Relations Since Machiavelli* (New Haven: Yale University Press).

Hasner, P. (1994), 'Beyond the Three Traditions: The Philosophy of War and Peace in Historical Perspective', *International Affairs*, 70 (4).

Hegel, G. W. F. (1946), *The Philosophy of Right*, trans. T. M. Knox (Oxford: Clarendon Press).

Heisbourg, F. (2004), 'A Work in Progress – the Bush Doctrine and its Consequences', in T. J. Lennon and C. Eiss (eds), *Reshaping Rogue States: Preemption, Regime Change and US Policy Towards Iran, Iraq and North Korea* (Cambridge, MA: MIT Press).

Held, V. (1991), 'Terrorism, Rights and Political Goals', in R. G. Frey and C. W. Morris (eds), *Violence, Terrorism and Justice* (Cambridge: Cambridge University Press).

Hendrickson, D. C. (1997), 'In Defense of Realism: A Commentary on *Just and Unjust Wars*', *Ethics and International Affairs*, 11 (1).

Herberg-Rothe, A. (2001), 'Primacy of "Politics" or "Culture" Over War in a Modern World: Clausewitz Needs a Sophisticated Interpretation', *Defence Analysis*, 17 (2).

Herby, P. and A. R. Nuiten (2001), 'Explosive Remnants of War: Protecting Civilians Through an Additional Protocol to the 1980 Convention on Certain Conventional Weapons', *International Review of the Red Cross*, 195.

Hernshaw, F. J. C. (1928), 'Chivalry and its Place in History', in E. Prestage (ed.), *Chivalry: A Series of Studies to Illustrate its Historical Significance and Civilizing Influence* (London: Kegan Paul, Trench, Trubner & Co.).

Herold, M. (2002), 'Counting the Dead: Attempts to Hide the Number of Afghan Civilians Killed by US Bombs are an Affront to Justice', *The Guardian*, 8 August.

Hershberger, G. F. (1969), *War, Peace and Nonresistance* (Scottdale, PA: Herald Press).

Higgins, R. (1994), *Problems and Process: International Law and How We Use It* (Oxford: Clarendon Press, 1994).

Himes, K. R. (1994), 'The Morality of Humanitarian Intervention', *Theological Studies*, 55 (1).

Hirst, P. (2001), *War and Power in the 21st Century* (Cambridge: Polity).

Hobbes, T. (1994), *The Leviathan*, ed. E. Curley (Cambridge: Cambridge University Press).

Hodges, D. C. (1956), 'Grotius on the Law of War', *The Modern Schoolman*, 34 (4).

Hoffman, B. (1998), *Inside Terrorism* (New York: Columbia University Press).

Holmes, R. (1989), *On War and Morality* (Princeton: Princeton University Press).

House of Commons International Development Committee (2005), 'Darfur, Sudan: The Responsibility to Protect', 5th Report of the 2004–5 Session, Vol. 1, HC67-1, 30 March.

Housley, N. (1995), 'The Crusading Movement: 1274–1700', in J. Riley-Smith (ed.), *The Oxford Illustrated History of the Crusades* (Oxford: Oxford University Press).

Housley, N. (2002), *Religious Warfare in Europe 1400–1536* (Oxford: Oxford University Press).

Howard, J. (2003), Transcript of the Prime Minister to the National Press Club, The Great Hall, Parliament House, Canberra, 14 March 2003, at http://www.pm.gov.au/news/speeches/speech74.html, accessed 23 March 2006.

Howard, M. (1976), *War in European History* (Oxford: Oxford University Press).

Howard, M. (1983), *Clausewitz* (Oxford: Oxford University Press).

Hudson, R. A. (2000), *Who Becomes a Terrorist and Why? The 1999 Government Report on Profiling Terrorists* (Guilford, CT: Lyons Press).

Human Rights Watch (2001), 'Cluster Bombs in Afghanistan', backgrounder, October.

Human Rights Watch (2002), 'Fatally Flawed: Cluster Bombs and their Use by the United States in Afghanistan', *Human Rights Watch Report*, 14 (7) (G), December.

Human Rights Watch (2004a), 'Rwandan Troops to Protect Civilians', news report, 17 August.

Human Rights Watch (2004b), 'Darfur: African Union Must Insist on More Troops', *Human Rights Watch Report*, 14 August.

Hurka, T. (2005), 'Proportionality in the Morality of War', *Philosophy and Public Affairs*, 33 (1).

Hyams, E. (1975), *Terrorists and Terrorism* (London: J. M. Dent and Sons).

Ignatieff, M. (1998), *The Warrior's Honor: Ethnic War and the Modern Conscience* (London: Chatto & Windus).

Ignatieff, M. (2004), *The Lesser Evil: Political Ethics in an Age of Terror* (Edinburgh: Edinburgh University Press).

Independent International Commission on Kosovo (IICK) (2000), *Kosovo Report: International Response, Lessons Learned* (Oxford: Oxford University Press).

International Campaign to Ban Landmines (ICBL) (2002), *Landmine Monitor Report 2002* (London: ICBL).

International Campaign to Ban Landmines (ICBL) (2004), *LM Report 2004: Afghanistan*, at http://www.icbl.org/lm/2004/afghanistan, accessed 23 March 2006.

International Commission of Inquiry on Darfur (2005), 'Report of the International Commission of Inquiry on Darfur to the United Nations Secretary-General', Geneva, January.

International Commission on Intervention and State Sovereignty (ICISS) (2001), *The Responsibility to Protect* (Ottawa: ICISS).

International Committee of the Red Cross (ICRC) (2001), 'Bombing and Occupation of ICRC Facilities in Afghanistan', press release 01/48, 26 October.

International Court of Justice (ICJ) (1986) '*Nicaragua* v. *United States* (Military and Paramilitary Activities in and against Nicaragua)' (The Hague: ICJ Reports).

International Criminal Tribunal for the Former Yugoslavia (ICTY) (2000), 'Final Report to the Prosecutor by the Committee Established to Review the NATO Bombing Campaign Against the Federal Republic of Yugoslavia', 15 June.

Iraq Survey Group (2004), 'Comprehensive Report of the Special Advisor to the Director of Central Intelligence on Iraq's WMD', 30 September.

Jackson, M. (2000), 'Imagined Republics: Machiavelli, Utopia and *Utopia*', *Journal of Value Inquiry*, 34 (4).

Jackson, R. (2000), *The Global Covenant: Human Conduct in a World of States* (Oxford: Oxford University Press).

Jacquard, R. (2002), *In the Name of Osama Bin Laden: Global Terrorism and the Bin Laden Brotherhood* (Durham, NC: Duke University Press).

Janda, L. (1995), 'Shutting the Gates of Mercy: The American Origins of Total War, 1860–1880', *Journal of Military History*, 59 (1).

Jenkins, P. (2003), *Ages of Terror: What We Can and Can't Know about Terrorism* (New York: Aldine de Gruyter).

John of Salisbury (1909), *Policraticus*, trans. C. C. J. Webb (Oxford: Oxford University Press).

John Paul II (1992), 'On Social Concern', in D. J. O'Brien and T. A. Shannon (eds), *Catholic Social Thought: The Documentary Heritage* (New York: Orbis).

John Paul II (1993), 'Address to the Diplomatic Corps', *Origins*, 22.

Johnson, J. T. (1973), 'Toward Reconstructing the *Jus ad Bellum*', *The Monist*, 57 (4).

Johnson, J. T. (1975), *Ideology, Reason and the Limitation of War: Religious and Secular Concepts, 1200–1740* (Princeton: Princeton University Press).

Johnson, J. T. (1981), *Just War Tradition and the Restraint of War: A Moral and Historical Enquiry* (Princeton: Princeton University Press).

Johnson, J. T. (1984), *Can Modern War be Just?* (New Haven: Yale University Press).

Johnson, J. T. (1987), *The Quest for Peace: Three Moral Traditions in Western Cultural History* (Princeton: Princeton University Press).

Johnson, J. T. (1999), *Morality and Contemporary Warfare* (New Haven: Yale University Press).

Johnson, J. T. (2000), 'Maintaining the Protection of Non-Combatants', *Journal of Peace Research*, 37 (4).

Johnson, J. T. (2001), 'The Just War Idea and the Ethics of Intervention', in J. C. Ficarrotta (ed.), *The Leader's Imperative: Ethics, Integrity and Responsibility* (West Lafayette, IN: Purdue University Press).

Johnson, J. T. (2004), 'From Moral Norm to Criminal Code: The Law of Armed Conflict and the Restraint of Contemporary Warfare', in A. Lang, Jr, A. C. Pierce and J. H. Rosenthal (eds), *Ethics and the Future of Conflict: Lessons from the 1990s* (Upper Saddle River, NJ: Prentice Hall).

Johnson, J. T. (2005), *The War to Oust Saddam Hussein: Just War and the Face of New Conflict* (Lanham, MD: Rowman and Littlefield).

Johnston, D. (2000), 'The Jurists', in C. Rowe and M. Schofield (eds), *The Cambridge History of Greek and Roman Political Thought* (Cambridge: Cambridge University Press).

Johnstone, D. and D. E. Sanger (2002), 'Yemen Killing Based on Rules Set Out by Bush', *New York Times*, 6 November.

Johnstone, I. (2004), 'US–UN Relations after Iraq: The End of the World (Order) As We Know It?', *European Journal of International Law*, 15 (4).

Juergensmeyer, M. (2001), *Terror in the Mind of God: The Global Rise of Religious Violence* (Berkeley: University of California Press, 2001).

Kaeuper, R. W. (1999), *Chivalry and Violence in Medieval Europe* (Oxford: Oxford University Press).

Kahn, H. (1962) *Thinking About the Unthinkable* (New York: Horizon Press).

Kahn, R. A. (1944), 'The Law of Nations and the Conduct of War in the Early Times of the Standing Army', *Journal of Politics*, 6 (1).

Kant, I. (1903), *Perpetual Peace: A Philosophical Essay*, trans. M. Campbell Smith (London: Simon Sonnenschein & Co.).

Kaplan, M. A. and N. de B. Katzenbach (1961), *The Political Foundations of International Law* (New York: Wiley and Sons).

Karsten, P. (1978), *Law, Soldiers and Combat* (Westport, CT: Greenwood Press).

Keegan, J. (1993), *A History of Warfare* (New York: Alfred Knopf).

Keegan, J. (1999), *War and our World: The Reith Lectures 1998* (London: Pimlico).

Keegan, J. (2000), *The First World War* (London: Vintage).

Keen, M. H. (1965), *The Laws of War in the Late Middle Ages* (London: Routledge & Kegan Paul).

Keen, M. H. (1967), *A History of Medieval Europe* (London: Routledge and Kegan Paul).

Keen, M. H. (1984), *Chivalry* (New Haven: Yale University Press).

Kegley, C. W. and G. A. Raymond (2003), 'Preventive War and Permissive Normative Order', *International Studies Perspectives*, 4 (4).

Kelsen, H. (1948), 'Collective Security and Collective Self-Defence Under the Charter', *American Journal of International Law*, 42 (3).

Kennan, G. F. (1985), 'Morality and Foreign Policy', *Foreign Affairs*, 64 (2).

Kenny, A. (1980), *Aquinas* (Oxford: Oxford University Press).

Kewley, G. (1984), *Humanitarian Law in Armed Conflicts* (London: VCTA Publishing).

Khatchadourian, H. (1998), *The Morality of Terrorism* (New York: Peter Lang).

Kingsbury, D. and A. Roberts (1992), 'Introduction: Grotian Thought in International Relations', in H. Bull, B. Kingsbury and A. Roberts (eds), *Hugo Grotius and International Relations* (Oxford: Clarendon Press).

Knight, W. S. M. (1925), *The Life and Works of Hugo Grotius* (London: Sweet & Maxwell).

Kolff, D. W. (2003), 'Missile Strike Carried Out With Yemeni Cooperation – Using UCAVs to Kill Alleged Terrorists: A Professional Approach to the Normative Bases of Military Ethics', *Journal of Military Ethics*, 2 (3).

Kramer, M. (2002), 'The Moral Logic of Hizballah', in W. Reich (ed.), *Origins of Terrorism: Psychologies, Ideologies, Theologies, States of Mind* (Baltimore: Johns Hopkins University Press).

Krasner, S. D. (1999), *Sovereignty: Organized Hypocrisy* (Princeton: Princeton University Press).

Kratochwil, F. V. (1989), *Rules, Norms and Decisions: On the Conditions of Practical and Legal Reasoning in International Relations and Domestic Affairs* (Cambridge: Cambridge University Press).

Kunz, J. L. (1947), 'Individual and Collective Self-Defence in Article 51 of the Charter of the United Nations', *American Journal of International Law*, 41 (4).

Kunz, J. L. (1951), 'The Chaotic Status of the Laws of War and the Urgent Necessity for Their Revision', *American Journal of International Law*, 45 (1).

Kuper, L. (1958), *Passive Resistance in South Africa* (New Haven: Yale University Press).

Lackey, D. (1989), *The Ethics of War and Peace* (Englewood Cliffs, NJ: Prentice Hall).

Lambeth, B. S. (2000), *The Transformation of US Air Power* (New York: Cornell University Press).

Lambeth, B. S. (2001) *NATO's Air War for Kosovo: A Strategic and Operational Assessment* (New York: RAND).

Laqueur, W. (2001), 'Left, Right and Beyond: The Changing Face of Terror', in J. Hoge, Jr and G. Rose (eds), *How Did This Happen? Terrorism and the New War* (Oxford: Public Affairs).

Lauterpacht, H. (1933), *The Function of Law in the International Community* (Oxford: Clarendon Press).

Lavoyer, J.-P. and L. Maresca (1999), 'The Role of the ICRC in the Development of International Humanitarian Law', *International Negotiation*, 4 (3).

Lawrence, T. J. (1908), *The Principles of International Law* (Boston, DC: Heath & Co.).

Lea, H. C. (2001), *Studies in Church History: The Rise of the Temporal Power – Benefit of Clergy – Excommunication* (Philadelphia: University of Michigan Library).

Lebow, R. N. (2003), *The Tragic Vision of Politics: Ethics, Interests and Orders* (Cambridge: Cambridge University Press).

Leggette, K. (1986), 'The Air Force's New Cluster Weapon – The Combined Effects Munition', *USAF Fighter Weapons Review*, Spring.

Lennox, D. (ed.) (1999), *Jane's Air Launched Weapons* (London: Jane's Defence Group).

Lepard, B. (2002), *Rethinking Humanitarian Intervention: A Fresh Approach Based on Fundamental Ethical Principles in International Law and World Religions* (University Park, PA: Pennsylvania State University Press).

Levie, H. S. (1961), 'Prisoners of War and the Protecting Power', *American Journal of International Law*, 55 (2).

Levie, H. S. (1962), 'Penal Sanctions for Maltreatment of Prisoners of War', *American Journal of International Law*, 56 (2).

Liddell Hart, B. (1934), *The Ghost of Napoleon* (New Haven: Yale University Press).

Lieber, F. (1839), *Manual of Political Ethics*, Vol. II (Boston: Charles C. Little and James Brown).

Linker, D. (1992), 'Machiavelli, Harrington and the Character of Modern Utopia', *Conference: A Journal of Philosophy and Theory*, 3 (2).

Linklater, A. (1990), *Men and Citizens in the Theory of International Relations* (London: Macmillan).

Linklater, A. (1998), *The Transformation of Political Community* (Cambridge: Polity).

Lowe, B. (1990), 'War and Commonwealth in Mid-Tudor England', *Sixteenth-Century Journal*, 21 (2).

Lumpkin, J. J. (2002), 'US Kills Senior al-Qaida Leader in Yemen with Missile Strike', *Associated Press*, 5 November.

Lustick, I. S. (1995), 'Terrorism in the Arab–Israeli Conflict: Targets and Audiences', in M. Crenshaw (ed.), *Terrorism in Context* (University Park, PA: Pennsylvania State University Press).

Lynch, A. C. (2001), 'The Realism of Russian Foreign Policy', *Europe–Asia Studies*, 53 (1) 2001.

MacAskill, E., M. White and L. Harding (2001), 'Bombs Go Astray, the Casualties Mount . . . and the Doubts Set in: Civilian Deaths Usher in the Feared "Kosovo" Moment', *The Guardian*, 29 October.

McCormack, T. (1996), *Self-Defence in International Law: The Israeli Raid on the Iraqi Nuclear Reactor* (New York: St Martin's Press).

McDougal, M. S. (1963), 'The Soviet–Cuban Quarantine and Self-Defence', *American Journal of International Law*, 57 (2).

McDougal, M. S. and F. P. Feliciano (1961), *Law and Minimum World Public Order: The Legal Regulation of International Coercion* (New Haven: Yale University Press).

McGwire, M. (2000), 'Why Did We Bomb Belgrade?', *International Affairs*, 76 (1).

Machiavelli, N. (1940), *The Prince*, trans. C. Detmold (Oxford: Oxford University Press).

Machiavelli, N. (1965), 'The Discourses', in *Machiavelli: The Chief Works and Others*, ed. and trans. A. Gilbert (Durham, NC: Duke University Press).

Machiavelli, N. (1969), *The Arte of Warre*, trans. P. Whichoine (Amsterdam: De Capo Press).

McInnes, C. (2003), 'A Different Kind of War? September 11 and the US–Afghan War', *Review of International Studies*, 29 (2).

McKeogh, C. (1997), *The Political Realism of Reinhold Niebuhr: A Pragmatic Approach to Just War* (London: Macmillan).

McKeogh, C. (2002), *Innocent Civilians: The Morality of Killing in War* (London: Palgrave).

Mackinney, L. C. (1930), 'The People and Public Opinion in the Eleventh-Century Peace Movement', *Speculum*, 5 (2).

McMahan, J. (1996) 'Realism, Morality and War', in T. Nardin (ed.), *The Ethics of War and Peace: Religious and Secular Perspectives* (Princeton: Princeton University Press).

McMahan, J. (1997), 'The Limits of National Partiality', in R. McKim and J. McMahan (eds), *The Morality of Nationalism* (Oxford: Oxford University Press).

McMahan, J. and R. McKim (1993), 'The Just War and the Gulf War', *Canadian Journal of Philosophy*, 23 (4).

Magnou-Nortier, E. (1992), 'The Enemies of the Peace: Reflections on a Vocabulary 500–1100', in T. Head and R. Landes (eds), *The Peace of God: Social Violence and Religious Response in France Around the Year 1000* (Ithaca, NY: Cornell University Press).

Markus, R. A. (1970), *Saeculum: History and Society in the Theology of St Augustine* (Cambridge: Cambridge University Press).

Marx, A. W. (1992), *Lessons of Struggle: South African Internal Opposition, 1960–1990* (Oxford: Oxford University Press).

Marx, S. (1992), 'Shakespeare's Pacifism', *Renaissance Quarterly*, 45 (1).

Mattern, S. P. (1999), *Rome and the Enemy: Imperial Strategy and the Magistrate* (Berkeley: University of California Press).

Mayer, H. E. (1988), *The Crusades*, 2nd edition, trans. J. Gillingham (Oxford: Oxford University Press).

Mearsheimer, J. J. and S. Walt (2003), 'An Unnecessary War', *Foreign Policy*, 134.

Meinecke, F. (1957), *Machiavellism: The Doctrine of Raison D'Etat and its Place in Modern History*, trans. D. Scott (London: Routledge and Kegan Paul).

Meron, T. (1987), 'The Geneva Conventions as Customary Law', *American Journal of International Law*, 81 (2).

Meron, T. (1992), 'Shakespeare's Henry the Fifth and the Law of War', *American Journal of International Law*, 86 (1).

Meron, T. (1998), *Bloody Constraint: War and Chivalry in Shakespeare* (Oxford: Oxford University Press).

Meron, T. (2000), 'The Martens Clause, Principles of Humanity, and Dictates of Public Conscience', *American Journal of International Law*, 94 (1).

Merrill, J. M. (1971), *William Tecumseh Sherman* (Chicago: Rand McNally).

Mertus, J. (2000), 'The Legality of Humanitarian Intervention: Lessons from Kosovo', *William and Mary Law Review*, 41 (4).

Mill, J. S. (1867), *Dissertations and Discussions*, 2nd edition, (London: Longman).

Mill, J. S. (1973), 'A Few Words on Non-Intervention', in G. Himmelfarb (ed.), *Essays on Politics and Culture* (Gloucester, MA: Peter Smith).

Miller, F. D., Jr (1995), *Nature, Justice and Rights in Aristotle's Politics* (Oxford: Clarendon Press).

Miller, L. H. (1964), 'The Contemporary Significance of the Doctrine of Just War', *World Politics*, 16 (2).

Miller, R. B. (1991), *Interpretations of Conflict: Ethics, Pacifism and the Just War Tradition* (Chicago: University of Chicago Press).

Miller, R. I. (1975), *The Law of War* (Lexington, MA: Lexington Books).

Millett, J. D. (1945), 'Logistics and Modern War', *Military Affairs*, 9 (3).

Minnear, R. H. (1971), *Victor's Justice: The Tokyo War Crimes Trial* (Princeton: Princeton University Press).

Moellendorf, D. (2002), *Cosmopolitan Justice* (Boulder, CO: Westview Press).

Moni, W. (2005), 'The UN Report on Darfur: What Role for the AU?', *Pambazuka*, 10 February 2005, at http://globalpolicy.igc.org/security/issues/sudan/2005/0210aurole.htm, accessed 12 April 2005.

Montross, L. (1960), *War Through the Ages*, 3rd edition (New York: Harper and Row).

Moorhead, C. (1998), *Dunant's Dream: War, Switzerland and the History of the Red Cross* (New York: Carroll and Graf Publishers).

Morgenthau, H. J. (1940), 'Positivism, Functionalism and International Law', *American Journal of International Law*, 34 (2).

Morgenthau, H. J. (1945), 'Evil of Politics and the Ethics of Evil', *Ethics*, LVI (1).

Morgenthau, H. J. (1948), 'The Twilight of International Morality', *Ethics*, 58 (2).

Morgenthau, H. J. (1951), *In Defense of the National Interest: A Critical Examination of American Foreign Policy* (New York: Alfred Knopf).

Morgenthau, H. J. (1969), *A New Foreign Policy for the United States* (Washington, DC: Council on Foreign Relations).

Morrall, J. B. (1960), *Political Thought in Medieval Times* (London: Hutchinson University Library).

Muldoon, J. (1972), 'The Contribution of the Medieval Canon Lawyers to the Formation of International Law', *Traditio: Study in Ancient and Medieval History, Thought and Religion*, 28 (2).

Muldoon, J. (1991), 'The Conquest of the Americas: The Spanish Search for Global Order', in R. Robertson and W. R. Garrett (eds), *Religion and Global Order* (New York: Paragon House Publishers).

Murphy, S. D. (2003), 'Use of Military Force to Disarm Iraq', *American Journal of International Law*, 97 (2).

Myers, R. (2001), 'Interview', ABC TV, 17 November 2001.

Myers, R. J. (1996), 'Notes on the Just War Theory: Whose Justice, Which Wars?', *Ethics and International Affairs*, 10 (1).

Myjer, E. and N. White (2002), 'The Twin Towers Attack: An Unlimited Right to Self-Defence?', *Journal of Conflict and Security Law*, 7 (1).

Nagel, T. (1972), 'War and Massacre', *Philosophy and Public Affairs*, 1 (2).

Nardin, T. (1992), 'Ethical Traditions in International Affairs', in T. Nardin and D. R. Mapel (eds), *Traditions of International Ethics* (Cambridge: Cambridge University Press).

Nardin, T. (2002), 'The Moral Basis of Humanitarian Intervention', *Ethics and International Affairs*, 16 (1).

Nardin, T. (2005), 'Justice and Coercion', in A. J. Bellamy (ed.), *International Society and its Critics* (Oxford: Oxford University Press).

National Security Strategy (NSS) (2002), *National Security Strategy of the United States*, Washington, DC, September.

Nederman, C. J. and K. Langdon Forhan (eds) (1993), 'Introduction', in C. J. Nederman and K. Langdon Forhan (eds), *Medieval Political Theory – A Reader* (London: Routledge).

Niebuhr, R. (1932), *Moral Man, Immoral Society: A Study in Ethics and Politics* (New York: Charles Scribner's Sons).

Niebuhr, R. (1936), *An Interpretation of Christian Ethics* (London: Student Christian Movement Press).

Niebuhr, R. (1940), *Christianity and Power Politics* (New York: Charles Scribner's Sons).

Niebuhr, R. (1953), *Christian Realism and Political Problems* (New York: A. M. Kelley).

Niebuhr, R. (1959), *The Structure of Nations and Empires: A Study of the Recurring Patterns and Problems of the Political Order in Relation to the Unique Problems of the Nuclear Age* (New York: Scribner).

Nielsen, K. (1981), 'Violence and Terrorism: Its Uses and Abuses', in B. M. Leiser, *Values in Conflict* (New York: Macmillan).

Norena, C. G. (1975), *Studies in Spanish Renaissance Thought* (The Hague: Martinus Nijhoff).

Norena, C. G. (1997), 'Francisco Suarez on Democracy and International Law', in K. White (ed.), *Hispanic Philosophy in the Age of Discovery: Studies in Philosophy and the History of Philosophy*, Vol. 29 (New York: Catholic University American Press).

Norman, R. (1995), *Ethics, Killing and War* (Cambridge: Cambridge University Press).

Norton-Taylor, R. and L. Ward (2001), 'Appeals to Halt Cluster Bombs', *The Guardian*, 8 November.

Nussbaum, A. (1954), *A Concise History of the Law of Nations* (London: Macmillan).

Nys, E. (1911), 'Francis Lieber – His Life and Work: Part II', *American Journal of International Law*, 5 (2).

O'Brien, W. V. (1981), *The Conduct of Just and Limited Wars* (New York: Praeger).

O'Connell, M. E. (2003), 'Re-leashing the Dogs of War', *American Journal of International Law*, 97 (2).

O'Connor, D. J. (1967), *Aquinas and Natural Law* (London: Macmillan).

O'Donovan, O. (2003), *The Just War Revisited* (Cambridge: Cambridge University Press).

Ober, J. (1994), 'Classical Greek Times', in M. Howard, G. J. Andreopoulos and M. R. Shulman (eds) (1994), *The Laws of War: Constraints on Warfare in the Western World* (New Haven: Yale University Press).

Observer, The (1999), 'Human Rights Index', at http://www.guardian.co.uk/Tables/4_col_tables/0,5737,258330,00.html, accessed 17 October 2003.

Odo of Deuil (1948), *The Journey of Louis VII to the East*, ed. and trans. V. Gingerick Berry (New York: W. W. Norton and Co.).

Orend, B. (2000a), *War and International Justice: A Kantian Perspective* (Waterloo, ON: Wilfrid Laurier University Press).

Orend, B. (2000b), 'Jus Post Bellum', *Journal of Social Philosophy*, 31 (1).

Orend, B. (2002), 'Justice after War', *Ethics and International Affairs*, 16 (1).

Osiander, A. (2001), 'Sovereignty, International Relations and the Westphalian Myth', *International Organization*, 55 (2).

Pape, R. A. (2003), 'The Strategic Logic of Suicide Terrorism', *American Political Science Review*, 97 (3).

Pappas, N. (1995), *Plato and the Republic* (London: Routledge).

Parekh, B. (1997), 'Rethinking Humanitarian Intervention', *International Political Science Review*, 18 (1).

Parel, A. J. (1990), 'Machiavelli's Notion of Justice: Text and Analysis', *Political Theory*, 18 (4).

Parker, G. (1988), *The Military Revolution: Military Innovation and the Rise of the West, 1500–1800* (Cambridge: Cambridge University Press).

Paskins, B. and M. Dockrill (1979), *The Ethics of War* (London: Duckworth).

Paton, H. J. (1962), *The Categorical Imperative: A Study in Kant's Moral Philosophy* (London: Hutchinson's University Library).

Paust, J. J. (2001–2), 'Use of Armed Force Against Terrorists in Afghanistan, Iraq and Beyond', *Cornell International Law Journal*, 35 (3).

Pennington, K. (1993), *The Prince and the Law, 1200–1600* (Berkeley: University of California Press).

Peterson, S. (2004), 'Sudan's Key Ties at the UN', *Christian Science Monitor*, 31 August.

Phillips, R. and D. Cady (1996), *Humanitarian Intervention: Just War vs Pacifism* (Lanham, MD: Rowman and Littlefield).

Pictet, J. S. (1951), 'The New Geneva Conventions for the Protection of War Victims', *American Journal of International Law*, 45 (3).

Pilger, J. (2002), 'The Great Charade', *The Observer*, 14 July.

Pitteloud, J. F. (with C. Barnes and F. Dubosson) (1999), *Procès-verbaux des Séances du Comité international de la Croix-Rouge, 17 février 1863–28 août 1914* (Geneva: Société Henry Dunant/International Committee of the Red Cross).

Plato (2003), *The Republic*, ed. and trans. D. Lee (London: Penguin).

Plato (2005), *The Laws*, trans. T. Saunders (London: Penguin).

Pojman, L. P. (2003), 'The Moral Response to Terrorism and Cosmopolitanism', in J. Sterba (ed.), *Terrorism and International Justice* (New York: Oxford University Press).

Posen, B. (2000), 'The War for Kosovo: Serbia's Political-Military Strategy', *International Security*, 24 (4).

Post, G. (1954), 'Blessed Lady Spain: Vincentius Hispanus and Spanish National Imperialism in the Thirteenth Century', *Speculum*, 29 (2).

Post, G. (1964), *Studies in Medieval Legal Thought: Public Law and the State, 1100–1322* (Princeton: Princeton University Press).

Price, J. J. (2001), *Thucydides and Internal War* (Cambridge: Cambridge University Press).

Pufendorf, S. (1934), *Of the Law of Nature and Nations*, ed. and trans. C. H. Oldfather and W. A. Oldfather (Oxford: Clarendon Press).

Pufendorf, S. (1994), 'On the Law of War', in *The Political Writings of Samuel Pufendorf*, ed. C. L. Carr, trans. (Oxford: Oxford University Press).

Ramsey, P. (1961), *War and the Christian Conscience: How Shall Modern War be Conducted Justly?* (Durham, NC: Duke University Press).

Ramsey, P. (2002), *The Just War: Force and Political Responsibility* (Lanham, MD: Rowman and Littlefield).

Rawls, J. (1993), *Political Liberalism* (New York: Columbia University Press).

Rawls, J. (1999), *The Law of Peoples* (Cambridge, MA: Harvard University Press).

Raymond, G. A. (1998–9), 'Necessity in Foreign Policy', *Political Science Quarterly*, 113 (4).

Raymond, J. M. and B. J. Frischolz (1982), 'Lawyers who Established International Law in the United States, 1776–1914', *American Journal of International Law*, 76 (4).

Record, J. (2004), 'Threat Confusion and its Penalties', *Survival*, 46 (2).

Reddy, F. S. (1975), *International Law in the Enlightenment: The Background of Emmerich de Vattel's Le Droit des Gens* (Dobbs Ferry, NY: Oceana Publications).

Reeves, J. C. (1909), 'The Influence of the Law of Nature upon International Law in the United States', *American Journal of International Law*, 3 (2).

Reichberg, G. M. (2003), 'Francisco de Vitoria: *De Indis* and *De iure belli relectiones*: Philosophy Meets War', in J. J. E. Garcia, G. M. Reichberg and B. N. Schumacher (eds), *The Classics of Western Philosophy: A Reader's Guide* (Oxford: Blackwell).

Reid, C. J. and J. Witte (1999), 'In the Steps of Gratian: Writing the History of Canon Law in the 1990s', *Emory Law Journal*, 48 (2).

Reisman, W. M. (1985), 'Criteria for the Lawful Use of Force in International Law', *Yale Journal of International Law*, 10 (2).

Remec, P. P. (1960), *The Position of the Individual in International Law According to Grotius and Vattel* (The Hague: Martinus Nijhoff).

Rengger, N. J. (2000), *International Relations, Political Theory and the Problem of Order: Beyond International Relations Theory?* (London: Routledge).

Rengger, N. J. (2002), 'On the Just War Tradition in the Twenty-First Century', *International Affairs*, 78 (2).

Renick, T. M. (1994), 'Charity Lost: The Secularization of the Principle of Double-Effect in the Just War Tradition', *The Thomist*, 58 (3).

Reus-Smit, C. (1999), *The Moral Purpose of the State: Culture, Social Identity and Institutional Rationality in International Relations* (Princeton: Princeton University Press).

Rhodes, R. (1995), *The Making of the Atomic Bomb* (New York: Simon and Schuster).

Rice, C. (2000), 'Promoting the National Interest', *Foreign Affairs*, 79 (1).

Ricks, T. E. (2002), 'Target Approval Delay Cost Air Force Key Hits', *Journal of Military Ethics*, 1 (2).

Rifaat, A. A. (1979), *International Aggression: A Study of the Legal Concept: Its Development and Definition in International Law* (Stockholm: Almqvist and Wiksell).

Riley-Smith, J. (1995), 'The Crusading Movement and Historians', in J. Riley-Smith (ed.), *The Oxford Illustrated History of the Crusades* (Oxford: Oxford University Press).

Riley-Smith, J. (1997), *The First Crusaders 1095–1131* (Cambridge: Cambridge University Press).

Riley-Smith, J. (1998), 'Raymond IV of St. Gilles, Archard of Arles and the Conquest of Lebanon', in J. France and W. G. Zajac (eds), *The Crusades and their Sources: Essays Presented to Bernard Hamilton* (Aldershot: Ashgate).

Riley-Smith, L. and J. Riley-Smith (1981), *The Crusades: Idea and Reality 1095–1274* (London: Edward Arnold).

Rist, J. M. (1994), *Augustine: Ancient Thought Baptized* (Cambridge: Cambridge University Press).

Roberts, A. (2002), 'Counter-Terrorism, Armed Force and the Laws of War', *Survival*, 44 (1).

Roberts, A. (2003), 'Law and the Use of Force After Iraq', *Survival*, 45 (2).

Roberts, A. and R. Guelff (2000), *Documents on the Laws of War*, 3rd edition (Oxford: Oxford University Press).

Roberts, B. (1998) 'NBC-Armed Rogues: Is there a Moral Case for Pre-emption?', in E. Abrams (ed.), *Close Calls: Intervention, Terrorism, Missile Defense, and 'Just War' Today* (Washington, DC: Ethics and Public Policy Center).

Roberts, G. (1999), 'The Counterproliferation Self-Help Paradigm: A Legal Regime for Enforcing the Norm Prohibiting the Proliferation of Weapons of Mass Destruction', *Denver Journal of International Law and Policy*, 27 (3).

Robertson, G. (1999), *Crimes Against Humanity: The Struggle for Global Justice* (London: Penguin).

Roblyer, D. A. (2004), 'Beyond Precision: Issues of Morality and Decision Making in Minimizing Collateral Damage', *ACDIS Occasional Paper*, University of Illinois at Urbana-Champaign.

Rodin, D. (2004a), *War and Self-Defence* (Oxford: Clarendon Press).

Rodin, D. (2004b), 'Terrorism without Intention', *Ethics*, 114 (4).

Rodin, D. (forthcoming), 'The Ethics of Preventive War', forthcoming publication in author's possession.

Rommen, H. A. (1947), *The Natural Law: A Study in Legal and Social History and Philosophy* (London: B. Herder Book Co.).

Roosevelt, T. (1916), *Fear God and Take Your Own Part* (New York: George H. Doran Co.).

Rossi, C. (1998), *Broken Chain of Being: James Brown Scott and the Origins of International Law* (The Hague: Kluwer).

Roszak, T. (1963), 'A Just War Analysis of Two Types of Deterrence', *Ethics*, 73 (2).

Roth, K. (2004), 'War in Iraq: Not a Humanitarian Intervention', *Human Rights Watch Report*, at http://hrw.org/wr2k4/3.htm, accessed 22 July 2004.

Rousseau, J.-J. (1927), *A Project for Perpetual Peace*, trans. E. M. Nuttall (London: Richard Cobden-Sanderson).

Rummel, R. J. (1994), *Death by Government* (New Brunswick, NJ: Transaction Books).

Rumsfeld, D. (2001a) 'Remarks at Stakeout Outside ABC TV Studio', 28 October 2001, at http://www.defenselink.mil/news/Oct2001/t10292001_t1028sd3.html, accessed 3 February 2005.

Rumsfeld, D. (2001b), 'Afghan Civilian Casualty Info Hard to Get, Says Rumsfeld', at http://www.defenselink.mil/news/Dec2001/n12042001_200112045.html, accessed 23 March 2006.

Russell, A. G. (1941), 'The Greek as a Mercenary Soldier', *Greece and Rome*, 11 (31).

Russell, F. H. (1975), *The Just War in the Middle Ages* (Cambridge: Cambridge University Press).

Russett, B. (1984), 'Ethical Dilemmas of Nuclear Deterrence', *International Security*, 8 (4).

Russett, B. (1993), *Grasping the Democratic Peace* (Princeton: Princeton University Press).

Sampson, P. (2002), 'Afghan Cluster Bombs Almost Cleared', Associated Press, 19 September.

Sandoz, Y. (1987), 'The Red Cross and Peace: Realities and Limits', *Journal of Peace Research*, 24 (3).

Santoni, R. E. (2003), *Sartre on Violence: Curiously Ambivalent* (University Park, PA: Pennsylvania State University Press).

Saunders, J. J. (1962), *Aspects of the Crusades* (Christchurch: University of Canterbury Press).

Schechtman, J. (1961), *Fighter and Prophet: The Last Years* (New York: Yoseleff).

Scheffer, D. J. (1992), 'Towards a Modern Doctrine of Humanitarian Intervention', *University of Toledo Law Review*, 23 (2).

Schmitt, M. (1999), 'The Principle of Discrimination in 21st Century Warfare', *Yale Human Rights & Development Law Journal*, 2 (1).

Schnabel, A. and R. Thakur (eds) (2000), *Kosovo and the Challenge of Humanitarian Intervention: Selective Indignation, Collective Action, and International Citizenship* (Tokyo: United Nations University Press).

Schneewind, J. B. (1990), *Moral Philosophy from Montaigne to Kant: An Anthology*, Vol. 1 (Cambridge: Cambridge University Press).

Schuman, F. L. (1932), 'The Ethics and Politics of International Peace', *International Journal of Ethics*, 42 (2).

Schwarzenberger, G. (1955), 'The Fundamental Principles of International Law', in G. Schwarzenberger (ed.), *Recueil des cours* (Leyden: A. W. Sijthoff).

Scott, J. (1992), 'The Law of War: Grotius, Sidney, Locke and The Political Theory of Rebellion', *History of Political Thought*, 13 (4).

Scott, J. B. (1908), 'The Work of the Second Hague Peace Conference', *American Journal of International Law*, 2 (1).

Scott, J. B. (1922) *The Spanish Origins of International Law*, Vol. 1 (New York: Carnegie Corporation).

Scott, J. B. (1924), 'The Codification of International Law', *American Journal of International Law*, 18 (2).

Scott, J. B. (1928), 'Associacion Francisco de Vitoria', *American Journal of International Law*, 22 (1).

Scullard, H. H. (1951), *A History of the Roman World: 753–146 BC* (London: Routledge).

Sewall, S. (2002), 'Understanding Collateral Damage', workshop report, workshop organized by Carr Center for Human Rights Policy, Washington, DC, 4–5 June.

Seward, D. (1972), *The Monks of War: The Military Religious Orders* (London: Eyre Methuen).

Shahid, A. (2001), *Legacy of the Prophet: Despots, Democrats and the New Politics of Islam* (Boulder, CO: Westview Press).

Shapcott, R. (2001), *Justice, Community and Dialogue in International Relations* (Cambridge: Cambridge University Press).

Shaw, M. (2003), *War and Genocide: Organized Killing in Modern Society* (Cambridge: Polity).

Shaw, M. (2005), *The Western Way of War* (Cambridge: Polity).

Shaw, M. N. (2003), *International Law*, 5th edition (Cambridge: Cambridge University Press).

Shaw, P. M. (1997), *Collateral Damage and the United States Air Force*, thesis written for the School of Advanced Aerospace Studies, Air University, June.

Sherman, W. T. (1957), *Memoirs of General William T. Sherman: By Himself* (Bloomington: Indiana University Press).

Shue, H. (1988), 'Mediating Duties', *Ethics*, 98 (4).

Shue, H. (2003), 'Bombing to Rescue? NATO's 1999 Bombing of Serbia', in D. K. Chatterjee and D. E. Scheid (eds), *Ethics and Foreign Intervention* (Cambridge: Cambridge University Press).

Shue, H. and D. Wippman (2002), 'Limiting Attacks on Dual-Use Facilities Performing Indispensable Civilian Functions', *Cornell International Law Journal*, 35 (3).

Sigmund, P. E. (1993), 'Law and Politics', in N. Kretzmann and E. Stump (eds), *The Cambridge Companion to Aquinas* (Cambridge: Cambridge University Press).

Silke, A. (2003), 'Becoming a Terrorist', in A. Silke (ed.), *Terrorists, Victims and Society: Psychological Perspectives on Terrorism and its Consequences* (London: Wiley).

Silverman, A. L. (2002), 'Just War, Jihad, and Terrorism: A Comparison of Western and Islamic Norms for the Use of Political Violence', *Journal of Church and State*, 44 (1).

Simpson, G. (2004), *Great Powers and Outlaw States: Unequal Sovereigns in the International Legal Order* (Cambridge: Cambridge University Press).

Skinner, Q. (1978), *The Foundations of Modern Political Thought, Vol. 1: The Renaissance* (Cambridge: Cambridge University Press).

Skinner, Q. (1984), 'The Idea of Negative Liberty: Philosophical and Historical Perspectives', in R. Rorty, J. B. Schneewind and Q. Skinner (eds), *Ideas in Context: Philosophy in History* (Cambridge: Cambridge University Press).

Skinner, Q. (1988), 'Analysis of Political Thought and Action', in J. Tully (ed.), *Meaning and Context: Quintin Skinner and his Critics* (Cambridge: Polity).

Slaughter, A.-M. (1995), 'International Law in a World of Liberal States', *European Journal of International Law*, 6 (3).

Slaughter, A.-M. (2000), 'A Liberal Theory of International Law', *Proceedings of the 94th Meeting of the American Society of International Law*.

Slaughter, A.-M. (2003a), 'Leading Through Law', *The Wilson Quarterly*, 27 (4).

Slaughter, A.-M. (2003b), 'Misreading the Record', *Foreign Affairs*, 82 (4).

Smilansky, S. (2004), 'Terrorism, Justification and Illusion', *Ethics*, 114 (4).

Smith, H. A. (1947), *The Crisis in the Law of Nations of International Law* (London: Stevens).

Smith, S. B. (1983), 'Hegel's Views on War, the State and International Relations', *American Political Science Review*, 77 (3).

Snyder, J. (2003), 'Imperial Temptations', *The National Interest*, Spring.

Sofaer, A. D. (2000), 'International Law and Kosovo', *Stanford Journal of International Law*, 36 (1).

Sofaer, A. D. (2003), 'On the Necessity of Pre-emption', *European Journal of International Law*, 14 (2).

Stevens, K. R. (2004), *Border Diplomacy: The Caroline and McLeod Affairs in Anglo-American–Canadian Relations, 1837–1842* (Montgomery: University of Alabama Press).

Strickland, M. (1996), *War and Chivalry: The Conduct and Perception of War in England and Normandy 1066–1217* (Cambridge: Cambridge University Press).

Stromseth, J. (1993), 'Iraq', in L. F. Damrosch (ed.), *Enforcing Restraint: Collective Intervention in Internal Conflicts* (New York: Council on Foreign Relations).

Suárez, F. (1944a), 'De Legibus', in *Selections from Three Works: De Triplici Virtute Theologica, Fide, Spe et Charitate*, ed. and trans. J. Williams (New York: Carnegie Classics on International Law).

Suárez, F. (1944b), 'On War', in *Selections from Three Works of Francisco Suárez*, Vol. II, ed. J. B. Scott (Oxford: Clarendon Press).

Suganami, H. (2005), 'The English School and International Theory', in A. J. Bellamy (ed.), *International Society and its Critics* (Oxford: Oxford University Press).

Sun Tzu (1963), *The Art of War*, trans. S. Griffith (Oxford: Oxford University Press).

Swift, L. J. (1970), 'St. Ambrose on Violence and War', *Transactions and Proceedings of the American Philological Association*, 101.

Swift, L. J. (1983), *The Early Fathers on War and Military Service* (Wilmington, DE: Michael Glazier).

Temple, W. (1940), *A Conditional Justification of War* (London: Hodder and Stoughton).

Tertullian (1885a), 'On Idolatry', in A. Roberts and J. Donaldson (eds), *The Anti-Nicene Fathers*, Vol. II (New York: Christian Literature Publishing).

Tertullian (1885b), ''On the Soldier's Crown', in A. Roberts and J. Donaldson (eds), *The Anti-Nicene Fathers*, Vol. II (New York: Christian Literature Publishing).

Tesón, F. (1992), 'The Kantian Theory of International Law', *Columbia Law Review*, 92 (1).

Tesón, F. (1997), *Humanitarian Intervention: An Inquiry into Law and Morality*, 2nd edition (New York: Transnational Publishers).

Tesón, F. (1998), *A Philosophy of International Law* (Boulder, CO: Westview Press).

Tesón, F. (2003), 'The Liberal Case for Humanitarian Intervention', in J. L. Holzgrefe and R. O. Keohane (eds), *Humanitarian Intervention: Ethical, Legal and Political Dilemmas* (Cambridge: Cambridge University Press).

Thomas, E. and M. Hosenball (2002), 'The Opening Shot: In a Show of Superpower Might, the CIA Kills Al Qaeda Operative in Yemen', *Newsweek*, 18 November.

Thomas, W. (2001), *The Ethics of Destruction: Norms and Force in International Relations* (Ithaca, NY: Cornell University Press).

Thompson, J. (2002), 'Terrorism and the Right to Wage War', in T. Coady and M. O'Keefe (eds), *Terrorism and Justice: Moral Argument in a Threatened World* (Melbourne: Melbourne University Press).

Thucydides (1954), *The Peloponnesian War*, trans. R. Warner (London: Penguin).

Tierney, B. (1964), *The Crisis of Church and State 1050–1300* (Englewood Cliffs, NJ: Prentice Hall).

Tierney, B. (1982), *Religion, Law and the Growth of Constitutional Thought 1150–1650* (Cambridge: Cambridge University Press).

Tilly, C. (2002), 'Violence, Terror, and Politics as Usual', *Boston Review*, 27 (3).

Tooke, J. D. (1965), *The Just War in Aquinas and Grotius* (London: SPCK).

Tuck, R. (1979), *Natural Rights Theories: Their Origins and Development* (Cambridge: Cambridge University Press).

Tucker, R. W. (1960), *The Just War: A Study on Contemporary Doctrine* (Baltimore: Johns Hopkins University Press).

Tucker, R. W. (1985), 'Morality and Deterrence', *Ethics*, 95 (3).

Turner, R. W. (1990), 'Changing Perceptions of the New Administrative Class in Anglo-Norman and Angevin England: The Curiales and their Conservative Critics', *Journal of British Studies*, 29 (2).

Tyerman, C. J. (1995), 'Were There Any Crusades in the Twelfth Century?', *The English Historical Review*, 110 (437).

Tyerman, C. J. (1998), *The Invention of the Crusades* (London: Macmillan).

UN Commission of Inquiry (2005), Report of the International Commission of Inquiry on Darfur to the United Nations Secretary-General, Geneva, 25 January.

UN News (2004), 'World is Responsible for Ending "Terrible Violence" in Sudan, Annan Says', 27 September.

United Nations High Commissioner for Human Rights (UNHCHR) (2004), *Situation of Human Rights in the Darfur Region of the Sudan*, advance edited edition, 7 May, E/CN.4/2005/3.

United Nations High Commissioner for Refugees (UNHCR) (2004), 'Chad: French Military Airlift Cuts Transport Time to Eastern Camps', 3 August 2004, at http://www.unhcr.org/cgi-bin/texis/vtx/news/opendoc.htm?tbl=NEWS&page=home&id=410f63e44, accessed 23 March 2006.

US Central Command (2003), 'Unclassified Executive Summary: Investigation of Civilian Casualties, Oruzgan Province, Operation Full Throttle, 30 June 2002', press release, 2 September 2003.

US Department of State (1999a), 'Daily Press Briefing', 18 March, DPB#34.

US Department of State (1999b), 'Erasing History: Ethnic Cleansing in Kosovo', human rights report, May.

Vagts, A. (1969), 'Intelligentsia versus Reason of State', *Political Science Quarterly*, 84 (1).

Van Der Molen, G. H. J. (1968), *Alberico Gentili and the Development of International Law: His Life, Work and Times*, 2nd revised edition (Leyden: A. W. Sijthoff).

Van Vollenhoven, C. (1919) *Three Stages in the Evolution of the Law of Nations* (The Hague: Martinus Nijhoff).

Vanderpol, A. (1919), *La Doctrine scolastique du droit de guerre* (Paris: Pedone).

Vattel, E. de (1916), *The Law of Nations or the Principles of Natural Law Applied to the Conduct and to the Affairs of Nations and of Sovereigns*, trans. C. G. Fenwick (Washington, DC: Carnegie Institution).

Verwey, W. (1998), 'Humanitarian Intervention in the 1990s and Beyond: An International Law Perspective', in J. N. Pieterse (ed.), *World Orders in the Making: Humanitarian Intervention and Beyond* (London: Macmillan).

Vesel, D. (2004), 'The Lonely Pragmatist: Humanitarian Intervention in an Imperfect World', *Brigham Young University Journal of Public Law* 18 (1).

Vincent, R. J. (1974), *Nonintervention and International Order* (Princeton: Princeton University Press).

Vincent, R. J. (1986), *Human Rights and International Relations* (Cambridge: Cambridge University Press).

Vitoria, F. de (1991a), 'On the American Indians', in *Vitoria: Political Writings*, ed. A. Pagden and J. Lawrence (Cambridge: Cambridge University Press).

Vitoria, F. de (1991b), 'On the Laws of War', in *Vitoria: Political Writings*, ed. A. Pagden and J. Lawrence (Cambridge: Cambridge University Press).

Vitoria, F. de (1991c), 'On Dietary Laws, or Self-Restraint', in *Vitoria: Political Writings*, ed. A. Pagden and J. Lawrence (Cambridge: Cambridge University Press).

Walker, H. (2005), 'The Case of Kosovo', *Civil Wars*, 7 (1).

Walker, W. (1997), *Prompt and Utter Destruction: President Truman and the Use of Atomic Weapons Against Japan* (Raleigh: University of North Carolina Press).

Wallace, G. (1991), 'Area Bombing, Terrorism and the Death of Innocents', in B. Almond and D. Hill (eds), *Applied Philosophy: Morals and Metaphysics in Contemporary Debates* (London: Routledge).

Walters, L. (1973), 'The Just War and the Crusade: Antitheses or Analogies?', *The Monist*, 57 (4).

Waltz, K. N. (1979), *Theory of International Politics* (Reading, MA: Addison Wesley).

Walzer, M. (1977), *Just and Unjust Wars: A Philosophical Argument with Historical Illustrations* (New York: Basic Books).

Walzer, M. (1994), *Thick and Thin: Moral Argument at Home and Abroad* (Notre Dame, IN: University of Notre Dame Press).

Walzer, M. (2000), *Just and Unjust Wars: A Philosophical Argument with Historical Illustrations*, 3rd edition (New York: Basic Books).

Walzer, M. (2004a), *Arguing About War* (New Haven: Yale University Press).

Walzer, M. (2004b), 'Just and Unjust Occupations', *Dissent*, Winter.

Warden, J. A. (1988), *The Air Campaign: Planning for Combat* (Norfolk, VA: National Defense University Press).

Watson, P. and L. Getter (2001), 'Silent Peril Lies in Wait for Afghanistan's People', *Los Angeles Times*, 1 December.

Watts, A. (2000), 'The Importance of International Law', in M. Byers (ed.), *The Role of Law in International Politics: Essays in International Relations and International Law* (Oxford: Oxford University Press).

Weibe, V. (2000), 'Footprints of Death: Cluster Bombs as Indiscriminate Weapons Under International Humanitarian Law', *Michigan Journal of International Law*, 22 (1).

Weigley, R. F. (1973), *The American Way of War: A History of United States Strategy and Policy* (New York: Macmillan).

Weisman, S. R. (2003), 'Pre-emption Evolves from an Idea into Official Action', *New York Times*, 23 March.

Weiss, P. (2002), 'Terrorism, Counterterrorism and International Law', *Arab Studies Quarterly*, 24 (2/3).

Weiss, T. G. (2004), 'The Sunset of Humanitarian Intervention? The Responsibility to Protect in a Unipolar Era', *Security Dialogue*, 35 (2).

Weller, M. (ed.) (1999), *The Kosovo Crisis 1989–1999: From the Dissolution of Yugoslavia to Rambouillet and the Outbreak of Hostilities* (Cambridge: Documents and Analysis).

Westhusing, T. (2002), 'Target Approval Delays Cost Air Force Key Hits: Targeting Terror: Killing Al Qaeda the Right Way', *Journal of Military Ethics*, 1 (2).

Westlake, J. (1894), *Chapters on the Principles of International Law* (Cambridge: Cambridge University Press).

Wheeler, M. (1952), 'Cicero's Political Ideal', *Greece & Rome*, 21 (62).

Wheeler, N. J. (2000), *Saving Strangers: Humanitarian Intervention in International Society* (Oxford: Oxford University Press).

Wheeler, N. J. (2001), 'The Legality of NATO's Intervention in Kosovo', in K. Booth (ed.), *The Kosovo Tragedy: The Human Rights Dimensions* (London: Frank Cass).

Wheeler, N. J. (2002), 'Dying for "Enduring Freedom": Accepting Responsibility for Civilian Casualties in the War Against Terrorism', *International Relations*, 16 (2).

Wheeler, N. J. (2003), 'The Bush Doctrine: The Dangers of American Exceptionalism in a Revolutionary Age', *Asian Perspective*, 27 (4).

Wheeler, N. J. (2004a), 'The Humanitarian Responsibilities of Sovereignty: Explaining the Development of a New Norm of Military Intervention for Humanitarian Purposes in International Society', in J. Welsh (ed.), *Humanitarian Intervention and International Relations* (Oxford: Oxford University Press).

Wheeler, N. J. (2004b), 'The Kosovo Bombing Campaign', in C. Reus-Smit (ed.), *The Politics of International Law* (Cambridge: Cambridge University Press).

Wheeler, N. J. and J. Morris (forthcoming), 'Justifying Iraq as a Humanitarian Intervention: The Cure is Worse than the Disease', in W. P. S. Sidhu and R. Thakur (eds), *The Iraq Crisis and World Order: Structural and Normative Challenges* (Tokyo: United Nations University Press).

Whittaker, D. J. (2002), *Terrorism: Understanding the Global Threat* (London: Longman).

Whittaker, D. J. (2003) (ed.), *The Terrorism Reader*, 2nd edition (London: Routledge).

Whittaker, D. J. (2004), *Terrorists and Terrorism in the Contemporary World* (London: Routledge).

Wieviorka, M. (1988), *The Making of Terrorism*, trans. D. G. White (Chicago: University of Chicago Press).

Wilkin R. N. (1947), *Eternal Lawyer: A Legal Biography of Cicero* (New York: Macmillan).

Wilkins, B. T. (1992), *Terrorism and Collective Responsibility* (London: Routledge).

Wilkinson, P. (1983), 'Armenian Terrorism', *The World Today*, September.

Williams, M. C. (2005), *The Realist Tradition and the Limits of International Relations* (Cambridge: Cambridge University Press).

Williams, P. L. (2002), *Al-Qaeda: Brotherhood of Terror* (New York: Alpha Press).

Williams, R. (2003), 'Just War Revisited', lecture to the Royal Institute of International Affairs, 14 October, at http://www.archbishopofcanterbury.org/sermons_speeches/2003/031014.html, accessed 23 March 2006.

Wilmhurst, E. (2005), 'Principles of International Law on the Use of Force by States in Self-Defence', *Chatham House*, International Law Programme Working Paper, ILP WP 05/01, October 2005.

Windass, S. (1964), *Christianity versus Violence: A Social and Historical Study of War and Christianity* (London: Sheed and Ward).

Wolfers, A. (1949), 'Statesmanship and Moral Choice', *World Politics*, 1 (2).

Wolff, C. (1934), *The Law of Nations Treated According to a Scientific Method*, trans. Joseph Drake (Oxford: Oxford University Press).

Wright, Q. (1924), 'Changes in the Conception of War', *American Journal of International Law*, 18 (4).

Wright, Q. (1953), 'The Outlawry of War and the Law of War', *American Journal of International Law*, 47 (3).

Wylie, N. (2002), 'The Sound of Silence: The History of the International Committee of the Red Cross as Past and Present', *Diplomacy and Statecraft*, 13 (4).

Yingling, R. T. and R. W. Ginnance (1952), 'The Geneva Conventions of 1949', *American Journal of International Law*, 46 (3).

Yoo, J. (2004), 'Using Force', *The University of Chicago Law Review*, 71 (3).

Young, R. (2002), 'Political Terrorism as a Weapon of the Politically Powerless', in T. Coady and M. O'Keefe (eds), *Terrorism and Justice: Moral Argument in a Threatened World* (Melbourne: Melbourne University Press).

Zeitlin, I. M. (1997), *Rulers and Ruled: An Introduction to Classical Political Theory from Plato to the Federalists* (Toronto: University of Toronto Press).

Zunes, S. (1999), 'The Role of Non-Violent Action in the Downfall of Apartheid', *Journal of Modern African Studies*, 37 (1).

Index

Note: Page numbers for figures and tables are denoted in italics

Abyssinia 102
Adrian VI, Pope 54
aerial bombing 11, 88, 103, 180–98
  discrimination 181, 182–5
  dual-use targets 180
  ethics and law 12, 180, 184, 230
  indirect consequences 180–1
  Kosovo 216–17
  moral responsibility 180–1
  proportionality 181, 182–5, 186
  targeting process 181, 186
Aetolians 19
Afghanistan 12, 120, 159, 170, 171–3,
    180–98, 205, 212
  Ainger 193–5
  civilian casualties 187
  cluster bombs 192
  failure rate of submunitions 195, 196
  Ishaq Suleiman 193–5
  Northern Alliance 171
  PGMs 187
  post-war reconstruction 225
  Qala Shater 193–5
  Taliban 146,171,185,188,191,193,198
  US intervention 161, 169
Africa, sub-Saharan 1
African National Congress
    (ANC) 136, 154–6
  banning of 155
  commitment to non-violence 155
  disclosing activities 156
  Freedom Charter (1955) 154–5
  jus ad bellum 156
  legitimate authority 156
  right intention 156

African Union (AU) 223, 224
  Constitutive Act 206
African Union Mission (AMIS) 222
aggressive war 101–2, 107, 229
al-Harethi, Qaed Salim Sinan 173,
    174–5
Al-Qaeda 143, 146–7
  casualty figures 147
  evidence against 171
  jus in bello 147
  missile attack on 170
  perceived threat 179
  principal objectives 146
  relation with Taliban 172–3
  use of human shields 188, 198
  and USS Cole 174
  in Yemen 173
Aldicott, J. 174
Alexander II, Tsar 98
Allied Force, Operation 189, 214–19
Ambrose of Milan 8
  justifying wars 24–5
American Civil War (1861–5) 91–2,
    95
American Indians 51
Amin, Idi 110, 227
Amnesty International 175
Anabaptists 62
ancient Greece 15–18
  city-states 16, 17
  customs and laws 7–9
  customs of war 40
  division of humanity 17
  Greek code 16
  philosophical ideas 15

Angell, Norman 101
Anglo, Sidney 58
Annan, Kofi 206, 224
anti-war demonstrations (Iraq) 220
Antioch 46
Antiochus III 19
apartheid 112, 136, 154–5, 156
Apology (Tertullian) 22–3
Aquinas, St Thomas 9, 37–40, 48, 54, 73, 124, 128, 129
Arab–Israeli war (1967) 151
arbitration 73
  compulsory 94, 98, 100, 101, 102
  impartial 60
  procedure 99
  voluntary 99
Arbre des battailes, L' (Bonet) 42
Arendt, Hannah 104
Aristotle 18
armed conflict 5, 110, 160–1, 167
  definition 173
  forms of 108
  internal 88, 89, 101, 109, 111
armies 88
  conscript 129
Art of War, The (Machiavelli) 58
Athenian Empire 16
Atlanta, US 92
Augsburg, Peace of (1555) 67, 68
Augustine of Hippo, St 8–9, 15, 24, 25–9, 33, 128, 132
  Christian doctrine of the Just Wars 25
  dualism 24, 25–8
  ethics of war 28
  four objectives for just war 28
  humanitarian intervention 202
authority
  consultation 53
  ecclesiastical 34, 42–3
  identifying 33
  legitimate 48, 146–7
  political 48
  secular 34–6, 42–3
  sovereign's belief 53
  temporal superior 48
Ayala, Balthazar 59, 65
Aztecs, limiting war 15

Bacon, Francis 69
Bainton, Roland 22
Balfour declaration (1917) 148, 149–50

Balkans 1, 205
Barber, Richard 43
Bartholomew, Peter 46
Begin, Menachem 148–9
Beitz, Charles 202
Belgium 91, 92
Bentham, Jeremy 131
Bernard, St 47
Bethmann-Hollweg, Theobald von 92
Biafra 205
bin Laden, Osama 146, 163
bishops 33, 35
Blair, Tony 171, 215, 219, 220
Blix, Hans 178
Bologna, school of law 31, 35
Bonet, Honoré 42, 43, 44
Bonizo, Bishop, of Sutri 44
Bosnia 201, 205
Brighton bombing (1984) 139
Britain 1, 99, 102, 161–2, 206
  Crimean War 91
  and Darfur 223–4, 225–6
  intelligence on Iraq 177
  and the Jews 150
  pacifying the Arabs 150
  and Palestine 148–9
  Saddam's regime and humanitarianism 175
  voluntary arbitration 99
British Foreign and Commonwealth Office 220
British House of Commons International Development Committee 222
British Joint Intelligence Committee 177
Brodie, Bernard 104
Brown, Chris 202
Brussels declaration (1874) 95
Bull, Hedley 3
Bullinger, Heinrich 69
Burma 213
Burundi 201
Bush doctrine (2002) 158
Bush, George H. W. 220
Bush, George W. 163, 167, 176, 219, 220
Butler, Lord, of Brockwell 177
Byers, Michael 170
Bynkershoek, Cornelius van 76, 81, 86
Byzantine Empire 45, 46

Cadoux, Cecil John 22
Cambodia 108, 205
Canada, British rule 162
canon law 9, 23, 31–7, 75–6, 80, 100,
    124, 128, 207
    peacetime roles 132
    reduced authority 49
Carnegie Council, ethics of war 50
Caroline, sinking (1837) 161–2
    criteria 168
Carr, E. H. 101
Carthage 19
Catholic Church 205–6
Catholic League 67
Catholicism 9, 47–8, 68
cavalry 41
Celsus 22
Chad 225
Charny, Geoffrey de 41–2
Chechnya 146, 213
Cheney, Dick 167, 177
China 132, 223
    and Sudan 224
Chinese Embassy, Belgrade bombing
    189–90
chivalric code 1, 9, 20, 31, 40–4, 48,
    75–6, 132
    conduct of war 43
    duties and origins of 41
    negative consequences 43
    religious to secular 43
    and wealth 42
Christendom
    natural law 203
    secular rulers 203
Christian Church 7
    eastern and western divide 45, 47
    eschatological expectations 23–4
    pacifism 15, 20, 22, 31
Christian Just War writers 8–9
Christianity
    Europe 47
    growth of 25
    and Rome 22
Christians
    Byzantine Empire 45
    centralizing society 30
    eschatology 21
    interpreting scripture 20–1
    military service 21–4, 25, 32, 38
    role through prayer 22–3
    and Roman Empire 22, 24

scripture interpretation 23, 62
    teaching and practice 21, 25
    war and conversion 51
    war and pagan idolatry 21, 22
Church
    and chivalric code 41
    legitimate authority 31, 35, 36, 51
    proper role of 9, 33–4
    and war 37
Cicero 1, 9, 19–20, 72
    civil war potential 20
    laws of war 18, 24
    limits on conduct 20
civil law 20
civil war 109, 199
    see also armed conflict
civitas maxima 78
Clark, Ian 5, 7, 229
Clarke, Richard 177
Clausewitz, Carl von 2, 88, 93
clerics, participation in war 34, 35, 37
Clinton, Bill 163, 215, 217
Cluny, Abbey of 31
cluster bomb 187, 198
    blast range 194–5
    CBU-87 196
    collateral damage 192
    due care 196
    indiscriminancy 192, 195
    non-combatant deaths 193
    proportionality 192
Coady, Tony 119, 135
Cohen, William 196
Cold War 89, 107, 165, 205
Colet, John 62–3, 64
collateral damage 192
    excessive 183
    target approval 187
collective responsibility 10, 142–3, 144,
    147, 148
collective security 98, 101, 102
Concordiantia Discordantum
    Canonum, see Dectretum (Gratian)
Conetta, Carl 187–8
Congo, Democratic Republic of 199,
    205
conscientious objection 28, 53–4, 55
consequentialism 141–2, 144, 147, 148
Constantine 22, 23
Contras, Nicaragua 136
Convention on Conventional Weapons
    (1980) 110

Convention on the Protection of
 Civilians 108–9
Convention on Terrorism 137
Côte d'Ivoire 209
Council of Bourges 32
Council of Clermont 45
Crenshaw, Martha 136
Crimean War 91
crimes
 against humanity 111–12, 206, 223
 of aggression 111
 see also war crimes
crusades 1, 31, 32, 44–8
cujus region ejus religio 67
Curzon, Lord 101
customary law 80, 82
customary practice 82, 120, 161, 201
 and new rules 133
Cyprian of Carthage 23
Czechoslovakia, invasion (1939) 200,
 205

Damrosch, Lori Fisler 201
Dar es Salaam 146
Darfur 12, 199, 205, 221–6
 duty to intervene 223–4, 226, 227–8
 just cause threshold 223
De Jure Belli et Pacis (Grotius) 69, 71,
 73
De Jure Belli (Gentili) 59
Dectretalists 34, 36–7
Decretists 34–6
Decretum (Gratian) 31, 32–6
defence
 of honour 60
 necessary 60
 of right religion 69
 of the state 69
 see also self-defence
Delian League 16
democracy
 and injustice 17
 political consensus for war 131
Deng, Francis 206
Déols, Odo de 32
Dier Yassin, 1948 massacre 149
Discourses (Machiavelli) 56–7
discrimination 12, 110
 intelligence failures 190
divine mandate 144, 147
 terrorism 144–5
divine war, evidence of 60

Donnelly, Jack 4
double-effect doctrine 9, 24, 38–9, 48,
 54–5, 75–6, 124, 183, 193
 conditions 124–5
 indiscrimination 182
 permissive interpretation 181
 Suárez 55
Droit des gens, Le (Vattel) 79
dual-use targets 186
 proportionality criteria 182–3
Dunant, Henry 97
Durban, SA, MK attacks 155–6

East Timor 199, 201, 205
Edessa, Syria 47
Egypt 169
 Israel's invasion of 151–2
Egyptian civilization 15, 132
El Fashir ceasefire agreement 224
Elshtain, Jean Bethke 104, 113,
 138
Enduring Freedom, Operation 12, 159,
 170, 172, 179, 180–98
 civilian casualties 187–8
 legitimacy 197–8
 pre-emptive self defence 172
 proportionality 172
 support for 173
 targeting mistakes 181
 weapon selection 181
England 64, 67, 68
English Civil War 66, 69
Erasmus, Desiderius 62, 63, 64–5
Erdmann, Carl 44
ethics 1, 28, 48, 50, 71, 103, 119, 229
 aerial bombing 12, 189, 184, 230
 humanitarian intervention 3, 11, 199,
 230
 Roman law 15, 20
ethnic cleansing 12, 112, 149, 201, 206,
 207, 209, 211
 Kosovar Albanians 215, 216, 217,
 218, 219
 Sudan 222
Europe
 holy war thinking 86
 political order 10
 Protestant and Catholic 10
 sovereign states 10
exceptionalist view 158–9
expansionist wars, justification
 19–20

Fadlallah, Sheikh 144
Faits d'armes et de chivalrie, Les (Pisan)
    42–3
Falk, Richard 201
Fanon, Frantz 143
Fatah 151–2
    guerrilla operations 152
    jus ad bellum 153
Feinstein, Lee 164
Feith, Doug 176
Feliciano, Florentino P. 169
fetial law 19, 124
feudal system 30, 35, 37, 52
Fischer, Joschka 212
Forsyth, John 162
France 64, 67, 99, 102, 103, 178, 226
    Dreyfus affair 91
    levée en masse 88, 91
French, Shannon 15
French Revolution 86, 88, 105

Gaius 20
Gallie, W. B. 82
Gaza 152, 153
General Orders No. 100, *see* Lieber
    code
Geneva arbitration (1872) 99
Geneva Conventions and Protocols 4,
    10, 94, 109–10, 132, 155, 193
    (1864) and ICRC 97
    (1948) 111
    (1949) 108–10
    and discrimination (Article 51) 182–3
    and due care 174
    gaps in 109
    and indiscriminate attacks 182–3, 192
    and proportionality (Article 51)
        183–5
    and target verification 187
    and weapons 103, 192
Geneva Society of Public Welfare 97
genocide 111, 144, 201, 206, 222, 223
Genocide Convention (1948) 110, 111
Gentili, Alberico 55, 59–61, 65, 86
Germany 1, 96, 99, 107, 132, 140, 178,
    212, 226
    and Belgium 91
    invasion of Norway 162
    national interest 104
    Nazi 104, 142, 148
    right cause 92–3
Glennon, Michael J. 165, 166

Goodin, Robert 138
Gospels 21
Gosson, Stephen 68–9
Grant, Ulysses S. 92
Gratian of Bologna 32–6
    identifying authority 33
    legitimate causes of war 33
    non-combatant immunity 34
Greece, *see* ancient Greece
Greenstock, Jeremy 136
Gregory VII, Pope 30, 44, 46
Grotius, Hugo 10, 50, 55, 66, 67, 78,
    86, 119–20, 129, 159, 200
    ethics of war 71
    humanitarian intervention 203–4
    jus ad bellum 75
    just causes 73–4
    just war images 72
    legalism 71–6
    permissions 72
guerrillas 108
Gulf War (1991) 175

Habsburgs 68
Hague Conventions (1899) 94, 98, 99
Hague Conventions (1907) 98, 99–100
    jus in bello restrictions 100
    level of protection 100
Hague rules (1923) 103
Haiti 199, 209
HALO Trust 192, 196
    de-mining 197
Hamas 152–3
    guerrilla attacks 152
    jus ad bellum 153
    targeting non-combatants 152
Hart, Liddell 93
Harward, Simon 68
Hebrew civilization 15, 132
Hegel, Georg Wilhelm Friedrich 89–90
Held, Virginia 140
Henry V (Shakespeare) 64
Henry VII 63
Henry VIII 52
Herat, Afghanistan, Taliban
        headquarters 192
Herold, Marc 187
Hershberger, Guy Franklin 22
Hindu civilization 15, 132
Hippolytus of Rome 23
Hiroshima 142
Hispanus, Laurentius 36

Hitler, Adolf 200
  humanitarian justifications 205
Hizbollah 140, 144
Hobbes, Thomas 10, 66, 67, 78, 117
  realism 69–71
  right authority 71
Holbrooke, Richard 216
Holland, T.E. 100
Holmes, Robert 27
Holocaust 88, 150
holy war 9–10, 31, 44–8, 66, 114
  chivalric code 44
  classic definition 47
  destructiveness 67
  to enlightenment 67–87
  Europe 68–9, 86
  Gratian on 34
  illegitimacy of 69
  and penance 45–6
  reaction to 69–76
Hospitallers 47
Hostiensis 36
Howard, John 219, 220
Hugo, Victor 97
Huguccio 35
  just cause 35
human law 71, 74, 86
human rights 108
  abuse by Saddam 175
  common rights 206
  equal rights to blacks 154–5
  right to life 143
  and sovereignty 206
  and use of force 201
  use as means 138, 147
  violations 202
  see also self-defence
human rights law 110, 206
Human Rights Watch 192, 193, 194,
    195, 197
humanism 65
  London Reformers 62
humanitarian emergency 130–3, 201,
    202
  ethics 3, 11
  immediate 216
  terrorism 143–4
  thresholds 130
humanitarian intervention 11, 12, 121,
    129, 199–228
  abuse of 200–1, 205, 207, 208, 214,
    221

anti-colonial movement 205
Augustine to Middle Ages 203
collective action 214
common values 214
communitarianism 200
controversy 199–203
counter-restrictionism 201, 215
delays 210
due care 213
duty to 203, 207, 211–12, 213
ends and means 211, 213, 227
ethics of 3, 11, 199
failure to intervene 227–8
from 1945 onward 205
imperfect duty 221–2
intentions 211–12
jus post bellum 211, 214
just cause 208–11
and just war 207–14
law and ethics 230
legal positivist 200–2
legitimacy costs 210
legitimacy of 199, 211–12
levels of responsibility 210
liberal cosmopolitanism 202
Middle Ages to 1945 203–4
military strategy 213
moral obligation 202
motivation for 211–12, 219–21
natural law 203–7
non-combatant protection 213
obligation in future cases 212, 222
positive law 203–7
precautionary principles 208
proportionality 12, 212–13, 222
prudence 12, 212–13, 222
responsibility for 207–8
restrictionist 200–1
right authority 203, 206–7, 208–11
right intention 211–12, 214
humanity 18, 38, 94
Hundred Years' War 42
Hussein, Saddam 176
  human rights abuse 175, 220, 221
Hussitism 62
Hutu, *Interahamwe* 227

ignorance, invincible 35, 53, 54, 55, 60,
    74–5, 86–7
imminence 159
  and action 166–7
  demonstrability 168–9, 170

imminence (*cont'd*)
  flexible concept of 168–9
  modified tests 11–12
  pre-emption 158, 162–3, 168, 170,
    171
  reinterpreting 179
  temporal 166, 168, 179
Industrial Age (1789–1945) 89–103
Innocent IV, Pope 47
internally displaced persons (IDP)
    camps 222
International Commission on
    Intervention and State Sovereignty
    (ICISS) 207
  just cause threshold 208–9, 211
  right authority 210
International Committee of the Red
    Cross (ICRC) 96–8, 108
  bombing of 190, 198
  positive law enforcement 109
International Court of Justice
    (ICJ) 120, 133, 162, 168
  Legality of Nuclear Weapons 110
  Nicaragua v. *United States* 160
  nuclear weapons 113
International Criminal Court (ICC)
    10, 108, 110, 120
  Darfur 222
  jurisdiction 111
  Rome Statute 111–12, 132
international justice 106
  domestic law 114
international law 55, 59, 65, 90, 93, 94,
    229
  binding power 82
  categorical imperatives 83–5
  customary 167
  decentralized 81
  enforcement 5, 164
  evaluating war 71
  functionalist 106
  human law 71, 72
  human rights 108, 201
  independence and equality 79
  indeterminacy 113
  interpretation 120
  liberal democracies 164
  mutual recognition 83
  and natural law 71, 84, 120
  and oppressive government 137
  political realities 72
  positive 10, 76–7, 105, 160

pre-emption 163
self-defence 158
sovereign consent 76
and state interests 82, 85, 86
Vattel and 79
Vitoria as father of 50
International Legal Commission (ILC)
    111
International Military Commission 98
international order 2–3, 6
international politics, moral
    restraints 117
international society 59, 131
  common good 200
  European 70
  genuine humanitarian
    intervention 200
  pre-emption 161
international treaties 94, 98
international tribunal, permanent 109
Intifada 148, 152
IRA 139
Iraq 12, 126, 132, 146, 147, 159, 165,
    166, 170, 175–8, 179, 199, 205, 212,
    219–21
  authority and just cause in 167,
    219–20
  breach of Resolution 687 175
  ceasefire violations 175
  civilian casualties 187
  human rights abuse 221, 227
  humanitarian conditions 220
  as imminent threat 177
  intervention strategies in 219
  invincible ignorance 178
  just cause threshold 221
  Kurdish and Shi'ite minorities 177,
    220
  link with Al-Qaeda 176–7
  mass murder (1988, 1991) 220–1
  Osirak nuclear reactor 161
  post-war reconstruction 219, 225
  and September 11 177
  terrorist training 177
  timing of humanitarian emergency
    220–1
  WMD 177–8
Iraq Survey Group 177
Irgun 148–9
  against the Arabs 151
  attacks on Arabs 149
  campaign of terrorism 149

jus ad bellum 149
  legitimate authority 150–1
  right intention 150
Irgun Zwei Leumi, see Irgun
Islam 147
  interpretation of 146
  Qur'an 152
  unified Islam caliphate 146
  see also Muslims
Islamic Jihad 152
Israel 140, 147, 148–54
  air strike on Iraq 161
  attack on Egypt 151–2, 161, 169
  casualty figures 152
  collective responsibility 152–3
  and international law 153
  jus ad bellum 148
  political violence 151–3
  proportionality 151
  terrorism 136, 151
  US support 143
  Zionist campaign 148
  see also Fatah; Hamas; Jewish
    nationalists
Israeli Defence Force 181
Italy 91, 102, 107
ius fetiale 19, 124
ius gentium 18, 20, 35, 81, 207
  voluntary positive law 55

Jabotinsky, Vladimir 148
Jackson, Mike 225
Japan 102, 107, 142
Jerusalem 1, 46
Jewish nationalists 150, 151
Jewish state, creation of 148–9
Jewish terrorism 150, 154
Jews, European 149, 150
John Paul II, Pope 205–6
John of Salisbury 41
Johnson, James Turner 53, 107, 181,
  229
Jordan 152
judges 6, 120, 126, 128, 129, 132, 134,
  168
juries 6, 120, 121, 126, 132, 134, 168
  global 126–8
  influence on judges 128
jus ad bellum 93–4, 139
  aggressor–defender concept 92
  Augustine 29
  declaration 87

ethics 1
  Grotius 75
  Kantian Just War theory 85
  legal constraints 1
  modern dilemma 108
  necessity 57
  permissive criteria 131
  procedural criteria 65, 80, 82, 87,
    102, 121–2
  proportionality 55, 58
  prudence 57, 121–2, 123–4
  raison d'état 92
  relation with *jus in bello* 11, 61–2,
    65, 81, 87, 101, 117, 128–30
  right authority 87
  Roman law and ethics 20
  rules 4, 121
  substantive criteria 121–2
  terrorism 145
  UN Charter 10
jus in bello 9, 36, 66, 81, 82, 98
  acts of terrorism 141
  canon law 32
  charity 81, 82
  chivalric code 48, 91
  codification 103
  determined by ends 93–4
  Geneva Conventions 109
  Grotius 76
  invincible ignorance 54
  Kantian Just War theory 85
  legalism 94
  military necessity 89
  'Peace of God' 37
  persistent breaching 145
  positive law 10, 76–7
  proportionality 55, 58, 80–1, 87
  prudence 57, 58
  Pufendorf 77–8
  relation with *jus ad bellum* 11, 61–2,
    65, 81, 87, 101, 117, 128–30
  rules 4, 121, 124–6
  system of laws 114
  Vattel 80
  Vitoria 54
jus post bellum 121
  Kantian Just War theory 85
  perpetual peace 85
just cause 35, 39, 48, 51, 52, 122–3, 146
  consultation 55
  defence 60
  Grotius 73–4

just cause (*cont'd*)
  judgement of 87
  legal positivism 122
  probabilism 53, 55
  proportionality 65, 156
  quasi-judicial 56
  subjective 102
  sufficient cause 123, 129
  Vattel 80
Just War tradition 2–5, 28, 33
  abuse of criteria 106
  advisability 80
  antiquity 15–29
  Aquinas 39–40
  Aristotle's five pretexts 18
  Christian 4
  common language 7
  and correcting religious error 69
  criteria 36, 106, 121–6
  degrees of 39–40
  European origins 4
  evolution of 1, 7
  expediency 80
  fought unjustly 73, 129
  fundamentalism 146
  Gratian 34
  and humanitarian intervention
    207–14
  just on both sides 35, 39–40, 52–3,
    59, 60, 65, 74–5, 80, 122–3
  law 73, 230
  legitimacy 3, 5–7, *8*, 229
  moral absolutes 131–3
  in practice 126–34
  present-day 117–34
  prudence 80
  Pufendorf 77
  quasi-judicial 72, 73
  relation between sub-traditions 5, 7,
    11, 126
  rules 5, 11, 117, 121, 132, 133
  secularized 49
  sixteenth century 9, 49–65
  sub-traditions 3–4, 117–21, 126, *127*,
    229
  Western traditions 4
justice
  and happiness 19
  and human relations 18
  and knowledge 17
  moral and legal 74
  objective 53, 59, 73, 74–5, 80, 122

  ostensible 59, 65, 74
  ostensible subjective 75
  simultaneous ostensible 53, 76, 87,
    204
  subjective 53, 80, 122

Kabul, Afghanistan 171
Kahn, Hermann 104
Kant, Immanuel 67, 77, 86, 121, 134,
  202
  abolition of war 83–4
  categorical imperatives 83–5
  humans use as means 138
  law of peace 85
  non-intervention 204
  obstacles to ideal 84
  reformism 82–5
Kantian Just War theory 85
Karthoum 226
Kashmir 146
Kaufman, Gerald 136
Keegan, John 93
Kellogg–Briand Pact 98, 103, 160
Khatchadourian, Haig 139
killing
  accidental 54, 55
  Augustinian justification 64
  Christian charity 64
  in defence of others 24
  domestic law 122
  inward disposition and outward
    action 24, 25–8, 33
  justification for 122
  legitimate intent 39
  level of 129
  mass murder 1, 12, 143, 201, 206,
    207, 209, 211, 216, 217, 218, 219,
    222
  mechanical mass murder 89
  non-combatants 147
  pre-emptive 55
  proportionality 54
  in self-defence 24, 26
  total justice vs total injustice 38
King David Hotel 151
  1946 bombing 149
knights
  rituals 41, 42, 43
  rules 1
  social class 40, 41, 43
  see also chivalric code
Knyghthode and Bataile 42

Korea, North 213
Kosovo 12, 165, 187, 199, 205, 212,
    214–19
  air campaign 217–18
  ceasefire violations 216
  collateral damage 217, 218
  just cause threshold 215
  refugees 218
  trigger to bombing of 215–16
  unauthorized intervention 214–15
  without intervention 218–19
Kosovo Liberation Army 215
Kuwait 132, 175

landmines 110, 192
  de-mining action group 192
  de-mining and due care 196–7
  inherent indiscriminance 195
Latin America 205
law 25–7
  see also canon law; customary law;
    fetial law; human law; human
    rights law; international law;
    military law; moral law; natural
    law; necessary law; peacetime law;
    positive law; Roman law; treaty law
Law of Nations
  constraining states 82, 83
  and Vattel 79
Law of Nature and Nations, The
    (Pufendorf) 77
Laws, The (Plato) 17
League of Nations 98, 101–3, 148–9
Lebanon, attack on US barracks 140
legal justice 74, 75
legal positivism
  law and ethics 103
  and natural law 95, 113
legalism 10, 48, 50, 58–62, 66, 67,
    94–103, 107–13
  bifurcation 68, 76
  distinction with moralism 86
  Grotius 71–6
  natural law focus 77–9
  positive law focus 79
legitimacy
  balance between sub-traditions 126
  balance of values 7
  and consensus 6
  level of indeterminacy 126–8
  procedural approach 5–6
  substantive approach 5–6

Leo IX, Pope 46
Leviathan (Hobbes) 69
liberal humanitarianism 94, 96–8
liberalism, new liberals 158–9
Liberia 199
Lieber, Francis 95
Lieber code 95–6, 98
Louis XIV (France) 87
Lucius II, Pope 34
Lull, Ramon 41

Macbeth (Shakespeare) 64
McDougal, Myers S. 160, 169
Machiavelli, Niccolò 56–8, 117
Machiavellian state 65
McKeogh, Colm 132
Manchuria, Japanese invasion 102
Mandela, Nelson 155
Martens, F.F. de 94–5
Martens clause 95, 119, 121
Marx, Steven 64
Mazar-e-Sharif, Afghanistan 171
Mazzini, Giuseppe 91
Meinecke, Friedrich 90–1
Melian dialogue 16–17
Melos 16
Memory of Solferino (Dunant) 97
mercenaries, motivation 58
Mézières, Philippe de 43
Middle Ages 1, 9, 30–48, 124
  political administration 30
militarism 64, 89, 90, 91, 93
military codes 94
military firepower 57, 88
military law 42–3, 44, 94, 95
  emerging codes 91
military necessity 3, 92, 95, 103, 181
  cluster bombs 196
  justification 96
military service 23, 33
militia Christi 46
militia sancti Petri 44
Mill, John Stuart 200, 204
Milošević, Slobodan 216, 218–19,
    227
Milvian Bridge 23
mitigation arguments 130–1
Molina 53, 55
Monroe Doctrine 99
moral justice 74–5
moral law 84
moral rights 214

moralism 105
  distinction between legalism and 86
  opinion and certainty 119
  and prudence 119
morality 6, 7, 23, 107, 118, 212
  international 119
Morgenthau, Hans 104–7, 114, 117
Moro, Aldo 139
Morris, Justin 219
Moynier, Gustave 97
Muslims 45, 147
  American oppression of 146
  in Spain 46
Myers, Robert 4
Myjer, Eric 172

Nagasaki, Japan 142
Nairobi, Kenya 146
Napoleon Bonaparte 93
Napoleonic wars 88
National Imagery and Mapping
  Agency, US 189
national partiality 118–19, 184, 191,
  198, 219
National Security Strategy, US (2002)
  159, 166–7, 176
nationalism 89, 90, 93, 104, 105, 106
NATO 171, 189, 214–19
  airstrikes and moral courage 217
  collateral damage 217
  duty of care 218
  ends and means 216–17, 219
  indirect consequences of
    intervention 216–17
  just cause 215
  Kosovo 166
  legitimacy in Kosovo 215
  national partiality 219
  right authority 215
  strategy 217–18
  targeting 216
natural law 4, 7, 10, 20, 59, 65, 66, 74,
  76, 86, 100, 113, 114, 215, 229
  authorizing war 124
  balance with positive law 10–11,
    119–21
  deontological rules 126
  discrimination 182
  duty to assist 78
  ethics 119
  Grotuis 71–2
  human or divine 49

intrinsic rights 202
jus in bello 75–6
  moral component 77, 113, 121
  murder of non-combatants 142
  of nations 79
  personal 70
  pre-emption 163
  presumption against injustice 108
  proportionality 182
  secular 76, 120–1, 201
  self-defence 69, 72–4, 158
  sources of 120–1
  survival and enrichment 56
  and terrorism 169
  theological 120–1
  in twentieth century 121
  universal 76, 203
necessary law 78, 80
necessary war 59–60
necessity 28, 104, 130–3, 230
  and arbitration 60
  perceived 117
  permanent justification 91
  pre-emption 158, 168, 170, 171
  self-defence 162–3
  tests 11–12
Negroponte, John 176
Netherlands, civil war 67
New Testament 21, 22
New York, US 146, 158
Niebuhr, Reinhold 104, 106–7, 114,
  117
Nielsen, Kai 142
Nigeria 224
Nightingale, Florence 97
non-combatant 109–10
  bomb casualties 192
  discrimination 124
  distinction from combatant 96
  distinguishing 92, 95, 140, 182
  enemy or friendly 118
  expectations and PGMs 185
  as human shield 180–1, 184
  humane treatment 15
  indirect harm responsibility 184–5
  indirect targeting 96
  innocence of 142–3
  justifying targeting 138, 141–5, 156
  legitimate targeting of 142–3
  massacre 110
  peacetime function 61
  systematic violence against 153

non-combatant immunity 11, 12, 40,
    43, 44, 76, 80, 87, 88, 117, 132–3,
    219
  absolutist view 132, 138, 139, 181
  acceptable risk 125
  aerial campaigns 218
  anti-oppression exception 142
  Bonet 42
  due care 125, 191
  grey-area 140
  intention and action 125
  medical personnel 97
  and military necessity 78
  military risk 182, 183–4
  overriding exemptions 34, 144
  positive commitment to 125
  proportionality 85, 157
  responsibility of deaths 181, 190–1
  Suárez 55
  wounded soldiers 97
non-intervention principle 131
non-state actors
  jus ad bellum criteria 138, 141
  rightful authority 137–8
North Atlantic Council 216, 218
Norway 162
nuclear weapons 88, 104, 110, 113
Nuremberg tribunals 94, 110–11, 162
Nussbaum, Arthur 50

O'Brien, William 181
O'Connell, Mary Ellen 173
O'Donovan, Oliver 113
Odilo, Abbot, of Cluny 32
Old Testament 21, 24
On the Soldier's Crown (Tertullian) 21
opinio juris 120
Oppenheim, L. F. L. 92–3
Ordene de chevalerie 41
Orend, Brian 84–5
Organization of American States, view
    of September 11 171–2
Origen 21, 22, 23, 33, 37
Othello (Shakespeare) 64

Pakistan 223
  East 205
Palestine 140, 146, 147, 148–54, 181
  al-Aqsa Mosque 152
  Hamas government 152–3
  Hebron massacre (1994) 152
  jus ad bellum 148

legitimate authority 153
  self-defence 153
  supreme emergency 144
  terrorism 136, 154
Palestine Liberation Organization
    (PLO) 151
Palestinian Muslim Brotherhood 152
papacy 30
  authority to wage war 48
  commanding the *militia* 44–5
  world empire 36
patria 36
Paust, Jordan 172
'Peace of God' 9, 31–2, 37, 44
peacetime law 5
Peloponesian War 16–17
penitential war 45–7
Permanent Court of Arbitration 99
Perpetual Peace (Kant) 82, 83
Perseus 19
Philippines, airline bombing (1944)
    146
Phillip V 19
Pisan, Christine de 42–3, 44
Plato 17, 132
Poland 132
political community 35, 203
  leaders' obligations 118
  moral relation 118
  morality and law 57
  right to defence 122
  self-interest and morality 106
  sovereign protection of 69
Political Ethics (Lieber) 95
political realism 7
political violence 5
  deligitimization 136
  jus ad bellum justification 137
Pol Pot 108, 110, 205, 227
Polybius 19
polygamy 72
positive law 4, 7, 49, 66, 76, 100, 215,
    229
  action and intention 113
  authorizing war 124
  discrimination 182
  enforcement of 89, 109
  humanitarian intervention 205
  international communities 106
  international politics 105
  ius gentium 55
  and justice 114

positive law (*cont'd*)
  legal 119
  murder of non-combatants 142
  of nations 80
  presumptions against aggressive war
    108
  primary sources 120
  process 120
  proportionality 182
  relation with natural law 10–11,
    119–21, 125
  terrorism 141
Powell, Colin 167, 176, 177, 178, 222
pre-emption 158–79, 230
  abuse of expanded concept 169–70
  case-by-case legitimacy 161
  expanded concept 174–5, 179
  imminence 158, 162–3, 168, 170, 171
  jus ad bellum criteria 167–8
  limited right to 159, 163, 170, 179
  necessity 158, 168, 169, 170, 171
  new liberals 164–5
  new realists 165–6
  non-violent alternatives 169
  and prevention 161, 167
  proportionality 158, 167, 168, 170
  revisionist arguments 163–70
  state power 170
  threat of terrorism 158
  traditional concept 179
  victims' rights 169
preventive war 159, 164, 165, 166, 167
Prince, The (Machiavelli) 57
princes 35, 124
  authority 9, 36
  and the law 59
  prudence 65
  rights 63
prisoners of war 1
  humane treatment 15, 96
  killing of 61
Pronk, Jan 222–3, 224
proportionality 9, 24, 38, 52, 54, 55,
  65, 77, 80–1, 85, 87, 109–10, 119,
  124, 129, 146, 151, 156, 157, 162–3
  aerial bombing 181–6, 192
  Erasmus 63–4
  level of force 172–3
  humanitarian intervention 12,
    212–13, 222
  moral 58
  and national partiality 118

pre-emption 158, 167, 168, 170
prudential 58, 123
subjectiveness 184
and terrorism 135, 141
and US 172, 174, 187
Protestantism 9, 47–8, 68
  approach to war 59
  union of principalities 67
prudence 57, 58, 65, 80, 121–2
  humanitarian intervention 12,
    212–13, 222
  moralism 119
  realism 123–4
  and states 91, 107
Pufendorf, Samuel 66, 76, 77–8, 159,
  204
Punic Wars 19
punitive war 204

Rabin, Yitzhak 144–5
raison d'état 56–7, 67, 90–1, 104
  hierarchy 91
  necessary and proportionate 57–8
Rambouillet settlement 216
Ramsey, Paul 181, 202
Rantisi, Abdul Aziz 152–3
Rastadt, Treaty of (1714) 87
Raymond of Aguilers 46
realism 4, 7, 10, 48, 50, 56–8, 66, 67,
  89–94, 103–7, 117–19, 229
  combatant risk 125
  consequential 126
  elemental realism dilemma 104
  Hobbes 69–71
  modified 104
  new realists 158–9
  and positive law 103
  prudence 123–4
  strategic over moral 93
Red Brigades 139
Red Cross, *see* International Committee
  of the Red Cross (ICRC)
Reformation 9
reformism 10, 48, 49–66, 67, 101
  Kant 82–5
Reisman, W. Michael 201
religion, believers and rights 51
religious absolutism 2
religious leaders, endorsement of war
  19
renaissance 10, 49–66
Renan, Ernest 97

Republic, The (Plato) 17
Reus-Smit, Christian 202
Revelations, Book of 22
Rice, Condoleezza 173
right authority 9, 20, 28–9, 33, 124, 230
  declaration of 73
  and judicial superior 36, 39
  last resort 73
  non-state actors 135, 138
  restriction of 34
  secular 10, 37
  and terrorism 135
right intention 24, 27–8, 36, 39, 40, 48,
  122–4, 146–7
  ANC 156
  judgement of 87
  and just cause 73
  subjective 102
  Vattel 80
Riley-Smith, Jonathan 46
rioters 108
Robinson, Mary 217
Rodin, David 122
Roman apologists 19
Roman Empire 15, 18–20, 67
  authority to wage war 35
  customs and laws 7–9
  declaration of war 19
  decline of 50
  fetial law 19
  particularist forces 30
  respublica Christiana 68
Roman law
  barrier to anarchy 22
  and ethics 15
  legal tradition 33
  pagan barbarians 23
Roman legion, recruiting
  Christians 23
Rome 18–19, 20
Roosevelt, Theodore 90
Roth, Kenneth 219
Royal Air Force 140
Rumsfeld, Donald 166, 180, 191
Russia 99, 216, 219, 223
  assault on Chechnya 213
  and Kosovo 215
  and Sudan 224
Rwanda 205, 223, 224
  ad hoc tribunal 111
  genocide 199, 201, 205
Ryswick, Treaty of (1697) 87

St John, Templars and Knights of 47
St Petersburg Declaration 98–9
Saladin 47
sanctions 6, 108, 205
scholasticism 9, 10, 37–40, 48, 86, 124
  decline 65
  development of 50–6
  methodology 49
  renaissance thought 62
Schroeder, Gerhard 212
Scott, James Brown 50, 100
Second Lateran Council 32, 34
Seddon, James 96
self-defence 10, 18, 24, 28, 38, 60, 69,
  73–4, 122, 139
  collective 169
  individual and state 78
  just cause 159
  Just War tradition 159–63
  legal right to 159
  natural law 72–3
  necessity and law 92–3, 162–3
  permissive 170
  pre-emptive 11–12, 74, 158–79
  revision after September 11 163
  right to 122, 158, 171
  rules 133
  traditional view 158
  vs state 73
September 11 11, 113, 133, 135, 136,
  146, 147, 158, 163
  Al-Qaeda 171
  and Iraq 176, 177
Serbia 215
Shakespeare, William 62, 64
Shamir, Yitzhak 148
Sharpeville, peaceful protest massacre
  155
Sherman, William T. 92
Sierra Leone 199
Simpson, Gerry 6
Sinai 152
Slaughter, Anne-Marie 164
slavery 72
soldiers
  code of ethics 48
  just war and salvation 63
  ordered to war 33
  sin vs common good 28–9
  strategy and tactics 58
Solferino, battle of 96–7
Somalia 199

South Africa 154
  apartheid 112, 136, 154–5, 156
  MK attack on air force HQ 155–6
  state violence 155
  Truth and Reconciliation
    Commission 156
sovereign, the
  abuse of citizens 205–6
  justification of war 107, 114, 204
  legal explanations 81
  modern conception of 83
  recognition of 131
  right authority 80, 89, 100
  right to judge 81
  source of law 70
  temporal authority 87
  ultimate authority 81
sovereign states 69, 124
  authorizing political violence 137
  moral and legal bonds 70
  preservation of 70
  relationships and duty 79
  war as lesser evil 75
  world society 78
sovereignty
  absolutist monarchies 204
  instrumental 206
  liberal regimes 204
  as responsibility 206
  tyranny and revolt 204
Spain 46, 64
  civil war 67
  legitimacy of American conquest
    50–1, 52
Sparta 16
Spear of the Nation (MK), *see
  Umkhonto we Sizwe* (MK)
states 19, 89–90
  Calvinist theories 59
  centrality of 94
  coercive diplomacy 138
  constraint on power 105
  customs and treaties 79
  democracy and legal mechanisms
    164
  free republican government 204
  government held to account 175
  host consent to intervention 209–10
  ideology 88
  and international society 58–9
  interstate consensus 131, 201, 202
  justice and arms 56–7, 58

justification to peers 102
  laws between 71
  legal right to wage war 114
  liberal 164
  liberal moral consensus 215
  monopoly of power 69
  moral standards 91, 201
  motivation for intervention 209–10
  natural law customs 77
  neutral 100
  own interests and international law
    82
  power and prudence 107
  power and survival 70
  preservation of 93
  primary duty of care 213
  prudence 91
  raison d'état 57, 78
  readiness for war 70
  reason to wage war 117
  restraints on right authority 101–3
  right authority 94
  right to govern 204
  rights and society of states 83
  self-governing sovereignty 79
  sovereign rights 202
  supreme emergency 130–3
  survival 57
  terrorism 135–6
  timeless ethical community 90
  value of 38, 73, 200
  victims' offensive strategy 178
  WMD proliferation 164
Stephen of Tournai 35
Stern, Joseph 148
Stern gang, right intention 150
Strickland, Matthew 43
Suárez, Francisco 55
Sudan 199, 201, 205, 223
  civil war 225
  human rights abuse 222–3
  Janjaweed 222, 227
  peace agreement 226
  see also Darfur
Sudanese People's Liberation Movement
  225
Suganami, Hidemi 4
suicide bomb attacks 152–3
Summa Theologica (Aquinas) 37
Sun Tzu 15, 132
Swift, Louis J. 24
Syria 111

Taliban 146, 171, 185, 191
  use of human shields 188, 193, 198
target identification 198
target selection 187–91, 213
target verification 187–91, 198
  due care 187
  process 190
  time for 189–90
targeting
  human error 187, 188
  incorrectly identified 188–9
  technological failure 187, 188
terror war 92
terrorism 11–12, 129, 133, 135–57
  acts of 135, 140–1, 145, 153, 156, 157
  against oppression 143
  against the state 137
  campaign of 145
  characteristics 136–7
  clear-cut 136, 145, 146–7
  commendable 147
  consistency test 145
  cost of 142
  counter-intuitive moral judgements 157
  defining imminence 163
  definition 135, 136–8
  everyday usage of word 136–7
  flawed justification of 135, 145
  global jurisdiction 169
  grey-area 136, 145, 148–54
  jus ad bellum 135, 157
  justification of 140, 141–5
  legitimacy of 136, 230
  mass casualties 163
  means and political outcomes 140
  moral definition of 135, 136, 139–41, 156
  non-state actors 137
  partial 136, 145, 154–6
  proportionality test 141
  reprehensible 147
  revolutionary 142
  as self-defence 142
  societal fear 138
  state support 161
  tactics 91, 135, 178–9
  threat of 130
  thresholds 154
  types of 140, 145–56
  universal crime 169
  weak against oppressors 142

terrorist organizations 135, 140–1, 146, 153, 156, 157
terrorists 108, 121
  Christian anti-abortion 144
  counter-intuitive outcomes 139–40
  as freedom fighters 136
  and human shields 182
  label of 157
  modus operandi 179
  moral connotation 136
  and non-combatants 180
  oppressed victim of 142
  prescriptive policy 136
  rights and Protocol II 110
  rules 12
  tactics 135
Tertullian 21, 22
Tesón, Fernando 82, 164, 200, 202
Thatcher, Margaret 139
Thebes 16
theology 10
  and philosophy 37
Thirty Years' War 1, 47–8, 66, 67, 68, 105
Thomas, Ward 185
Thucydides 16–17
Tokyo, Japan 110–11
Tooke, Joan 38
total war 89, 92, 101, 105
treaties 68, 79, 82, 87, 120, 133
treaty law 80, 82
'Truce of God' 9, 31, 32

Uganda 205
Umkhonto we Sizwe (MK) 155–6
UN Charter 4, 10, 107–8, 124, 200, 201, 207, 227
  Article 2(4) 205
  Article 51 158, 160–1, 162–3, 165
  broken rules 165–6
  indeterminacy 107–8
UN Human Rights Commission 223
UN Mine Action Group 196
UN Mine Action Programme 197
UN Security Council 107, 109, 111, 114, 124, 161, 164, 166
  ability to protect 165
  and Afghanistan 171
  authorizing intervention 201, 205, 207, 209, 210–11
  Chapter VII Resolutions 209
  collective enforcement 227

UN Security Council (*cont'd*)
  committee on terrorism 136
  and common good 209
  control 112
  Darfur 222, 223
  domestic law jurisdiction 112
  humanitarian emergency 208–9
  Iraq 176, 220–1
  Kosovo 215
  legal authority in intervention 207–8
  primary responsibility for
    intervention in Darfur 224
  Resolution 687 175
  Resolutions 1368 and 1373 171
United Nations 149, 223
Universal Declaration of Human
  Rights 108
universal international society 55, 81
universal legal restraints 18
unjust war
  and divine retribution 28
  uniting against 16–17
Urban II, Pope 44–5, 46
US 99, 103, 161–2, 206
  alternatives to force 175
  atomic terror attacks 142
  cluster bombs 192
  coercive diplomacy 171
  and Darfur 223–4, 225–6
  democracy 147
  discrimination 187
  due care 195, 197, 198
  due care and de-mining 196–7
  due care in Afghanistan 194
  due care in Iraq 178, 179
  due care in Yemen 174
  embassy bombings(1998) 146
  ICRC bombing, Kabul 190
  imminence in Iraq 176
  imminence in Yemen 174
  indirect indiscriminance in
    Afghanistan 195
  information failure 190, 195
  intelligence in Afghanistan 188–9
  intelligence failure 188–9
  intelligence on Iraq and Al-Qaeda
    176
  intelligence as proof 174
  invasion of Afghanistan 12, 169,
    171–3, 191
  jus in bellum in Yemen 173–4
  justification for Iraq 175

  and Kosovo 216
  in Middle East 143
  and Muslims 147
  necessity in Iraq 176
  power and pre-emption 170
  pre-emption for Iraq 167, 176
  pre-emption and right to decide
    165–6
  pre-emptive action 158
  proportionality 174, 187
  redesigning right of self-defence
    158–9
  sanctions on Vietnam 205
  targeting and legal advice 186–7
  targeting process 186–7, 197
  unexploded submunitions 195–6
  in Yemen 173–4
  see also Allied Force, Operation;
    Enduring Freedom, Operation
US Air Force
  effects-based strategy in Afghanistan
    185–6
  failure rate of submunitions 196
  targeting process 191
US Congress 222
US Defence Department, unitary
  bombs 194
US Special Forces 185
USS *Cole*, attack on (2000) 146, 173,
  174
utilitarianism, anti-oppression
  exception 141–2
Utrecht, Treaty of (1713) 87
Uzbekistan 213

Vattel, Emmerich de 66, 76, 79–81, 83,
  86, 119–20, 159–60, 201
  humanitarian intervention 204
  proper motives 80
Vietnam 108, 126
  ICRC access 109
  invasion of Cambodia 205
Vietnam War 105, 181
violence, types of 137
Vitoria, Francisco de 10, 50–6, 60, 61,
  73, 119, 122–3, 129
  double-effect 54–5
  humanitarian intervention 203
  just cause 52
  practical application 52
  precedent and proof 144–5
  proportionality 55, 65

volitional law 57, 59, 72, 78, 86
  legal right of sovereigns 73
voluntary law 79–80

Waldock, Sir Humphrey 160
Wallace, Gerry 139
Walzer, Michael 2–3, 5, 125, 128,
  132–3, 143, 144, 151, 181, 183–4,
  200
war
  abolition of 83
  abuse of pretexts 73
  accidental 101
  aggression and defence 160, 165
  articulation of case for 39
  basic rights 84
  breakdown of customs 17
  canonical truth 62
  codifying laws of 99
  commanded by God 9, 28, 33, 42,
    43, 44
  declaration of 100, 124
  decline of inter-state 108
  defensive 60
  desire for just peace 27
  dilemmas of contemporary 1, 11
  genocidal violence 1
  for glory 19
  humane conduct of 4
  ideological absolutism 2
  immunity 32
  judgements on 2, 12
  jurisdiction over 9
  justice and legitimacy 107
  justice and limitations 53, 59
  justification framework 2, 23
  last resort 123
  laws of 96, 108
  legal prohibition 101
  legitimacy of 2, 5, 12, 29, 39
  as lesser evil 3, 75, 105, 117
  limitations 1, 4, 17, 40, 93, 105,
    128–9
  maintaining community 90
  maintaining religious orthodoxy 28
  mechanized 114
  minutiae of 181
  monopoly on justice 35, 61
  moral dilemmas 20–1, 104, 113
  new war 110
  non-international 108
  objectively just 60–1

offensive 60
  one true faith 10
  opposition and treachery 68
  overriding rules 92, 118, 130
  for peace 17
  presumption against 38
  pretexts for 19
  procedurally correct 76
  protests against 126
  quasi-judicial 52
  ransom system 43
  reason to wage 131–2, 230
  reducing likelihood 101
  and religious faith 69
  response to prior injury 34
  rule change 117, 130, 133–4
  rules 2, 6, 12, 106, 134
  sin of 26–7
  social practice and mass murder 133
  strategy 110
  test of self-government 90
  to force regime change 172–3
  to preserve society 71
  to right a prior wrong 52
  type of 18, 19, 102
  universal moral limits 93
  victor's justice 112
  victor's rules 59
  see also aggressive war; civil war;
    divine war; expansionist wars;
    holy war; necessary war;
    penitential war; preventive war;
    punitive war; terror war; total war
war convention 2–3
war crimes 111–12, 206, 215, 223
war on terror 130, 180
  global 173–4
Warden, John 185
warfare, modern 88–114
warrior
  class 40, 44, 48
  code 15
  ideal just 36
  traditional customs 16
Washington, US 146, 158
Watts, Arthur 3
weapons
  biological 103, 176, 177
  BLU-82 191
  CBU-87 196
  chemical 103, 176, 177
  crossbow ban 36

weapons (*cont'd*)
'dum dum' bullets 98
failure rate 196
indiscriminate 110
in Iraq 220
manufacture and failure rate 196
mass destruction (WMD) 164–5, 167, 176, 177–8, 179
missing target 193–4
precision guided missiles (PGMs) 217–18
prohibited 99, 124
selection 191–7, 213
unexploded submunitions 198
unitary bombs 194
use of artillery 49
see also cluster bomb; nuclear weapons
Webster, Daniel 161–2, 169
Weiss, Thomas 201
West Bank 152, 153
Westlake, John 105
Westphalia, treaties of 67, 69, 70
Wheeler, Nicholas 183, 201, 219
White, Nigel 172
Wilkins, Burleigh 142–3

William III (England) 87
Williams, Rowan (Archbishop of Canterbury) 38
Wilson, Woodrow 101
Wolff, Christian 66, 76, 78, 79, 204
Wolfowitz, Paul 174, 176
world empire 36
World War I 1, 88
impact on legalism 101
number killed 101
World War II 1, 88–9, 103, 107, 110, 140

Yassin, Sheik 152
Yemen
Al-Qaeda 173, 175
missile attack (2002) 159, 170, 173–5, 179
Young, Robert 139
Yugoslav Federal Directorate 189
Yugoslavia 199
arms embargo 209–10
non-compliance 218
tribunal 111, 216

Zimbabwe 213